Visual Culture in
Twentieth-Century Germany

T0339274

Visual Culture in
Twentieth-Century Germany

Text as Spectacle

Edited by Gail Finney

INDIANA UNIVERSITY PRESS

Bloomington and Indianapolis

This book is a publication of

Indiana University Press

601 North Morton Street

Bloomington, IN 47404-3797 USA

http://iupress.indiana.edu

Telephone orders 800-842-6796
Fax orders 812-855-7931
Orders by e-mail iuporder@indiana.edu

The paper used in this publication meets the minimum requirements of American National Standard for Information Sciences—Permanence of Paper for Printed Library Materials, ANSI Z39.48-1984.

Manufactured in the United States of America

Library of Congress Cataloging-in-Publication Data

Visual culture in twentieth-century Germany : text as spectacle / edited by Gail Finney.
p. cm.
Includes bibliographical references and index.
ISBN 0-253-34718-1 (cloth : alk. paper) — ISBN 0-253-21833-0 (pbk. : alk. paper)
1. Arts, German—20th century. I. Finney, Gail.
NX550.A1V57 2006
306.4'709430904—dc22

2005028353

1 2 3 4 5   11 10 09 08 07 06

Contents

Contents

Acknowledgments

I would like to thank Robert Scheetz, whose computer ingenuity greatly facilitated the formatting of the manuscript and whose love and support sustained me throughout my work on this volume.

G. F.

Illustrations

Illustrations

x

Introduction

Gail Finney

At first glance the title of this volume—*Visual Culture in Twentieth-Century Germany: Text as Spectacle*—appears purely descriptive. But its terms are not simple; like Japanese paper flowers that expand when dropped into water, they unfold on closer examination into multilayered concepts. Elaborating these terms will offer an entrée into the collection at hand. To begin with the subtitle: the oxymoronic phrase "text as spectacle" points to the fact that in twentieth-century culture, visual activity—the acts of seeing, looking, watching, gazing—assumed the prominence and complexity previously associated with reading. W. J. T. Mitchell has called this shift the "pictorial turn," thus putting its importance for the human sciences on a par with that of the "linguistic turn" and earlier turning points in the history of philosophy as characterized by Richard Rorty (Mitchell 1994, 11–34). One aspect of Mitchell's definition of the pictorial turn in particular justifies his placing of this shift in the second half of the twentieth century: "a postlinguistic, postsemiotic rediscovery of the picture as a complex interplay between visuality, apparatus, institutions, discourse, bodies, and figurality" (16). Yet the following collection is guided by the conviction that, while the pressure of the visual is enormous and omnipresent during the postmodern era, the entire twentieth century can be characterized as the visual age—the era in which the image becomes paramount.

The term "spectacle" in the collection's title is not intended, or at least not exclusively, to evoke associations with *The Society of the Spectacle* (1967), in which the Situationist thinker Guy Debord defines the spectacle as the "perfect image" of the capitalist order (15). In the title

1

of this collection, by contrast, "spectacle" is used in its broad sense—with varying degrees of self-consciousness—as that which is presented to sight. Consciously and unconsciously, the ascendance of visual media in the West—above all, film, television, and digital—has shaped the way we look at the world and at other media, such as the plastic arts. The extent to which today's children and adolescents are visually conditioned has been much discussed. Often one medium bleeds into another, as when comic book characters become the subjects of cinematic megahits. Lisa Cartwright employs the term "media convergence" to describe the phenomenon of film "disintegrating into, or integrating with, other media" (Cartwright 2002, 8). Now more than ever, spectacle abounds.

Martin Jay's recent coinage of the phrase "visual turn" to characterize the "advent of visual culture" takes Mitchell's notion of the pictorial turn to a further level of breadth. But the place to which this latest turn leads is not always easily located. The visual is a consciously invented code that changed according to technological developments of the twentieth century, and it is correspondingly eclectic. And "visual culture" is variously understood as the culture we live in, as the visible phenomena within this culture, and as the interdisciplinary field that studies these phenomena. Although this confusion derives in part from the ambiguous quality of the term "culture," which Raymond Williams characterizes as "one of the two or three most complicated words in the English language" (Williams 1985, 87), the difficulty in defining visual culture stems at least as much from the diversity of the objects of investigation, in terms of both medium and period. Subjects ranging from television soap operas to urban architecture to canonical painting, all having something to say about visual culture, are equally worthy of treatment. While the concept of visual culture in itself suggests universality, its purview is frequently limited to recent decades. In introducing his edited collection *The Visual Culture Reader* (1998), Nicholas Mirzoeff claims that "Postmodernism is visual culture," and that visual culture is "a tactic with which to study the genealogy, definition and functions of postmodern everyday life" (4, 5). His own study from the following year, *An Introduction to Visual Culture*, likewise focuses on the past few decades, as do the selections in *The "Block" Reader in Visual Culture.*

If the definition and scope of visual culture are contested, there does appear to be consensus that its origins lie in art history. In one of the landmark documents on visual culture, a collection of brief statements from experts responding to a "Visual Culture Questionnaire" and published in the journal *October* in summer 1996, Thomas DaCosta Kaufmann traces the origins of the concept of visual culture to art historian Michael Baxandall's book *Painting and Experience in Fifteenth-Century Italy* (1972). Highlighting Baxandall's notion of the "period eye" and its relation to broader aspects of culture, Kaufmann credits this study with addressing social history as well as the history of art (Kaufmann 1996, 45). Similarly, Kaufmann notes that the same year—1972—art historian Svetlana Alpers uses the term "new art history" to refer to the discipline's embracing of sociocultural perspectives (Kaufmann 1996, 45). Alpers is generally regarded as responsible for the dissemination of the term "visual culture," and her writings point to the importance of theories of vision, image-making devices, and visual skills as cultural resources (Evans and Hall 1999, 5). And art historian Jonathan Crary calls for a linkage between an emphasis on vision per se and a consideration of historical dimensions: "I have tried to show how vision is never separable from larger historical questions about the construction of subjectivity" (Crary 1996, 33).

Yet visual culture can be said to have outgrown the discipline of art history. As Mieke Bal summarizes, "[Visual culture] has emerged primarily because [art history] has largely failed to deal with both the visuality of its objects—due to the dogmatic position of 'history'—and the openness of the collection of those objects—due to the established meaning of 'art'" (Bal 2003, 5). This doctrinaire assessment of the situation does not take into account the fact that, as we have seen, art historians themselves began crossing the boundaries of their discipline as traditionally circumscribed, but Bal's use of the term "visual culture studies" (6) to distinguish the practice from its object is judicious. Both the interdisciplinarity and the sociohistorical orientation of visual culture studies reflect its indebtedness to cultural studies; indeed, visual culture studies may be viewed as a subdomain of the older field. The disciplinary borders of cultural studies, as a much larger area, are even more fluid than those of visual culture studies; as defined by Lawrence Grossberg, Cary Nelson, and Paula Treichler, "cultural studies is an interdisciplinary, transdisciplinary, and sometimes counter-disciplinary field that operates in the tension between its tendencies to embrace both a broad, anthropological and a more narrowly humanistic conception of culture. . . . Cultural studies is . . . committed to the study of an entire range of a society's arts, beliefs, institutions, and communicative practices" (Grossberg, Nelson, and Treichler 1992, 4). Television's MTV can reveal as much about the cultural practices of American adolescents today as could be discovered through systematic interviews with high-school guidance counselors.

Not surprisingly, as with its subfield of visual culture studies, the eclecticism of cultural studies has generated a degree of uncertainty about precisely what it is and does. Its focus on popular and contemporary culture has led many to associate it exclusively with these areas, but cultural studies includes work on high cultural topics as well. Contemporary work in cultural studies may be only distantly inspired, or not at all, by the British origins of the field, which was shaped by thinkers like Raymond Williams and Richard Hoggart in the 1950s and given official status by the founding in 1964 of the Centre for Contemporary Cultural Studies in Birmingham, directed first by Hoggart and then by Stuart Hall. Yet if cultural studies today is not always concerned with oppressed groups—above all the working class—or aimed at social change, as was the case in its formative days, it is still unified by its interest in social transformation and cultural change, as reflected for example in the relationships between cultural domains that appear distinct but prove on closer examination to be interdependent.

To date, the topic of visual culture in twentieth-century Germany[1] has not received comprehensive attention, although its potential contribution to the field of cultural studies is considerable. In recent years three important collections devoted to German cultural studies have appeared: *German Cultural Studies: An Introduction* (1995), edited by Rob Burns; *A User's Guide to German Cultural Studies* (1997), co-edited by Scott Denham, Irene Kacandes, and Jonathan Petropoulos; and *Contemporary German Cultural Studies* (2002), edited by Alison Phipps. The Burns volume is structured chronologically, the *User's Guide* and the Phipps collection by topic, and none of these anthologies emphasizes visual culture. On the other hand, there are relevant books that do not focus on Germany, such as *Vision in Context: Historical and Contemporary Perspectives on Sight* (1996), co-edited by Teresa Brennan and Martin Jay; *Visual Culture: The Reader* (1999), an anthology of texts collected by Jessica Evans and Stuart Hall on issues pertinent to the title subject, such as the gaze, the image, and the theory and practice of photography; and the Mirzoeff volumes mentioned earlier. Neither is there a focus on Germany in the special issue on visual culture published by the journal *October* (Summer 1996) or the British periodical *Journal of Visual Culture,* to mention some prominent examples.

By contrast, the following collection concentrates solely on German visual culture, which is especially rich and varied during the twentieth century. As indicated earlier, this collection does not share the view of Mitchell, Mirzoeff, and others that visual culture studies should focus on the second half of the twentieth century and on postmodernism in particular. Numerous developments during the 1900s, inflected by the idiosyncrasies of German history, favor a cohesive conception of the entire century as the visual age. In the course of the century the introduction and development of cinema and television, as well as the refinement of photography and printmaking, profoundly shaped the way people in the industrialized West saw and interacted with the world around them. Living as we now do in a culture saturated with images, we tend to forget that the ability to reproduce them by mechanical means rather than through manual copying is a relatively recent phenomenon. The florescence of visual culture in the West during the twentieth century is indebted above all to three technological developments: the mass production of prints, evolving from newspaper illustrations and pictorial broadsheets in the eighteenth century to lithographs and color prints in the nineteenth; photography, descended from the daguerreotype as conceived in the 1830s in France; and film, whose birth is associated with the moving picture apparatus that the brothers Auguste and Louis Lumière introduced in Paris in 1895. All three inventions were furthered by the unprecedented urbanization and industrialization that took place in nineteenth-century Europe, and all three advanced immeasurably during the twentieth century. As early as 1914, for example, Germany had some 2,500 cinemas.

In Germany these developments, like so much else in German history, were affected by the belated establishment of the German nation. During the centuries when Germany consisted of an agglomeration of small states, a discourse of cultural unity often took the place of nationhood and national power. After the founding of the German Empire beneath Bismarck in 1871, the strong compensatory impulse to create a unified national culture—to make up for lost time, as it were—had a decisive impact on visual culture in the following century. To mention only two instances: the art market gradually evolved from a system of royal patronage to one in which artists were supported by public and state funding, a transformation that was of crucial benefit to the arts. By way of illustration, one thinks in particular of Alfred Lichtwark, the first director of the Kunsthalle Hamburg (from 1886–1914), who in building the collection there expressly sought to contribute to the artistic education of the population. Lichtwark's beliefs—that art can function to counteract social ills and that the emphasis of art education should be visual pleasure rather than erudition—look ahead to twentieth-century debates in Germany and elsewhere about the role of art (Burns 1995, 36–37). Secondly, in a different vein, the linking of visual culture with national identity found its most extreme and most insidious manifestation during the 1930s, when the National Socialists exploited to the fullest the propagandistic potential of film.

These instances point to the especially close connection in the German tradition between visual studies and modern cultural conditions—in other words, to the rationale for the concept of "visual culture in twentieth-century Germany." During the 1900s Germany produced a wealth of offerings in a wide range of visual media. These developments include German technology's decisive contribution to photography and photojournalism at the turn of the century, cabaret culture, influential innovations in expressionist painting and cinema, pioneering experiments in modern dance between the world wars, powerful propaganda films of National Socialism; and the post-1990 cross-pollination between theaters from the former East and West Germany. In all these instances, German visual culture functioned as a vehicle through which important political, aesthetic, sexual, economic, and racial debates were played out.

Endeavoring to reflect this diversity, this collection spans a temporal spectrum from 1905 to 1999. Despite its focus on visual culture in a single linguistic tradition, this anthology manifests a degree of the eclecticism characteristic of cultural studies in general. Taken together, the contributions are not reducible to one model, to one subject, to the (pre-twentieth-century) past or present, or to high or low/popular culture, but instead they examine a spectrum of German cultural artifacts. The seventeen new essays collected here[2] treat film, photography, cabaret performance, architecture, painting, television, theater, print advertising, dance, and cartography. The essays range not only across these visual media but also temporally through individual media. To cite the case of film: Valerie Weinstein discusses comedic films of mistaken identity by Ernst Lubitsch from the first two decades of the century; Ingeborg Hoesterey explores interrelations between painting and film, notably *The Cabinet of Dr. Caligari*, in the 1910s and 1920s; Dagmar von Hoff studies the impact of training as a dancer on the cinematic aesthetics of director-actresses Leni Riefenstahl and Dorothy Arzner in films from the 1930s and 1940s; Patrick Greaney reads queer montage in a 1970s film by Rainer Werner Fassbinder through the lens of Brechtian theater; and Dagmar Lorenz illuminates the tensions between the West and the Muslim world as portrayed in a recent film by the Austrian director Ruth Beckermann.

Divided into sections on methodology and aesthetics, gender and sexuality, and political dimensions, this volume can be read either thematically, synchronically (according to visual medium), or chronologically (within the three sections). Taken together and in some cases individually, the essays form a truly interdisciplinary collection. This book thus responds to the question of how German studies can make the transition to German cultural studies. As in earlier cultural studies, the analyses are not merely textual but contextual, here illuminating the resonances of the media treated in terms of aesthetics, gender and sexuality, and politics. To mention only one example from each category: Janet Ward's essay explores the actual and metaphoric influence on post-*Wende* Berlin of American architecture as epitomized by Las Vegas, the quintessence of commercialization, commodification, and imitation; Barbara Kosta shows the ways in which cigarette advertisements in Weimar Germany open up new possibilities for the performance of gender, using the growing prominence of the New Woman and of the female consumer to attract potential smokers; and Kristin Kopp elucidates the subjective strategies through which post–World War I revisionist geopolitical maps function as tools of persuasive communication, downplaying Germany's defeat and aggrandizing its territorial dominion. But before turning to this volume's close studies of these and other facets of German visual culture, it will be helpful to take a look at some twentieth-century German thinkers whose insights into the aesthetic, political, and gender dimensions of visual culture provide an illuminating background to the essays collected here.

The interdisciplinary possibilities of visual culture were explored as early as 1917 by the German literary scholar Oskar Walzel, whose *Wechselseitige Erhellung der Künste* (Mutual illumination of the arts) suggested ways in which painting and literature or painting and music could shed light on each other. But as Ingeborg Hoesterey points out in her contribution to this volume, "The Interarts Experiment in Early German Film," Walzel's study remained unknown outside the academy (p. 23, this volume). Much better known and significantly more influential is the work of literary theorist and cultural critic Walter Benjamin, who, like Walzel, anticipated the power of the interdependent relationship between word and image. Of particular importance for visual culture studies, especially in Germany, are Benjamin's insights into the effects that modern technologies of reproduction—above all, printing, lithography, photography, and film—have had on art. These thoughts are elaborated in his classic essay "The Work of Art in the Age of Its Technological Reproducibility" (1936–1939), but are largely anticipated in a lesser-known piece he wrote in 1931, "Little History of Photography." A central thesis of the two essays is that the reproduction of works of art for mass consumption destroys what he calls a work's aura, which he defines as "[a] strange weave of space and time: the unique appearance or semblance of distance, no matter how close it may be" (Benjamin 1999, 518). Contributing to the decay of the aura is the growing need on the part of consumer—a need both driven and appeased by modern technology—to "possess the object in close-up in the form of a picture, or rather a copy" (Benjamin 1999, 519).

It is not difficult to recognize the aptness of Benjamin's aesthetic observations to the behavior of contemporary tourists, whether manifested as the desire to purchase a mouse pad replicating the Rosetta Stone or as the compulsion to own a piece of the Berlin Wall. A similar wish to collect, possess, interpret, and label a piece of the past, Benjamin argues, characterizes the treatment of photographs. The destruction of the photograph's aura is epitomized in his prediction that the caption will become the most important component of the shot. In sum, Benjamin associates original works of art with authenticity, uniqueness, embeddedness in tradition, a basis in ritual cult, and an aura that manifests distance from the observer and demands his or her concentration; whereas he links objects reproduced by technological means with commercialization, reproducibility, ahistoricity, the lack of an aura, proximity, and the function of distraction. In the later essay, inflected by the intervening rise of fascism, the political implications of this dichotomy are more evident. In contrast to the basis in ritual culture that Benjamin associates with genuine works of art, he notes here that technologically reproduced objects are based in politics, insofar as technological reproduction facilitates the politicization of art—another observation with far-seeing relevance to our media-dominated age.

Never one to see things one-sidedly, however, Benjamin also discerns a creative potential in modern media of technological reproduction. With reference to a photograph of the nineteenth-century photographer Karl Dauthendey and his fiancée, who (as Benjamin was aware) would commit suicide years later, he writes: "[T]he most precise technology can give its products a magical value, such as a painted picture can never again have for us. . . . the beholder feels an irresistible urge to search such a picture for the tiny spark of contingency, of the here and now, with which reality has (so to speak) seared the subject, to find the inconspicuous spot where in the immediacy of that long-forgotten moment the future nests so eloquently that we, looking back, may rediscover it" (Benjamin 1999, 510). On the one hand, then, photography, which Benjamin later terms the "first truly revolutionary means of reproduction" (Benjamin 2003, 256), appears to provide the most verisimilar reproduction of reality ever conceived; on the other hand, to the imaginative spectator it reveals nuances that lie beneath or beyond the surface of the image, truths of which it is unaware. In Benjamin's pithy formulation, "It is through photography that we first discover the exis-

tence of this optical unconscious, just as we discover the instinctual unconscious through psychoanalysis" (Benjamin 1999, 510–512).

Benjamin evokes the notion of the optical unconscious again in "The
Work of Art in the Age of Its Technological Reproducibility" in connection with film, thereby anticipating the prominent contemporary metaphor of Hollywood as a dream factory. He shows uncanny insight into
the uniqueness of film as a medium, suggesting that because film consists of scenes that can be isolated from each other, a process facilitated
by slow motion, close-ups, and other camera techniques, the new medium would lend itself to analysis better than painting did. One recognizes a modern parallel to the distinction in Lessing's "Laocoön" essay
(1766) between the fluid nature of literary representation and the static
quality of the plastic arts, the former moving the reader through the
emotional effects it produces whereas the latter freezes the viewer's focus and hence response. Whether Benjamin is writing about photography or cinema, the source of innovation is the camera, possessing unprecedented manipulative abilities. As is evident in the volume at hand,
the dialectic between "technology and magic" (Benjamin 1999, 512)
through which the camera's images circulate remains central to visual
culture studies seven decades later.

Benjamin's analyses of the groundbreaking effects of photography
and cinema find a next step in Max Horkheimer and Theodor Adorno's
Dialectic of Enlightenment, in the chapter entitled "The Culture Industry: Enlightenment as Mass Deception," expressly conceived as a reply
to "The Work of Art in the Age of Its Technological Reproducibility."
Written while the two thinkers were in exile in Los Angeles in 1944, the
essay is a politically motivated, strikingly prescient critique of the mass
entertainment business, or culture industry, which they conceive as
comprising film, photography, magazines, radio, and recordings of
popular music. Although their analysis is not limited to visual culture,
it has been so important for subsequent discussions of German (and
other) popular culture and its reception that it provides useful background to this volume.

Horkheimer and Adorno's assessment of the workings of the culture
industry is shaped by the Marxist orientation of their thinking and
their concomitant opposition to Hitlerian fascism: they attack the culture industry because of its basis in capital and because of its homogenizing influence, which Benjamin had earlier recognized as both a primary attraction and a major effect of mass culture as epitomized in
fascism. Horkheimer and Adorno regard the media of mass entertainment solely as businesses, possessing no social or other use value but

rather only exchange value. The chapter's subtitle—"enlightenment as mass deception"—reflects their view that the common people of the working class, enslaved to the ideology of mass entertainment, are deceived because "[t]he culture industry perpetually cheats its consumers of what it perpetually promises"—a true escape from their problems (Horkheimer and Adorno 1991, 139). Horkheimer and Adorno's attack on the culture industry is part of their larger Marxist critique of the capitalist system: "The idea of 'fully exploiting' available technical resources and the facilities for aesthetic mass consumption is part of the economic system which refuses to exploit resources to abolish hunger" (Horkheimer and Adorno 1991, 139). These insights have wide-ranging and far-seeing applicability: precisely the same argument is made today with reference to digital technology.

Horkheimer and Adorno analyze not only the physical and economic effects of the culture industry but also its psychological ramifications. For them, the mass entertainment business represents not genuine culture but the union of culture and entertainment, a "bloated pleasure apparatus" that "adds no dignity to man's lives" (Horkheimer and Adorno 1991, 139). The degree to which their analysis again anticipates the effects of digital visual culture is strikingly evident in Emily Apter's description of the "oneiric, anamorphic, junk-tech aesthetic of cyber-visuality" (Apter 1996, 27). Echoing Benjamin, Horkheimer and Adorno point out that insofar as the products of the culture industry— technologically reproduced and therefore standardized—are never originals but always copies, they in fact embody a corruption of culture. Plots of films and short stories in magazines are uninspired and predictable, failing to stimulate the imagination. Its every detail "stamped with sameness" (Horkheimer and Adorno 1991, 128), the culture industry has a homogenizing influence on its consumers, undermining their individuality and reducing them to a common (lowered) denominator: in consuming copies, they become copies of each other.

If Horkheimer and Adorno's critique appears harsh, it should be kept in mind that they conceived it in the throbbing heart of the culture industry, Los Angeles. Like Benjamin, they were forward-looking about the future of popular media. Although television was in its infancy at the time their essay was written, they foresaw its power to manipulate viewers, above all through advertisements, and predicted that it might someday deliver films right to people's homes, just as radio had brought them symphonies—and the speeches of the Führer.

As a final stage in this brief background survey of thinkers who shed particular light on German visual culture, Andreas Huyssen's *After the Great Divide: Modernism, Mass Culture, Postmodernism* genderizes the terms we have been looking at: he demonstrates the ways in which mass culture, which he regards as the "hidden subtext of the modernist project" (Huyssen 1986, 47) from which it is typically distinguished, is increasingly associated in the course of the nineteenth century with women, while "authentic," high culture remains the province of men. Huyssen cites political, psychological, and aesthetic examples from the turn of the century, when this dichotomy was especially visible, and observes that its rhetoric is no longer persuasive because the exclusion of women from high culture and its institutions on which this gender split was based has now been overcome. While this is of course true, the fact that in Germany fewer women than men as yet participate in high culture and its attendant institutions of power and that fewer women function as principal breadwinners could explain, at least in part, their greater consumption of selected forms of mass culture, such as television soap operas and certain types of popular film and fiction. This contemporary instance, highlighting the mutual influence of visual culture and gender patterns and the relation of both to socioeconomic realities, illustrates the heuristic potential of German visual culture, a potential whose multifaceted resonance this volume explores.

Notes

1. "Germany" refers to all nations in which German is the dominant language, i.e., Austria and Switzerland as well as Germany, both prior to and since 1990.

2. None has been published previously except a much longer version of Blake Stimson's "The Photographic Comportment of Bernd and Hilla Becher," which appeared in volume 1 of the online journal *Tate Papers* (Spring 2004).

Works Cited

Apter, Emily. "Anamorphic Art History." "Visual Culture Questionnaire." *Visual Culture.* Special issue of *October* 77 (Summer 1996): 26–27.

Bal, Mieke. "Visual Essentialism and the Object of Visual Culture." *Journal of Visual Culture* 2, no. 1 (2003): 5–32.

Baxandall, Michael. *Painting and Experience in Fifteenth-Century Italy: A Primer in the Social History of Pictorial Style.* Oxford: Clarendon Press, 1972.

Benjamin, Walter. "Little History of Photography." Vol. 2 of Benjamin, *Selected Writings: 1927–1934,* trans. Rodney Livingstone et al. and ed. Michael W.

Jennings, Howard Eiland, and Gary Smith, 507–530. Cambridge, Mass.: Belknap Press, 1999.

———. "The Work of Art in the Age of Its Technological Reproducibility." Vol. 4 of Benjamin, *Selected Writings: 1938–1940*, trans. Edmund Jephcott et al. and ed. Howard Eiland and Michael W. Jennings, 251–283. Cambridge, Mass.: Belknap Press, 2003.

Brennan, Teresa, and Martin Jay, eds. *Vision in Context: Historical and Contemporary Perspectives on Sight*. New York: Routledge, 1996.

Burns, Rob, ed. *German Cultural Studies: An Introduction*. Oxford: Oxford University Press, 1995.

Cartwright, Lisa. "Film and the Digital in Visual Studies: Film Studies in the Era of Convergence." *Journal of Visual Culture* 1, no. 1 (2002): 7–23.

Crary, Jonathan. "Visual Culture Questionnaire." *Visual Culture*. Special issue of *October* 77 (Summer 1996): 33–34.

Debord, Guy. *The Society of the Spectacle*. Trans. Donald Nicholson-Smith. New York: Zone, 1994.

Denham, Scott, Irene Kacandes, and Jonathan Petropoulos, eds. *A User's Guide to German Cultural Studies*. Ann Arbor: University of Michigan Press, 1997.

Evans, Jessica, and Stuart Hall, eds. *Visual Culture: The Reader*. London: Sage, 1999.

Grossberg, Lawrence, Cary Nelson, and Paula A. Treichler, eds. *Cultural Studies*. New York: Routledge, 1992.

Horkheimer, Max, and Theodor W. Adorno. *Dialectic of Enlightenment*. Trans. John Cumming. New York: Continuum, 1991.

Huyssen, Andreas. *After the Great Divide: Modernism, Mass Culture, Postmodernism*. Bloomington: Indiana University Press, 1986.

Jay, Martin. "That Visual Turn: The Advent of Visual Culture." *Journal of Visual Culture* 1, no. 1 (2002): 87–92.

Kaufmann, Thomas DaCosta. "Visual Culture Questionnaire." *Visual Culture*. Special issue of *October* 77 (Summer 1996): 45–48.

Lessing, Gotthold E. *Laocoön: An Essay on the Limits of Painting and Poetry*. Trans. Edward Allen McCormick. Baltimore: Johns Hopkins University Press, 1984.

Mirzoeff, Nicholas. *An Introduction to Visual Culture*. London: Routledge, 1999.

———, ed. *The Visual Culture Reader*. London: Routledge, 1998.

Mitchell, W. J. T. *Picture Theory: Essays on Verbal and Visual Representation*. Chicago: University of Chicago Press, 1994.

Phipps, Alison, ed. *Contemporary German Cultural Studies*. London: Arnold, 2002.

Robertson, George, et al., eds. *The "Block" Reader in Visual Culture*. London: Routledge, 1996.

Walzel, Oskar. *Wechselseitige Erhellung der Künste: Ein Beitrag zur Würdigung kunstgeschichtlicher Begriffe*. Berlin: Reuther and Reichard, 1917.

Williams, Raymond. *Keywords: A Vocabulary of Culture and Society*. New York: Oxford University Press, 1985.

PART I
Questions of Methodology and Aesthetics

1

Questions of Methodology in Visual Studies

Nora M. Alter

That German studies would formalize its interest in visual studies as an official category for interrogation some ten to fifteen years after the concept, or area, has been problematized by other scholarly fields points to the general lag time that it often takes national, foreign-language-based disciplines to acknowledge theoretical and academic trends adopted in English, comparative literature, or theory programs. That said, it should be emphasized that German studies is ahead of other foreign language concentrations in altering its curriculum offerings to include and reflect broader changes in the humanities. Many German departments in the United States include cultural studies as an integral part of their programs, and almost all regularly teach film in a rigorous way. It is therefore only natural that the discipline should now turn to visual studies—an area that is ascendant in that part of the academy that likes to think of itself as avant-garde. Visual culture, as defined by Douglas Crimp, "is the object of study in visual studies, which is a narrower area of cultural studies" (Crimp 1998, 31). A visual studies approach is viewed as an innovative means by which to update sleepy and conventional fields. However, like cultural studies before it, visual studies is a hotly contested new disciplinary formation whose adaptation is anything but seamless.

Rosalind Krauss and Hal Foster, in their "Introduction" to a special issue of the journal *October* devoted to "Visual Culture," propose that it is "both a partial description of a social world mediated by commodity images and visual technologies, and an academic rubric for interdisciplinary convergences among art history, film theory, media analysis, and

15

cultural studies" (Krauss and Forster 1996, 3). A brief history of visual culture would have to begin in Europe during the fifties with the theorization of the society of the spectacle by Guy Debord and the Situationists, who argued that the image has become primary in the era of advanced capitalism. As Debord put it in *The Society of the Spectacle*, "The Spectacle is *capital* to such a degree of accumulation that it becomes an image" (Debord 1967, Thesis #34). This was followed in the late fifties and sixties by a series of texts by the French sociologist Jean Baudrillard that further investigated the production of the media-saturated society, as well as by the writings of literary theorist Roland Barthes. The latter's essays on images as diverse as the face of Garbo and the *Paris Match* cover of a Senegalese soldier saluting the French flag grafted a theory of image interpretation onto cultural analysis. While this approach to visuality was based on a sociohistorical model of criticism, a different one was taken up in the next decade in the British film journal *Screen*. Enormously influential in the seventies, *Screen* featured an array of critical texts that theorized concepts of visuality and the gaze from a psychoanalytic and feminist viewpoint.

The late eighties and nineties saw an explosion of publications on the topic of visuality coming from a variety of disciplines: philosophy, literary studies, art history, anthropology, ethnography, gender studies, and more. Indeed, critics such as W. J. T. Mitchell have gone so far as to propose that a "pictorial turn" has supplanted the "linguistic turn" (Mitchell 1994). This, of course, resurrects the debate initiated by Lessing in the eighteenth century, which opposed the linguistic (poetry and literature) and the plastic arts (painting and sculpture). Visual culture has roots in such diverse, linguistically based theoretical paradigms as, among others, structuralism, iconography, hermeneutics, semiotics, psychoanalysis, aesthetics, and reception theory. This heritage has led some to ask whether or not visual culture should be accounted for in linguistic or discursive terms. By relying on a textual model to examine the visual, the argument goes, one automatically subsumes and transforms the visual into the linguistic, thereby ignoring the irreconcilable differences between these two cultural modes. However, others such as Jacques Derrida insist that pure realms of either language or visuality do not exist, and that rather than being distinct, these constructs are fully interdependent. I do not want to engage with this debate at this particular theoretical level. Rather, I would like to signal a number of issues that may have more practical consequences in our use and practice of visual culture.

One of the overarching claims for visual culture, as with cultural studies, is that we live in an era characterized by a proliferation of images. These range from fine art and architecture to film, advertisements, and other visual media—from the highest cultural expression to the lowest and most popular. This diversity has led some to warn against visual studies as a "pseudopopulist leveling of all cultural values" (Jay 1996, 44). This line of argumentation, which in essence seeks to shut down meaningful discussion about a nascent field of study, is by no means new. In fact, it is to a certain extent predictable, for it echoes precisely the same charges that were brought against cultural studies and the scholarly examination of popular and mass cultural texts some years ago by more traditional literary scholars and theorists in the academy. However, a more productive approach is adopted by Foster, who, while acknowledging the dangers of blurring "high" and "low" objects of study in the "shift from history to culture" that "may promote, in art as well as in criticism, a posthistorical reduction," goes on to argue that at the same time these approaches allow for a "multihistorical complication" (Foster 1996, 105). Thus, for Foster, cultural studies and, by extension, visual culture promote a field of investigation that rightly includes alterity. There is no point in rehearsing the culture war debates in detail, since they are by now quite familiar. Briefly stated, the logic contra cultural studies maintained that if programs devoted to the teaching and researching of texts with high cultural "value" were infiltrated by the study of other cultural objects—some of them not even literary—the entire field would lose its standards and become less rigorous, less specialized, and increasingly politicized. The assault against cultural studies came primarily from literary historians, and the attack on visual culture has been voiced most vociferously by art historians. That art historians would have strong objections to the establishment of an interdisciplinary field of visual studies is not surprising, for such a formation would directly threaten their disciplinary boundaries in terms of enrollments, publications, and influence in the art world. By the latter, I refer not only to the writing of art history and criticism, but also to guest curating, catalogue publishing, and the like. However, the point made by art historians and critics—that learning to read the visual in all of its complexities is equivalent to learning another language and should be treated as such by colleagues in other fields—is well taken. We all have a basic knowledge of how to read written texts. But we generally accept that literary scholars have spent a considerable amount of time studying the operation of texts and are better equipped than most to analyze textual complexities. It follows that the same should hold true for the scholar of visual images, such as the art historian or critic. Along these lines, it is important not to subordinate a formal reading to a thematic or sociocritical one. Although, as Mitchell has recently observed, the concept of form is historically obsolete, it is still a key to unlocking a text's meaning (Mitchell 2003).

Scholars not trained in the study of images tend to adopt a synchronic or "snapshot" approach to their objects of study. This horizontal manner of examining visual texts, while producing many invaluable insights, ultimately falls short, since it neglects the vertical or diachronic analysis of the elements that led to the production of the objects in question. Rather than attempt to determine how images negotiate the conventional codes established over time, the synchronic study of images is primarily concerned with decoding. By contrast, the field of literary studies has long maintained the importance of synthesizing a synchronic with a diachronic approach. Thus, for example, to study a contemporary novel, the literary scholar will keep in mind a whole history and genealogy of the novel and its developments. Yet this is not the case with visual images. The iconography of a particular photograph is read, but not the manner in which the photograph negotiates either the genre of which it is a part (for example, portraiture, still life, landscape) or its own proper medium. This disregard for how a visual object is constructed within its own specific field of possibilities produces an unbalanced and incomplete critical analysis—one weighted entirely in the direction of horizontality. And it is precisely such endeavors that provide fuel for those who seek to prevent extradisciplinary intervention in the realm of the visual. The scholar who neglects the manner in which an image negotiates the conventions of its genre or the limits of its medium is at best dismissed, at worst ignored. Hence it is crucial for those entering the realm of visual studies to learn how to interpret both the genealogical and the iconographical aspects of the discipline and to treat it respectfully.

Since many in the field of German studies are textually trained and oriented, there is a tendency to read visual culture either theoretically or thematically through a linguistic lens. However, visual texts are inherently dynamic, often involving the audial and the tactile as well as the optical sense, and substantial meaning is lost if the focus is exclusively on the visual component. Indeed, in German studies we must be careful not to do to architecture, film, or the fine arts what was done by traditional drama criticism to theater, where the live performative component was neglected in favor of a concentration on written form. Even from its inception, film was meant to have sound, and a large number of artworks in the second half of the twentieth century require a phenomenological or otherwise participatory interaction with the viewer for their full meaning to unfold. Clearly, to concentrate an analysis solely on the surface visual effect in these works produces a superficial reading at best.

Let me now turn to another problematic issue in the study of twentieth-century visual culture, one that is primarily historical. Writing about early-twentieth-century visual art is obviously very different from writing about contemporary culture. Here I am referring to a certain consciousness or awareness of the image that has evolved over the course of the century. As noted earlier, there has been a rise in both the production and the critique of visual culture in the second half of the twentieth century. Within the fine arts, this has been manifest in the move away from the visual aesthetic object toward a condition in which art is no longer defined primarily by optical faculties. Therefore, any study of visual culture must be alert to the often self-reflexive critique against visuality performed by these texts. For example, much conceptual art, generally considered to be the most influential art of the last third of the twentieth century, eschews visual representation. Thus even within the area of investigation considered to be the purview of the visual, the term "visual culture" has a limiting effect.

This brings me to another point, which concerns the actual visual texts that preoccupy us. Whereas no text is too difficult, obscure, hermetic, avant-garde, or experimental within the field of literature and theory, the opposite seems true in the visual realm. In the rush to embrace visuality, we seem to be rooted in the representational, the "easy-to-read." For example, in German studies our tastes often turn to the works of painters such as Gerhard Richter, whose *18 Oktober 1977* series has been the object of a great deal of analysis. Yet equally if not more significant artists such as Bernd and Hilla Becher, Martin Kippenberger, or Hans Haacke have tended to remain obscure to us and out of reach. Haacke's work in particular, considered to be among the most influential in the late twentieth century (though, in stark contrast to works by artists such as Richter, they are anathema to the art market), negates aesthetic conventions. It is "anti-aesthetic," yet fully visual. Indeed, one might have thought that his art, with its many textual components, would have been of interest to those with literary backgrounds. Similarly, when architect Daniel Libeskind's Jewish Museum in Berlin is treated by scholars interested in visual studies, it is usually only the architectural structure that is subjected to critique and not his writings. The latter are presented in an unproblematized way, read as factual documents, a treatment we would never grant a literary text. Why this discrepancy? Are we blinded by the very spectacle we seek to deconstruct? Or does market value drive our visual analyses? Within film studies, again it is narrative film that is of interest; whether Weimar, Third Reich, New German Cinema, Postwall, or exile cinema, the films that attract our attention are the ones that are most successful. Ignored is the rich experimental tradition of nonnarrative avant-garde film, initiated by, among others, Hans Richter and Oskar Fischinger, which is understandably marginalized in mass society but less understandably so within the academy. Thus, I would urge that we not look at the most familiar products of visual culture, but rather tackle visual texts that are challenging, that elude facile interpretative or predictable glosses. However, this can only be achieved if we adopt a diachronic as well as a synchronic perspective.

Finally, I would like to raise one more cautionary word—namely, that when we develop theories in visual studies, we move beyond Western models as the sole interpretive lens. To limit ourselves to canonical Western texts is shortsighted and not in step with multicultural German studies that have shifted the focus from exclusively German texts to include hybrid Turkish-German, Afro-German, and other minority discourses. To take the canon as our point of critical reference runs the risk of folding these vibrant syncretic texts back into a Pan-Germanic means of understanding. Instead, not only the objects we examine but also our entire theoretical apparatus should reflect an opening of the field.

What then is to be done in order to develop our practice of visual studies successfully? Let us look at two models that have, to my mind, achieved success. I am referring on the one hand to feminism, and to the crucial role that the organization Women in German has played in altering and shaping not only German studies but also women's and gender studies programs, and on the other hand to German film studies, which I single out because of my own familiarity with its genealogy as well as its close affiliation with visual culture. In both instances, Germanists are leaps and bounds ahead of other foreign language departments, as evidenced by the reputations of the two disciplines both nationally and internationally. The best scholarship in German feminist and gender studies and in German film is regularly published by American or British university presses, authored by individuals whose primary departmental affiliation is German. French, Italian, and Spanish departments offer no parallel. Scholars trained in the United States regularly participate in relevant annual conferences and often form an integral part of their institution's interdisciplinary studies programs, which are usually dominated by English professors.

In this sense, success for Germanists in the field and practice of visual studies would manifest itself in the following three areas: (1) active participation in debates on visual studies at conferences, seminars, and symposia; (2) the establishment of, and the full involvement by, Germanists in inter- and transdisciplinary university or college visual studies programs; and (3) the production of critical texts (in the form of publications or publicly presented papers) capable of interweaving several disciplines and thereby providing rich analyses and interpretations that illuminate and push forward several disciplines.[1]

Why do I feel that this is necessary? My answer is unavoidably connected to a larger problem, one that is part of the general "crisis in the humanities" and related to the changing function of the university as we enter the twenty-first century. If we in German departments do not want to find ourselves reduced to language service, then it is crucial that we play an active role institutionally, nationally, and internationally as intellectuals. In order to survive, it is imperative that we transcend the boundaries of our relatively closed departments and function as scholars whose ideas and writings are also of interest to other fields. This takes a lot of hard work—the success of German film studies was due, in part, to the tireless efforts of Anton Kaes and Eric Rentschler, among others; in women's and gender studies, the contributions of Patricia Herminghouse, Sara Lennox, and Susanne Zantop, to mention but a few, have been invaluable. In both instances dedication to advancing the field has been continued by the next generation. This community of scholars works, and encourages others to work, collaboratively, and I think that this is a key to avoiding some of the pitfalls that I raised earlier. Here we might heed the advice of Sander Gilman, who often stresses the importance of collaborative work. Collaborations, he argues, are of great benefit to scholars, insofar as they aid in crossing disciplines effectively and increase the likelihood of reaching a larger public. If Germanists are to play a significant role in visual culture, which I think we should, then we will need to produce responsible texts based on rigorous scholarship that is knowledgeable about and respectful of the complexities of all the relevant fields involved.

Notes

1. The essays in this volume can be viewed as responses to this last call, as well as to Alter's exhortations in this essay that Germanists venture beyond familiar objects of study and adopt a diachronic approach in their investigations of visual culture. *Ed.*

Works Cited

Crimp, Douglas. "Lost: Cultural Studies, Visual Culture." In *Lecture in the Visual Arts 1996–1997: Samuel P. Harn Eminent Scholar Lecture Series*, 27–38. Gainesville, Fla.: Samuel P. Harn Museum of Art, 1998.

Debord, Guy. *The Society of the Spectacle*. 1967. Reprint. Detroit: Black and Red, 1983.

Foster, Hal. "The Archive without Museums." *Visual Culture*. Special issue of *October* 77 (Summer 1996): 97–119.

Jay, Martin. "Visual Culture Questionnaire." *Visual Culture*. Special issue of *October* 77 (Summer 1996): 42–44.

Krauss, Rosalind, and Hal Foster. Introduction. *Visual Culture*. Special issue of *October* 77 (Summer 1996): 3–4.

Mitchell, W. J. T. "The Commitment to Form; or, Still Crazy after All These Years." *PMLA* 118 (2003): 321–325.

———. *Picture Theory: Essays on Verbal and Visual Representation*. Chicago: University of Chicago Press, 1994.

2

The Interarts Experiment in Early German Film

Ingeborg Hoesterey

It's a fitting scenario for our age of crossover priorities: a prominent literary scholar at Humboldt University introduces the concept of "Wechselseitige Erhellung der Künste" (Mutual illumination of the arts) in a lecture given in 1917 before the Kant-Gesellschaft, Berlin, and published the same year. The idea moves a few blocks and is taken up by a group of stage designers at the Deutsches Theater, who subsequently apply it to the making of a silent movie.

Alas, no such juncture occurred. Oskar Walzel's project, the Magna Charta of the comparative study of the arts (Weisstein 1992, 10), never traveled beyond academe. The creation of *The Cabinet of Dr. Caligari* in the summer of 1919 in Berlin-Weissensee was nourished by a cultural climate in which the stimuli of the new were disseminated from art scene to stage to cinematic production, enhanced by a general enthusiasm for the formal experiment and a rupture with tradition.

Throughout the twentieth century and up to today, *Caligari* has been hailed by aficionados of various persuasions as the exemplar of intermedia aesthetics in cinema. It was, however, not without some hesitation that the director, Dr. Robert Wiene, himself knowledgeable about art, underwrote the move to crossover proposed by set designer Walter Reimann and film architect Hermann Warm. A question rarely asked is, what sort of creative energies in German visual culture helped shape this breakthrough? To be sure, despite World War I, the Berlin art scene was buzzing with new directions. French cubism was shown at Herwarth Walden's gallery, Der Sturm, and influenced expressionist artists; futurist art made its appearance soon after the publication in German of

Marinetti's *Manifesto del futurismo* in the journal *Der Sturm*. At this point, it is worthwhile to contextualize briefly. What energized the art community (in Europe and beyond) was nothing less than the most significant paradigm shift in the genre of painting since the Renaissance: the move by the first modernists from mimetic representation to semi-abstract and abstract modes.

Some German artists felt the modernist drive as a challenge to extend the traditional object character of the painted canvas, no matter how abstract it had become, by transposing the properties of the fine arts genre into the cinematic medium—to create paintings on the move. Thus the painters Walter Ruttmann and Hans Richter proposed that the language of the visual be the essential property of the new medium. In a programmatic essay of 1914, Ruttmann defined the film medium as *Malerei mit Zeit* ("painting in time"), which for him was superior to the atemporal, reductive formulas of painting (Goergen 1989, 74). The future author of abstract film went so far as to predict that cinematography would succeed the centuries-old form of painting.

In the second decade of the twentieth century, art-oriented filmmaking in Germany established its identity by means of a dialogue with a "classical" plastic art genre that it proceeded to deconstruct. A motion picture, however, limited in scope, was envisaged as *bewegte Malerei* ("motion painting") that should affect the senses like the temporality of music and dance (Diebold 1921). Walter Ruttmann's earliest "absolute film," *Lichtspiel Opus 1* of 1921, exemplified this program of cinema as visual art and inaugurated what would later become known as the German avant-garde film (see below). The movement included the makers of abstract films Hans Richter and Oskar Fischinger, whose development profited considerably from the bold conflation of the painting genre with the kinetic medium undertaken by the artists of *The Cabinet of Dr. Caligari.*

After its premiere on February 27, 1920 at the Marmorhaus on Kurfürstendamm, the movie was hailed by most critics as the first expressionist film, as the savvy press campaign of the production company Decla-Bioscop had suggested. (For several weeks, posters on walls and in subway stations had featured an enticing line from the movie: "Du musst Caligari werden!" [You must become Caligari!]). The often brief and anonymous reviews in the Berlin papers praised the "painterly vigor" with which the bizarre images were rendered. A preview in the popular *BZ am Mittag* on the day of the film's premiere suggested that the vaguely unreal mood and the distortions of a soul could have been achieved only by painterly means, through *Flächenkunst* ("flat decorative painting"). Those who had argued that the poet of the cinema would be a painter were emphatically applauded by the reviewer of the renowned *Vossische Zeitung*. Signing as "My," Dr. Wilhelm Meyer proclaimed that finally a work of art had been achieved that followed the natural laws of the new kinetic medium while pursuing its strongest means of expression, the painterly (Meyer 1920).

The argument for cinematography as a kind of painting needs to be seen as a point in the evolutionary phase of the new medium when sound had not even been conceived of as a future integral aspect of film. Furthermore, many in the visual arts community deplored the way in which hundreds of productions relied on turning cheap, melodramatic plots into petty-realist moving pictures at the neglect of a more demanding visual semiotics. *Caligari* introduced this potential in spectacular fashion.[1]

From the beginning, the reception was split as to the meaning of the conspicuous presence of modernist art displayed by the painted sets. Most reviewers saw the sets as furnishing a kind of *Seelenlandschaft* ("landscape of the soul"), pictorial signs to be read as symbolic objectivations of Francis's hallucinations. To paraphrase Rudolf Kurtz, the plunging surfaces, agitated linearity, crooked streets and winding stairs, ghostlike barren trees, forces animating doors that are greedy, hollow openings—all these elements of the fantastic and the scary were deemed to enhance the *Stimmung* of the tale (Kurtz 1926, 66). Many critics saw in the distorted space and contours a congenial representation of the inner workings of a deranged mind; after all, the initial subtitle of the film had been "Wie ein Wahnsinniger die Welt sieht" (How a madman sees the world). A special *Caligari* issue of the *Illustrierte Film-Kurier* (no. 6, 1920) described both the visuals and the plot as "krankhaft, Zickzack, verrückt" (sick, zigzag, crazy).

Those familiar with modernist art recognized the flaw in the appropriation of this innovative visual style for a psychological narrative. In the prestigious *Berliner Börsen-Courier*, Herbert Jhering pointed to the dangerous equation of expressionist form and mental illness: "Impressionismus ist da, wo man zurechnungsfähig, Expressionismus, wo man unzurechnungsfähig bleibt" (impressionism = sound mind; expressionism = insanity) (Jhering 1920). A promoter of the expressionist cause, Jhering complained that in *Caligari* this cultural movement was placed in service to the portrayal of a demented mind. The famous theater critic would have liked to see the expressionist interpretation evolve organically rather than as a sensational novelty. Similarly, the French writer Blaise Cendrars warned that *Caligari* might be received as "a film that casts discredit on all modern art" (Cendrars 1922, 351).

As far as the artist-craftsmen Warm, Reimann, and Walter Röhrig were concerned, their foremost aim was to heighten the fantastic quality of the plot rather than to depict a case of insanity. In an interview given to the *Illustrierte Film-Kurier* (no. 6, 1920), Reimann commented that, speaking in cinematographic terms, expressionism for him meant the "rhythmic intensification of the script's dramatic idea, though no longer on a naturalist basis, but generated by a purely artistic sensibility." The stage designer from the Deutsches Theater, who authored the slogan "Filmkunst ist Bildkunst!" (Film art is pictorial art!) (Kaul 1971, 11), was not primarily interested in the psychological function of the decor, but rather in applying the styles of modernist visual art so as to convey an extravagant mood. We know that Reimann was actively pursuing a career as a painter and showed his art nouveau drawings and expressionist oils in public art exhibitions in Berlin (Kamps 1997, 25). A minor artist, Reimann was a typical receptor type, picking up formal innovations wherever he could; it is more than likely that he regularly saw advanced art at the gallery Der Sturm.[2]

The pragmatics of the production situation—the need to complete the movie in four weeks while cutting costs wherever possible—led Hermann Warm to opt for painted rather than modeled sets and prompted him to hire Walter Reimann (who in turn hired his colleague from the Deutsches Theater, Walter Röhrig). The dilemma allowed the designers to produce painterly *Flächenkunst* in the manner of expressionist and other semi-abstract canvases. The pointed shapes so frequently displayed on the painted sets in *Caligari* recall the "Gothic" style of Ernst Ludwig Kirchner's Berlin "street pictures," whereas the zigzag pattern on Cesare's path echoes the artist's 1910 *African Nude* (Bremen) as well as a Klee watercolor, *Play of Forces*, which had just appeared in the *Sturm* journal in 1919. Exaggerated high hats such as the one worn by Dr. Caligari populate Lionel Feininger's painting *Pink Sky* (*Street in Paris*) of 1909 (Iowa Art Museum); the crooked houses that make up the little town of Holstenwall are most often associated with Ludwig Meidner's apocalyptic cityscapes, although a 1916 picture by Johannes Itten, *Houses in Spring* (Thyssen-Bornemisza Collection, Madrid), left its traces as well. Kandinsky's early abstract compositions are ubiquitous; the swirling, joyous movements on his canvases are visibly present in the frames depicting the fair, a fact that refutes Siegfried Kracauer's rather odd reading of the scene as reflecting the chaos after World War I (Kracauer 1947, 74).

The German reception of French cubism after 1912, mostly work by minor artists such as Albert Gleizes and Jean Metzinger, can be detected in the asymmetrical windows, walls, and roofs. It gave the designers the aesthetic license to *paint* light and shadows instead of shaping and dramatizing space by modeling, which allowed the cameraman, Willy Hameister, to get by with using merely diffuse light. (The savings, in turn, pleased production manager Rudolf Meinert, as it reduced the expense of securing lighting from the severely rationed electrical facilities in postwar Berlin.)

The question of attribution, who created what, is complex and by no means clear. Hermann Warm was the only member of the team still alive after 1945. (He died in 1976 at the age of eighty-seven.) In interviews in the sixties, Warm promoted the claim that it was he who had conceived of the expressionist style of *Caligari*, because the "droll" screenplay needed *skurrile Malerei* (Kaul 1970, 11–12). The notion of visual expressionism as "droll painting," to fit the script by Carl Mayer and Hans Janowitz, does not suggest an acute awareness of visual modernism on the part of Warm, in contrast to his film architecture for Carl Dreyer's *La passion de Jeanne d'Arc* of 1928.[3] In one of the interviews, Warm did concede that it was Walter Reimann who had proposed and pushed for painted sets done in the expressionist style when the three of them were sitting over the script during the first exhilarated night of planning (Engel 1964, 30).

In 1968 Warm reconstructed for the Stiftung Deutsche Kinemathek (now part of the Berlin Filmmuseum) thirty sketches for the sets of *Caligari*, as well as a small-scale model of the Lixie studio. The drawings give only a rough impression of the genesis of the *Caligari* style. They are generally referred to as "originals" by Warm and as "reconstructions." Warm's "design" titled *Dächer*, on view in the Berlin Filmmuseum, echoes one of the most striking sketches for *Caligari*, depicting Cesare dragging Jane over a steep incline of rooftops, that is displayed in Berlin as a still only. It is, however, well documented as being by Walter Reimann; a stunning color print, it accompanies an article by the set designer in the September 1925 issue of *Filmtechnik* (vol. 1, no. 9).[4]

To be part of an artistic breakthrough is symbolic capital. Robert Wiene was the first to capitalize on *Caligari*'s success by making two more pictures using painted, modernist sets, *Genuin* (1920) and *Raskolnikov* (1922), both unsuccessful. The unique symbiosis of painting and film in *The Cabinet of Dr. Caligari* meanwhile led to the film's being chosen to open the first art house cinema in the United States, the Fifth Avenue Playhouse in New York, in 1926. At the same time, Walter Reimann wrote articles for *Filmtechnik* elaborating on his significant contribution to the movie—and was invited to work in Hollywood in 1928.[5] And Hermann Warm effectively circulated a statement in his later career that he had originally made in 1920, "Das Filmbild muss Graphik werden" (The cinematic image must become graphic), which to this day

Figure 2.1. Walter Reimann, sketch for *Caligari*.
Courtesy Deutsche Kinemathek (Filmmuseum Berlin).

adds to his reputation as the originator of the *Caligari* style.[6] To be sure, none of the players in this game for fame could have been aware at the time that their experimentalism would mark a watershed in the evolving culture of motion pictures. It was after the discursive event of *Caligari* that film split into two structurally and aesthetically different genres: narrative film, featuring mimetic representation, invisible editing, and so forth; and absolute film, representing nothing but the transposition of abstract art, that is, modernist art, onto the filmstrip (cf. Messel 1928, 240).

Narrative cinema, as we know, conquered the world, whereas abstract film remained a minority aesthetic, albeit a highly sophisticated idiom.[7] A detour via a prominent postmodern revival of *The Cabinet of Dr. Caligari* may provide an enticing introduction to both the debt to and the fascination for *Caligari* on the part of the emerging makers of abstract film. In 2002 the American Robert Wilson, notorious for his aesthetic promiscuity, created an ingenious pastiche of the 1920 film for the Deutsches Theater in Berlin, titled *Dr. Caligari*. Wilson's theater tends toward pure visuality, often via an emphatic language of projected light, which is used in this production to turn silent cinema, complete with accompanying pianist, into stage performance. Figures move about as if in a tableau, albeit with exaggerated expressiveness as in a silent film. Colorful geometric shapes light up magically—as if on a canvas.

Wilson's hybrid spectacle pays homage not only to the restored, tinted, and toned version of *The Cabinet of Dr. Caligari* but also to those painted props that appear isolated from the general cubo-expressionist decor, especially in the black and white copies.[8] They are the asymmetrical window in Caligari's shack, in particular the jagged triangular window that dynamizes the space (and the frame) where the murdered town clerk is found As is so often the case in the multidiscursivity of culture, a style revival in the plastic arts or a remake of a literary classic brings out features of the original work in a more intense, more visible way. Wilson's revival, executed in a taut neoconstructivist style, makes us more aware of a certain underrated aspect of the 1920 movie—that, unintentionally on the part of its makers, its decor does nothing less than synthesize the major avant-garde directions of the day: cubism, futurism, and constructivism. French cinéastes did their work of significant condensation earlier, celebrating the film's intermediality as *caligarisme* (Courtade 1984).

Constructivism, Russian and Dutch, was the movement of importance for Walter Ruttmann and his *Lichtspiel Opus* series, made between 1921 and 1925. In a Frankfurt Ufa theater, before a few invited artists and critics, Ruttmann's *Lichtspiel Opus 1* was premiered in April 1921,

Figure 2.2. The jagged window in *Caligari*.
Courtesy Deutsche Kinemathek (Filmmuseum Berlin).

with music played by Max Butting. Bernhard Diebold, an editor with the *Frankfurter Zeitung,* hailed the *Lichtspiel* as "Eine neue Kunst. Die Augenmusik des Films" (A new art: The visual music of the film, April 2, 1921). His description, with remnants of expressionist language, grasps the excitement elicited by the first German "absolute" film. A few paraphrasing glimpses must suffice here: Round blue shapes open into elliptical ones; angular shapes push from the edge of the frame toward the middle. Pink and light green ribbons wave over the surface as if dancing around, and pointed forms sting combatively. There is a red sun—in labor. Diebold, who was Swiss, applauded the artist for "painting" his film, driven to movement by expressionist painting, and drawing "his speed from the cinematic rush of the futurist canvas." The oxymoron *bewegte Malerei* should become the "signature" label not only for Ruttmann's *Opus* films, but for German abstract film of the early twenties.

With *Opus 3,* Ruttmann arrived at his constructivist idiom: squares, rectangles, trapezoids, and circles—in black and white. It was first shown in May 1925 together with *Opus 2* and *Opus 4,* during a matinee entitled *Der absolute Film* organized by the *Novembergruppe,* and in collaboration with Ufa, which had provided artists with equipment for the production of animated films since 1920. The authentic avant-garde event, which featured other now-historical reels, had to be repeated a week later, this time with Hans Richter's *Film ist Rhythmus* (a.k.a. *Rhythmus 25*) on the program, which had been finished just days before.[9] In 1921 his *Rhythmus 21* competed with Ruttmann's *Opus 1* and its avid reception; Richter's short would become better known during the artist's American exile than that of his colleague who remained in Nazi Germany.[10]

Hans Richter, who died in 1976, was a cubist painter in Berlin with ambitions to introduce musical structures into his canvases—not unlike Kandinsky in spirit. His oils *Cello Player* (1914) and *Music* (1915) show a familiarity with the French cubists who were exhibited at Herwarth Walden's gallery Der Sturm. In 1916 Richter joined the Dada group in Zurich, where he befriended Tristan Tzara and worked with the Swede Viking Eggeling on merging the visual code of painting with structures derived from music (for example, from Busoni's compositions) in a filmstrip, an artistic collaboration they continued after the war in Berlin.

Rhythmus 21 is four minutes of nonobjective film on which rectangular and square shapes move rhythmically toward each other—constructivist painting in rhythmic motion. Inspired by Mondrian and other De Stijl artists, as well as the suprematist compositions of Malevich, the piece predated Ludwig Hirschfeld-Mack's attempts at abstract animation in

Figure 2.3. Hans Richter, *Rhythm 21*, filmstrip.
Courtesy Deutsche Kinemathek (Filmmuseum Berlin).

the Bauhaus. As Standish Lawder wrote: "Perhaps more than any other avant-garde film, [*Rhythm 21*] uses the movie screen as a direct substitute for the painter's canvas, as a framed rectangular surface on which a kinetic organization of purely plastic forms was composed" (Lawder 1975, 49).

In a letter to Alfred Barr Jr. at the Museum of Modern Art in New York (November 16, 1942), Richter describes how he moved from painting to film: "I used the square (or rectangle) as the simplest way of dividing the square *film-screen,* after I had discovered that our scrolls [his and Eggeling's] were painting and followed the laws of painting not filming. The simple square gave me the opportunity to forget about the complicated matter of our drawings and to concentrate on the orchestration of movement and time" (Russett and Starr 1988, 49).

Rhythm 21 became a staple of American avant-garde film culture because, according to Elena Pinto Simon, it resonated with the ideas of modernism in all its permutations (Simon 1977). By "animating the image, putting it into motion, and playing it against the very notion of cinema frame and illusions of space," Richter's 1921 filmstrip reflected the visual preoccupations of Mondrian and the De Stijl group. Moreover, it seemed to prefigure the cinematic self-reflexivity of Michael Snow's *Wavelength* of 1967.

In 1922 Hans Richter attended the congress of international constructivists in Weimar and subsequently founded the journal *G—Zeitschrift für elementare Gestaltung* (G—Journal for Elementary Formation), which appeared at irregular intervals between 1923 and 1926. As editor, Richter was aided by board members such as the young and rather politicized Mies van der Rohe in the practice of implementing a collectivist constructivism—as a social utopia. Contributions in the form of texts and images by artist colleagues—Dutch, French, Hungarian, and Soviet—were published if they were deemed relevant to the constructivist ideal of a technically rationalized and holistic organization of life. Several of the participants in the 1922 Weimar conference supplied essays and statements; Laszlo Moholy-Nagy, who had just joined the Bauhaus faculty, offered a graphic work, *Construction,* for reproduction in one of the 1923 issues; and from Moscow, Nathan Altmann sent a missive in which he acerbically condemned modernist directions such as cubism, suprematism, and expressionism as *l'art pour l'art* and unsuitable for the new Soviet Republic (Altmann 1924, 35).

Special issues dealt with topics such as "Die neue Wohnung" (the new home) and architecture, the latter edited by Mies van der Rohe. It was Hans Richter whose intellectual and entrepreneurial energy managed to hold the heterogeneous corpus of the journal together, aided, no doubt, by the use of the typographical anarchism developed by the Dadaists, which made for a progressive, optically unconventional appearance. Richter was noticeably in the process of retrieving his Dada past, occasionally interjecting irreverent phrases in large bold typeface such as: "Es gibt noch keinen Film, nur eine perverse Abart photographierter Literatur!" (There is no film as yet, only a perverse, degenerate species of photographed literature!) (Richter 1926, April 5/6).

Although Richter continued to reproduce sequences from his *Rhythm* series in *G*, he turned away from the purism of his constructivist work in 1926. The (originally cubist) technique of *collage* had been adopted and redefined by the Dadaists before 1920; John Heartfield discovered that he could create visually provocative political comments by developing collage into *photomontage*.[11] In a number of shorts that Hans Richter made between 1927 and 1929, these innovations in the art scene had a significant impact on his new style of "intellectual montage" (Bordwell and Thompson 1986, 383). The 1927 piece *Inflation*, for example, was commissioned as an introduction to the feature film *Die Dame mit der Maske* (The lady with the mask, 1928), whose theme was inflation; the collage-montage style of *Inflation* is nothing less than an effective political statement. The short film also features the kind of shock effects that Walter Benjamin will later identify in the "Work of Art" essay and elsewhere as providing the self-protective mechanisms that human beings develop against the threatening aspects of contemporary society.

Superimposition, negative film, cinematic photomontage—Richter experimented with filmic form in a way that thirty years later would strike members of the American "underground" film movement as highly original in its distance from the cinematic orthodoxy of the "classical" Hollywood movie. *Everything Turns* of 1929 is a marvelous study in filmic self-reflexivity, and the whimsical surrealism cum Dada in *Vormittagsspuk* (Ghosts before breakfast, 1927–1928) not only testifies to the symbiotic relationship of the two movements, but also introduces us to several of the Berlin avant-garde personalities in action, the best-known of which were Werner Graeff, Paul Hindemith, and Hans Richter.

The climate of reception that awaited Hans Richter in his American exile in the early forties privileged the Dadaist and modernist artist alike, which resulted in Richter's being offered the directorship of the Film Institute at City College of New York in 1942. Many of the students he trained there in the techniques of producing experimental films became prominent members of the "underground" movement.[12] One of them, Frank Stauffacher, invited him in 1947 to be the plenary speaker at a symposium called "Art in Cinema" at the San Francisco Museum of Art. Richter's lecture, "A History of the Avantgarde" (*his*

German spelling), was for the most part a survey of experimental film-making in Europe after 1921 and of its vitality in the United States in the 1940s (Richter 1947). The hybrid modernist asserts in the conclusion of his essay that "the Avantgarde Movement may be historically regarded as an outgrowth of Modern Art, even if it belongs technically to the film" (Richter 1947, 21).

In his brief catalogue listings of work in experimental animation, Richter grossly understates the achievement of a younger German colleague, Oskar Fischinger, who was also in American exile. "[Fischinger's] film consists of different abstract compositions as illustrations of classical and modern music. All sound films" (Richter 1947, 17). "All sound" referred to the synchronization process that Fischinger invented to create his musico-visual synthesis, which set a new artistic standard for experimental animation. As a trained engineer, Fischinger was the technical virtuoso of the Berlin group. He developed an array of technical innovations in the twenties, from a fabulous "wax machine," to a device for tracking records for synchronization, to the generation of synthetic sound from ornament strips (Moritz 1993, 9, 32).[13] Walter Ruttmann was among the admirers of Fischinger's technical genius; the latter, in turn, was greatly influenced by *Opus 1* (1921).

Until *Studie No. 12,* much of Fischinger's work in black and white was tentative and fragmentary. When the wax-produced short was first shown in May 1932 at Kamera Unter den Linden, Bernhard Diebold, already a champion of Fischinger, hailed the abstract "filmlet" as a splendid example of animation—*Augenmusik* (Moritz 1993, 31). Instant success came with the advertising feature *Muratti greift ein* (Muratti marches on, 1934) and the four-minute short *Composition in Blue* (1935). For someone who repeatedly got in trouble with the *Reichsfilmkammer* for making absolute films, it was consoling to know that Hollywood's animation industry was interested. (Fischinger emigrated in 1936.) At the first showing of *Composition in Blue,* viewers stamped their feet, chanting his name: "Fisch-in-ger!" (Fischinger was hiding in a nearby pub for fear that Nazi agitators would apprehend him [Moritz 1993, 43].)

To some eyes, *Composition in Blue* is still exhilarating today, with its brilliantly colored shapes that move in constructivist, sometimes Kandinsky-inspired formation to the music of the overture to Otto Nicolai's *Merry Wives of Windsor.* While the piece delights as "visual music" and "optical poetry," as Freudians we are amused at the sight of pistons pushing up vigorously, taking phallic shape.

In the summer of 2000, the Museum of Modern Art in New York mounted a retrospective of Fischinger's work curated by John Canemaker, an expert on animation film. "A Fischinger Centennial Celebration" featured quality presentations of the artist's shorts made in Germany and in Hollywood. In his survey in the *New York Times* (July 2, 2000), Canemaker called the artist "the original laureate of an abstract poetry," someone who knew how to tightly match patterns and color to music and created "elegant, mesmerizing and influential short films."[14] The critic singled out a 1947 work, *Motion Painting No. 1*, which was entirely executed by painting on glass. Computer animators such as Larry Cuba, who worked on the original *Star Wars*, are among those who value these early examples of experimental animation—surely not because of the painstaking work involved in processing as many as 3,000 wax-sliced images for each of the abstract films Fischinger created.

Because Fischinger integrated painting, the kinetic medium, and music into a unified whole, his pieces are sometimes referred to as "*Gesamtkunstwerk*." In its basic definition, a *Gesamtkunstwerk* is a work of art on a large scale (opera, ballet, and so forth) in which several arts participate in a major way (Weisstein 1992, 317); the grandiose claim for aesthetic totalization, as Richard Wagner inaugurated it, does not seem pertinent to the small-scale artistic endeavors discussed here. *The Cabinet of Dr. Caligari* might possibly qualify, but its multimediality has regressive features that were detected by some commentators. Thus Rudolf Arnheim, in a 1925 review, critiqued the lack of stylization in the figures and the acting (Arnheim 1977, 177); Lotte Eisner mocked herself with regard to the "utterly bourgeois furniture—the chintzy armchairs in Lil Dagover's sittingroom" (Eisner 1973, 25). Furthermore, the sheer craft and technological complexities of bringing forth a motion picture prevent it from attaining *Gesamtkunstwerk* status. All in all, it is not a desirable entity for thinkers such as André Vladimir Heiz, who consider it an ideological construct that lays claim to offering a vision of the world complete with the potential for quasi-mystical transformation (Heiz 1984, 181 ff.).

It would be wrong, however, to agree with Scott MacDonald, who writes in his *Avant-Garde Film: Motion Studies* that "in Germany . . . , the cinematic apparatus was seen as a tool with which artists working in the fine arts could expand their repertoire and, by doing so, attract more of the public than visited art galleries and salons" (MacDonald 1993, 2).

This is an amazing observation that makes one aware of cultural difference regarding aesthetic priorities in general and the desideratum of interarts experimentation in particular. How German is it? To be sure, German Romanticism, with its diverse efforts toward establishing a unity of the arts, may have outfitted German artists with a stronger than usual desire for a symbiosis of the arts. It is typical for German cultural discourse to be quick to fashion a new metaphor for states of intermediality—*Vernetzung der Künste,* a term awaiting translation. Older expressions such as mutual illumination of the arts, the sister arts, cross-pollination, conflation of genres, and symbiosis of the arts with an academic pedigree are rewritten by young artists with deconstructive flair: a Berlin group who present themselves as six *Wahnsinnsfrauen* dealing in "picture, word, dance" call their act *Wackelkontakte* (Loose connections). The pursuit of artistic interconnectivity is reinventing itself. When *Kino* meant film, in 1918, the Dadaist Raoul Hausmann coined a most poetic slogan for the interarts experiment in early German cinema:[15]

synthetisches CINO der Malerei.

Notes

1. In an earlier article, "Intertextuality of Film and Visual Arts in Weimar Culture," *Kodikas/Code* 14, nos. 1–2 (1991), I was mainly concerned with deconstructing Kracauer's reading of the film in *From Caligari to Hitler,* using little-known archival material. I am pleased to note that recent scholarship has come to similar conclusions (cf. Kasten 1994, 49, n. 7). Translations in the following are mine.

2. Herwarth Walden later indirectly confirmed this when he complained in exile in London that the set designers of *Caligari* had plagiarized one of his painters, Arnold Topp (cf. Carter 1930, 250). In a letter to Gero Gandert, Stiftung Deutsche Kinemathek, Berlin, the art historian Eberhard Roters resolutely refuted Walden's claim (November 2, 1977).

3. Cf. Jürgen Kasten, who looked in vain for the "bizarre style" (Hermann Warm) and the supposedly expressionist language (Lotte Eisner) in the screenplay for *Caligari* (Kasten 1994, 48); in his introduction to the published typescript as handed in by the team of Janowitz/Mayer in 1919, Siegbert S. Prawer also proceeds to destroy the myth that their screenplay was an important document of literary expressionism (Belach and Block 1995, 16).

4. See Kurtz 1926, frontispiece; Barr 1936, ill. 159. The drawing, signed by Reimann, is in the Gerhard Lamprecht archive of the Stiftung Deutsche Kinemathek.

5. Sabine Wilke has discussed Reimann's work for Nazi ideology, such as *Ewiger deutscher Wald* (Wilke 2001, 355). Walter Röhrig, who primarily assisted his colleagues, was employed during the Third Reich in the "Unterhaltungsfilm" genre; since Eric Rentschler's *The Ministry of Illusion,* we know that this was not an innocent category.

6. This statement, originally made in the interview with *Illustrierter Filmkurier* (no. 6), can be found in *Caligari* criticism in several different versions, including "Das Filmbild muss graphisch werden" (Kaul 1971, 5)

and "Das Filmkunstwerk muss eine lebendige Graphik werden!" (The cinematic work must become a lively piece of graphic art!). It is odd that in later years Warm continued to use the technical term *graphic* to describe the visual code of *Caligari,* since the film's decor turned out to be predominantly *painterly.*

7. The so-called underground film movement in the United States in the 1950s and 1960s is only one such outcome; the unconventional style of recent Hollywood filmmakers such as David Lynch is informed by the tradition of film-as-art.

8. Original copies of *Caligari* were "*viragiert*"; i.e., the colors of blue and amber were directly applied to the celluloid by hand. Generations of viewers saw the movie in black and white; with hardly a tinted nitro copy left in the world, those involved in the restoration project faced almost insurmountable challenges. For a detailed account of this thrilling meta-scenario, see Regel 1985, 2–4. The restored copy now contains the original intertitles, which were previously available for viewing only in the Stiftung Deutsche Kinemathek. According to the list of credits prefacing Robert Fischer's introduction to *Caligari* in *Focus-Film-Texte,* no. 3 (1985), it was Walter Reimann who created the intertitles. Stylistically their cubo-futuristic, dramatic opticality relates to the jagged window discussed in the following.

9. Excluding Ruttmann's shorts: Viking Eggeling's *Symphonie Diagonale,* René Clair's *Entr'Acte,* and *Images mobiles* by Fernand Léger and Dudley Murphy.

10. After his *Neue Sachlichkeit* masterwork *Berlin. Die Sinfonie der Grosstadt* (1927), Ruttmann had to conform to the cinematic conventions of the Nazis. He made a number of *Kulturfilme,* such as *Deutsche Panzer* (German tanks, 1941) and *Die Volkskrankheit Krebs* (The disease cancer, 1941).

11. This is Bordwell/Thompson's term to differentiate a method such as Richter's from the regular film-editing process (Bordwell and Thompson 1986, 383). When Richter expressively states: "Wir montieren!" (Richter 1981, 24), he is referring to the deliberate juxtaposition of images, which he later contextualizes in his lengthy discussion of Pudovkin's theory of montage as an aesthetic device (Richter 1979, 57–59).

12. Maya Deren, Shirley Clarke, and Jonas Mekas are students of Richter's.

13. The "wax machine" was a labor-saving animation machine that produced wax-sliced images. Dr. William Moritz, who has devoted a life of scholarship to the work of Oskar Fischinger, gives the most detailed description of this process in his important catalogue for a retrospective of Fischinger films and paintings at the Frankfurt Filmmuseum (Moritz 1993, 9); a shorter version in English can be found in Moritz 1974, 41. In 1922 Ruttmann acquired the license from Fischinger to use the wax machine commercially.

14. Although Fischinger became an icon for West Coast experimental filmmakers, his studio career in Hollywood was full of misfortunes, including

the fate of *his* version of *Fantasia* (1940), of which only a short segment survived the final cut by Disney.

15. I much appreciated how Jean-Paul Goergen graphically foregrounded the Hausmann motto in his essay on Dada and "Kino" (Goergen 1990, 20–26).

Works Cited

Altmann, Nathan. "Elementare Gesichtspunkte." *G—Material zur elementaren Gestaltung* 3 (1924): 35–36.

Arnheim, Rudolf. "Dr. Caligari redivivus." In *Rudolf Arnheim*, ed. Helmut H. Diederichs. 1925. Reprint. Munich: Hanser, 1977.

Barr, Alfred, Jr. *Cubism and Abstract Art.* 1936. New York: The Museum of Modern Art. Reprint. Cambridge, Mass.: Harvard University Press, 1986.

Belach, Helga, and Hans-Michael Block, eds. *Das Cabinet des Dr. Caligari.* Screenplay. Materials by Uli Jung and Walter Schatzberg. Munich: edition text+kritik, 1995.

Bordwell, David, and Kristin Thompson. *Film Art: An Introduction.* New York: Knopf, 1986.

Canemaker, John. "The Original Laureate of an Abstract Poetry." *New York Times,* July 2, 2000.

Carter, Huntley. *The New Spirit in the Cinema.* London: Harold Shaylor, 1930.

Cendrars, Blaise. "The Cabinet of Dr. Caligari." *Broom* II (Rome), no. 4 (1922): N.p.

Courtade, Francis. *Cinema expressioniste.* Paris: Henri Veyrier, 1984.

Diebold, Bernhard. "Eine neue Kunst: Die Augenmusik des Films." *Frankfurter Zeitung,* no. 2 (April 1921). Reprinted in Jean-Paul Goergen, *Walter Ruttmann: Eine Dokumentation,* 98–99. Berlin: Freunde der deutschen Kinemathek, 1989.

Diederichs, Helmut H., ed. *Rudolf Arnheim.* Munich: Hanser, 1977.

Eisner, Lotte. *The Haunted Screen.* Berkeley: University of California Press, 1973.

Engel, Otmar. "Hermann Warm." *Civis* 7 (1964): 30–31.

Fischer, Robert. "Hinter den Augen." In *Focus-Film-Texte,* no. 3, 4–7. Stuttgart: Focus Verlagsgemeinschaft, 1985.

Goergen, Jean-Paul. "Dada-Berlin und das Kino." *epd film* 7 (1990): 20–26.

———. *Walter Ruttmann: Eine Dokumentation.* Berlin: Freunde der deutschen Kinemathek, 1989.

Heiz, André Vladimir. "Zur totalen, totalitären Tendenz des Gesamtkunstwerks." In *Unsere Wagner: Joseph Beuys, Heiner Müller, Karlheinz Stockhausen, Hans Jürgen Syberberg,* ed. Gabriele Förg, 164–189. Frankfurt: Fischer, 1984.

Janowitz, Hans, and Carl Mayer. *Das Cabinet des Dr. Caligari.* Screenplay. Ed. Helga Belach and Hans-Michael Block. Munich: edition text+kritik, 1995.

Jhering, Herbert. "Ein expressionistischer Film." *Berliner Börsen-Courier,* February 29, 1920. Reprinted in *Das Cabinet des Dr. Caligari,* ed. Helga Belach and Hans-Michael Block, 144–145. Screenplay. Materials by Uli Jung and Walter Schatzberg. Munich: edition text+kritik, 1995.

Kamps, Johannes. "Reimann, Walter. Kunstmaler." In *Walter Reimann: Maler und Filmarchitekt*. Kinematograph 11, ed. Walter Schobert and Hans Peter Reichmann. Frankfurt: Deutsches Filmmuseum, 1997.

Kasten, Jürgen. *Carl Mayer: Filmpoet*. Berlin: Vistas, 1994.

Kaul, Walter, ed. *Caligari und Caligarismus*. Berlin: Deutsche Kinemathek, 1970.

———. *Schöpferische Filmarchitektur*. Berlin: Deutsche Kinemathek, 1971.

Kracauer, Siegfried. *From Caligari to Hitler: A Psychological History of the German Film*. Princeton, N.J.: Princeton University Press, 1947.

Kurtz, Rudolf. *Expressionismus und Film*. Berlin: Verlag der Lichtbildbühne, 1926.

Lawder, Standish D. *The Cubist Cinema*. New York: New York University Press, 1975.

MacDonald, Scott. *Avant-Garde Film: Motion Studies*. Cambridge: Cambridge University Press, 1993.

Messel, Rudolph. *This Film Business*. London: Ernest Benn, 1928.

Meyer, Wilhelm. "Filmkunst des Malers." *Vossische Zeitung*, February 29, 1920.

Moritz, William. "The Films of Oskar Fischinger." *Film Culture* 58–60 (1974): 37–188.

———. "Oskar Fischinger." In *Optische Poesie: Oskar Fischingers Leben und Werk*, 7–90. Kinemathograph 9. Frankfurt: Deutsches Filmmuseum, 1993.

Regel, Helmut. "Das Cabinet des Dr. Caligari (Rekonstruktion)." Brochure. Berlin: 15. Internationales Forum des jungen Films, 1985, 2–4.

Rentschler, Eric. *The Ministry of Illusion: Nazi Cinema and Its Afterlife*. Cambridge, Mass.: Harvard University Press, 1996.

Richter, Hans. "Es gibt noch keinen Film." *G—Zeitschrift für elementare Gestaltung*, nos. 5/6 (April 1926): N.p.

———. *Der Kampf um den Film: Für einen gesellschaftlich verantwortlichen Film*. Ed. Jürgen Römhild. Frankfurt: Fischer, 1979. Based on 1939 manuscript.

———. *Filmgegner von heute—Filmfreunde von morgen*. Frankfurt: Fischer, 1981. Text for 1929 photo exhibition in Stuttgart.

———. "A History of the Avantgarde." In *Art in Cinema*, ed. Frank Stauffacher, 6–24. San Francisco: San Francisco Museum of Art, 1947.

Russett, Robert, and Cecile Starr. *Experimental Animation: Origins of a New Art*. New York: Da Capo Press, 1988.

Simon, Elena Pinto. "Dada on Film: Richter's 'Rhythmus.'" *Thousand Eyes* 2 (1977): N.p.

Von Hofacker, Marion. "Introduction." In *G. Material zur Elementaren Gestaltung*, 1923–1926. Reprint. Munich: Kern, 1986.

Weisstein, Ulrich. *Bildende Kunst und Literatur*. Berlin: Erich Schmidt, 1992.

Wilke, Sabine. "'Verrottet, verkommen, von fremder Rasse durchsetzt': The Colonial Trope as Subtext of the Nazi 'Kulturfilm' *Ewiger Wald* (1936)." *German Studies Review* 24 (2001): 353–376.

3

From Dance to Film
The Cinematic Art of Leni Riefenstahl and Dorothy Arzner

Dagmar von Hoff

"May one perceive expressive motion and the visual in
general as the very specific material of cinematography?"
—Béla Balázs, *Der sichtbare Mensch*
oder die Kultur des Films[1]

In the book *Der sichtbare Mensch* (1924), Béla Balázs asks the above
question in order to point out that the gestures of the actor on film
fundamentally differ from those of the dancer and that they also bear
nothing in common with the speech of the theater performer. The actor
on film does not dance, nor does his expression correlate directly to the
word. Between the gesticulations of the speaker and the expressive
movements of the dancer, there appears to be a third form of expression
that is determinant for film's specific interiority. The two filmmakers to
be discussed in the following essay are pioneers of film history, and they
uniquely explored this third area of expression. Dorothy Arzner is Hollywood's classic female film director, and Leni Riefenstahl is perhaps one
of the most interesting women ever to have stood behind a camera. The
American filmmaker Dorothy Arzner influenced classical Hollywood
over a period of fifteen years during which she made sixteen films, beginning with *Fashions for Women* in 1927. Leni Riefenstahl is one of the
most controversial German artists of the twentieth century. The greatest controversy revolves around her film of Hitler's assembly of the Nazi
party in 1934, *Triumph des Willens* (*Triumph of the Will*). The film depicts and celebrates Hitler's victory over opponents within his party
(whom he had slaughtered). For this film, which expresses Hitler's notion of absolute power in opulent and perfect images, Riefenstahl was
honored at the World's Fair in Paris in 1937.

One can object to Riefenstahl's film aesthetics on moral or aesthetic
grounds, but one must recognize that she profoundly influenced the matrix of relations between thought and visual expression in our time.

Siegfried Kracauer repudiated Riefenstahl's film artistry in 1947, and in the same tradition, Susan Sontag disputed any justification for Riefenstahl's symbolic imagery. Yet since Ray Müller's documentary *Die Macht der Bilder* (The power of images, 1994), the Leni Riefenstahl exhibition in Potsdam 1999, and Rainer Rother's book *Leni Riefenstahl: Die Verführung des Talents* (2000; translated into English as *The Seduction of Genius* in 2002), evaluations of her work have become ambivalent. What Susan Sontag referred to as "fascist longing" is now labeled "romantic ideal," "antimodern," or guided by the concept of the "noble savage." In contrast, Dorothy Arzner has long been perceived as the heroine of feminist film. As Judith Mayne demonstrated in a study published in 1994, Arzner critically explored gender-specific constellations of the gaze to an unprecedented degree at an early point in history.

On the surface, then, the two filmmakers appear worlds apart. An emancipatory quality in Arzner's cinematic works stands in contrast to a retrograde fascination with myth and visions of power in Riefenstahl's films. For Riefenstahl, the human being is a slave of fate, wholly determined by destiny. Arzner, on the other hand, focuses on the individual as a subject within a community, who may exercise freedom of consciousness on a path of interaction. But in spite of such fundamental differences, there are commonalities between the approaches that the two artists took in order to express themselves cinematically. They both looked to dance to form their paths. Both women studied dance as an art form and both innovatively influenced dance with their respective work on the potential of expression and motion within the modern medium of film. For both directors, questioning conventional manifestations of the gaze in relation to the dancing woman was paramount. But before discussing two films from the early period of sound cinema that demonstrate this similar motivation, I would like to detour briefly into the eighteenth century to examine a paradigmatic constellation of the gaze.

In 1787 Johann Wolfgang von Goethe was quite captivated by a particular style of representation that involved posing female bodies. This popular style was called *Attitüde* and consisted in having a woman assume certain historically coded poses for an audience. The images were intended to summon up cultural memories of mythical or biblical female figures. In his *Italian Journey*, Goethe describes how he had the opportunity to observe such a presentation. Lady Hamilton, who was soon to be recognized as the most famous mime of this creative style, performed for Goethe the strangely muted dance that reenacted postures and gestures that had become symbolically meaningful in cultural history. It must have been quite something to have observed this woman dressed in the garb of antiquity going through motions that her husband, Sir Hamilton, had choreographed. Goethe writes:

> She is very beautiful and well-proportioned. [Sir Hamilton] had a Greek gown made for her that dresses her exquisitely, and she lets her hair down, takes a few shawls and makes a variety of poses, gestures, expressions, etc. in such a manner that one ultimately actually thinks that one is dreaming. Here one observes what so many thousands of artists would like to have achieved, fully completed in motion and surprising variation. Standing, kneeling, sitting, lying, serious, sad, playful, licentious, penitent, enticing, threatening, fearful, etc., one thing follows upon the other and from within the other. For every expression she knows what folds of the veil to choose, to change, and she makes herself a hundred types of headdress with the same cloths.[2]

In reminiscing about this frequently discussed moment of Goethe's travels, I would like to focus briefly on the status of Lady Hamilton. Her husband has assigned movements to her. Her task is to assume meaningful gestures for those who have come to appreciate art. Here she is clearly an eroticized art object. Yet in stating, as Goethe does, that she herself knows how to "choose" and to "change" the "folds of the veil" appropriate to each "expression," he also casts light on the fact that this body is indeed a subject capable of expressing itself in the given medium. Somewhere in the medium, the objectified female body remains a subject, but the possibilities for that body to represent itself as subject are strongly limited by the medium. This problem, of course, never goes away. But it is certainly quite differently posited in the entirely new medium of film as it was developed at the beginning of the twentieth century. As a medium, film is dramatically different from the play of poses that Goethe was able to witness, in that the gaze itself has become emphatically thematized in and by the medium. Yet by recalling the way in which Goethe described Mrs. Hamilton's dance, we might be better able to perceive what happened when women began to use a creative medium to take charge not only of the postures that they assumed as art, but of the entire field of representation, including the gaze that came to rest on them.

It is no accident that I draw upon Goethe as a historical reference point for my conjectures, because the women whose films are under scrutiny here looked toward precisely such classical moments of aesthetic appreciation and reflection in history in order to make their way. They were fundamentally interested in exploring relationships between the male gaze and the female body as these occur in art. In very different ways, they asked themselves how they might remember, dramatize, and innovatively alter such relationships within and by means of their medium. Like Lady Hamilton, they appear to have been quite capable of choosing the "veils" appropriate to their expression, and beyond that, they worked toward unveiling the fundamental problem of female bodies as they are captured in aesthetic representations.

In attempting to depict females in front of the camera in new ways, both Dorothy Arzner and Leni Riefenstahl drew upon the tradition and the expressive force of modern dance. Both women had a background in expressive dance (*Ausdruckstanz*) and the modern dance of the 1920s. When Dorothy Arzner made her film *Dance, Girl, Dance* in 1940, she oriented her representation of the female body to a great extent around American modern dance as it continued to be developed in the lineage of the dance pioneer Isadora Duncan (1878–1927). Arzner made her film together with Marion Morgan, who was herself a dancer and a choreographer. Leni Riefenstahl also began as a dancer. After a knee injury that prevented her from ever seriously pursuing her passion to dance again, Riefenstahl made the movie *The Blue Light* (*Das blaue Licht*). In this 1932 film she stages a "dance on the mountain." Riefenstahl's own training as a dancer was also oriented around the teachings of Isadora Duncan, whose turning away from classical dance with its firmly established notion of the purely executing subject released enormous creative potential.

In Riefenstahl's work destiny takes precedence over the concept of human liberty. *The Blue Light* is set in a mystical world beyond the metropolis. In contrast to Arzner's lavish Hollywood production, this film was low-budget. Riefenstahl founded her own company and provided most of the financing for the project herself. Harry Sokal, the film's coproducer, financed the rest. It should be recalled that it was very unusual at this time for a woman to want to make her own movie. There were actresses, female script writers, and women working in the copying stations, but very few women directed. Alice Guy and Germain Dulac had made movies in France, and Lotte Reiniger presented animated movies with scissor-cut silhouettes in Germany. But Riefenstahl was determined to achieve her aim, and she defied the common mechanisms governing how films could be made by organizing things differently. To create *The Blue Light*, Riefenstahl worked with a small team. She not only directed the film but also played the lead role of the gypsy-like Junta, aided by scriptwriter Béla Balázs and Hans Schneeberger, who sat behind the camera. There are multiple versions of the film, and it is difficult today to determine how extensively individual contributions influenced their overall character. The 1932 version is presented as

a collective piece by Leni Riefenstahl, Béla Balázs, and Hans Schneeberger. In this version the sociocritical signature of the Jewish communist Balázs is clearly legible. Balázs was forced to emigrate to Moscow
shortly after the filming had been completed and was unable to attend
the premiere in 1932 in Berlin. In a version of the film from 1952, Riefenstahl signs alone for script, direction, and art production. This second, more widely known version is reedited and synchronized. Without
expounding on differences between the two versions, it can be noted
that the 1932 version clearly has a more critical edge, insofar as a modern, urban woman reads and presents the legend of Junta that is depicted without such framing in the 1952 version of the film.

At the center of the narrative we find Junta, who is at home in the
mountains. She is the epitome of the wild woman. When she descends
from her mountain to the village, the simple and superstitious folk of
the valley chastise her for being a witch and chase her off. More than in
any social or ethnic sense, Junta appears to be "strange" aesthetically.
She is portrayed as a mythical, erotic woman mysteriously linked to nature and living beyond the limitations of a closed society whose structure is determined by men. The painter Vigo (played by Mathias Wie-
mann), who has come to the mountains in order to "breathe more
freely," chances upon this unusual woman. He is magically attracted to
her and follows her into the mountains. On this path, his heart becomes
set on solving the mystery of why the mountain on which Junta lives
radiates blue light whenever the moon is full. Ultimately, he will discover that strange crystals in a fairy-tale-like cave produce the unusual
blue radiance when they are struck by rays from the full moon. But the
act of disclosing the source of the magic will also destroy precisely what
attracted Vigo's gaze in the first place.

In one sequence we watch Vigo follow Junta into the mountains. The
dance-like climbing sequence dramatically demonstrates Riefenstahl's
choreographic sensibility. As a now lamed dancer and a rather accom-
plished choreographer, Riefenstahl was familiar with the abstract character of Mary Wigman's expressive dance, with the erotic morbidity of
dancers like Anita Berber and Valeska Gert, and with the silhouette
films of Lotte Reiniger. Riefenstahl's climb up the mountain as Junta—
always toward the light—is full of references to these and other artists,
emerging as a walk through cultural history. It begins with a shadow,
comparable to the reliefs and depictions on Greek urns. In a further
scene, we see her ascending a pinnacle in a manner reminiscent of silhouette imagery. In contrast to Junta's feline, dance-like light-footed-
ness on the mountain, Vigo's ascent seems cumbersome and challenged.
He always comes from darkness. But he will nonetheless conquer the

object of his pursuit in the end. He finally discovers her secret when he follows her into a cave. In the last scene we see wonderful crystals sparkling like insect eyes—an effect that was cinematically realized by shifting in and out of focus.

This technique was only one of the extraordinary effects Riefenstahl employed in order to achieve her "image vision." For example, the nighttime takes were filmed during the day using particular filters, the so-called R-material from Agfa, to transform the sun into the full moon and to allow for filming without artificial lighting. In the cave scene, Riefenstahl is seemingly obsessed with light. One can almost perceive blue light in the layered, atmospheric gray tones. And the scene is loaded with symbolism. Drawn into the cave, the viewer recognizes that Junta has gone into a trance. Her posture resembles that of the sphinx. Gustave Moreau's famous painting of *Oedipus and the Sphinx* (1864) might have served as inspiration here. Vigo, who has entered the cave, is unable to achieve Junta's dreamlike state. Suddenly he steps into the crystals, and Junta awakens and crosses her arms in front of her face. In this moment, the secret source of the blue light is revealed, but all magic and mystery are destroyed as well. Junta's power has ceased to be. It is no wonder that after the painter has had the mysterious treasure excavated from the mountain—supposedly as a demonstration of his love for her—she suffers a fatal fall in the region that she once so gracefully traversed.

One can hardly avoid being impressed by the unusual dramatization of light effects and the astonishing editing technique of Riefenstahl's "dance on the mountain," which has in fact been looked to as an inspiration for music video productions. *The Blue Light* differs starkly from mountain films by her contemporaries. Riefenstahl often distances the viewer from images by means of slight blurring effects—some scenes appear to have been filmed through gauze—an antithesis of the contoured hardness and precision of images in conventional mountain films of the day. Rather than wanting to demonstrate the magnificence of nature, Riefenstahl was concerned with expressing Junta's "inner landscape." She was interested in representing not the mountain world but a dream world.

Dorothy Arzner presents quite a different case. Her work can be seen as the consequence of a genuine dance revolution that began in America. The screenplay of Dorothy Arzner's film *Dance, Girl, Dance* was adapted from a book written by Vicki Baum, who immigrated to the United States to escape persecution by the Nazis. Arzner decisively altered the script prepared by Tess Slesinger and Frank Davis by turning Basiloff, the male director of the dance group, into Basilova, a female manager, thereby drawing relationships between women into thematic focus and consequently developing a most unusual drama of the gaze.

In Hollywood Arzner worked first as a cutter and then as a scriptwriter before directing for Paramount. After making several silent movies, she directed *Dance, Girl, Dance* in 1940 for RKO studios (Radio Keith Orpheum) with Erich Pommer as producer. The film appears to ask how female dancers can discover their own unique expression, how they can translate their own desire within the realm of artistic representation into reality. With regard to this endeavor, stereotypical gender roles appear clearly as barriers that must be overcome. The story depicts how women in search of modes of expression for themselves must always submit to a designated performance style. Arzner shows us various dance scenes: the hula dance, which is performed for an all-male audience; certain movements of classical ballet; dance steps from a vaudeville show; and musical dance. Progressing through such dance steps, Judy, played by Maureen O'Hara, makes her way against the odds to find her own artistic self-expression. In light of such an unusual scenario, it is no wonder that Dorothy Arzner is perceived as an icon of feminist film. This status is all the more justified when one considers that she was also the only woman to have produced her own films in Hollywood for over three decades. *Dance, Girl, Dance* is one of Arzner's most famous movies, and it has generated a good deal of secondary literature. Among others, Laura Mulvey and Claire Johnston have analyzed it specifically in terms of gender representation.

A closer look at the plot can help to measure the intensity of the film's emancipatory impulse. Bubbles, played by Lucille Ball, and Judy, played by Maureen O'Hara, are both members of a dance troupe led by Madame Basilova. The troupe performs various numbers in bars and night clubs. Bubbles makes her career as "Tiger Lily" in burlesque performance. By contrast, Judy is a serious student of ballet. In an early scene we see Judy performing a dance in the attic. She has created the dance herself and calls it "The Morning Star." Madame Basilova observes the dance and decides to call the attention of Mr. Adams, who is the director of a modern dance theater, to Judy's talent. It is an interesting feature of this scene that Madame Basilova breaches conventional gender expectations both in role and appearance, since she assumes the voyeuristic gaze commonly reserved in Hollywood films for males and is furthermore dressed in a markedly masculine manner. Be that as it may, as luck would have it, Madame Basilova has a fatal accident on the way to see Mr. Adams, temporarily halting Judy's chances for entering the performing arts.

In a later scene Judy has acquired a mediocre job as a dance clown in a variety show in order to make some money. She is performing some ballet steps to set the stage for Bubbles, whose dance as Tiger Lily is the main attraction. In this scene there is a notable break in the manner in which the gaze is consolidated. Judy looks back at those looking at her. She steps out of her performance role, in which she has been submitting herself to a male gaze, and confronts the audience with a reflection on the entire constellation of observer and observed. She turns to her audience in a fit of anger and tells them how she sees them. This breach of protocol is applauded by the audience. We see how both Mr. Adams and his assistant witness this seriously artful exchange. This doubling back of scrutiny in what is normally a one-way process, that is, a spectacle to be consumed by men, constitutes a direct attack not only on the audience depicted in the film but also on the audience that is viewing the film. The entire notion of spectacle as such is challenged. This turnabout completes Judy's development. She is accepted into Mr. Adams's school of modern dance, where everyday New York street scenes become part of dance performance.

The aesthetic dance expression for which Judy will ultimately obtain recognition is formulated along the way. At one point, Mr. Adams and Judy are unaware that they pursue related interests. We see the two of them standing on a street in New York in the pouring rain. Mr. Adams offers Judy a taxi and she suddenly begins to run—yes, to dance. At this moment the camera connects up with impulses that are at the core of modern dance. This is Arzner's contribution on celluloid to an aesthetics of dance.

Thus Arzner draws on dance as a medium for reflecting on and for legitimizing her cinematic expression. In *Dance, Girl, Dance* this expression encompasses abstract reflections on sexual difference. The viewing audience is explicitly drawn into this process of reflection. The "Morning Star" that Judy dreams of dancing is a clear antithesis of the burlesque performance perfected by her friend Bubbles. But the opposition of the two dancing styles and the confrontation between Bubbles as "vamp" und Judy as "straight girl" do not serve to cancel out these antipodes. Arzner appears to be more concerned with a synthesis between the two feminine lifestyles and between two types of art, high and low. In pursuing her dream, the young dancer is able to achieve artistic expression beyond stereotypes. Hence Arzner's film is about dance, but it is also a plea for contemporary art as a mode of expression capable of breaking down barriers that restrict both social and aesthetic possibilities.

What Dorothy Arzner and Leni Riefenstahl have most strikingly in common is that they both draw upon dance traditions to thematize problems of gender and the gaze in the process of seeking their own artistic expression in the medium of film. They have both come a long way since the ideal of statically posed femininity epitomized in Mrs. Hamilton and celebrated by Goethe, but they have gone very different ways. Riefenstahl participates in an artistic tradition of the sublime in which the feminine is nearly always synonymous with nature and myth. Her leading figure conjoins with the mountain, the cave, and the sparkling crystals, with light and the moon. The sparkling of the crystals functions like a gaze with which the heroine communicates. Riefenstahl stages a form of femininity that is bound to the forces of nature and that must ultimately fail when it comes into contact with masculine rationality. Whereas in *The Blue Light* no one really dances her- or himself free of anything, *Dance, Girl, Dance* speaks to a more individualized notion of freedom. Arzner's film is about dance, and it pleads for the urbanity of dance as an art form. She is not concerned with entering the sphere of the gods, with immortal art, but with establishing creative contact with the everyday conditions and concerns of the modern world. With her camera, the gaze is directed into a near-perfect aestheticized totality of rhythm and spaces. In her film Arzner seeks out a vibrant contact with the pulse of the modern world along the lines of a personal artistic expression, much like the expression that Isadora Duncan aimed for in her dance performances.

In many ways *The Blue Light* and *Dance, Girl, Dance* reflect cultural influences specific to the 1930s in Germany and the United States, respectively. Yet both films represent serious endeavors by women behind the camera to explore the aesthetic potential of integrating dance into film and of developing their own new, unconventional dramas of the gaze—Riefenstahl in a mythical language and Arzner in a gender-critical discourse. Both languages work dynamically with relationships between the gaze and the figure of the dancing woman to transform the screen into an ambivalent location that defies its common dimensionality.

Notes

1. "Darf man die Ausdrucksbewegung und überhaupt das Visuelle als ganz spezielles Material der Filmkunst betrachten?" (Balázs 2001, 209).

2. "Sie ist sehr schön und wohlgebaut. Er hat ihr ein griechisch Gewand machen lassen, das sie trefflich kleidet, dazu löst sie ihre Haare auf, nimmt

ein paar Schals und macht eine Abwechslung von Stellungen, Gebärden, Mienen etc., daß man zuletzt wirklich meint, man träume. Man schaut, was so viele Künstler gerne geleistet hätten, hier ganz fertig in Bewegung und überraschender Abwechselung. Stehend, kniend, sitzend, liegend, ernst, traurig, neckisch, ausschweifend, bußfertig, lockend, drohend, ängstlich etc., eins folgt aufs andere und aus dem anderen. Sie weiß zu jedem Ausdruck die Falten des Schleiers zu wählen, zu wechseln, macht sich hundert Arten von Kopfputz mit denselben Tüchern" (Goethe 1998, 209).

Works Cited

Balázs, Béla. *Der sichtbare Mensch oder die Kultur des Films.* 1924. Reprint. Frankfurt a.M.: Suhrkamp, 2001.

Goethe, Johann Wolfgang von. *Die italienische Reise.* Vol. 11 of *Goethes Werke. Hamburger Ausgabe.* Munich: Beck, 1998.

Johnston, Claire, ed. *The Work of Dorothy Arzner: Towards a Feminist Cinema.* London: British Film Institute, 1975.

Kracauer, Siegfried. *From Caligari to Hitler: A Psychological History of the German Film.* Princeton, N.J.: Princeton University Press, 1947.

Mayne, Judith. *Directed by Dorothy Arzner.* Bloomington: Indiana University Press, 1994.

———. *The Woman at the Keyhole: Feminism and Women's Cinema.* Bloomington: Indiana University Press, 1990.

Rother, Rainer. *Leni Riefenstahl: Die Verführung des Talents.* Berlin: Henschel, 2000.

Sontag, Susan. *Under the Sign of Saturn.* New York: Farrar, Straus and Giroux, 1980.

Filmography

The Blue Light / Das blaue Licht (1932)

Directed by	Béla Balázs	
	Leni Riefenstahl	
Writing credits	Béla Balázs	
	Leni Riefenstahl	
Cast	Leni Riefenstahl	Junta
	Mathias Wiemann	Vigo
	Beni Führer	Tonio
	Max Holzboer	Innkeeper
	Martha Maire	Lucia
	Franz Maldacen	Guzzi

Produced by	Leni Riefenstahl
	H. R. Sokal
Original music by	Giuseppe Becce
Cinematography by	Hans Schneeberger
	Heinz von Jaworsky
Film editing by	Leni Riefenstahl

Dance, Girl, Dance (1940)

Directed by	Dorothy Arzner
Writing credits	Vicki Baum
	Frank Davis
	Tess Slesinger

Cast (in credits order)

Maureen O'Hara	Judy "Irish" O'Brien
Louis Hayward	James "Jimmy" Harris
Lucille Ball	Bubbles, a.k.a. Tiger Lily White
Virginia Field	Elinor Harris
Ralph Bellamy	Steve Adams
Mary Carlisle	Sally
Katharine Alexander	Miss "Olmy" Olmstead
Edward Brophy	Dwarfie
Walter Apel	Judge
Harold Huber	Mr. Kajulian, Hoboken Gent
Maria Ouspenskaya	Madame Lydia Basilova
Ernest Truex	Harry, Bailey #1
Chester Clute	Larry, Bailey #2
Lorraine Krueger	Dolly
Lola Jensen	Daisy
Emma Donn	Mrs. Simpson
Sidney Blackmer	Puss in Boots
Vivien Fay	Vivian, the Ballerina
Ludwig Stössel	Caesar, Burlesque Violinist
Ernö Verebes	Fitch

Produced by	Harry E. Edington (executive)
	Erich Pommer
Original music by	Chet Forrest
Cinematography by	Russel Metty
Film editing by	Robert Wise
Art director	Van Nest Polglase
Set decoration	Darrell Silvera
Costume design by	Edward Stevenson
Sound department	Hugh McDowell Jr.

4

The Photographic Comportment of Bernd and Hilla Becher

Blake Stimson

Bernd and Hilla Becher first began their still-ongoing project of systematically photographing industrial structures—water towers, blast furnaces, gas tanks, mineheads, grain elevators and the like—in the late 1950s. The seemingly objective and scientific character of their project was in part a polemical return to the "straight" aesthetics and social themes of the 1920s and 1930s in response to the subjectivist photographic aesthetics that arose in the early postwar period. This latter position was epitomized in Germany by the entrepreneurial, beauty-in-the-eye-of-the-beholder aestheticism of Otto Steinert's *Subjektive Fotografie* and globally by the one-world populist humanism of Edward Steichen's tremendous Cold War extravaganza, *The Family of Man*. While many photographers followed Robert Frank's critical rejoinder and depicted the seamier, chauvinistic underbelly of the sentimental universalism advocated by Steichen and Steinert, the Bechers simply rejected it and returned to an older, prewar paradigm.

Their project was based primarily on two prewar influences. The first of these was the systematic, pseudoscientific studies of Karl Blossfeldt, Albert Renger-Patzsch, and, particularly, August Sander, whose life-project making sociological portraits of Germans from all classes and occupations provided the methodological and affective structure for the Bechers' own typological procedure and a logical alternative to the sentimental individualist and familial framing systems adopted by their humanist predecessors. The second major influence, the source for the distinctive subject matter to which they chose to apply Sander's system, was the industrial iconography popular with many photographers and

52

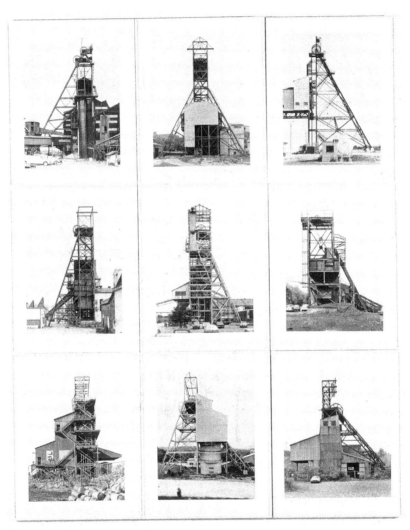

Figure 4.1. Bernd and Hilla Becher, *Winding Towers* (1967). Nine silver gelatin developed-out prints, 60 ¼ × 48 in. (153 × 121.9 cm). Courtesy The Museum of Contemporary Art, Los Angeles. Gift of Lannan Foundation.

artists in the 1920s and 1930s. They might have had in mind one of the many well-known photographs by Renger-Patzsch, such as his *Chimney Seen from Below, Herrenwyk Blast Furnace Works, Lübeck* from 1928, for example, but it could have just as well been photography by Charles Sheeler or Margaret Bourke-White or Laszlo Moholy-Nagy or many, many others equally or less well known.

To varying degrees among the Bechers' Machine Age forebears—from around the industrialized world and across the political spectrum— scientific method, industrial subject matter, and the mechanical advantage of photography all drew on and supported a challenge to the perceived anachronism of aestheticism and promised a new place and new importance for artists in the modern world. That ambition was developed in many places—for example, by Aleksandr Rodchenko in 1928, when he wrote: "Art has no place in modern life. It will continue to exist as long as there is a mania for the romantic and so long as there are people who love beautiful lies and deceptions. . . . Every modern cultured man must make war against art as against opium" (241). The antidote to such decadent self-deception and weak-willed addiction, he concluded in a rather overwrought directive, was as simple as it was modern: "Photograph and be photographed!" (Rodchenko 1989, 241). Not all members of the once-labeled "engineer generation" were as antipathetic to the older ideals as Rodchenko (Renger-Patzsch, for one, sought something more like reconciliation between modern life and art and set himself against such modernist polemics, particularly as they were developed in Germany by Moholy-Nagy), but all did share in the claim for photography's machine-age advantage, responsibility, and entitlement (Graeff 1923, n.p.). All agreed that representation needed to be mechanical if it was to be modern, and all agreed that art needed to be somehow sober, objective, *sachlich*, at a remove from any simple expressiveness unto itself and at a remove from any claim that the art object might be a bearer of value in and of itself.

This tension between art as an autonomous and self-contained value, on the one hand, and modern life, on the other, has, of course, regularly given definition and distinction to the social role played by photography. From the beginning, photography was not only a passive product or sign or symptom of modernity but also worked actively as an engine of modernization. Beginning already with the official, state-sponsored birth of photography in 1839, both civic duty and marketplace opportunity alike were pinned to its capacity for bringing vision as an ideal and visual representation as a material resource into the workaday world of the masses. Photography was credited with the ability to bring visual imagination up to speed with the ever-accelerating, ever-expanding industrial revolution and thereby to modernize the archaic, pseudoreligious, would-be aristocratic presumption of art in its role as herald of the private life of the bourgeois subject.

The mantle assumed by photography is carried forward in the Bechers' work, albeit in a complex fashion. While their career has been almost exclusively a function of the international art market and art publishing industry and the German art education system, their photographic studies regularly have been characterized as "industrial archeology" or "a contribution to the social history of industrial work" and are routinely assumed to support such extra-artistic ambitions and accomplishments. These assumptions are misleading, however: the Bechers' photographs offer little sociohistorical or archeological interpretation and do not detail the particulars of design, operation, and social function that might be useful for such areas of study.[1] Indeed, they often go to great lengths to ensure the absence of such detail: "We want to offer the audience a point of view, or rather a grammar, to understand and compare the different structures," they have said: "Through photography, we try to arrange these shapes and render them comparable. To do so, the objects must be isolated from their context and freed from all association" (Touraine 1989, 9) (see fig. 4.1). They do employ a method, like much historical or archeological analysis, that is strict in its consistency and sense of purpose, but that purpose avoids "context" and "association" by design and thus has little to offer understanding in the manner traditionally given by such extra-artistic, analytically minded aims. Their more properly artistic characterizations of the structures they photograph—their terms they have used are "anonymous sculptures" (1969) and "basic forms" (1999)—suggest a more useful understanding of their project by drawing us away from the simpler, more transparent notion of representation assumed in such archaeological and sociohistorical characterizations and throwing us into the murkier waters of the aesthetic.

The Bechers have emerged as a leading influence in postwar art history, not only for their own work and its interweaving with other artistic developments such as Minimalism and Conceptual Art, but also, particularly in the last decade, for the extension of their project by a string of extraordinarily successful students.[2] Indeed, the "point of view" or "grammar" developed by the Bechers—"countless interrelated micro and macrostructures are woven together, determined by an overall organizational principle," is how one of the students describes this grammar, perhaps giving it a bit too much of an executive tone—has gained a significant measure of dominance within contemporary art practice (Gursky 2000, n.p.). My effort here will be to read that "grammar" as embodied expression, as a form of "comportment" or bearing toward the world. In so doing, this grammar will be understood as a sign or symptom of a social relation, yet one not listened to or viewed from the perspective of the executive manager or planner but instead from that of the worker or constituent subject, which serves as one of the elements brought together within that larger organizational principle. The distinctive orientation and determination of that systemic body language or photographic comportment, which in the Becher scholarship is sometimes said to be found midway "between distance and proximity," has taken on imposing proportions in the epic continuity of their own work and in the stilled grandeur typical of the work of their students. Considering the strong debt of this comportment to artistic developments of the 1920s and 1930s, its powerfully consistent elaboration as a form in the 1950s and 60s, and its artworld success in the 1980s and 90s, I will be asking how it has been able to, "at a stroke," in the words of one philosopher of comportment, "incorporate the past into the present and weld that present to a future" (Merleau-Ponty 1962, 392). Or, framing the problem more narrowly, I will be asking how the Bechers have transformed photography's Enlightenment promise of rigor and transparency, its promise to "make war against art as against opium," as Rodchenko put it, into that promise's inversion or return to its homeland category of art, that is, to the same category it had originally taken as its foil.

Commitment

The most obvious feature of the Bechers' work is its disciplined commitment to a singular vision—a commitment that has been consistent over nearly a half-century's duration, consistent across many different countries and regions, and consistent from each to the next of many thousands of photographs. As one critic has put it, the pattern of "rhythms and repetitions" established between the individual pictures (and, we might add, between individual series as well) is "very much the idea of the work" (Sobieszek 1971, 12). Such, the artists have admitted, is their goal—"to produce a more or less perfect chain of different forms and shapes"—and, indeed, something like this "perfect chain" or pattern of serial rhythms and repetitions is the initial impression given to the beholder when facing a Becher installation or book for the first time or when moving from one to the next of any of their twelve books—from *Water Towers* to *Framework Houses* to *Gas Tanks* to *Industrial Landscapes*, for example—or in and between any of the numerous exhibition catalogs (Becher and Becher 1970, 56).

Their system is based on a rigorous set of procedural rules: a standardized format and ratio of figure to ground; a uniformly level, full-frontal view; near-identical flat lighting conditions or the approximation of such conditions in the photographic processing; a consistent lack of human presence; a consistent use of the restricted chromatic spectrum offered by black and white photography rather than the broad range given by color; precise uniformity in print quality, sizing, framing, and presentation; and a shared function for all the structures photographed for a given series. There is another obvious rule too, although one their project systematically denies—their industrial history is exclusively and resolutely a history of the West. What they do *not* do is to group the images by geographic or historical categories, which would bring a more detailed historical consciousness to bear on the material at hand, nor do they arrange them in a manner that would chronicle the development of the project. The term they generally use to describe their method is "typological," and they freely state that it has "much to do with the 19th century," that is, they say, with "the encyclopedic approach" used, for example, in botany or zoology (Ziegler 2002, 97).

While an individual Becher photograph seen on its own without attribution could be mistaken easily for a transparent illustration of the kind used in trade journals, annual reports, or books on the history or design of industrial architecture, the same photograph seen in its intended setting alongside tens or hundreds of nearly identical others could not support any similar instrumental goal. Unlike similar approaches used in botany or zoology, the cumulative effect of the typological method as it is applied in the Bechers' life-project does not provide greater knowledge of the processes or history of their subject. Instead, the use of rhythm and repetition endows the buildings they photograph with the "anonymity" or abstract form they seek rather than with scientific specificity and, in turn, allows us to read them ahistorically and extra-socially and appreciate them as autonomous aesthetic objects or "sculpture."

This distinctive method of cultivating aesthetic response is consistent with the 1920s' and 1930s' project of aesthetic appropriation of scientific or systemic method, but it is also different. Perhaps the most significant measure of difference between the Bechers and their forebears is artistic ambition. Even today the Bechers' work (and its legacy in the art of their successful students) makes reference to this phantasm from the prewar past. Unlike their artist cum engineer predecessors, however, the Bechers' sensibility relies on melancholy rather than innovation or allegiance to make its point: tied to the loss of an idealized past, their work gains its emotional power, its expressive force as art, from the extent to which it conveys that sense of loss to the beholder. Their photographs present us with a transformed image of the avant-garde ambitions of the 1920s and 1930s: in their view, the great industrial structures that served as monuments to the "gigantic schemes" of collective life, monuments to technological, social, and political modernization, have aged and are now empty of all but memory of the ambition they once housed. Likewise, their postwar rehashing of the "New Vision" is now drained of all but memory of the heroic affect that went along with artists' sense of their own "indispensable" contribution. They have stated their position outright: "We don't agree with the depiction of buildings in the '20s and 1930s. Things were seen either from above or below which tended to monumentalize the object. This was exploited in terms of a socialistic view—a fresh view of the world, a new man, a new beginning" (Grauerholz and Ramsden 1981, 18).

This postwar critique of the New Vision and related artistic ambitions of the prewar past is generally consistent across an entire generation of artists and intellectuals whose historically distinct critical vision continues to serve as a foundation for the range of critical perspectives available to us today. We do not have to go far for such testimony— witness, for example, Michel Foucault in one of his most-cited essays: we "know from experience," he writes, "that the claim to escape from the system of contemporary reality so as to produce the overall programs of another society, of another way of thinking, another culture, another vision of the world, has led only to the return of the most dangerous traditions . . . to the programs for a new man that the worst political systems have repeated throughout the twentieth century" (Foucault 1984, 46). The Bechers, like many of their contemporaries, have made an obsession of this disagreement with the past. By returning to those views again and again and again for nearly a half-century with even greater sobriety, even greater assiduousness, even greater industry than the *Neue Sachlichkeit* that inspired them, by shooting the grand icons of the Machine Age "straight-on" so they do not, they have claimed, "hide or exaggerate or depict anything in an untrue fashion," by committing themselves to an ethic of representation free of bogus political elevation or degradation, they realize one leg of their generation's postmodern affect (Grauerholz and Ramsden 1981, 18). In so doing, the Bechers' commitment sits wedged between a passionate, trance-like fascination with the great progressive democratic ambitions of modernism and an equally ardent renunciation of them.

Delight

The promise of the aesthetic as a realm of experience separate from the instrumental thinking of daily life has served many different purposes since it was first elaborated by the Enlightenment philosophers. It has given rise, for example, to the ideal of "publicness"—in German, *Öffentlichkeit*—or a public sphere of proto-political discourse independent of undue influence from church, state, and, later, the marketplace. In Habermas's formulation, this public sphere "provided the training ground for critical public reflection"; art and the experiences it provided were "claimed as a serviceable topic of discussion through which a [newly] publicly-oriented subjectivity communicated with itself" rather than achieving its political being only "in the service of a patron" (Habermas 1989, 29, 33–34; translation modified). So too, the aesthetic has long given rise to the contrary ideal of a bohemian preserve where a delicately cultivated aristocratic balance of taste and tastelessness, convention and transgression, suffers the brute indifference and smug naiveté of its bourgeois audience.

The Bechers' transformation of the iconography and methodology of social ambition from the 1920s and 1930s into "anonymous sculptures" relies just as much as their forebears on this counterpoint between aesthetic and instrumental world views, but in an opposite manner. The Bechers' aesthetic program is no war against the opiate of the elite, as Rodchenko had advocated. They have made themselves and their audience into connoisseurs of an industrial past providing us all with opportunity for unexpected visual delectation, with opportunity to delight in the play of fine distinctions and subtle variations between the appearances of many different structures which all perform the same instrumental function.[3] They offer their audience the opportunity, as one viewer has testified, for example, to delight in "differences in composition, rhythm and formal solutions where an ordinarily distracted eye would see only indifference and standardization" (Becher 1999, 15). In the words of another viewer, the Bechers' work is said to allow us "to regard a single line of rivets as equally significant a marking as a full-blown mannerist conceit" (Sante 1995, 29). In so doing, they revitalize the claims of taste and tastelessness by exercising those claims on the turf of instrumental reason, that is, by making art out of industry.

One interpretation of the Bechers' contribution, one that has deep roots in modernist critical theory, might argue that such connoisseurship represents the aestheticization of politics, the transformation of a publicly oriented sensibility into a rarefied product aimed at an elite market that ambivalently and obsessively draws succor from an earlier, more political moment for its legitimation. "Their work is a fraud," a certain school of criticism might once have alleged, "a mere *neo* avant-garde." Andreas Huyssen, for example, has made a broader statement that might be retrofitted to this context, particularly if we grant the Bechers nothing more than their disaffected pastiche of the past: "The obsessive attempts to give utopia a bad name," he writes, "remain fundamentally ideological and locked in a discursive battle with residual and emerging utopian thinking in the here and now" (Huyssen 1995, 86). Another, more openhanded interpretation, however, might see that same act of aestheticization as in its own way liberating, as both cathartic and invigorating, as an attempt to serve equally two pressing and contradictory concerns: to both remember and let go of a failed political program and failed attempt to upgrade artists' social status in the name of the possibility for other, more viable investments. As such, the unexpected finery afforded by the Bechers, the part of their work that declares itself to be art in the most conventional decorative or ornamental sense, the systemic delight in the play of form, might well be valued (even, perhaps, by that group one critic has labeled "the last partisans of the avant-garde") as a refuge from political cynicism for an age in which such refuge is often unavailable (de Duve 1996, 455).

This question about the place of the aesthetic in the Bechers' work can also be phrased in more general terms: How is it that we move beyond the critical negation of failed political attachments from the past? How can old commitments be rendered sympathetic beyond their inadequacy, heroic beyond their failing, forward-looking beyond their obsolescence, cherished beyond not being believed? The issue here is thus one of political memory, of a "talking cure" for false consciousness, of the way in which the political past is negotiated within our sense of the present and how that settlement inhabits the realm of the aesthetic. In light of such a question, the Bechers' mastery of their craft and the obsessiveness of their fascination—their tight, standardized formal rigor and their fixed commitment to a grueling, lifelong study—might be prized precisely for the way the aesthetic appeal of their work can emancipate an earlier political ideal from its anxiety-ridden status in the present and resituate it in the past. The distinguishing beauty of the Bechers' craft would thus not be found in the way it shares our period's still-vital critical distance from the old utopianisms but instead in its seemingly indefatigable preservationist impulse, in its attempt to hold on to and find delight in the great beleaguered promise of the modernist past over and above the critique of that past that is still vital in the present.

It is the fantasy life of this work, its capacity to take delight in an opening in the past which leads forward into the future, then, that might be said to have sustained it and driven its rhythm and repetition onward, maintaining its commitment to producing nearly the same picture over and over and over again for almost a half-century. Bernd Becher was clear about his fascination in a 1969 interview: "These things are so full of fantasy there is absolutely no sense in trying to paint them; I realized that no artist could have made them better," he said. "This is purely economic architecture. They throw it up, they use it, they misuse it, they throw it away" ("Beauty in the Awful," 1969, 69). A term the artists return to periodically is "nomadic architecture": the structures are "not like the pyramids," they have said, they are not "for eternity" (Zorpette 1994, 166). Their vision is of an architecture free of the burden of culture, free of the burden of identity: "An Italian gasometer does not look Italian and a Chinese blast furnace does not look Chinese," they have said, and it is this form of looking that is so appealing; it is this form of looking that delights (Morris 1974, n.p.).

The strongest reference for identity-thinking for anyone growing up in Germany during the war, of course, would be the construction of Germanness and its others, and this was formative for the Bechers: "the industrial world is completely divorced from" such identity thinking, Bernd has said. "It has absolutely nothing to do with ideology. It corresponds more to the pragmatic English way of thinking" (Ziegler 2002, 143). As the artists note, their nineteenth-century approach itself, like the structures they photograph, is drawn from "the soul of industrial thought" (Ziegler 2002, 143). Method and subject matter, form and content, serve as reciprocal homologous support for each other: just as with industry, so photography in their hands is assumed to be "by its very nature free of ideology" (Ziegler 2002, 143). This sense of freedom, this delight in the industrial as an alternative to ideology, is the engine sustaining their distinctive photographic comportment.

All similar end-of-ideology claims that developed in the 1950s were born of similar assumptions. Each arose with a theory of ideology based on the principle of identity—as in Nazi ideology, for example, or Communist ideology—and any cultural development that weakened or diluted identity was understood also to weaken the ideology that sustained that identity. As Raymond Aron put it the same year the Bechers embarked on their project, for example, ideology was supposed to draw its authority from "the longing for a purpose, for communion with the people, for something controlled by an idea or a will" (Aron 1957, 46). This identity-thesis was embraced across a wide political spectrum from Aron leftward, and in many respects it continues to form our own moment now. But it is important for our purposes to recall how this model of ideology was different from that first developed by Marx, which subtended the ambitions of the engineer generation.

What the modernists of the 1920s and 1930s wanted was a kind of materialist foothold that would sustain the progressive development of identity—in social planning, in the machine, in their productivism itself—and that could hold its own against the vagaries of taste in a world increasingly dominated by consumerism. Such consumerism was a big part of the modernity of artists like Rodchenko, Moholy, Renger, and others, of course, but as a group they had no aspiration for an anti-aesthetic per se (as would later be the case with Pop Art, for example), no aspiration to abandon the claims of science, no aspiration for negation that rested on its own laurels. In the Marxian schema that they had inherited, the very moment that ideology in its identity-based sense is said to be negated is itself the turning point into ideology proper or the moment when, as *The Communist Manifesto* put it famously, "all that is solid melts into air, all that is holy is profaned" and identity is given over to process, social relations are given over to relations between things, and politics is given over to economics.

This type of ideology is given not by propagandists and ideologists—in an important sense there can be no such thing as a capitalist Goebbels—but is given instead always already right in the technology. "Modern Industry never views or treats the existing form of production process as the definitive one," Marx wrote. "Its technical basis is therefore revolutionary, whereas all earlier modes of production were essentially conservative. By means of machinery, chemical processes and other methods, it is continually transforming not only in the technical basis of production, but also the functions of the worker and the social combinations of the labor process. . . . [It] incessantly throws masses of capital and of workers from one branch of production to another" (Marx 1992, 617). This movement is the "nomadic" quality of modern industry that the Bechers rely on to make their point, and their project speaks equally to Marx's account of industry as progressive social change as it does to his account of it as bearer of false consciousness, alienation, and exploitation.

The Bechers work this boundary between promise and threat differently, however. Their project provides a systematic manner of viewing the world that wagers its own system of value, and thereby its distinctive form of autonomy, against its architectural subject: where the architecture promises pure instrumentality, they provide a purity of aesthetic form. As such, while their work makes its own claim to be free of ideology, its own claim to being apolitical, it does so differently than does the industry they photograph. Their method as artists is to pit one modern form against another, to pit the nomadism of aesthetic delight against the nomadism of industry, to pit the (idealistic, German) soul of aesthetic experience against the (pragmatic, English) "soul of industrial thought." In so doing they have produced a full-blown nineteenth-century archive exactly in the manner that Foucault would describe. It is an archive not of bodies but of machines, however, not of the formal, physiognomic variations of deviance but of industriousness, not of those discarded by modernity but of what modernity has shed of itself. The delight offered by their art—in its mechanical rhythms and repetitions, in the play of form across the registers of its objectivity and systematicity—is therefore realized only *against* the revolutionary promise of the modern industry it depicts.

Enlightenment

Art and industry thus stand opposed in the Bechers' work in a manner different from, even contrary to, their Machine Age forebears: put schematically, their project is one of aestheticizing industry rather than industrializing art. This, it might be said, is the other leg of postmodernism in their work, the way in which it engages in the play of signification with diminished concern for its attachment to some properly material reality.

But this turn away from modernism's politics and science of industry is in no way the whole story. Art and industry also rely on a common foundation in the Bechers' work, and it is this that can be said to be its embrace of modernism, its faith in the power of representation to reveal and comprehend the hidden material conditions of the world it addresses, its faith in the project of Enlightenment. Even though the Bechers' work distances itself from most of the affective attachments of the engineer ideal of their forebears, it does share with that ideal (in a manner that is fully modern) faith in the more abstract aim of *system.* Their work cares little for the mimicking of the consumer world that emerged as a program side-by-side with theirs in the pre-Pop and Pop movements of Britain and the United States in the 1950s and early 1960s. Their detachment is not founded on irony, and the pleasure taken in their project is not the consumer's pleasure of expenditure without return, of process without aim. Indeed, it might be said, if there is one thing the Becher project is more than anything else, one thing that distinguishes it from the core critical motif of their pop-culturalist contemporaries, it is the apparent earnestness with which it embraces systematicity, the way in which it holds onto modernism's seriousness of purpose and concentration of aim even as it abandons the purpose or aim itself.

What then has this residual modernist ideal of systematicity meant for the Bechers and their audiences, and what might it mean for us now? What, in the end, is the value of their archive? Certainly it has taken on the form and weight of the ethical principle of commitment, as argued above. Certainly, too, it has provided the formal conditions for aesthetic experience or delight. But these standards on their own are abstract forms and empty of historical content, empty of any claim for why such an ethic or such an aesthetic might appeal or serve its constituency and its time. The historical promise of systemic form had been clear enough for their Machine Age forebears: it was to carry the new vision, the society planned by artists; it was to be scientific management raised to the level of social engineering through its visual forms. Its promise, in short, was that it would produce, as the Bechers have said disapprovingly, "a socialistic view—a fresh view of the world, a new man, a new beginning."

From our latter-day perspective, it is important to remember that this critique is really a product of the generation of the Bechers and Foucault and did not emerge immediately after the war but instead only arose in the 1950s. In the earlier postwar period, the old prewar project for a new man was actually revitalized and given a new mission, if only for a moment. Against the fluctuating political passions aroused by the emerging anticommunist bunker culture of the late 1940s and early 1950s, many public intellectuals came to approach the question of political subjectivity with a renewed sense of urgency and purpose. Much-discussed statements, derived from such works as *Modern Man Is Obsolete* by *Saturday Review* editor Norman Cousins and *The Real Problem Is in the Hearts of Men* by leading world-government advocate Albert Einstein, set the tone in the United States and paralleled the more immediately pressing self-scrutiny in Germany, institutionalized in the reeducation program and developed in a more philosophical manner by intellectuals such as Karl Jaspers: "Brainwork is not all this requires," Jaspers wrote in *The Question of German Guilt;* "The intellect must put the heart to work, arouse it to an inner activity which in turn carries the brainwork" (Jaspers 1947, 16). "Our poisoned hearts must be cured," as Camus put it; we must "remake our political mentality" (Camus 1961, 61).

Photographers once again assumed a special role for this reconstruction, this production of a new, new vision and a new, new man. Such was the mission adopted programmatically by Edward Steichen for *The Family of Man*, for example, and it was the mandate assumed by Otto Steinert for his *Subjektive Fotografie:* "As the most widely-spread vehicle of expression up to the present day," he wrote, "photography is called upon to mold the visual consciousness of our age. And as the pictorial technique most generally comprehensible and most easily accessible to lay hands on, it is particularly fitted to promote the mutual understanding of the nations" (Steinert 1952, 5).

In a significant sense the search for a "visual consciousness of our age" promoted by Steichen and Steinert, like the heart-work called for by Cousins, Einstein, Jaspers, and Camus, was similar to that of the war consciousness that it promised to move beyond, at least structurally. In both cases—in the wartime German *Volk*, for example, and in the post-war *Family of Man*—the primary ideological goal was to produce a powerful and passionate sense of belonging, to produce the affective experience of nation. The structure of the social bond, in both cases, thus, was based on the principle of identity or passionate attachment to a shared sense of self, even if the later attachment was to be built around shared guilt. It was a social form generated through ideological means of the first, identity-driven variety discussed above rather than by the second, Marxian account. The structural correspondence of wartime and postwar approaches to political subjectivity was an insight not lost on the Bechers' generation and one that motivated their rejection of the one-world, hearts-of-men model.

There are, of course, other possible levers for generating a "visual consciousness of our age" than that of the passionate attachments of one-world nationalism. On the idealistic end of the spectrum, for example, there is the old philosopher's dream of collectively generated enlightenment or communicative reason developed through the search for shared interest. More soberly, perhaps, and far closer to our own experience now, there is the capitalist's dreamworld of individual interest, or a fluid collective economy of individual wagers, risks, investments, losses, and gains brought into commerce through the market-logic of exchange. As discussed above, however, the Bechers' own practice and the model of sociality it promises is not vested in either of these systems. Neither collectivist nor individualist, they work the principle of systematicity to their own alternative "rhythms and repetitions," that is, to their own aesthetic ends.

Through this differential setting of form against content, aesthetic against instrumental aims, the Bechers deploy the original promise of the aesthetic: the development of "the faculty for judging an object . . . *without any interest*," as Kant described it (Kant 2000, 96). Judgment, in their work, assumes the abstract form of a concept which allows for aesthetic response to take place in a manner similar to cognition but through which "no thing is actually cognized" (Kant 2000, 57). The experience of their work is thus realized as satisfaction (or dissatisfaction) in the object without any specific individual aim or purpose being satisfied (or frustrated), without any notion of individual interest or collective will. The experience of delight that conveys satisfaction, thus, is generalized and endowed with the presumption of universality or "common sense" (Kant 2000, 122–123).

It is this experience of universality that the Bechers' project courts and posits as its systemic aim; it is this experience that serves as an alternative "visual consciousness of our age," different from either the collective passions of political identification or the individual interests of the consumer. The key to their system, to the particular form of social value they produce, lies in the fact that the objects they photograph are "anonymous." The Bechers present modern industry in a manner that disavows its social, political, and economic value to the beholder and, in so doing, makes it available anew via an alternative category—aesthetic value or value "*without any interest.*" In creating the circumstances for such experience by using aging industrial structures still resonant with the memory of all their great modern ambitions, the Bechers create a powerful sense of that disavowal of instrumental value, that purposiveness without purpose, as *loss*, as the experience of *no interest* where interest was once housed, of *no passion* where passion once resided. In so doing they give us a fully elaborated neo-Kantian judgment made melancholy, a fully developed archive structured around an absent ideal, and the old promise of Enlightenment is once again resurrected, but now on the foundation of its own lost materialist soul.

Notes

1. Asked why their work exists in an art context rather than being made available in public archives for research purposes, the Bechers responded, "We did offer it to the government but they weren't interested. The work is about visual considerations, therefore it was only natural to show it in art galleries" (Grauerholz and Ramsden 1981, 18).

2. E.g., Thomas Ruff, Thomas Struth, Candida Höfer, and Andreas Gursky.

3. For an extended analysis using this feature of the Bechers' work to argue for the redemption of "the name of art" in the wake of the anti-aestheticism and politicization of functionalism, see Becher, *Basic Forms*, 1999.

Works Cited

Aron, Raymond. *The Opium of the Intellectual.* New York: Doubleday, 1957.

Becher, Bernd. "Beauty in the Awful." *Time,* September 5, 1969, 68–69.

———. *Bernd and Hilla Becher: Basic Forms.* Text by Thierry de Duve. New York: te Neues, 1999.

Becher, Bernd, and Hilla Becher. "Anonymous Sculpture." *Art and Artists* 5 (1970): 56–57.

Camus, Albert. "Defense of Intelligence." *Resistance, Rebellion, and Death.* New York: Alfred A. Knopf, 1961.

de Duve, Thierry. *Kant after Duchamp.* Cambridge, Mass.: MIT Press, 1996.

Foucault, Michel. "What Is Enlightenment?" In *The Foucault Reader,* ed. Paul Rabinow. New York: Pantheon, 1984.

Graeff, Werner. "Es kommt der neue Ingenier." *G* 1 (1923): N.p.

Grauerholz, Angela, and Anne Ramsden. "Photographing Industrial Architecture: An Interview with Hilla and Bernd Becher." *Parachute* 22 (1981): 14–19.

Gursky, Andreas. " . . . I generally let things develop slowly." Interview with Veit Görner. In *German Open: Contemporary Art in Germany,* ed. Gijs van Tuyl et al. Ostfildern: Hatje Cantz, 2000.

Habermas, Jürgen. *The Structural Transformation of the Public Sphere: An Inquiry into a Category of Bourgeois Society.* Cambridge, Mass.: MIT, 1989.

Huyssen, Andreas. *Twilight Memories: Marking Time in a Culture of Amnesia.* New York: Routledge, 1995.

Jaspers, Karl. *The Question of German Guilt.* New York: Dial, 1947.

Kant, Immanuel. *Critique of the Power of Judgment.* New York: Cambridge, 2000.

Marx, Karl. *Capital: A Critique of Political Economy.* Vol. 1. New York: Penguin, 1992.

Marx, Karl, and Frederick Engels. *The Communist Manifesto.* London: Verso, 1998.

Merleau-Ponty, Maurice. *Phenomenology of Perception.* New York: Humanities, 1962.

Moholy-Nagy, Sibyl. *Moholy-Nagy: Experiment in Totality.* 2d ed. Cambridge, Mass., and London: MIT, 1969 [1950].

Morris, Lynda. *Bernd and Hilla Becher.* London: Arts Council of Great Britain, 1974.

Rodchenko, Alexander. "Against the Synthetic Portrait, For the Snapshot." In *Photography in the Modern Era: European Documents and Critical Writings, 1913–1940,* ed. Christopher Phillips. New York: Metropolitan Museum of Art, 1989.

Sante, Luc. *The New Republic,* July 3, 1995, 213, n.1.

Sobieszek, Robert A. "Two Books of Ultra-Topography." *Image* 14 (1971): 12–18.

Steinert, Otto. *Subjektive Fotografie: Ein Bildband moderner europäischer Fotografie.* Bonn: Brüder Auer, 1952.

Touraine, Liliane. "Bernd and Hilla Becher: The Function Doesn't Make the Form." *Artefactum* (April/May 1989): 6–9.

Ziegler, Ulf Erdmann. "The Bechers' Industrial Lexicon." *Art in America* (June 2002): 92–101, 140–143.

Zorpette, Glenn. "Dynamic Duos: How Artist Teams Work." *Art News* (Summer 1994): 164–169.

5

Ready, Set, Made!
Joseph Beuys and the Critique of Silence

Jan Mieszkowski

Few postwar artists can rival Joseph Beuys for the range of experimentation he displayed in his immense repertoire of sculptures, installations, and performance pieces. Still more unique was the scope of Beuys's engagement with the intellectual, social, and political events of his day. His knack for generating publicity and his uncanny ability to ally himself with one aesthetic movement after another kept him in the headlines for decades. Even taken in the context of the diverse and idiosyncratic German left of the Cold War era, Beuys brought the role of the engaged artist to a new level as he assailed the hierarchical structures of bourgeois institutions through *Aktionen* ("actions") championing democracy and individual self-determination. His proselytizing tendencies culminated in a call to subsume every dimension of human experience under a paradigm of creativity, a position encapsulated in his well-known claim that he did "not want to carry art into politics, but make politics into art" (Adriani 1979, 277).[1]

Beuys's detractors have identified him as part of a larger neo-avant-garde tendency to appropriate the radical strategies of early twentieth-century movements such as Dada and Surrealism for thoroughly conventional purposes. These projects are said to betray their aesthetic predecessors by reinforcing rather than challenging the institutional parameters of art and the status of the artwork as a fetishized commodity.[2] On the occasion of a major Beuys retrospective at the Guggenheim Museum in 1979, Benjamin Buchloh went further and dismissed the artist as a naive utopian:

Everybody who was seriously involved in radical student politics during the 1960s in Germany, for example, and who worked on the development of a new and adequate political theory and practice, laughed at or derided Beuys' public-relations move to found the Grand Student Party, which was supposed to return an air of radicality to the master who was coming of esthetic age. Nobody who understands any contemporary science, politics, or aesthetics, for that matter, could want to see in Beuys' proposal for an integration of art, science and politics—as his program for the Free International University demands—anything more than simple-minded utopian drivel lacking elementary political and educational practicality. (Buchloh 2001a, 201)

Buchloh went on to propose that Beuys's "political ideas fulfill the criteria of the totalitarian in art just as they were propounded by Italian Futurism on the eve of European fascism" (Buchloh 2001a, 211). The artist's ostensibly left-wing program, he concluded, was based on an abstraction of universal subjectivity that could lead only to the kind of aesthetics of self-destruction against which Walter Benjamin had warned. To this day, Buchloh's attack remains extremely influential and is frequently cited as the reason Beuys has never attained the widespread popularity in America that he enjoys in Europe.

Even read with a sympathetic eye, there is much in Beuys's pronouncements that may strike us as anachronistic and out of step with the agendas of contemporary cultural criticism. At the same time, we should not assume that the liberatory potential of his project has been fully understood, either by Beuys or by his most stalwart supporters. To make a case for the progressive elements of his art will require considerably more than some assertions about the originality or beauty of his work. To this end, the following essay seeks to recast the Beuys Debate by focusing on one of the most popular and controversial facets of his polemical agenda: his attack on Marcel Duchamp. Although the prevailing view is that Beuys profoundly misunderstood Duchamp's innovations, we will argue that he radicalizes his predecessor's insights into the nature of the aesthetic act, thereby revealing a new understanding of art as a political praxis.

One of the great challenges in discussing Beuys's politics lies in overcoming the view that one of his primary aims was to construct an aesthetic religion that featured himself as privileged visionary or shaman. The Fluxus artists with whom Beuys cooperated in the early 1960s frequently criticized him on these grounds, arguing that his work was too egotistical and amounted to no more than a form of blatant self-promotion—a conclusion to which Beuys appears to give credence when he criticizes Allan Kaprow's Happenings for their failure to make clear the distinction between the artist and audience, as if the very idea that the onlookers might take on the most minor role in Beuys's show was sheer blasphemy. From this perspective, Beuys's actions are designed to parody the semiotic systems organizing spiritual or political authority, but they fail to undermine the symbols of power they deploy and confirm only the self-perceived virtuosity of their performer. When Beuys says that "it is important to know of man that his freedom and its conscious implementation lead to recognition of the 'Ego' as the sovereign, determining power" (Beuys 1986b, 42), many critics would argue that there can be no doubt as to whose "ego" he has in mind.

On the other hand, it is worth considering whether the ease with which Beuys's pretensions to irony have been dismissed betrays a reluctance to engage with the real challenges of his work. Perhaps the most striking aspect of Beuys's contributions to 1960s European performance art was his conviction that the diverse range of experiments taking place needed to be underwritten by a theory, "a recognizable, underlying structure, with a clearly marked goal" (Adriani 1979, 86). These remarks may betray a misunderstanding of the attempts in Fluxus and Neo-Dada to free artistic expression from the authority of teleological thought. Nevertheless, there is no reason to assume that such efforts were successful or to condemn Beuys for pointing towards the difficulties in—if not the impossibility of—escaping the specter of telos.

How, then, does Beuys conceive of the ends of art? Commenting on his frequent use of fat as a sculptural material, he highlights its status as a fluid that may harden at the same time as it continues to hold out the possibility of further decomposition. Expanding on these dynamics of formation and deformation, he explains:

> The totalized concept of art, that is the principle that I wanted to express with the material, which in the end refers to everything, to all forms in the world. And not only to artistic forms, but also to social forms or legal forms or economic forms, or agricultural problems, or to other formal and educational problems. All questions of man can be only a question of form, and that is the totalized concept of art. (Adriani 1979, 283)

In his quest for a fundamental form capable of grounding the social sciences and the humanities in their entirety, Beuys couples an Enlightenment predilection for the encyclopedic systematization of thought with a Romantic interest in the primordial figures that govern all discourse. It is worth noting that he has little to say about why this basic form should be treated as a concept of art rather than one of economics, jurisprudence, or epistemology. Nor does he explain why concepts should be exclusively matters of form in the first place. Indeed, it is precisely the form of totality itself that Beuys never questions, the form in virtue of which a concept could become the form of forms. It is difficult to see how someone so concerned with the nature of political action could have failed to entertain even the possibility of resistance to the totalizing imprimatur of such a Master-form. From this perspective, Beuys's conception of human freedom seems quite sinister, as he abandons the notion of spontaneous autonomy or whim that has been at the heart of our ideas about liberty since Rousseau: "[F]reedom," he proclaims, "cannot be arbitrary. Freedom must be fulfilled in accordance with strict forms" (Beuys 1986b, 48). The vision of Beuys as the proponent of a totalitarianism of form appears to be confirmed.

Despite these damning conclusions, I would like to propose that Beuys's artistic praxis also reveals the possibility of another understanding of form according to which the expressive powers of art do not have absolute sovereignty. In an interview given near the end of his life, Beuys speaks of "the expanded concept of art" not as a "theory" but as "a way of proceeding" (Beuys 1986a, 34). He elaborates: "I go back to the sentence: in the beginning was the word. The word is a form. That is the evolutionary principle as such" (Beuys 1986a, 34). While Beuys goes on to explain that this principle springs out of the creative potential of man, his customary emphasis on the totalizing nature of human art is at least momentarily complemented by a decision to accord language primacy as the originary power of form-giving.

To explore the implications of this move more fully, we must now turn to what was to become one of Beuys's most famous actions. By its nature, performance art is notoriously difficult to study after the fact, since it is typically not filmed and detailed records of individual events generally do not exist. Indeed, it has been suggested that the basic provocation of performance work lies in its challenge to the primacy of the visual fixity we take for granted in painting, sculpture, or photography. Some of Beuys's actions have become widely known thanks to excellent photographic documentation, for example, "How to explain pictures to a dead hare" or his several days of cohabitation with a coyote in a New York gallery space. In contrast, the performance from December 1964 that concerns us here is renowned not for the relics of its visual instantiation, but for the quotation to which it gives rise, the gnomic claim "Das Schweigen von Marcel Duchamp wird überbewertet" (The silence of Marcel Duchamp is overrated).

**Figure 5.1. Joseph Beuys, *The Silence of Marcel Duchamp Is
Overrated* (1964).**
**Courtesy Stiftung Museum Schloß Moyland, Collection van
der Grinten, MSM 01610. © 2005 Artists Rights Society (ARS),
New York/VG Bild-Kunst, Bonn.**

Although the action involved a number of elements that were standard features of Beuys's work at the time, including the construction of a *Fettecke* (a corner of fat), the use of felt and walking sticks, and multiple participants, this sentence written in oil and chocolate (see fig. 5.1) has obliterated nearly every trace of the activities from which it emerged. In the process, it has become one of Beuys's most frequently cited slogans, if not the cornerstone of his theoretical agenda.[3] Twenty years after its appearance, Beuys offered a gloss on the line:

> I criticize [Duchamp] because at the very moment when he could have developed a theory on the basis of the work he had accomplished, he kept silent. And I am the one who, today, develops the theory he could have developed. He entered this object [the urinal]

into the museum and noticed that its transportation from one place to another made it into art. But he failed to draw the clear and simple conclusion that every man is an artist. (Quoted in de Duve 1999, 285)

It is interesting that the suggestion that Duchamp is to be reprimanded for having failed to become a public figure is never taken particularly seriously, as if Beuys's own overindulgence in the public sphere makes it a foregone conclusion that he will criticize everyone else for their failure on this score. Instead, the debate has concentrated on Beuys's misunderstanding of the implications of Duchamp's ready-made. Divorcing a prefashioned object—whether a urinal, bicycle wheel, or snow shovel—from its customary context and renaming it as "art" continues to be regarded as one of the groundbreaking aesthetic gestures of the twentieth century. In contrast to Beuys's claim that Duchamp reveals "every man to be an artist," it is generally assumed that the latter's goal was to ridicule the very idea of artistic creation as a privileged event. As Duchamp himself put it, the ready-made is "a work of art for which there is no artist" (Duchamp 1968, 62). From a slightly different perspective, the ready-made has also been characterized as an attempt to collapse the distinction between the genius who makes art and the cultured observer who has the taste necessary to differentiate between art and everything else.[4]

It can be argued that Beuys's misunderstanding of Duchamp's legacy manifests itself in his own ready-mades. To the extent that he makes use of prefabricated items, Beuys appears not to be trying to alter the status of a work of art qua art, but to be incorporating preexisting objects into conventional pieces of sculpture. As Buchloh writes:

> Unlike his European peers from the late 1950s—Piero Manzoni, Arman or even Yves Klein—Beuys does not change the state of the object within the discourse itself. Quite to the contrary, he dilutes and dissolves the conceptual precision of Duchamp's ready-made by reintegrating the object into the most traditional and naïve context of representation of meaning, the idealist metaphor: this object stands for that idea, and that idea is represented in this object. (Buchloh 2001a, 206)

For Buchloh, the ready-made remains outside the control of the "artist" who appropriates it and thus challenges his or her capacity to employ it in a meaningful way. It is this resistance to the artist that Beuys appears not to respect. He takes a bathtub, a stool, or a chair and elides its status as preconstructed by completely integrating it into his own idiosyncratic web of icons and motifs. In the process, he forecloses on the ironic possibility that all art might be "just" a chair or a bathtub. As Tony Godfrey has observed, "[Beuys's] use of the readymade was always dominated by his signature: it is true that the readymade cannot exist without the signing or naming of it, but Beuys took it to greater extremes so that the readymade seemed no more than a support for the signature, as the canvas is for a painting" (Godfrey 1998, 183). A self-styled purveyor of spiritual truths, Beuys once again appears to be the advocate of an art grounded in an outmoded model of genius.

On the most basic level, Beuys ostensibly domesticates Duchamp's project by refusing to acknowledge that the concept of art itself may fundamentally be open to attack. Still, the debate begins to look somewhat different once we realize that both Beuys and Duchamp share a concern with a more basic change in the focus of art theory, a shift from the idea of art as an object passively viewed to an emphasis on art as an act or an event. Duchamp insisted that the ready-made could only be fully appreciated if one grasped the randomness that was inherent in the project. Thus, he comments that his *Bicycle Wheel,* a wheel mounted on a stool, did not proceed from a given plan but "had more to do with the idea of chance" (Schwarz 1970, 442). In an extremely influential move, the Dadaist Hans Richter maintained that the key to Duchamp's gesture was the singularity of its shock value: whether they remain on display in a museum or are safely put back in the bathroom or the tool shed, the urinal, the shovel, and the bike wheel are neither aesthetic nor anti-aesthetic the second time around (Richter 1966, 208). As a consequence, the ready-made combines two seemingly divergent features: as a provocation, it is a onetime event, but as the appropriation of a mechanically reproduced object, it is an overt meditation on the nature of mass production, addressing both the status of the artwork as a commodity and the status of all objects as always-already derivative or premade.[5]

The fact that Duchamp's ready-made becomes one of the most imitated gestures of twentieth-century art is one of its most obvious paradoxes. If nothing else, it makes it more difficult to disparage Beuys's tactics in working with ready-made objects, for what his procedures actually question is whether the ready-made's "random" dimension can ever be standardized into a practice to be repeated by others. Why, Beuys asks, should we celebrate those artists who seek to establish themselves as Duchamp's inheritors by displaying ready-mades "like" those of the master, rather than criticizing them for failing to understand the inherent singularity of his project? Far from naively incorporating ready-made objects into traditional symbolic pieces, Beuys's insistence that their semantic value does not represent an attack on "art" reveals the pitfalls of attempting to participate in Duchamp's legacy.

In the process, Beuys invites us to reconsider how ready-mades function in a broader field of signification.[6] Of particular importance is Godfrey's claim, cited above, that "the ready-made cannot exist without the signing or naming of it." This observation reminds us that the accent falls on *says* in Duchamp's notorious suggestion that art is "what an artist says it is." In these terms, the ready-made must be considered not only as the recontextualization of a material object, but also as an overtly linguistic act—specifically, an act of naming. Duchamp makes it clear that the decisive step in producing the first ready-mades was the gesture whereby he gave the object a quasi-title: "In New York in 1915, I bought at a hardware store a snow shovel on which I wrote 'in advance of the broken arm.' It was around that time that the word 'readymade' came to mind to designate this form of manifestation" (Duchamp 1966, 47). Even from this brief account, it is clear that the activity of "naming" the object was not simply a matter of "stating the obvious"—that is, labeling a can "can" or a pipe "pipe." Duchamp explains: "One important characteristic was the short sentence which I occasionally inscribed on the 'readymade.' Instead of describing the object like a title, the sentence was meant to carry the mind of the spectator towards other regions more verbal" (Duchamp 1966, 47).[7] No mere presentation of an epithet or appellation, the move to inscribe a phrase on the ready-made is intended to shift the creative medium from the visual to the verbal. From this point on, the medium of the artwork is neither wood, nor stone, nor metal, but language itself.

Octavio Paz, one of Duchamp's most influential supporters, has underscored the notion that the paradigm of the ready-made is linguistic. Speaking of the gesture whereby one calls an "anonymous object" art, Paz writes, "Contradiction is the essence of the act; it is the plastic equivalent of the pun: the latter destroys meaning, the former the idea of value" (Paz 1975, 84). For Paz, the semantic capacities of a ready-made rest not on the fact that it attacks the sanctity of the fabricated object, but on the way it highlights the absence of any simple one-to-one correspondence between a physical entity and what it represents. It is from this perspective that one should interpret the "label" that emerges from Beuys's 1964 action, the "short sentence" that comes to define his aesthetics as a whole: "The silence of Marcel Duchamp is overrated." In his comments on this utterance, Beuys is plainly aware of the degree to which the lapidary pronouncement confronts us not simply as a catchy proverb we will never tire of repeating, but as a ready-made in its own right, a piece of language that can never be reduced to the expressive intentions of the person who reads or writes it. It is not by chance that the poster from the action is often described as a piece of graffiti, as if it were something Beuys had stumbled across on the wall of an alley. From the moment it is articulated, the sentence emerges as prefabricated; it is a slogan that can be taken up and reappropriated time and time again, but it is never entirely in hand.

We must therefore distinguish ourselves from those critics who accuse Beuys of claiming absolute sovereignty over his art, as if he could dictate every resonance of its meaning in isolation from its social or historical field of production. "The silence of Marcel Duchamp is overrated" is nothing if not a testimony to the impossibility of understanding an event of performance art through a fixed form of control. What Buchloh heralds as the innovation in Fluxus performances that Beuys failed to grasp—their ability to bring the art object "back into a completely new circuit, into a complete new discourse, into a completely different type of viewer-author exchange" (Buchloh 2001b, 87)—describes very well the way in which artist and viewer participate together in the repetition and recoding of Beuys's silence slogan, to the point that the word "Duchamp" itself becomes less a reference to a historical figure than a confirmation that there is no boundary between the plastic and the performing arts.

At the same time, Beuys does not follow Buchloh in celebrating Fluxus for its search for an "interactive model in which participant and producer are equals" (Buchloh 2001b, 87). The word "Duchamp" designates an event of art as anti-art that may be impossible to replicate. Ostensibly the clumsiest humanist of his era, Beuys thus reminds us that the ready-made is an attack on the anthropocentric conception of art as a product of the human hand. Artist and audience are only equal in their mutual status as secondary with respect to the event of art they both confront. Buchloh has argued, "what Beuys lacks most of all is the understanding that artistic languages are public entries into the symbolic order, and as such they are both historically overdetermined and socially constructed" (Buchloh 2001b, 89). In contrast, we insist that the strange legacy of the silence slogan in the 1964 action confirms precisely that an act of art emerges into a symbolic order in such a way that no one—Duchamp, Beuys, or any member of the public—is able to establish what it means to say (or even to write in chocolate): "The silence of Marcel Duchamp is overrated." If Duchamp's ready-made mocks us with the implicit speech act that declares something to be an aesthetic object—"I proclaim this urinal to be a work of art"—Beuys's pronouncement on Duchamp mocks us by revealing that the reduction of Duchamp's project to a pure assault on art misses the fact that nobody can prevent a ready-made from being reincorporated into a semantic field in which it may function as the epitome of high art.

Like Walter Benjamin, Beuys recognizes that the very gestures that destroy the cult of beauty and the aura of the artwork may become the means for their vigorous return.[8] In this regard, we must reject Buchloh's positivistic treatment of the "symbolic order" as a kind of empirical given. Avoiding such a reification, Beuys's work directs us to examine the verbal acts, the acts of power, whereby such an order is constantly being constituted and dismantled, formed and deformed. Unlike his Fluxus contemporaries who sought to develop a performative *object* that would resist traditional aesthetic hierarchies and conventions, Beuys provides a verbal performance, an exercise in the fetishism of the slogan that continues to this day to organize the semiotics of social hegemony.

From this perspective, Beuys's work allows for a broader reconsideration of the ready-made. Duchamp proposes that any form of making is essentially the deployment of ready-mades, even going so far as to claim that "the painter is really making a readymade when he paints with a manufactured object that is called paints" (Duchamp 1968, 62).[9] Taken to its limit, this argument makes it difficult to distinguish between two ideas: the notion that Duchamp's work proves that what has traditionally been called art is no different from any other kind of craft or construction, and the notion that everything is essentially derivative of a prior construction such that there is no such thing as a making in the present but only the deployment of what has already been fashioned in the past. Here, we should recall our earlier concern with Beuys's notion of a Master-form under whose stamp all discourses are to be legitimated as contributions to the sum total of human experience. To claim that everything is always-already ready-*made* is not necessarily to claim that any object or sentence is always-already *ready*. What is often overlooked in Duchamp's argument is its subtle theory of use. The ready-made logic implies that any and every object is necessarily open to appropriation by a project that will employ it as part of a construction. Resistance to this transformative assimilation is evidently futile.

The question, then, is whether Beuys's emphasis on art as a linguistic act rather than the fashioning of an object in a physical medium offers insight into what may not allow itself to be made use of in this way, whether in a sculpture, an installation, or a performance piece. Much closer to Dada or to Kaprow than he himself would ever allow, Beuys appears to offer an answer in a single word: silence. Written on a poster in the 1964 action, the word "silence" functions as the poster child for a language that does not do what we try to use it to do. The word "silence" is never as good as its name and cannot be part of a speech act that can make good on a declaration of quietude. In the sentence "The silence of Marcel Duchamp is overrated," the word "silence" is thus thoroughly ironic, for the real lesson of the Duchamp action is that no art can speak loud enough to guarantee that it will remain art.

Charges of mysticism notwithstanding, Beuys does not simply turn silence into a privileged category of experience or an ultimate value on the basis of which one could assess all the other elements of his art. In 1973, he made use of galvanized copper and zinc to encase five reels of an Ingmar Bergman film called *The Silence*. Far from simply "silencing" the cinematic work of that name and thereby holding it to the promise of its title, Beuys's "sculpture" forces us to consider the implications of reducing a film to the status of an object. Can an artwork be turned into a ready-made? Or does Beuys simply take us from one artwork to another, allowing us to avoid the problem of the "ordinary" object entirely? The products of the gesture, the galvanized reels, are easy to situate among the motifs that govern Beuys's work, lining up with his meditations on encasement, storage, and stored potential. We might imagine, then, that Beuys's piece is a sort of reverse ready-made in which the aesthetic authority of the film is dismantled from within rather than from without. The problem is that it is not clear that its aesthetic authority is being dismantled or even that we successfully shift aesthetic media in the process of altering the reels. Like Bergman's *The Silence*, Beuys's *The Silence* is a multiple of which fifty copies exist; and in this respect, it mimes the structure of repetition and reproduction that defines the cinematic medium and does not expose its banality or dispel its aura.[10] *The Silence* may reveal that film shares with ready-mades an investment in technologies of reproducibility, but it hardly exposes film as being in any way less than art. Moreover, the fact that Beuys renders the films unplayable is clearly contingent with respect to the artistic medium under analysis, that is, the fact that one can seal a reel inside a canister and thereby make it impossible to run it in a projector is of no more interest than the fact that fire or water can destroy a painting.

Is Beuys's point, then, that "silence"—be it a word, an idea, or a physical (non)phenomenon—is the only thing that can truly escape the fate of being exposed as ready-made because it is never actually "made" or because it never "happens" and can therefore never be repeated? Or is he simply trying to tell us that silence marks the limit of the plastic arts and performance art—hence, the limit of the visual arts as such—because it names an absence rather than a positive presence? To this last suggestion, one can respond that silence plays a central part in all music—most notoriously in John Cage's composition in which the pianist sits at the keyboard doing nothing for four minutes and thirty-three seconds.[11] In fact, we might argue that if Beuys and other performance artists are interested in realizing *live* art, silence is the most eminently live phenomenon of all.

Even as we are quick to affirm that silence is a crucial feature of the paradigms of performance debated by Beuys and his contemporaries, we begin to realize that we have been poor readers of the 1964 Duchamp action. We have missed the joke, for we have failed to recognize that Beuys has reminded us that Duchamp's predicament is our own and that silence is always overrated and overvalued (*überbewertet*). The moment we treat silence as part of an auditory event or as a concept in a theory of art, we turn it into something that is given or made, in which case it ceases to be silent. Insofar as it can only be articulated through a surrogate—whether felt, fat, or Marcel Duchamp—silence interests Beuys because it reveals the limits of our models of representation. In this respect, Beuys's silence is not an object or a theory but, as he tells us in explaining his "expanded concept of art," a "way of proceeding." For Beuys, silence is a *political* ideal because it is the one process that can never be incorporated into another project or put to use for an external end. Conceived in these terms, silence has nothing to do with an individual artist's withdrawal from the public eye or with his or her refusal to account for the implications of a given creative project; nor is it a form of quietism. This is a silence that never gets noticed, much less criticized or written down in oil and chocolate. To the question of whether or not such a "way of proceeding" is something to which we can actually aspire, Beuys has both everything and nothing to say.

Ultimately, then, Beuys's confrontation with Duchamp reveals that in his actions, interviews, and manifestoes, the postwar German artist who was so notorious for being anything but quiet may have been striving to perform something one could never hear. Ironically, this means that Beuys is far closer to Duchamp than are those critics who have been trying to protect Duchamp from him. Hardly a formalist, much less a mere showman, Beuys is true to the heritage of his Dadaist forerunners in undertaking a broad reconsideration of our most basic ideas about the means and ends of art. Pitting the representational against the performative, the expressive against the inexpressive, his *Aktionen* require us to think about aesthetic praxis not as a process generating material objects but as an event that in challenging our paradigms of signification holds out at least the possibility of an escape from the dominion of commodity culture.

Notes

1. "[Teaching] is my most important function," said Beuys. "To be a teacher is my greatest work of art" (quoted in Godfrey 1998, 195).

2. "Beuys," writes Donald Kuspit, "is the grand climax of a long line of self-contradictory avant-garde narcissists in conflict with a society they want as their audience. Each idealizes himself while showing society that it is far from ideal, especially compared to himself" (Kuspit 1993, 98). See also Biro 2003, 118–119.

3. Few descriptions of this action seem to agree on the details of what was actually involved, or even on what day it took place. The best available account can be found in Schneede 1994, 80–82.

4. See de Duve 1999, esp. 285.

5. Rosalind Krauss has argued that "the ready-made's discursive form is that of the commodity-in-circulation, which is to say an exploitation of the commodity's own economic condition as an object of exchange now redoubled by its location in the pages of a magazine and thus ready for dissemination within the world of high culture" (Krauss 1996, 250).

6. Some positive assessments of the differences between the ready-mades of Beuys and Duchamp have proceeded along similar lines. Commenting on Beuys's reaction to Duchamp's *Bicycle Wheel, Is it about a bicycle?* (a piece that consists of a bike next to some inscribed slates), Alain Borer writes:

   Duchamp's bicycle turns on itself, albeit *free*wheeling, whereas Beuys' brings a series of measures in its wake. Duchamp *takes his leave:* he places (flings) the urinal in the museum, in the freezer, on its end; Beuys *moves into action,* dynamizes objects, sets their thermal energy free, and takes us under his wing. (Borer 1997, 22)

   In these terms, Beuys's ready-made is designed to move the art installation beyond the realm of static entities and into a context of motility or even performativity.

7. On ready-made sentences and the language experiments of Duchamp and Walter Arensberg in general, see Nesbit, "Duchamp's Readymades," esp. 255–256, and Nesbit and Sawelson-Gorse 1996.

8. See Benjamin's comments on film in "The Work of Art in the Age of Its Technological Reproducibility," esp. 263–270.

9. In a 1961 interview Duchamp was again less than silent: "Let's say you use a tube of paint; you didn't make it. You bought it and used it as a ready-made. So man can never expect to start from scratch; he must start from ready-made things like even his own mother and father" (Kuh 1962, 90). For a broader analysis of painting and the readymade, see de Duve 1999, esp. 147–196.

10. Many of Beuys's most famous objects exist as multiples—for example, the

wooden and felt box he made with the Fluxus artist Nam June Paik or the coke bottle he placed in a box.

11. Beuys and his contemporaries repeatedly paid homage to this piece. Beuys, for example, sewed a piano up in felt, while Bruce Nauman filled a piano with honey.

Works Cited

Adriani, Götz, et al. *Joseph Beuys: Life and Works.* Trans. Patricia Lech. Woodbury, N.Y.: Barron's Educational Series, 1979.

Benjamin, Walter. "The Work of Art in the Age of Its Technological Reproducibility." Vol. 4 of Benjamin, *Selected Writings: 1938–1940,* trans. Edmund Jephcott et al. and ed. Howard Eiland and Michael W. Jennings, 251–283. Cambridge, Mass.: Belknap Press, 2003.

Beuys, Joseph. "In Conversation with Friedhelm Mennekes." In *In Memoriam Joseph Beuys: Obituaries, Essays, Speeches,* trans. Timothy Nevill, 29–34. Bonn: Inter Nationes, 1986a.

———. "Talking about One's Own Country: Germany." In *In Memoriam Joseph Beuys: Obituaries, Essays, Speeches,* trans. Timothy Nevill, 35–55. Bonn: Inter Nationes, 1986b.

Biro, Matthew. "Representation and Event: Anselm Kiefer, Joseph Beuys, and the Memory of the Holocaust." *Yale Journal of Criticism* 16, no. 1 (2003): 113–146.

Borer, Alain. "A Lament for Joseph Beuys." In *The Essential Joseph Beuys,* ed. Lothar Schirmer, 11–34. Cambridge, Mass.: MIT Press, 1997.

Buchloh, Benjamin H. D. "Beuys: The Twilight of the Idol, Preliminary Notes for a Critique." In *Joseph Beuys: Mapping the Legacy,* ed. Gene Ray, 199–211. New York: Distributed Art Press, 2001a. The article was originally published in *Art Forum* 18 (January 1980): 35–43.

———. "Reconsidering Joseph Beuys: Once Again." In *Joseph Beuys: Mapping the Legacy,* ed. Gene Ray, 75–89. New York: Distributed Art Press, 2001b.

de Duve, Thierry. *Kant after Duchamp.* Cambridge: MIT Press, 1999.

Duchamp, Marcel. "Apropos of 'Readymades.'" *Art and Artists* 1, no. 4 (July 1966): 47.

———. "I Propose to Strain the Laws of Physics" (interview with Francis Roberts). *Art News* 67 (December 1968): 62.

Godfrey, Tony. *Conceptual Art.* London: Phaidon Press, 1998.

Krauss, Rosalind. "The Object Caught by the Heel." In *Making Mischief: Dada Invades New York,* ed. Francis M. Naumann, 248–251. New York: Whitney Museum of American Art, 1996.

Kuh, Katharine. *The Artist's Voice Talks with Seventeen Artists.* New York: Harper and Row, 1962.

Kuspit, Donald. *The Cult of the Avant-Garde Artist.* New York: Cambridge University Press, 1993.

Nesbit, Molly. "Duchamp's Readymades." In *Making Mischief: Dada Invades New York,* ed. Francis M. Naumann, 252–257. New York: Whitney Museum of American Art, 1996.

——, and Naomi Sawelson-Gorse. "Concept of Nothing: New Notes by Marcel Duchamp and Walter Arensberg." In *The Duchamp Effect,* ed. Martha Buskirk and Mignon Nixon, 131–175. Cambridge, Mass.: MIT Press, 1996.

Paz, Octavio. "The Ready-Made." *Marcel Duchamp in Perspective,* ed. Joseph Masheck. Englewood Cliffs, N.J.: Prentice-Hall, 1975. 84–89.

Richter, Hans. *Dada: Art and Anti-Art.* London: Thames and Hudson, 1966.

Schneede, Uwe M. *Joseph Beuys, die Aktionen: Kommentiertes Werkverzeichnis mit fotografischen Dokumentationen.* Stuttgart: G. Hatje, 1994.

Schwarz, Arturo, ed. *The Complete Works of Marcel Duchamp.* 2d ed. New York: Abrams, 1970.

6

Las Vegas on the Spree

The Americanization of the New Berlin

Janet Ward

There is a Las Vegas metaphor of city-creation—that is to say, the Strip's reputation of instant architectural *bricolage,* of ahistorical fabrication and unashamed self-invention, of a hyperreal so strong that it has become substantial. The success of Las Vegas's "architecture of seduction" not only has influenced urban design worldwide in the direction of the "tourist city" but also has given rise to the United States' fastest-growing area of urban agglomeration, even after the economic impact of September 11 (Leach 1999, 76–78). Because it stands for Americanization in its most blatant sense, the Vegas metaphor has long inspired a "fear and loathing" among the cultural-intellectual elite, particularly those whose raison d'être is provided by cities established in modern industrial times. Increasingly, however, there is now a recognition of the pervasive reach of the Vegas metaphor of commodification into the root of all architectural practice. Architect Rem Koolhaas and his Harvard students have reflected on how the whole built world seems to have become a mall, with shopping the "last remaining form of public activity. . . . The traditional European city once tried to resist shopping, but is now a vehicle for American-style consumerism. . . . Perhaps the end of the twentieth century will be remembered as the point where the city could no longer be understood without shopping" (Koolhaas 2000, 125, 127). It is in the context of this latest urban condition that the new Las Vegas, postmodernity's infamous fantasy destination for Middle America and purveyor of the Baudrillardian simulacrum, or realm of the hyperreal, has modified itself again into a supra-reality, this time of "substance" and "sheer mass" (Koolhaas 2000, 165).

In Germany, meanwhile, most critics both on the right and the left would never admit openly or willingly to any complicity in the increasing degree of Americanization (or globalization) in their own urban design, even as they bemoan the spread of "big box" or "container" architecture and Walmartization on the suburban fringes, especially in the former East Germany. The electronically enhanced cinematic billboard on the new C&A store on the Ku'Damm is as effective as those in Singapore or Vegas. Nonetheless, a degree of resistance is understandable given the fact that Europe has four square feet of retail space per capita for the United States' thirty-one. And the city that used to have the moniker of Frederick the Great's *Spree-Athen* ("Athens on the Spree") still prefers to not notice the degree to which even this high-cultural epithet betrays a healthy dose of city marketing: for it was by means of a national art culture that the nineteenth-century Prussian capital wished to ground itself, specifically via the Schinkel-era founding of Berlin's Museum Island.

During the years since the fall of the Berlin Wall, it is the Vegas metaphor that has stepped in to fill that which Andreas Huyssen has called the many "voids" of the reunified Germany's regained capital city. Indeed, there is now also such a thing as a Berlin metaphor for Vegas: artist Dave Hullfish Bailey recently claimed that Berlin is worth copying by Las Vegans intent on designing new, meaningful theme architecture, because Berlin is the only city that has followed the Strip casinos' three main tenets: namely, nostalgia, exoticism, and futurism. With inadvertent hilarity, Bailey suggests a "Scholle Vaterland"-themed casino that could help transform impoverished North Las Vegas; the basic theme of such a hotel project would be Berlin's insignia of an unfinished demolition cum building site (Bailey 1999, 7, 19). The New Berlin, then, can even be a model for Vegas.

Now that the 1990s are over, we can assess why the drive to fill in reunified Berlin was as aggressive as it was. Public and private development in Berlin rose from under $5 billion in 1990 to $15 billion by the end of the decade. "The New Berlin," as the capital's own marketing company has called it, hearkens back to the use of the term in the 1920s, in an era when Berlin truly ranked among the largest world-cities. As such, the latest reincarnation of the New Berlin represented an irresistible opportunity to rebuild and re-form the face of Germany for the post–Cold War era. The investment in post-Wall Berlin was extremely high, politically speaking, as a declaration of intent from Chancellor Gerhard Schröder's inaugural speech of 1998 makes clear: "For some people, 'Berlin' still sounds too Prussian, authoritarian, too centralistic. We intend to oppose this image with our completely unaggressive vision

Figure 6.1. C&A department store at the new "Ku'damm-Eck,"
Kurfürstendamm, Berlin. Designed by von Gerkan,
Marg & Partner (completed 2001).
Photo by Janet Ward.

of a 'republic of the new center [*Mitte*]' . . . symbolically, this new center is taking shape in Berlin—at the center of Germany and the center of Europe" (Becker 2001, 2). As part of the initial euphoria of building the Berlin Republic into being, tax breaks and city loans were given far too readily to real estate developers, who promptly overbuilt and over-renovated both on the commercial and residential levels, and then waited during most of the 1990s for a reluctant government to relocate in 1999. They are still waiting for the major German corporations to do the same, because the West German federalist system is holding out on Berlin. The city is now nearly $70 billion (€53.9 billion) in debt. Berlin's population has 16 percent unemployment and has been shrinking from pre-*Wende* levels to below 3.4 million as residents move out to fulfill their suburban dreams on the affordable Brandenburg periphery.

Berlin, as an economically weakened and, among Germans, a traditionally unloved, reborn capital, is under siege, so to speak, from both the East and the West. But these respective senses of geocultural infiltration are based on quite different sets of anxieties. Many West Germans, as if fearing an impending "Easternization" upon contact with their fellow East Germans, have yet even to visit their new capital only fifty miles from the Polish border; likewise, many West Berliners have yet to venture into any part of East Berlin other than the theaters and museums of the newly gentrified Mitte. Uwe Rada (an editor at the liberal Berlin daily, *taz*) gives ironic treatment in his book, *Berlin Barbarians*, to the fact that far from turning into a new capital for (Western) Europe, post-Wall Berlin is bringing with it an invasion of Eastern Europeans and their uncivilized Slavic mores into the West. The Polish bazaar that sprang up on the site of Potsdamer Platz during the Wende was just the beginning, Rada mockingly warns Western sensibilities (Rada 2001, 14).

Given the fact that Berlin was always precariously positioned as the former outpost of Western democracy right in the middle of Eastern Europe, it is understandable that the early intoxicated rush toward architectural reunification included an impetus to make Berlin look more "Western" as quickly as possible, as if to provide three-dimensional evidence that the West had won. Yet this (American) "West" appears as an alien, or at best uncomfortable, source of influence, or belated anti-Loosian "cladding," for Europe's latest capital. Huyssen pinpoints this problematic thus: "The issue in central Berlin, to use Venturi, Scott Brown, and Izenour's by now classic postmodern terms from *Learning from Las Vegas* in this very different context, is how best to decorate the corporate and governmental sheds to better attract international attention: not the city as multiply coded text to be filled with life by its dwellers and its readers but the city as image and design in the service of displaying power and profit" (Huyssen 1997, 69). Two key transformational aspects can be identified in the Americanization of post-Wall Berlin: first, commercial architecture, including office space, is exerting a "considerable influence on the new face of Berlin"—perhaps more than any other building type (Burg 1995, 25). Second, formerly public properties are being sold to privately owned investor groups; increasingly, as urban sociologist Hartmut Häussermann has noted, the market is saying what goes up where (Häussermann 2000, 11).

As it tries to stand on its own two feet in these imported clothes, Berlin appears to be outpacing even Vegas in the maelstrom of urban mythmaking. Hullfish Bailey's proposal for a Berlin-themed casino in Vegas illustrates how post-Wall Berlin's strongest identificatory principle has been building-site tourism, a phase first promoted by the developers of Potsdamer Platz: the Info-Box celebrated this condition of incessant building and becoming, and helped to forge the site as both the world's largest construction site (*Baustelle*) and the world's greatest display site (*Schaustelle*). Such a degree of educating the public about Potsdamer Platz was deemed necessary given that it had been so laid to waste as a bombed-out, emptied field of nostalgia and homeless Odyssean wandering on the no man's land of the Wall. It was, in short, the epitome of the (West) German postwar condition, and as such remained unrecognizable for the old man, Homer, who yearned for the intersection's pre–World War II days in Wim Wenders's pre-*Wende* film *Wings of Desire* (1987): "Aber ich gebe solange nicht auf, bis ich den Potsdamer Platz gefunden habe!" ("But I won't give up until I have found Potsdamer Platz!")[1]

The entire area was sold for a song to Daimler-Chrysler (then Daimler-Benz) and Sony in the immediate post-Wall era of unbounded optimism. Today, its three modest high-rises by Renzo Piano, Hans Kollhoff, and Helmut Jahn are marketed as signifying a compensatory power of regained centrality and function for the boosterist commercialism of the New Berlin. Even though claims were made that the Daimler terrain, in particular, followed the building styles of the "European city" model (in comparison, that is, with the glass-walled Sony Center opposite), all of Piano's alleys and side streets serve to frame such rather American locales as the casino or the Potsdamer Arkaden Mall, which rather puts that theory to rest. Nor is the area finished yet: the Lenné-Dreieck (Beisheim Center) opened in late 2003, and the adjoining octagonal Leipziger Platz is still under construction.

Potsdamer Platz's strongest statement is surely Jahn's Sony atrium, with its transparent roof, lit up at night as a beacon, linking the en-

Figure 6.2. S-Bahn station entrance at Potsdamer Platz, Berlin.
Designed by Hilmer & Sattler with Modersohn & Freiesleben
(completed 2000). The three skyscraper office towers behind it
were designed by (left to right) Renzo Piano (1999), Kollhoff &
Timmermann (1999), and Murphy/Jahn Architects (2000).
Photo by Janet Ward.

circling buildings. This permanent circus-tent of privately monitored
(hence only semi-) public space that is both outside and inside has become a new square in its own right—despite the traditional understanding of what a public space for *flânerie* ought to be (namely, non-
corporate). The Sony suspended roof bears an obvious resemblance with
the interior view of Sir Norman Foster's dome for the new Reichstag,
an accidental similarity that only helps point up the functional kinship
of these two arenas in helping to provide new centers for Berlin on the
commercial and governmental levels, respectively.

If we recall the unfulfilled skyscraper competition of 1922 to build a
tower on the Friedrichstrasse, we can see how this dream has now been
brought to a belated fruition by the substitution of site and era: at
Potsdamer Platz, Berlin has finally realized its modernist wish to build
a mini-Manhattan. But in so doing it became a mini-Vegas, a citational
package that comes with a simulacrum of Europe's first traffic light in-
stalled at Potsdamer Platz in 1924 as well as entombed remains of the
Kaisersaal and the front façade of the Hotel Esplanade within the Sony
complex. Essentially, Potsdamer Platz bears the hallmarks of the New
Berlin's most "American sector." It encapsulates the post-Wall process

whereby the former *Spree-Athen* of Frederick the Great is on the way to becoming an instantly created "Vegas on the Spree." As a result, German intellectual reactions to this constructed intrusion that post-dated the 1994 withdrawal of the bulk of U.S. troops from German soil have been predominantly harsh. While Piano has referred to the city-in-the-city as a Phoenix arising from the "desert," Berlin-based architectural sociologist Werner Sewing calls it, less charitably, a "test-tube city" (Sewing 2000, 47). Similarly, urban critic Frank Roost critiques Potsdamer Platz's monocorporate development for masquerading as multiplicity, especially in Piano's "superficial collage of elements of European old town quarters (alleys, squares, side streets, steps to entrances)" which only "serves the cliché" and "does not create any real urban variety, but functions only as a decorative frame around the shopping mall and the office center" (Roost 2001a, 5). For Roost, there can be no authentic urbanity arising from such a staging of urban tourism as the backbone for metropolitan renewal and economic prosperity.

Architect Daniel Libeskind brings attention to the underlying problem raised by Potsdamer Platz, despite its relative success. Libeskind remains highly skeptical of the ability of Potsdamer Platz to transform the city's image for itself and abroad, and he denigrates the use of this site for the promotion of millennial architectural commodity fetishism: "I believe that Berlin, like any city which deserves to be called that, is no commodity. It is not something which can be bought in a store like a refrigerator, washing machine, or computer. A city is something which you really need, like the air we breathe. That quality is something which you can't always say of commodities" (Libeskind 1997, 161). Many of us might well prefer to imagine what would have been had Daniel Libeskind been permitted to build his own design at Potsdamer Platz— a fantasy land of zigzagging structures celebrating the site's Cold War status of voids and divisions, and leaving untouched the destroyed street plan of old, with a "one kilometer long wilderness . . . , in which everything," states Libeskind, "can remain as it is" (Libeskind 1997, 162). However, this "as is" is suspect: it neglects Potsdamer Platz as it actually used to be before it was bombed, cut in two, and leveled as a no man's land. It seems that all post-Wall imaginings concerning Potsdamer Platz, whether arguing for its refashioning as a commercial city or for its memorialization as a broken monument, have arisen from an imagined original condition of urban fullness and completeness. This imaginary fullness is what is most missed in the new Potsdamer Platz, even if it was never there. As Gerwin Zohlen states, the busy traffic junction of pre–World War II Potsdamer Platz was rather the very opposite of presence," the non-form [*Un-Form*] . . . the non-square [*Un-*

Platz] par excellence," careening full of tempo, traffic, and Einsteinian relativity" (Zohlen 1994, 17).

If the image of Berlin counts for more than any actual street-level experience, then a fitting microcosmic example is a pop-up book of the architectural events since the *Wende: Das Berlin-Paket*, published in the fall of 2001. Another building site on the verge of becoming a pop-up display site—that is to say, a victim of its own commodification—is the Kunsthaus Tacheles, a ruined building on East Berlin's Oranienburger Strasse famous for its alternative arts scene initiated by squatters during the *Wende*. After its purchase by the Fundus development company, it was sanitized and literally propped up like a page from the *Berlin-Paket*. Fundus intends to turn both Tacheles and the mostly empty city block on which it stands into a massive, neotraditional "New Urbanism" project by Andres Duany and Elizabeth Plater-Zyberk (better known as the American architects of Seaside, Florida). Fundus will rename this area the "Johannisviertel," a new mixed-use collection of retail, offices, penthouses, and a hotel, all clustered around *flânerie*-inducing court-yards and squares; and the Tacheles association will continue to pay its symbolic one mark (now perhaps half-a-euro?) rent and be housed within it. For critics like Sewing and Roost, this would amount to an inauthentic Disneyfication of the site on the level of the *Truman Show* movie (which was filmed in Duany and Plater-Zyberk's Seaside). Evi-dently, such critical voices of this fate for Tacheles suspect the unwel-come American import of New Urbanism of the same crimes against authentic representation as those committed by Critical Reconstruction, that now somewhat infamous conservative blueprint initiated over a de-cade ago by Berlin city building director Hans Stimmann.

Nonetheless, let us hope that Duany and Plater-Zyberk can make a success of their new urbanist "Johannis Quarter," even if the Tacheles artists will end up like exotic animals in a "natural" habitat at the zoo, on show for the urbanism thrill-seekers in the theme park of the new pop-up Berlin. We have to hope this because too much of Berlin's boosterism has gone terribly wrong. One scenario of this failure has been the attempt to make the Friedrichstrasse into an Oxford Street alternative to the Regency Street of the Ku'Damm. The error lay, per-haps, in the boosterist attempt to create something far greater than Friedrichstrasse had ever been before (in the 1920s, for example, it was an entertainment and retail district with a decidedly seedy reputation at night). At present one can count at least forty office and retail spaces for rent on the Friedrichstrasse along the dozen or so small blocks be-tween its eponymous train station and the former Checkpoint Charlie at Kochstrasse. This dangerously high ratio of empty commercial spaces

includes offices in the three glamorous Quartier buildings built by
Jean Nouvel, Pei, Cobb & Freed, and O. M. Ungers above the Friedrich-
stadtpassagen (the underground mall or rival "street" extending parallel to the Friedrichstrasse itself). Entire buildings (both new and reno-
vated ones) on blocks of the Friedrichstrasse further south of this trio
stand empty, plaintively awaiting occupancy according to the ascending cocktail-mix of retail, office, and residential occupants. The late
Aldo Rossi's city block building, Quartier Schützenstrasse, just east of
Checkpoint Charlie, stands about 50 percent empty even though it was
finished in 1997. Even the flagship building designed by Josef Paul
Kleihues at the reconstructed site of Checkpoint Charlie stands part-
empty next to the commemorative photo billboards of Soviet and U.S.
soldiers created by artist Frank Thiel.

With the lack of confidence in corporate growth for Berlin, all of
Mitte will at this rate succumb to the alternative commodification model,
namely, history as theme park—as epitomized by the trendily refash-
ioned courtyards of Hackesche Höfe, a fate that Roost terms "final
commercialization," based on the hyping of the "myth" of what the
area used to be in the days before World War II (Roost 2001b, 91, 89).
In the impulse to make Berlin into its previous images—especially in
Wilhelmine-Weimar days, when huge sections of the city were built to
accommodate a population boom from two to four million between the
1900s and the 1920s—we can find a too-neat elision of all the disrup-
tions to the city caused by Nazism, wartime bombing, and Cold War
division. In Critical Reconstruction's purported reach back into history,
or modernity, neither history nor modernity is, of course, brought forth.
Rather, the broken series of ruined palimpsests that is the Berlin city-
scape is being made over into a seamless simulation of historical continuity. Former Getty Center director Kurt W. Forster asks us to recall
how determined Peter Behrens, the most famous Wilhelmine-Weimar
architect of German industrial buildings, had been to use the modern
building style (*Neues Bauen*) in order to facilitate the ineluctable change
of modern Berlin into "a new business city." By contrast, critiques Forster, the Critical Reconstruction policy is too timid, and it is lacking any
real engagement with or *Umgestaltung* ("reformation") of the actual
"historical ground" of Berlin, especially the most transformed area of
all, Mitte. Forster's view is echoed by journalist Helmut Böttiger, who,
smiling at the many bars and restaurants in Mitte with their newly invented layers of *neue Geschichtlichkeit* ("new historicity"), perceives that
the current emulation of the Weimar world-city effect in Berlin is des-
tined to fall short, lacking as it does modernity's "shattering" effect
that gave rise to new forms mirroring such radical social changes. That

Figure 6.3. Checkpoint Arkaden, Friedrichstraße,
Berlin (formerly Checkpoint Charlie).
Designed by Josef Paul Kleihues (completed 1996).
Photo by Janet Ward.

which reflected Weimar Germany's sense of engagement with the processes of industrial modernization back to itself (namely, the rise of urban surface culture) can today only be invoked in the form of nostalgic simulacra of that same modernity.

The application of Critical Reconstructionist tenets—rehashing the old street plan, lot sizes, façade materials, and building height limits (twenty-two meters for cornice lines, and thirty meters for rooftops)—is leading to an instant-history "stage-set" impression of fake spatial completion and historical cohesion that the New Berlin will simply have to live with. Paul Virilio's recent comment on the post-Wall German capital rings true in this regard: "As with the reconstruction of Warsaw in the 1950s, behind the desire to wipe out the past there lurks an incredible transformation of history into a mere STAGE SET, *a transformational stage set* capable of including everything and anything. . . . [T]here is the urge to destroy, to wipe out not only what is really ugly, but anything which spoils the prospect of a glorious globalization" (Virilio 2001, 154; emphasis in original). In this sense, commercial and noncommercial sites alike have been or are being reconstructed to fit the now-requisite stage-set appeal (as in Stimmann's phrase: "Berlin must look like Berlin" [cited by Goldberger]) that alone today seems to guarantee economic growth for urban centers. The many examples of this include the Pariser Platz's Haus Sommer and Haus Liebermann, designed by Kleihues, adjoining the Brandenburg Gate; the neoconservative reconstruction of the Adlon Hotel nearby, much derided by critics yet *the* address for rich tourists and visiting dignitaries; the Lutter & Wegener restaurant on the Gendarmenmarkt, a dining experience of "fake old" ambience that has an uncannily close parallel in Las Vegas's Red Square restaurant at the Mandalay Bay hotel, with its aged interior and a "forged" statue of a headless Lenin; the rebuilt Kommandatur for the media company Bertelsmann; Schinkel's Bauakademie according to the desires of Berlin's architectural elite; and, especially, the city palace, Stadtschloß, promoted by (*inter alia*) the Stadtschloß Berlin Initiative and the Gesellschaft Historisches Berlin. Any future Stadtschloß (with a palace-replica outer wall encasing exhibition rooms designed along contemporary guidelines, as well as a remnant-room from the GDR-era Palast der Republik, which stole its site after a politically motivated demolition of the palace remains) will surely provide as much of a mélange through architectural time and taste as can be found by Vegas's urban tourists as they walk within (or go on foot or by monorail from and to) ancient Egypt, New York, Paris, and Venice on the Strip—or, more specifically, when they access the new Koolhaas-designed Guggenheim-Hermitage galleries that are located inside the urban mock-up of the

Venetian Hotel's intricate exterior façades. Berlin's Critical Reconstruction has thus let in the American bogeyman by mistake—all the more ironic since Stimmann once defined the European City model's main aim as that of warding off such U.S. icons as malls (Burg 1995, 17). The Stimmann-effect will prove to be, most inadvertently, a "Las Vegasizing" one.

Another unintended "Americanizing" irony of this conservative, controlled approach to urban renovation has been more than just stylistic: as in the Wilhelmine and Weimar eras, commercial interests have ended up "planning" the New Berlin (rather than any slower-moving governmental agency), because key areas were rebuilt according to the highest bidders who conformed with the Critical Reconstructionist regulatory building and zoning styles. (The process of land release was essentially led by Wolfgang Nagel, who managed many of the sale transactions of Berlin land after the fall of the Wall, or by the Treuhandanstalt, a governmental body convened to decentralize and sell off GDR-owned businesses.) Berlin's speculative real estate boom of the early 1990s only strengthened the inadvertent parallelism of Critical Reconstructionist Berlin to the United States' style of market-driven urban planning. As political scientist Elizabeth A. Strom emphasizes in her book *Building the New Berlin* (2001), "*capitalist urban development doesn't require the mobilization of political support*" (235, emphasis in original).

Ultimately, however, and despite such an underlying open-market operative, what we are finding in the reconstituted Mitte in former East Berlin is an "over-encoding." By "over-encoding" I refer to a process of sociogeographical mapping through which too many adjoining sites are developed too swiftly and homogeneously, producing a rigid network of fixed urban interfaces that remain bounded, or separate, one from the other. This is what lies ahead as a possible danger for Berlin. Such is the composition, most obviously, of the grand new plazas like Potsdamer Platz and its separateness from the other Berlin areas all around it, but it also applies to the less obvious theme-park-style historicization of Berlin's New-Old Mitte (a downtown equivalent of master-planned community planning). When the Wall fell, Berlin went through an initial phase of promoting both boosterism (or space-filling) as well as the "fragile and fragmentary network" of the urban voids of its Cold War heritage (La Varra 2000, 428). Now these spaces are being bought out, developed, and gentrified, as Berlin searches in vain for its lost modernist city centers. In contrast, architectural critic Giovanni La Varra writes in praise of the "Post-It City" of alternative European city spaces, whereby provisional, unplanned sites can be adapted via a "temporary rewriting" of the more "tightly woven structures" represented by the likes of Potsdamer Platz: "In this constellation of spaces, which continually 'light up' and 'go dark,' the public life of the European city seems to find the energy of regeneration" (La Varra 2000, 431). But urban historian Françoise Choay, in her book *The Invention of the Historic Monument*, points out that the filling-in of voids is a general phenomenon, indeed part of the very "modernization" of a city's "ancient urban tissue"—a renewing process that "is brought about by filling existing voids, or voids created for the purpose" (Choay 2001, 154). In this sense, then, the New Berlin might be more easily forgiven for fulfilling, if in too rushed a fashion, an age-old tendency in urban transformation.

This is what critics of all the void-filling—of New Urbanism, of Critical Reconstruction, and so forth—are missing out on. While it is true that Potsdamer Platz was the focal point of the strange emptiness that filled postwar Berlin (it was full of marks and traces of its former structures and movements), it is also true that we cannot hold on to the voids and the wounds in a state of eternal petrification. They are all but impossible to memorialize as such, indeed to do so would work against urban life, not assist it (think here of Ground Zero, the destroyed site of the World Trade Center: its radical voidedness can and should be cited in a memorial to the thousands crushed and burned at the spot, but for the sake of New York City and beyond, the entirety of this site *qua* catastrophe obviously could not be maintained in stasis). Such is the fallacy behind Werner Sewing's otherwise justified complaint that "50 years of recent history are being completely ignored [in the New Berlin]: the divided city, the Wall-city, the city of the Cold War" (Sewing 2001, 6). Or again, there is more than a dose of petrified stasis in the nostalgic longing for German urban cum collective "homelessness" in the character of Eduard, the protagonist in Peter Schneider's post-Wall Berlin novel of 1999, *Eduards Heimkehr* (*Edward's Return Home*): Eduard bemoans the lack of city-identity or *Stadtbild* that once was Potsdamer Platz, yet feels distrustful of the overly radical surgical changes underway there to reincarnate the closure that a "new center" would entail (Schneider 1999, 164). One interesting recent alternative to the overt negativity (or typical Berlin depressiveness!) of such critiques can be found in the recent documentary film *Berlin Babylon* (dir. Hubertus Siegert, 2001), in which the major point of camera-eye fascination is reserved not for the sense of nostalgic spatial loss, but rather for the exciting processes of building on, over, and under the former voids of Berlin.

The general intrusion of the commodification of architecture, whether for retail or for tourism theme-park purposes, into the urban fabric of

Berlin is part of what architecture now does, and what cities now do, even if this means building in the image of a former urban identity (now: myth). These critics' melancholic nostalgia over the demise of Berlin's voids is based on a somewhat selective memory of a dreamed-of "authenticity" not only of the very patchiness and walled up separations of Cold War Berlin but also of the city's pre-Wall (and especially, pre-Nazi) era of rapid modernization—a time marked more by Blochian *Ungleichzeitigkeit* than by inherent cohesion. Hence a balanced view needs to be found that does not demonize economic and infrastructural renovation and the concomitant commercial development that has to accompany the city's long path to growth.

Reactions against the American-style methods used in the rebuilding of Berlin are being voiced on this side of the Atlantic as well. After an initial phase of idealistic euphoria, it now seems fashionable after the first decade of celebrating the various phases of transformational building to castigate poor New Berlin's bid to remake itself as a global player, rather than to indicate the more patient, and surely wiser, path of waiting another ten to fifteen years or so for the city's long-term post-Wall identity to emerge. One such example is a recent attack by the *New York Review of Books* on post-Wall Berlin's "lost" architectural "opportunities": the critique is based on a knee-jerk condemnatory citing of American urban and consumer practices as the root of Berlin's diseased condition. In this review essay, Berlin's vast, spread-out terrain is cause for the author, Martin Filler, to pinpoint Berlin's affinity to Los Angeles more "than any other European capital"; Potsdamer Platz is singled out by Filler for its inward turn of public space by means of "atriums and multilevel shopping malls as anti-urban as anything on the American roadside strip"; Helmut Jahn's Sony Center at Potsdamer Platz is decried as a "glitzy, glass-skinned shopping and entertainment center better suited to L.A. or Las Vegas"; and the view from the Kultur-Forum, complains Filler, "might as well be in Texas as in Brandenburg." The Vegas metaphor pops up yet again between the lines in Filler's concluding condemnation of the "grotesque speculative frenzy of the classic boomtown" that "overwhelmed all other impulses in 1990s Berlin" (Filler 2001, 29, 28, 31). In short, Filler claims that Berlin has failed because it has become, or (more mysteriously) always already was, simply too American—even though a considerable part of his negative reaction is obviously an East Coast reaction to the growing economic and social influence of the American West. In point of fact, Filler is closer to the historical truth of Berlin's identity than he himself realizes: for such was Wilhelmine Berlin's growth spurt that it was dubbed "Chicago on the Spree," and Berlin of the 1920s owed much of its

world stature to a massive post–Versailles Treaty shift toward American-
ism in business and consumer practices (in the shape of, for example,
Fordism, Taylorization, New Objectivity, and the Hollywood-Babelsberg
connection).

The "case" of the Critics versus Americanized New Berlin is in several respects a reflection of the recent fallout against American-style
globalization. European anti-Americanism, which has become much
sharper in the wake of 9/11 and (more justifiably) after Gulf War II,
contains within it seeds of a deeper, more disturbing phenomenon. As
philosopher Bernard-Henri Lévy remarked in an interview with *Der
Spiegel,* anti-Americanism in Europe is now a thin mask for anti-
meritocracy and anti–racial-mixing beliefs, themselves Europe's own
bugbear issues (Lévy 2001). Lévy is reacting to Baudrillard's article in
Le Monde in which Baudrillard irresponsibly blamed the Islamic terror-
ist acts of September 11, 2001, on America itself (specifically, a suicidal
desire wrought by the guilty power of U.S.-based globalization). In the
wake of the attacks, ex-cultural minister Michael Naumann likewise
felt the need, in an editorial article for *Die Zeit,* to take the growing
number of German anti-Americanists to task. Henryk Broder, writing
for *Der Spiegel* online, found himself in a lot of trouble when he haz-
arded the guess that at this rate, German anti-Americanism (and its
accompanying undercurrent of antisemitism) would end up siding with
the Islamic extremist terrorists (Broder 2001; Broder 2002, 13).

Given this overall unfortunate context, it may yet prove to be the
case that Berlin's areas of commercial design are, for all their faults,
the best available counterbalance to fears of a renascent Teutonia-city
emerging as a symbol of the Berlin Republic, as Roger Cohen recently
implied in a *New York Times* critique of Axel Schultes's new Chancel-
lery building. It is a regrettable academic tendency to feel somehow superior to commerce and to despise the mass culture of consumerism
(and consumers themselves). The title for the German edition of a collection of Mike Davis's essays makes the case against *Casino Zombies.*
Is the fate for an "Americanized," that is, commercialized New Berlin
in general, or Potsdamer Platz in particular, that of casino-cultural
"zombification"? Can we approach the matter of today's architectural
realities in a less defensive, atrophied way? A forerunner to such debates
is Richard Sennett, who, in *The Spaces of Democracy,* rejects the "all-at-
once, massive development of urban centers" like Berlin's Potsdamer or
Alexanderplatz, saying he wants a decentralized collage as the space of
democracy, in the fashion of Aristotelian "*synoikismos*—a coming together of differences." This is Sennett's understanding of the Athenian
agora as the origin of fragmented, mixed social space for (albeit origi-

nally male) democratic interaction. "The result of visual, decentralized democracy should be," states Sennett, "to shatter those images which attempt to represent the city as a whole" (Sennett 1998, 41, 19, 41). We can reflect on the degree to which the redone Potsdamer Platz, as a microcosm of the New Berlin, offends against Sennett's concept of democratic urban space. It tries to be both the *agora* and a recentralization of urban commercial power. The question remains: Can it retain both functions?

Notes

1. Except where otherwise indicated, translations are my own.

Works Cited

Bailey, Dave Hullfish, ed. *Union Pacific: Berlin's Neue Mitte and the Fringes of Las Vegas*. Künstlerhaus Bethanien/Philip Morris Kunstförderung/Art Center College of Design (Pasadena). Berlin: Vice Versa, 1999.

Baudrillard, Jean. "The Spirit of Terrorism." Originally published in *Le Monde*, November 2, 2001; trans. Rachel Bloul. http://www.egs.edu/faculty/baudrillard/baudrillard-the-spirit-of-terrorism.html (accessed May 29, 2005).

Becker, Jochen. "Planet Berlin: In the History Park of the New Center." In *Union Pacific: Berlin's Neue Mitte and the Fringes of Las Vegas*, ed. Dave Hullfish Bailey. Künstlerhaus Bethanien/Philip Morris Kunstförderung/Art Center College of Design (Pasadena). Berlin: Vice Versa, 1999.

Böttiger, Helmut. "Das alte Chaos: Zeitreise in eine ganz andere Krise oder Warum die Sehnsucht nach den Zwanziger Jahren ein Missverständnis ist." *Der Tagesspiegel* (June 10, 2001): 26.

Broder, Henryk. *Kein Krieg, nirgends: Die Deutschen und der Terror*. Berlin: Berlin Verlag, 2002.

———. "Warum wir die Amerikaner hassen." *Der Spiegel-Online* (September 17, 2001).

Burg, Annegret. "The Commercial Building: An Urban Component." In *Berlin Mitte: Die Entstehung einer urbanen Architektur*, ed. Annegret Burg. Basel: Birkhäuser, 1995.

Choay, Françoise. *The Invention of the Historic Monument*. Trans. Lauren M. O'Connell. New York: Cambridge University Press, 2001.

Cohen, Roger. "A Shrine to Power: Is Berlin Ready?" *New York Times*, February 16, 2001.

Davis, Mike. "Las Vegas gegen die Natur." In *Casino Zombies und andere Fabeln aus dem Neon-Westen der USA,* 29–51. Berlin: Schwarze Risse, 1999. In English in *The Grit Beneath the Glitter: Tales from the Real Las Vegas,* ed. Mike Davis and Hal Rothman. Berkeley: University of California Press, 2002.

Filler, Martin. "Berlin: The Lost Opportunity." *New York Review of Books,* November 1, 2001.

Forster, Kurt W. "Berliner Balance." *Die Zeit* 4 (January 28, 1994): 14.

Goldberger, Paul. "Reimagining Berlin." *New York Times Magazine,* February 5, 1995.

Häussermann, Hartmut. "U-Bahn und Urban: Wie die europäischen Städte immer amerikanischer werden." *Süddeutsche Zeitung* (June 30, 2000): 11.

Huyssen, Andreas. "The Voids of Berlin." *Critical Inquiry* 24 (1997): 57–81.

Koolhaas, Rem, with Tae-Wook Cha, Judy Chang, et al. "Shopping: Harvard Project on the City." In *Mutations,* ed. Rem Koolhaus, Stefano Boeri, and Sanford Kwinter, 124–183. Bordeaux: ACTAR, 2000.

La Varra, Giovanni. "Post-It City: The Other European Public Spaces." In *Mutations,* ed. Rem Koolhaus, Stefano Boeri, and Sanford Kwinter, 426–431. Bordeaux: ACTAR, 2000.

Leach, Neil. *The Anaesthetics of Architecture.* Cambridge, Mass.: MIT Press, 1999.

Lévy, Bernard-Henri. "Ein Krieg um die Aufklärung." *Der Spiegel* 49 (December 3, 2001): 208–212.

Lewitscharoff, M., ed. *Das Berlin-Paket.* Munich: ars Edition, 2001.

Libeskind, Daniel. "Potsdamer Platz." *radix-matrix: Architecture and Writings.* New York: Prestel, 1997.

Naumann, Michael. "Seid nicht so German." *Die Zeit* 40 (2001): 37.

Rada, Uwe. *Berliner Barbaren: Wie der Osten in den Westen kommt.* Berlin: Basis Druck, 2001.

Roost, Frank. "Die Disneyfizierung Berlins: Stadtumbau nach den Wünschen der Entertainmentindustrie." *scheinschlag* 11, no. 2 (February 22–March 21, 2001a): 5.

———. "Themenpark am Tacheles. 'New Urbanism' in Berlin." *Architektur in Berlin: Jahrbuch 2001,* ed. Architektenkammer Berlin (Hamburg: Junius, 2001b), 86–91.

Schneider, Peter. *Eduards Heimkehr.* Hamburg: Rowohlt, 1999.

Sennett, Richard. *The Spaces of Democracy.* Ann Arbor: University of Michigan, College of Architecture + Urban Planning, 1998.

Sewing, Werner. *Der Potsdamer Platz: Urban Architecture for a New Berlin.* Ed. Jochen Visscher et al. Berlin: Jovis, 2000.

———. Interview, "Schöne neue alte Stadt." *scheinschlag* 5 (May 17–June 14, 2001): 6.

Strom, Elizabeth A. *Building the New Berlin: The Politics of Urban Development in Germany's Capital City.* Lanham, Md.: Lexington Books, 2001.

Virilio, Paul. "Open Skies over Berlin." In *Remake Berlin,* ed. Kathrin Becker and Urs Stahel. Winterthur: Steidl, 2001.

100

Zohlen, Gerwin. "Erblast des Mythos: Das Verfahren Potsdamer/Leipziger Platz. Rückblick nach vier Jahren." In *Ein Stück Großstadt als Experiment: Planungen am Potsdamer Platz in Berlin,* ed. Vittorio Magnago Lampugnani & Romana Schneider. Stuttgart: Verlag Gerd Hatje, 1994.

PART II
Gender and Sexuality

7

Magnus Hirschfeld and the Photographic (Re)Invention of the "Third Sex"

David James Prickett

Introduction

The cover of Dr. Magnus Hirschfeld's *Geschlechts-Übergänge* (*Gender-crossings*, 1905) would be nothing but a blank slate were it not for two fields of text. The first—a French quotation of Leibniz—renders the mysterious title even more esoteric: "Motto: Tout va par dégrés dans la nature et rien par sauts" (Everything in nature appears by degrees and not by leaps).[1] The reference to Leibniz reminds the reader of Hirschfeld's theory of sexual intermediaries: between the two poles of male and female, an almost indefinite number of sexual types exists. The second text at the left of the cover refers to "83 Abbildungen und eine Bunttafel" (83 pictures and a color table). These visual aids help the reader to better understand the detailed, fine degrees in which the gender crossings reveal themselves in human form. Truly, these photographs mark an intersection of the political, gender, and aesthetic discourses that constitute early twentieth-century German visual culture.

Magnus Hirschfeld was an established physician and sexologist in Wilhelmine and Weimar Germany; his politics were social-democratic, and he was of Jewish background. A binary impulse defines Hirschfeld's gender paradigm. His motto, "per scientiam ad justitiam" (through science to justice), is at once born of an ethical impulse and also exhibits a subversive structure. Hirschfeld was "doing justice" to gender and self-perception by breaking down socially acceptable gender performances and proposing alternative gender structures with his model of homosexuality, the *Uranier* and *Uranierin* (Uranian) of the Third Sex. Photography is key to Hirschfeld's analysis of sex and gender. The photograph acts as testimony, as narrative, and as memory of those who stood at the periphery of patriarchal, heterosexist German society. Whereas Krafft-Ebing and many of his contemporaries would classify Hirschfeld's subjects under the rubric of *psychopathia sexualis,* for Hirschfeld, his photographic archive would represent merely a subcategory—a degree—of human sexuality.

The subversive structure of Hirschfeld's "photographic message" is analogous to the relation of sign to signified in Roland Barthes's essay, "The Photographic Message." The sign becomes performative: for Hirschfeld, it is not important that the photographed subject is a man or a woman, but how the subject performs his/her gender. It is the materiality of the gesture that is of interest to Hirschfeld, which he in turn enters into a catalogue. In my essay, I will illustrate that the ultimate goal of Hirschfeld's photographic message is dependent on the freedom of the sign from the signified—in this case, divorcing "masculinity" from the "male." Only when the representation no longer would be, or never need be brought to the signified, could Hirschfeld's concept of sex and sexuality in degrees, or a Third Sex, be conceivable.

Queering Early-Twentieth-Century German Visual Culture: Magnus Hirschfeld's "Photographic Message"

At the last turn of the century, medicine (particularly psychoanalysis) was, as Eric Santner writes, "in a state of emergency, meaning a state of emergence, of coming-into-being, as well as one of crisis and endangerment" (Santner 1996, 24). The age of modernity and the rapid technological advances that accompanied it gave rise to a sense of unease in Western society. This unease often manifested itself in hysteria in both men and women, as well as in nervous disorders such as "railway spine."[2] Although technology fostered rapid economic growth that translated to national political power, it was this same rapidity that traumatized the public and that threatened to undermine masculinity.[3] George Mosse explains that "the traditional outsiders . . . were joined by those who by rights should have been part of the mainstream, otherwise respectable middle-class men who could not live up to the manly ideal because in some manner they were considered sick or unmanly" (Mosse 1996, 83).

Thus, at this time of emergence and crisis, the crucial defining boundary between the societal Other and the respectable bourgeois male was in danger of collapsing. However, in the case of the homosexual in Germany, legal discourse buttressed this boundary with §175, the law which outlawed male-male sexual relations. Those persons who could exercise power via German legal and/or medical discourse and identified with the German patriarchy firmly maintained the legitimacy of §175. However, Magnus Hirschfeld utilized medical discourse in an attempt to disprove §175's legitimacy and to legalize homosexuality within legal discourse.

In the Foreword to *Geschlechts-Übergänge*, Hirschfeld simultaneously addresses and defines his audience: "den ärztlichen Kollegen, den Juristen und dem gebildeten Publikum" (medical colleagues, the lawyers, and the educated public) (3). Like his audience, Hirschfeld's essay is tripartite in structure. The first section is an explanation of Hirschfeld's theory of sexual intermediaries. He bases this on other "Naturerscheinungen" (occurrences in nature), thereby underscoring variance in sexual determination and orientation as natural (3). In the second section, Hirschfeld presents case histories of a "female" and a "male" sexual intermediary who have visited Hirschfeld's clinic. The "male" sought Hirschfeld's aid, because "er erfahren hatte, daß [Hirschfeld] Personen seiner Art, die er als 'Lebewesen letzter Klasse' bezeichnete, besonders Interesse entgegenbrächte" (he had heard that [Hirschfeld] would offer people like him, people whom he classified as "life forms of the lowest class," special care) (26).

It is the third and final section, however, that marks Hirschfeld's highest priority: "einmal in zusammenhängender bildlicher Darstellung die Haupttypen der Geschlechtsübergänge ad oculos zu demonstrieren" (for once to demonstrate, via related visual representation, the main types of the gender crossings *ad oculos*) (4). He guarantees that the photographs that comprise this section are "größtenteils aus eigener Beobachtung" (for the most part the results of my own observation), and that they will prove the existence of sexual intermediaries between the "normal" male and female forms.[4] Hirschfeld is a product of modernity who seizes upon the photograph as visual verisimilitude. His medical degree, which legitimizes his knowledge of medical and legal discourses, also legitimizes his visual observations. In medical photography, the gaze of the doctor simultaneously validates and manages the camera, which in turn manages the distribution of information. What this would mean for the visual conception and representation of the homosexual at the dawn of the twentieth century will be discussed in the following sections.[5]

Rendering the Homosexual Visible:
The Photograph as Political Testimony

The impetus behind Hirschfeld's *Geschlechts-Übergänge* is to demonstrate the varied manifestations of *sex* that can occur in the body and
gender that can be performed according to or against societal norms.
James Steakley writes that Hirschfeld "intuitively grasped that the universal legitimacy of heterosexuality was based on an unquestioning acceptance of sexual dimorphism, and indeed that each individual's development of a harmonious sexual and gender identity *took the body as its
starting point*" (Steakley 1997, 141; emphasis mine). Hirschfeld explains
that "[a]lles was das Weib besitzt, hat—wenn auch in noch so kleinen
Resten—der Mann und von allen männlichen Eigenschaften sind beim
Weibe zum mindesten Spuren vorhanden" (everything that the woman
possesses, the man—even if in very small degrees—also has, and at
least traces of all male characteristics can be detected in woman) (8).
With this statement, Hirschfeld presents the polarities of "man" and
"woman" in a new light, thereby allowing for "natural improvisations"
of gender, sex, and sexuality.
    When discussing the "male" sexual intermediary,[6] he writes that

> [d]ieses Beispiel ist besonders wichtig, weil es zeigt, wie voreilig es
> war, im neuen Bürgerlichen Gesetzbuche vom Jahre 1900 den
> Paragraphen über Zwitter fortzulassen, mit der Begründung, es
> gäbe in Wirklichkeit keine Personen zweifelhaften Geschlechts.
> [this example is especially important, because it shows how rash a
> move it was to omit the paragraph concerning hermaphrodites in
> the new Civil Law Book of 1900, with the reasoning that in reality
> there were no people of ambiguous sex.] (3)

Based on medical and legal discourse, *Geschlechts-Übergänge* offers
Hirschfeld's "medical colleagues, lawyers and educated public" visual
"proof" that this omission was indeed unfounded. If such persons did
exist, it is only just that such persons be incorporated in legal discourse.
    With its reliance on written and visual testimony of hermaphrodites
and homosexuals, it is possible that Foucault would categorize *Geschlechts-
Übergänge* as an "effort to define a statutory form of correlation between
the gaze and language" (Foucault 1973, 112). The difficulty in establishing such a correlation presents itself in Hirschfeld's analysis of the
"male" sexual intermediary. Interestingly, no photographs of this subject were taken. Hirschfeld only offers the reader a textual account of

this baffling case: that which is perceived on the body by Hirschfeld's eye cannot be expressed in a photograph. He writes that the patient

> war nicht wenig enttäuscht, als ich entgegen meinem Versprechen ihm die Antwort schuldig bleiben mußte, ob er denn nun eigentlich ein Mann oder ein Weib sei, ihm also wie er in der ihm eigentümlichen Art meinte, "auf die Sektion vertröstete." [was more than a little disappointed when I, contrary to my initial promise, still owed him an answer to the question of whether he was actually a man or a woman; indeed, as he once remarked about himself in his own particular manner, he would only "find peace in his own autopsy."] (32)

In this case, it seems that not even the camera could provide the doctor further insight into the patient's condition. Lacking a definable sex, the patient remains an alienated Other in medical and legal discourse, a "type" whose characteristics defy integration into the space of visual representation.

In lieu of a visual representation of the subject, Hirschfeld's "legible" analysis proves the existence of sexual intermediaries, establishes a record of "knowledge" about the sexual intermediary, and manages and disseminates such knowledge in a manner much like a camera.[7] The process could be described as follows: "I, the doctor, have *seen* and *examined* this patient, and my credentials as a doctor of medicine *legitimize* my findings. You, the reader, *see* the 'truth' *through my writing*, much as I have *seen* the 'truth' firsthand." This analysis integrates the subject somewhere along the spectrum of sexual intermediaries, despite Hirschfeld's inability (or refusal) not only to render a visible, photographic representation of the subject but also to determine whether the subject was actually a man or a woman.

Despite ambiguous genitalia, the subject performs masculinity as understood by societal norms. Indeed, the subject had been baptized as a boy (25). He bore a strong resemblance to his mother, and his effeminate nature drew him to the company of girls. His androgynous, hermaphroditic nature was something of an "open secret" at an early age: "[Die Eltern] sowohl wie die älteren Geschwister wußten von seiner zwitterhaften Beschaffenheit, vermieden es aber, mit ihm darüber zu sprechen" (The parents as well as the older siblings knew of his hermaphroditic condition; however, they avoided discussing it with him) (26). The visual knowledge of the family has been repressed up to this point in time, when Hirschfeld records his visual encounter with this patient.

Yet the question begs to be asked: "Whose testimony are we reading?" Much like Freud's "reading" of Dora's oral and later textual testimony, Hirschfeld's "reading" of Franz K.'s body-testimony (visual testimony; the body as image, text) is an interpretation of the "text" that the patient provides. However, part of the patient consciously withholds information, and his/her "visible" and therefore "legible" testimony presents obstacles to the doctor. These include episodes of amnesia in Dora's case and physical manifestations in Franz K.'s case, which both defy visible representation. Exercising power via medical discourse, the doctor (Freud, Hirschfeld) can legitimately fill these gaps in the narrative.

For example, not only are the subject's gender and sex ambiguous, but so is his age: "Das Auffallendste beim ersten Eindruck war, daß es fast unmöglich schien, über das Alter der sich vorstellenden Person ein Urteil zu fällen. Man konnte ihn ebensogut für 17, wie für 40 Jahre halten" (The thing I noticed most from my first impression was that it was almost impossible to judge the age of the person. One could take him for 17 just as easily as for 40 years of age) (26). In his day-to-day life as a bookkeeper, the subject keeps his age a secret, "damit die Leute ihm nicht zum Heiraten zureden" (so that people don't try to persuade him to marry) (27). In order to find a place for himself in a strictly gendered, patriarchal society, the subject must perform the role of the respectable, heterosexual male. His reluctance to visit a doctor illustrates the performative nature of his existence. Whereas the layperson might be "fooled" by his "performance" of a "respectable" sex and gender, a clinical examination would expose these as ambiguous.

If textual, visual, or bodily testimony can be considered to be "performance," the following question arises: is this "performance" a moment of parody, or is it an expression of authenticity? Why performative discourse inevitably leads us back to this question, or why this issue is of such importance for Hirschfeld and his contemporaries, must be examined. Basing Charcot's mistrust of his patients' hysteric episodes on their theatrical nature, Georges Didi-Huberman explains that "'deceit . . . is an integral part of the classical theater . . . to recite that which is true via scenic means; that is, facts, lies and, deception in a *bodily* answer" (Didi-Huberman 1997, 16). Similarly, I propose that the same fear of "deceit" informs Hirschfeld's mistrust of the hermaphroditic "performance." Hirschfeld expresses his reservations as to the factual nature of the testimony of his hermaphroditic patients: "man [hat] Zwittern vielfach und wohl auch nicht mit Unrecht den Vorwurf gemacht, die Angaben über ihr Leben, ihre Triebe und Neigungen seien unzuverlässig" (hermaphrodites have often—and indeed not unjustly—

been accused that the statements about their life, their drives, and inclinations are unreliable) (32–33).

A case similar to that of Franz K. is represented in both text and picture in the third section of *Geschlechts-Übergänge*. This study of a nineteen-year-old "'jungen Manne,' der vor einigen Jahren viel in den homosexuellen Lokalen Berlins verkehrte" ("young man" who, some years ago, frequented the homosexual bars in Berlin) is problematic for Hirschfeld: "Es war nicht möglich, diese Angaben auf ihre Richtigkeit zu prüfen, da P. wenn auch nicht nachweislich lügenhaft, so doch sehr unklar und zerfahren war" (it was not possible to check the accuracy of these statements, since the patient—if not proven to be deceitful—was certainly unclear and flighty) (Hirschfeld 1905, Tables IX and X). On what does Hirschfeld base this subjective analysis? He mentions that the young man regularly visited the *Friedrichstraße* at night,[8] for which he had been chased out of Berlin as a "lästiger Ausländer" (undesirable alien; that is, an undesirable Other) (Hirschfeld 1905, Tables IX and X). Hirschfeld had since lost track of the young man, whose performative nature is interpreted by Hirschfeld as dishonest. Due to a sudden, painful swelling of the breast, the subject consulted Hirschfeld. Hirschfeld writes that "[i]m Bestreben, sich noch interessanter zu machen, wie er war, behauptete er, es hätte die angeschwollene Brust 'viel Milch' abgesondert" (in an attempt to make himself more interesting than he actually was, he maintained that the swollen breast had expressed "a lot of milk") (Hirschfeld 1905, Tables IX and X). Attempts to express milk during the examination failed to produce a secretion of any kind, indicating to the reader that the testimony of the young man was truly deceitful.

The photographs of the young man look more like studio portraits than clinical photographs (see fig. 7.1). In the first photograph, the subject is well dressed and poses to the right with his hand resting on a chair. In the other three pictures, the subject is naked and rests his hand on a bar that is mounted on the wall. The subject stares defiantly at the camera in the full-frontal shot. The side- and rear-views are theatrically posed and are intended to illustrate the subject's "weibliches Benehmen" (female manner) and "weibliches Becken bei im übrigen männlichen Figur" (female pelvis in an otherwise male figure) (Hirschfeld 1905, Tables IX and X). A fifth picture shows a scar from an operation incision. Hirschfeld's caption reflects Hirschfeld's mistrust of the patient's testimony: "Patient gab an, daß ihm hier von einem Arzt ein Eierstock herausgenommen sei, derselbe habe vor der Operation geglaubt, es läge eine Geschwulst vor" (Patient alleged that an ovary was

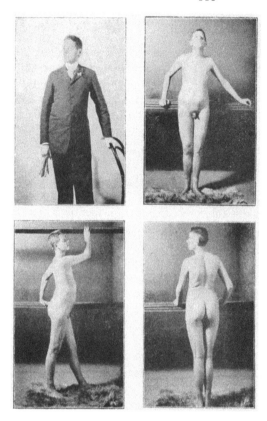

Figure 7.1. Tafel IX. "Gynandrie (sexus incertus)" [Table IX. Androgyny (sex ambiguous)]. From Magnus Hirschfeld, *Geschlechts-Übergänge. Mischungen männlicher und weiblicher Geschlechtscharaktere (Sexuelle Zwischenstufen.)*. Leipzig: Malende, 1905. By permission of the Magnus-Hirschfeld-Gesellschaft e.V., Berlin.

extracted here by a doctor, who believed before the operation that it was a tumor) (Hirschfeld 1905, Tables IX and X). Hirschfeld's doubt of the relation between sign (scar) and signified (the subject's testimony) throws the validity of the case into question.

In contrast to the problematic testimony of this young man, Hirschfeld defends Franz K.'s testimony based solely on Franz K.'s character, class, and education (33). Although an Other in terms of sex, gender, and sexual orientation, Hirschfeld sees part of his respectable Self in this bourgeois bookkeeper, who is "von sittlichem Ernst und großer Ordnungsliebe . . . ein großer Verehrer von Bismarck" (of respectable seriousness and a great love of order . . . a great admirer of Bismarck) (30). Hirschfeld is also quick to stress that "[e]s überwiegen die männlichen Charakterzüge. . . . Starke Affekterregbarkeit ist nicht vorhanden; Thränen fließen fast nie; er kann dagegen leicht zornig werden" (male character traits are dominant . . . strong affectation cannot be detected, he almost never sheds a tear; he can, however, become easily enraged) (30). Franz K. performs his masculine gender in accordance with societal standards of virile masculinity so well that no one questions whether he is indeed strictly of the male sex.

Whereas Hirschfeld chooses to discredit not only the legible, but also the visible testimony of the young man in Figure 7.1, he quite literally engenders and affirms Franz K.'s performance of masculinity. Although the patient's genitalia refuse visual definition, Hirschfeld creates a legible testimony from the fragments of information that he gleans from the subject's secondary characteristics. In other words, it is Franz K.'s masculine behavior that makes him a man. In addition, he is patriotic, loves order, and is respectable—the ideal male German bourgeois. Therefore, Franz K. deserves legal protection just like any other law-abiding citizen.

Having deemed Franz K.'s gender to be masculine and his sexual orientation to be "weiblich passivisch" (feminine passive) (30), Hirschfeld seems to have solved the riddle of Franz K. But what of Franz K.'s sex? Hirschfeld cannot classify him as a man "wie die Behörden und seine Umgebung annehmen" (as generally accepted by the officials and those in his environs) based on "der überwiegenden Anzahl weiblicher Geschlechtscharaktere, dem Mangel männlicher Keimzellen und dem ausgesprochenen weiblichen Geschlechtstrieb" (the overwhelming number of female sexual characteristics, the lack of male germ-cells, and the pronounced female sex drive) (31). Since Franz K. cannot be defined as a man, he also cannot be classified as a homosexual man, as he categorizes himself (31). Since he has never menstruated and exhibits male secondary characteristics, he cannot be a woman. He is not of no sex, since he displays "Geschlechtsstigmata in großer Fülle" (a large number of genital stigmata) (31). Neither is he of two sexes, because no reproductive cells are present in his genital secretions (31).

Hirschfeld ultimately declares that the subject is "weder Mann noch Weib" (neither male nor female) (33). It would seem that Hirschfeld's *Übergangstheorie* would "solve" this instance of "gender trouble": if the subject is neither man nor woman, then the subject must be of the Third Sex. However, Hirschfeld's resigned tone indicates, or anticipates, the frustration felt by him, his patient, and his reader resulting from this diagnosis. "Neither man nor woman" is as ambiguous as it is precise. Hirschfeld still relies on conventional medical and gender discourse in order to create a testimony for people of the Third Sex. From such a diagnosis, it would seem to the reader that the successful performance of masculinity takes precedence for the ambiguous body. If, like Irigaray's "woman," the hermaphroditic body "represent[s] the sex that cannot be thought," Hirschfeld's "inclusive" *Übergangslehre* is marked by a "linguistic absence and opacity" (Butler 1999, 14).

Visualizing the Homosexual: The Photograph as Gendered Narration / Narration of Gender

When the camera is introduced to the doctor–patient relationship, the camera amplifies the perception of the doctor's gaze, which has predominantly been a male gaze. As the object of the male clinical gaze, the patient assumes the passive role of a body of information: symptoms, gestures, and other signs to be "read" by the doctor. Therefore, the medical photograph is largely a male narration of the patient's characteristics. This visual moment provides the opportunity for further analysis at a later date, either alone or in the company of colleagues. The photograph also indicates that gender can be performed; that a person of indeterminate sex can choose and perform a gender most suitable to him/herself. Such relationships among photograph, narration, and gender issues present themselves in Hirschfeld's case study of "Friederike S.," the "female" sexual intermediary featured in *Geschlechts-Übergänge*.

As Foucault writes, "nineteenth century medicine . . . was regulated more in accordance with normality than with health" (35). In other words, in medical discourse, the term "healthy" is a normative signifier. "Healthy" people are considered "normal," "respectable" citizens. Conversely, the undesirable Other is defined as "degenerate" or "sick." Hirschfeld takes great pains to stress the respectability of Friederike, her parents, and her family vis-à-vis their "normal" bodily conditions. The parents are defined as "gesund, nicht blutsverwandt . . . beide sind sittenstrenge, sehr fromme und biedere Leute" (healthy, not blood-related, moral, pious, and upright); the siblings are married, thus performing a "normal" sexuality; and their children have always been strong and healthy (19). In the family, there are no psychological illnesses, deformed body developments, fractures, wens, syphilis, alcoholism, tuberculosis; neither were there ever any cases of suicide (19). Hirschfeld declares the family as "healthy" and therefore "normal" when he states: "Eine Belastung im degenerativen Sinne ist nicht nachweisbar" (A handicap in the degenerate sense is not ascertainable) (19). The family has maintained "normality" vis-à-vis their bodily condition, and in doing so, remains a healthy cell of society.

In her childhood, Friederike was healthy, but she exhibited "masculine" traits such as playing boys' games and climbing trees. However, she also learned "feminine" activities such as needlework (19). At the

onset of puberty, her body began to develop as a boy's would: "die
Brüste blieben völlig unverändert, Menses traten nicht ein, im 17. Jahr
veränderte sich die Stimme. Im Beginne der zwanziger Jahre kamen
Barthaare an Oberlippe und Kinn" (the breasts remained unchanged,
menstruation did not set in, and at seventeen her voice changed. In her
early twenties, facial hair grew above her upper lip and on her chin)
(19). She also displayed a "masculine" love of smoking and could con-
sume large amounts of alcohol (20). Hirschfeld describes Friederike S.'s
sex drive as

> männlich aktivisch, die Stärke ihres Geschlechtstriebes groß, nach
> dem Verkehr mit einer Frau fühlt sie sich erfrischt und gesund-
> heitlich gefördert. Sie war der Meinung, daß sie homosexuell ver-
> anlagt sei. Wenn die Gelegenheit zum sexuellen Verkehr mit einem
> Weibe lange fehlte, griff sie zur Selbstbefriedigung. [male-active,
> the intensity of her sex drive is great; after intercourse with a
> woman she feels refreshed and that her health has been strength-
> ened. She was of the opinion that she was of homosexual orienta-
> tion. If the opportunity for sexual intercourse with a woman did
> not present itself for a long time, she turned to masturbation.] (21)

Like Franz K., Friederike S. has a uniform fetish and a strong desire
to be a soldier. Unlike Franz K., Friederike S. "besitzt einen Revolver
und scharfe Patronen, schießt gern, . . . auch hätte sie gern als Sol-
dat gedient" (possesses a revolver and cartridges, likes to shoot; . . . she
also would have liked to serve as a soldier) (20). One might say that
Friederike S.'s masculinity is more successful than that of Franz K.: she
performs more like a man than he does. Most telling of her predominately masculine sexual determination is her "virile" sex drive, as demonstrated by frequent masturbation, "bis in die jetzige Zeit fortgesetzt"
(which she has practiced up through the present) (20). Friederike S.'s
penile clitoris, her "performances" of frequent masturbation, wet dreams,
and enjoyment of sex with women receive special attention in Hirschfeld's narrative: "sie träumte, daß sie ein Mädchen küßte und an sich
drückte, wobei Erektionen der 'Clitoris' eintraten" (she dreamt that she
kissed a girl and pressed her to herself, which brought about erections
of the "clitoris") (21).

With respect to the penile clitoris, such dreams are largely *heterosexual* in nature. The subject is well past the Oedipal stage and should
be consciously aware of difference between male and female genitalia.
In her attraction to women, Friederike S. is performing heterosexual
desire in terms of her sex. Although Friederike chooses to perform her
gender as a woman based on the assumption that she is a woman,

114

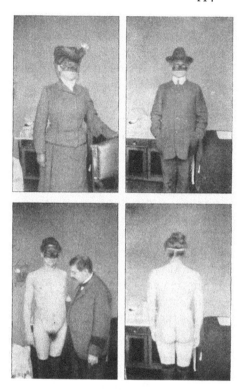

Figure 7.2. Tafel III.
"Pseudohermaphrodit-
ismus masculinus bei
überwiegend männ-
lichem Habitus (Error in
sexu)" [Table III. Mascu-
line pseudohermaphrod-
ism in a predominately
masculine habitus (Sex
determined erroneously)].
From Magnus Hirschfeld,
Geschlechts-Übergänge.
Mischungen männlicher
und weiblicher Geschlechts-
charaktere (Sexuelle
Zwischenstufen). Leipzig:
Malende, 1905.
By permission of the
Magnus-Hirschfeld-
Gesellschaft e.V., Berlin.

Hirschfeld judges her to be more man than woman. If Friederike were more man than woman, her desire to have intercourse with women would not be proof of *homo-*, but rather *heterosexual* orientation.

It is at this point where the photograph becomes of great importance. The photographs of Friederike S. pinpoint her performances of female gender and her predominately male sex (see fig. 7.2). In "Little History of Photography," Walter Benjamin illustrates the photograph's visual exactitude in his example of how one would record how people walk. Details that the conscious eye might miss upon first examination would be captured by the camera. The viewer would finally see information that has been repressed by the unconscious eye, information that the viewer has always known without knowing. The tall, strong, "virile" Friederike S. is indeed more man than woman. When presented with the photographs, the viewer is apt to think: "She only *acts* like a woman; I knew her secret all along."

In the first photograph, Friederike poses as a woman in her "normal" street garments. To the right of this photograph, she appears "in dem ihrer Natur mehr entsprechenden, ihr auch sympathischeren Männeranzug, den sie aber in ihrem Leben nur drei Mal entliehen und angelegt hat" (in her men's suit, which better suits her nature and which is also more pleasing to the eye; however, she has borrowed and worn this only three times in her life) (Hirschfeld 1905, Tables III and IV). In the first picture, Friederike avoids looking at the camera, yet in the second, her pose is confident, almost inviting the camera's eye. As in Figure 7.1, both photos resemble studio portraits rather than medical photographs. If they were presented individually, the conscious eye might not see the similarity—indeed the identical nature—of the subject in both pictures. However, as they are placed side by side, the viewer can exercise his/her "unconscious eye" and critically examine the subject, who could pass for a woman as well as a man.

Benjamin explains, "No matter how artful the photographer, no matter how carefully posed his subject, the beholder feels an irresistible urge to search such a picture for the tiny spark of contingency, of the here and now" (510). The viewer seeks such an "accident" in order to "see through" Friederike S.'s largely successful performance of gender. The photograph presents the viewer with Friederike's past by capturing the residuum, the present absence, the inability to represent everything that has gone on in Friederike's life. The viewer also brings a piece of the photographic subject's futurity to the subject—something that the subject was not aware of at the time of the photograph. In this instance, this "something" is the viewer's present knowledge that due to her "masculine" gender and sex, Friederike will never find peace as long as she performs female gender in society.

Beneath these two pictures are two pictures of Friederike in the nude. In the full-frontal shot, Hirschfeld also appears in the photograph. Here, the photograph functions on various levels. Hirschfeld's presence accentuates Friederike's height ("1.72 m") and her physical strength: Hirschfeld remarks that "mich selbst (85 Kilo) hob sie ziemlich leicht empor" (she was able to lift me up [85 kilos] rather easily) (22). In addition, Hirschfeld's presence legitimizes the photograph as scientific evidence and validates not only that this examination did take place, but also that Friederike S. does exist. The viewer also now *sees* (in the sense of *knowing*) the doctor-patient relationship: Hirschfeld, clothed, actively examines Friederike S., while she, naked and masked (even her identity is ambiguous) stands upright, yet in a passive manner. The final photograph is a rear shot, which illustrates Friederike's "masculine" shoulders and pelvis. This invites comparison by the reader to the rear shot of the effeminate nineteen-year-old man, which is intended to illustrate his "feminine" body (see fig. 7.1).

Hirschfeld's medical diagnosis—and the power vested in it—can be compared to Freud's diagnosis of his patient "Dora" in his *Bruchstück einer Hysterie-Analyse* (*Fragment of a Case of Hysteria*, 1905). In order to alleviate her hysterical symptoms, Dora must accept Freud's narration of her testimony. The case remained a fragment because Dora refused to do so and broke contact with Freud. Similarly, Hirschfeld, who has pieced together a legible and visible narration based on the pieces of Friederike S.'s testimony, offers Friederike S. his diagnosis of her severe depression.[9] Since medical examinations have proven her to be more man than woman (spermatozoa can even be found in her genital secretions), and since she has expressed a desire to be (or perform as) a man, Hirschfeld suggests "ihre Metrik zu ändern und als Mann weiter zu leben" (that she walk to a different beat and to live henceforth as a man) (25). Although Friederike's reaction is not as strong as Dora's rejection of Freud's diagnosis, Friederike also refuses Hirschfeld's advice. She does this for the simple reason that "sie das mit dieser Umänderung verknüpfte Aufsehen scheute und fürchtete, die ihr angenehm gewordene geschäftliche Stellung zu verlieren" (she shrank from the idea of assuming a masculine appearance and was afraid of losing the position in society to which she had grown accustomed) (25). Having performed as a woman in society for so long, to perform a gender more true to her nature would prove socially disastrous for Friederike S.

Conclusion

The camera proved to be a vital tool for Hirschfeld as a medical doctor, as a political activist, and as an aesthete. The goal of his work is to prove that those persons who had once been seen as rarities or curiosities due to their sex, gender, and/or sexual orientation are just as natural as the average German citizen. Although Hirschfeld would indeed argue that such persons are the exception to the norm, *Geschlechts-Übergänge* is a textual and visual normative message, intended to guarantee those of "abnormal" gender performance, sex, and/or sexual orientation the same legal rights as those in "normal" society enjoyed.

The photograph is "visual proof" of sexual intermediaries: persons who existed between the accepted polarities of "male" and "female." These same citizens suffered unjustly due to their natural condition. Legal discourse, epitomized in §175, discriminated against ostensibly homosexual males and went so far as to deny the existence of sexual intermediaries. The visual testimony of people such as Friederike S. translates to the legible testimony as narrated by her doctor, Magnus Hirschfeld. Hirschfeld's exercise of medical discourse, as authorized by his legal medical title, legitimizes her testimony, as well as the textual testimony of Franz K. Via Hirschfeld's textual and photographic message, the grave omission in the 1900 German Civil Law Code is revealed, and additional evidence is presented that addresses the injustice of §175.

Notes

1. All translations of Hirschfeld's text by the author.

2. Freud writes about "railway spine" in "Jenseits des Lustprinzips" (Beyond the Pleasure Principle) and compares this to trauma experienced by World War I veterans resulting from "mechanical force": "Nach schweren mechanischen Erschütterungen, Eisenbahnzusammenstößen und anderen, mit Lebensgefahr verbundenen Unfällen ist seit langem ein Zustand beschrieben worden, dem dann der Name 'traumatische Neurose' verblieben ist. Der schreckliche, eben jetzt abgelaufene Krieg hat eine große Anzahl solcher Erkrankungen entstehen lassen und wenigstens der Versuchung ein Ende gesetzt, sie auf organische Schädigung des Nervensystems durch Entwicklung mechanischer Gewalt zurückzuführen" (After severe mechanical concussions, railroad accidents, and other life-threatening accidents, a condition has long been described to which the name "traumatic neurosis" has stuck. The terrible war that has just come to an end also brought about a large number of such illnesses. This has at least ended any temptation of tracing such diseases back to organic impairments through the development of mechanical force) (Freud 1999b, 9).

3. Although such disorders certainly bear on the concept of masculinity in turn-of-the-century Germany, a lengthy discussion of them would have no direct relevance to the thesis of this essay. For a detailed explanation of the link between technology, nervous disorders, degeneration, and masculinity, see Mosse 1996, especially chap. 5, "Masculinity in Crisis: The Decadence."

4. According to Hirschfeld, intermediaries of sexual orientation, sex, and gender are related. As James Steakley explains, "The theory of sexual intermediacy, as Hirschfeld emphasized repeatedly, was not at all a theory in the strict sense of the word, but instead simply a type of systematics that made it possible to order the multiplicity of individual cases. To order the gradations between the sexes, he investigated sexual differentiation along four lines: 'I. the sex organs [hermaphroditism], II. other bodily qualities [androgyny], III. the sexual drive [metatropism (per Steakley, a term coined by Hirschfeld that "designated a reversal of the sex drive in terms of gender, for example, in a heterosexual couple between a dominant female and a passive male"), homosexuality, and bisexuality], IV. other psychological qualities [transvestism]'" (Steakley 1997, 144).

5. Since the original submission of this essay, Katharina Sykora has published an article of central importance not only to the specific topic at hand in this article, but also to the topic of visual culture in twentieth-century Germany in general. See Sykora 2004.

6. Here, "intermediary" should be read as "hermaphrodite" or "intersexual"; cf. n. 4.

7. Foucault explains that language is charged with a "dual function" in medical analysis: "To describe is to follow the ordering of the manifestations, but it is also to follow the intelligible sequence of their genesis; *it is to see and to know at the same time, because by saying what one sees, one integrates it spontaneously into knowledge; it is also to learn to see, because it means giving the key of a language that masters the visible*" (Foucault 1973, 113–114, emphasis mine).

8. Hirschfeld's reference to this area in the nineteen-year-old's case study relegates the nineteen-year-old to this degenerate milieu that lies beyond bourgeois respectability: "A favorite cruising ground of gays was the intersection of *Friedrich-/Behrenstraße nach den Linden*. Next to the *Panopticum* there were also stores with erotic postcards and books, in front of which young hustlers waited for customers. John Henry Mackay describes this milieu in his novel *The Puppet-Boy*" (Herzer 2001, 20; author's translation).

9. Hirschfeld does not give the exact reason why Friederike S. came to him, but she displayed signs of depression and had thoughts of suicide due to her physical makeup: "Sie fühlte sich oft sehr unglücklich, litt an Lebensüberdruß, kaufte sich daher einen Revolver, hat aber keinen Selbstmordversuch gemacht. Am liebsten wäre sie 'als Mann geboren,' angekämpft gegen ihre Natur hat sie nicht, weil sie es für aussichtslos hielt. Trotz sehr religiöser Erziehung hat sie ihren Glauben verloren, weil 'in der Bibel steht, Ihr sollt Euch vermehren' und sie nicht an einen Gott glauben kann, der so unvollkommene Geschöpfe geschaffen habe, wie sie eines sei'" (She often felt very unhappy, and suffered from satiety of life. For this reason she bought herself a revolver, but to date has not attempted suicide. Most of all, she wished she "had been born as a man." She has not tried to fight against her nature, since she considers that to be futile. Despite her religious upbringing, she has lost her faith, because "in the Bible it is written that you should go forth and multiply," and she cannot believe in a god who supposedly created such imperfect creatures as she believes herself to be) (Hirschfeld 1905, 21–22).

Works Cited

Benjamin, Walter. "Little History of Photography." Vol. 2 of Benjamin, *Selected Writings: 1927–1934*, trans. Rodney Livingstone et al. and ed. Michael W. Jennings, Howard Eiland, and Gary Smith, 507–530. Cambridge, Mass.: Belknap Press, 1999.

Butler, Judith. *Gender Trouble: Feminism and the Subversion of Identity.* 1990. Reprint. New York: Routledge, 1999.

Didi-Huberman, Georges. *Erfindung der Hysterie: Die photographische Klinik von Jean-Martin Charcot.* Trans. Silvia Henke, Martin Stingelin, and Hubert Thüring. Munich: Fink, 1997.

Foucault, Michel. *The Birth of the Clinic: An Archaeology of Medical Perception.* Trans. M. Sheridan Smith. London: Tavistock, 1973.

Freud, Sigmund. "Bruchstück einer Hysterie-Analyse." In *Gesammelte Werke* 5. 1905. Reprint. London: Imago, 1940. Frankfurt a.M.: Fischer, 1999a.

———. "Jenseits des Lustprinzips." In *Gesammelte Werke* 13. 1920. Reprint. London: Imago, 1940. Frankfurt a. M.: Fischer, 1999b.

Herzer, Manfred. *Magnus Hirschfeld: Leben und Werk eines jüdischen, schwulen und sozialistischen Sexologen.* Hamburg: Männerschwarm Skript, 2001.

Hirschfeld, Magnus. *Geschlechts-Übergänge: Mischungen männlicher und weiblicher Geschlechtscharaktere (Sexuelle Zwischenstufen.).* Leipzig: Malende, 1905.

Mosse, George L. *The Image of Man: The Creation of Modern Masculinity.* New York: Oxford University Press, 1996.

Santner, Eric L. *My Own Private Germany: Daniel Paul Schreber's Secret History of Modernity.* Princeton, N.J.: Princeton University Press, 1996.

Steakley, James. "Per scientiam ad justitiam: Magnus Hirschfeld and the Sexual Politics of Innate Homosexuality." In *Science and Homosexualities,* ed. Vernon Rosario, 133–154. New York: Routledge, 1997.

Sykora, Katharina. "Umkleidekabinen des Geschlechts: Sexualmedizinische Fotographie im frühen 20. Jahrhundert." *Fotogeschichte: Beiträge zur Geschichte und Ästhetik der Fotografie* 24, no. 92 (2004): 15–30.

8

(Un)Fashioning Identities

Ernst Lubitsch's Early Comedies

of Mistaken Identity

Valerie Weinstein

Early German film offers many examples of *Verwechslungskomödien*, or comedies of mistaken identity. These filmic *Verwechslungskomödien* draw on a well-established theatrical tradition in order to engage with contemporary discourses of modernization. Early German cinema adapts this narrative structure to address alleged shifts in gender, sexuality, race, and class, attributed to their changing visibility in the modern world. Such a gesture can be seen in two of the *Verwechslungskomödien* made by Ernst Lubitsch in 1919: *Ich möchte kein Mann sein* (I wouldn't like to be a man) and *Die Austernprinzessin* (The oyster princess). These films engage in early-twentieth-century debates about mass production of clothing undermining traditional class and gender distinctions. Where Lubitsch's films first seem to stage blurrings or confusions of classes and genders and to perpetuate discourses of social homogenization, a closer examination of their style will show how they actually parody such discourses and reinforce class and gender difference. They do so, however, by way of a humorous, ironic style that leaves open the potential for some flexibility in the same boundaries that they seem to uphold. Ultimately then, Lubitsch's *Verwechslungskomödien* do not simply protect or dissolve preexisting social structures, but rather subtly modify them.[1]

Dress and fashion remained central components of Lubitsch's films throughout his career (Grafe 1984, 82–83, 86–87). Indeed, Lubitsch literature abounds in references to costume, dress, and fashion. Critics and biographers repeatedly point to Lubitsch's own family origins in the clothing industry and his training as an apprentice in that industry

(Prinzler 1984, 8–11). Even the Berlin clothing industry itself has been proud to claim Lubitsch as one of its own (Dopp 1962, 47–48). But, as Sabine Hake demonstrates, one should be careful not to let the biographical smother other kinds of critical analyses, which is too often the case in Lubitsch criticism (Hake 1992, 3–15). Yet fashion plays a pivotal role in Lubitsch's work, particularly in his German comedies. Here I intend to press beyond the clear linkages between this manifest interest and Lubitsch's background and inquire about the function of dress—and the problems of mistaken identity caused by changes in dress—in Lubitsch's early films. Although not set in the garment industry, as are many of Lubitsch's early films, *Ich möchte kein Mann sein* and *Die Austernprinzessin* feature elaborate scenes of dressing and undressing, and the choice of what to wear initiates the intrigues of mistaken identity. These films not only reflect Lubitsch's lifelong interest in fashion but also participate in contemporary discussions of fashion. By examining these films alongside concurrent debates, we can see that the mistakes caused by exchanged clothing in these films operate in tandem with the irony and humor characteristic of Lubitsch's style in order to critique contemporary discourses of social homogenization and force the audience to recognize modern distinctions between social groups.

Discussions of the garment industry in Wilhelmine and Weimar Germany were socially and politically charged. All who mention Lubitsch's origins in Berliner *Konfektion* (ready-to-wear) highlight its "Jewishness." Jews played an important role in Berliner *Konfektion* and were more represented in the fashion industry than in the German population as a whole. Estimates range from 50 percent (Westphal 1992, 96) to as high as 80 percent (Dopp 1962, 50). Furthermore, some of the most successful and visible leaders of the industry were Jews (Waidenschlager 1993, 31; Guenther 2004, 79–80). Around 1880, antisemites directly attacked a perceived overrepresentation of Jews in the garment industry (Guenther 2004, 82; Westphal 1992, 11, 26–28). There was a dramatic rise in antisemitism around the fashion industry during and after World War I (Guenther 2004, 50–52), and *Konfektion* remained a target of antisemites up through the process of its "Aryanization" in the 1930s.[2]

Fashion was not only associated with Jews (often negatively) but was also a site of contention as a marker of class, gender, and sexuality. We can see this in symptomatic contemporary texts by German fashion historian Max von Boehn. In 1918, Boehn attributes *Einförmigkeit* (uniformity) to mass production by the ready-to-wear clothing industry, which results in a "democratization" of clothing (Boehn 1918, 70).[3] Boehn argues that industrialization of fashion by capitalism produces dress that "erases" difference of class and rank and "renders uniform" all social groups (Boehn 1918, 83). In 1925, Boehn complains that there is not as much variation in men's fashion—the key to mistaken identity in *Ich möchte kein Mann sein* and *Die Austernprinzessin*—in the late Wilhelmine and early Weimar eras as there has been in the past, and that choice in color and pattern have been so reduced that there is no more room for individual taste (Boehn 1976, 319). Contemporaries attribute this *Gleichförmigkeit* (monotony) in part to an American *Modediktatur* (fashion dictatorship) (C. A. Bratter in Boehn 1976, 322) and consider it to be part of a new technological age, not only because it results from industrial production but also because the new fashions echo other forms of technology. We see this logic at work in Boehn's comparison of the abbreviation of language in a telegram to the reduction of formal mourning garb to a single armband (Boehn 1918, 71). The Americanization and industrialization of fashion allegedly foster a pace described as *rasend* (racing).[4] The wealthy keep switching fashions to keep ahead of the poor, but *Konfektion* follows close on their tails (Boehn 1918, 81, 83). Furthermore, in 1911 the *Verein zur Reform für männliche Kleidung* (Club for the Reform of Men's Clothing) was founded, not only to advance the hygienic notions of the Reform Movement (Boehn 1918, 100) but also to combat "tedious egalitarianism" (Boehn 1976, 322). The upper classes also defended their class privilege by building an elaborate system of social dress based not only on what one needed to own but also on knowing what was appropriate to wear and when (Boehn 1976, 322).

We can find more than fear of Jewish capitalists and of the erasure of class structures in discussions of fashion in this period. Just as mass production was construed as blurring class boundaries, changes in women's fashion were perceived by some as threatening distinctions between male and female (Guenther 2004, 53–58, 63–64, 67–70, 72; Kessemeier 2000, 84, 188–270). Pants were slowly making their way into women's fashion, because of the increase in women's participation in sports and the workplace (Boehn 1976, 301–307). This new form of women's dress stirred debate and redefinition of the boundaries between masculine and feminine gender (Kessemeier 2000, 201, 209–211, 251–256; Guenther 2004, 57–58). In 1911 Eugen Isolani published *Die Frau in der Hose: Ein Beitrag zur Kultur der Frauenkleidung* (The woman in pants: a contribution to the culture of women's clothing). That an entire book defends this latest development in women's fashion testifies to the public outrage over it, which included mockery, public demonstrations, and rules banning women in pants from public places (Isolani 1911, 5–6). Isolani attributes this public outrage to a notion deeply imbedded in public consciousness, namely that pants are a primarily masculine form of dress (6; see also Kessemeier 2000, 209). Isolani shows the embeddedness of this notion through the widespread use of pants metaphors in popular aphorisms such as "Sie hat die Hosen an" (She wears the pants). Moreover, he claims that among articles of clothing, pants uniquely signify masculinity to his contemporaries (Isolani 1911, 7). Thus men perceive pants worn by women as a violation of men's rights (Isolani 1911, 7). The opponents of women's pants, according to Isolani, fear the "*Vermännlichung*" (masculinization) of women[5] and interpret pants as a sign of conflict between the sexes.

Thus, Lubitsch's contemporaries treated fashion as making class and gender conflict visible. They also viewed fashion as a marker of sexual orientation. Before World War I, some lesbians had developed a style of dress based on the men's suit (Hacker 1987, 185–211; Kokula 1980, 38–39; Waidenschlager 1993, 26). This style eventually became part of mainstream Weimar women's fashion, but only in the 1920s did it become widespread among non-lesbian women as a sign of independence (Waidenschlager 1993, 26–27; Kessemeier 2000, 50–62). Although there was no absolute correlation between lesbian sexuality and "masculine" dress on a woman, it was often read this way. We see such a reading in the 1906 edition of Richard von Krafft-Ebing's popular *Psychopathia Sexualis:* "Uranism [homosexuality] may nearly always be suspected in females wearing their hair short, or who dress in the fashion of men . . . also in opera singers and actresses, who appear in male attire on stage by preference" (Krafft-Ebing 1906, 398). The courts also adopted this reading of "masculine" dress on a woman; in the late 1890s a lawyer divorced his wife in a "sensational" divorce proceeding in Berlin because he believed that her predilection for wearing pants to masquerade balls showed "homosexual leanings" (Isolani 1911, 90). Furthermore, German courts often charged women in masculine dress with fraud, and particularly marriage fraud (Isolani 1911, 57). In late Wilhelmine and early Weimar Germany, "masculine" fashion choices not only seemed to render lesbian sexuality and a lesbian social identity increasingly visible, they also signified a confounding of gender binaries, for some scientists and activists saw homosexuals as members of a "third sex."

According to these discourses about fashion, differences among classes, ethnic groups, and even genders would shrink or disappear, simply because they would no longer be seen. Lubitsch's *Verwechslungskomödien* stage these concerns in a fictional setting. On the one hand, they seem partially to echo worries that clothing can erode social difference. On the other hand, they parody visions of homogenization.

Lubitsch's films temporarily destabilize categories of gender and class and make visible alternative sexual combinations and desires. Yet they also have other functions. They posit gender and class reversals as fleeting and superficial and ultimately reshape and reestablish preexisting social distinctions.

Ich möchte kein Mann sein examines female cross-dressing and concludes that changes in dress do not irreparably confound gender difference or heterosexuality, even if these look a little different from the way they have looked in the past. In this film, the protagonist Ossi's uncle and governess can no longer discipline her, so they hire Dr. Kersten, a strict new guardian. To escape Kersten, Ossi dresses herself as an elegant young man. When she meets Kersten coincidentally in a dance hall, he does not recognize her, and the two get drunk together. By way of various plot devices, Ossi is unveiled and the two declare their love for each other.

Alice Kuzniar claims that *Ich möchte kein Mann sein* destabilizes gender and sexuality through Ossi's "third sex position" (Kuzniar 2000, 35), and that in doing so, the film criticizes the current social order and "seem[s] to say that single-gendered identity and single-vectored desire are restrictive and inhibiting" (Kuzniar 2000, 39). While this interpretation rings true during some moments where Ossi is in drag, it is not in tune with the entire film. Lubitsch does indeed invest Ossi's escapades with much comic and visual pleasure, and this partially affirms the eroticism and the potential for a fluid gender system evoked by her cross-dressing. This threat to gender and sexual norms is akin to what contemporary critics fear from the woman in pants. Yet rather than wholeheartedly promoting this social disruption, Lubitsch illustrates and domesticates it.

A series of scenes in which the film spectators see something different from the spectators in the film characterizes the cross-dressing narrative of *Ich möchte kein Mann sein*. When Ossi first leaves her home dressed as a boy, her governess finds her to be "ein reizendes Kerlchen" (a charming lad), without registering that "he" came from inside the house. This initiates Ossi's comedy of pragmatic errors, which—strangely enough—no one but the film audience seems to notice. Several actions draw comment from figures in the film as being inappropriate to Ossi's (male) gender. Yet her disguise functions well enough, and people around her still take her for a boy. Inside a crowded subway, a well-dressed lady standing next to the seated Ossi glares at her. Other men in the subway hassle Ossi until she stands up, but soon thereafter she gets her foot stepped on and begins to howl. An older gentleman tells her to stop howling, reminding her that she is a man. "Das sagen Sie so!" (You say that so easily) exclaims Ossi, who continues to howl under his indignant gaze.

Ossi has actually made three mistakes in this scene. She has failed to exhibit the chivalrous behavior appropriate to the class and gender suggested by her frock coat and formal wear. Furthermore, she has displayed an inappropriately emotional response. Finally, her response to criticism comes riskily close to revealing that she might not be a man. In fact, all the comments center on her *unmanly* behavior, yet no one but the film audience can see that this is indeed *not* a boy. Similar scenes take place later, when Ossi continues to make incriminatory errors noticed by others in the dance hall, as when she powders her nose in a public mirror—to the intense amusement of the women around her—or when a waiter needs to steer her away from entering the women's restroom.

Although the public around her recognizes Ossi's behavior as inappropriate to a young man in a frock coat, and this behavior invites censure or mockery, the grammar and content of the responses show that the public still reads Ossi as a man. "Sie sind doch ein Mann!" (You are, after all, a man) rebukes the indignant elderly man in the subway. "Kuck mal den da!" (Look at him) exclaims a lady, who invites her friends to join her laughter at the young man powdering his nose. Although all of Ossi's behavior is legible as appropriate to a young girl in 1919—remaining seated in the subway, crying when she is yelled at and her foot is stepped on, powdering her nose, and lining up for the ladies' restroom—those around her in the film do not read it as such. The costume she wears—short wig, suit, top hat, monocle, and walking stick—signifies maleness to her public far more strongly than her behavior signifies femininity for them. For this public the frock coat is more important as a sign of upper-class masculinity than as a sign of female transgression. Furthermore, the surface signs of dress are more important to them in "reading" Ossi than whatever legible signs are produced by her feelings and behavior.

These scenes create a gap between that which figures in the film see and that which the film's spectators see, a gap that can be described as dramatic irony. Not only is this irony comic, but it also sets up two apparently divergent viewing positions. This split allows the audience to view the fictional figures' viewing process from an allegedly detached position. Where the narrative shows the spectators that the suit functions as a sign of Ossi's (female) emancipation and rebellion, these ironic moments also highlight the function of the suit as a sign of upper-class masculinity that is more important than behavior for the dupes in the film. This invites a mildly humorous criticism of a particular kind of viewing. In this case, the public "mis-reads" Ossi by focusing on her dress, on surface appearances, and ignoring other signs of her femininity. The dramatic irony here foregrounds how surface and performance function as gender in social spaces and mocks society's superficial epistemology. Yet, the irony also positions the film audience as more clever than that, because the audience knows more about the context and can see the public's error. This warns the audience not to jump to conclusions based on easily changeable surface appearances, such as dress, but rather to consider other signs as well. This superior knowledge is not necessarily liberatory, for it suggests that gender may be more fixed than critics of *Konfektion* fear, that it is absurd to think that just anyone can change genders. While the film concedes that clothing may be used to masquerade temporarily as a member of another gender, it implies that there remains a true and immutable gender underneath.

Although Lubitsch's use of irony seems to admit the possibility of multiple spectatorial positions, his directorial style actively intervenes to position spectators, and in this case does so to insist on Ossi's "true" gender. It is a well-known feature of Lubitsch's style that by requiring the spectators themselves to fill in the punch line of a joke he integrates them into the narrative (Grafe 1984, 83; Truffaut 1984, 121; Wilder 1984, 123). Lubitsch uses this technique in the scene where Ossi goes to buy her suit, and the audience is slowly lured into ultimately delivering the punch line of a dirty joke. Rather than relying upon spectatorial identifications to ensure a particular perspective, this scene uses an ellipsis to draw the audience into the scene and drive home its point. The style and humor in this scene highlight, and render funny, the contradiction—and the socially charged topic—of a woman dressing herself up in men's clothing. They also insist upon Ossi's femininity and heterosexuality and thus seek to belittle the threat of her cross-dressing.

The scene in the men's clothing store introduces the possibility that a girl who does not want to conform to conventional femininity might want to put on men's dress. That Ossi can consider this option points to a particular economic and social circumstance. She has access to money, and *Konfektion* makes mass-produced suits available to all who want to buy and who have at least some means. This dress has multiple potential meanings. It not only can suggest that its wearer is a young man of the "right sort." If recognized as on a woman, it may also evoke the associations described above: the modern girl who rejects older notions of femininity, or the girl who goes so far as to reject the (hetero)-sexuality associated with feminine dress and wants to mark herself as a lesbian. Ossi's dressing herself as a man stages an incongruity that threatens the conventions of gender and sexuality of her time and also arises from economic and social circumstances that belong to it.

Despite the techniques that distance spectators from figures in this film, the spectator can possibly identify with Ossi in this scene. She is, after all, the protagonist, and the spectator may have become invested in her narrative. For the spectator who identifies with Ossi, this scene is more fun and mischief. For some, this scene could also evoke a vicarious pleasure of getting to live out this particular fantasy. This could partially undermine the preexisting gender and sexual boundaries that Ossi's antics seem to transgress. Yet it would be foolish to assume that all spectators—regardless of background or subject position—would identify with Ossi, for other techniques in the scene also make Ossi the object of humor and sexual desire. Humor relieves the burden on the spectator to take any of this too seriously. At the same time it presents the woman in pants and cuts her down to size. Ossi is constructed as a feminine, flirtatious, and desirable sexual object; then she is symbolically dismembered by the dialogue and editing, rendering her less harmful than before. (The humor in the scene should also remind us not to take this threat *to* Ossi any more seriously than the threat posed *by* Ossi.)

This takes place by way of a gag—the centerpiece of the scene—in which the salesmen fight over who gets to measure Ossi. The salesmen crowd around her, flirt, and play with their measuring sticks. Particularly when one of them mimes a violin, this recalls an earlier scene in the film where schoolboys "played" a serenade outside Ossi's window, miming instruments with their walking sticks. This play sexualizes the scene not only by evoking an earlier one where Ossi was the object of male desire but also, in addition, through conspicuous play with an obvious phallic symbol. In the face of the men's desire, the boss asks Ossi whom she would like to have (measure her). She cedes the decision to the men in a gesture that seems out of place for someone who until now has clearly shown what she wanted and gone after it. Her facial expressions and body language suggest that she is flirting with the salesmen the way she did with the schoolboy serenaders. Finally each salesman picks a part that needs measuring, with both gestures and intertitles naming arms and legs, leaving the last salesman to ask, "Was bleibt denn für mich übrig?" (What's left for me?). They all start to measure, and black converges from the edges of the screen, the image shrinking like a pupil, in an iris out. In the gap left by the iris, the audience must imagine what the last salesman should measure. The humor in the scene comes from the salesmen's antics and mad scrambling to measure Ossi, as well as the punch line of the whole interaction—the imagined answer to the question of what is left for the last salesman after all the others have chosen the "decent" parts. This joke, then, like the editing, asks the audience to re-view Ossi Oswalda in parts: the arms, legs, and that which is left. The chuckle this elicits is grounded in sexual innuendo. The audience is invited to imagine the unmeasurable body parts of a very popular film actress. The iris here leads the audience to manufacture the humorous punch line that underscores the thrust of the entire film—under Ossi's frock coat will always be that body part that we understand to define her as female. Clothing cannot erase gender distinctions in the way critics of modern fashion fear.

While *Ich möchte kein Mann sein* indulges in the pleasures of cross-dressing, it implies that there remains a true sex underneath. This is revealed again at the close of the film where Ossi, hair long and loose, cries that she doesn't want to be a man, and abandons herself to heterosexual bliss with Dr. Kersten. Nevertheless, her costume and behavior still show that she is the one wearing the pants. Thus, the ambivalence of this film allows the viewer to engage with potential shifts in gender and sexuality, signified by masculine trends in women fashion. Yet it does so in a way that diffuses anxiety by both providing pleasure in the potential shifts and partially disavowing them through humor, irony, and a happy ending.

Die Austernprinzessin functions in a similar way to deal with the potential blurring of class distinctions. The protagonist in this film is also named Ossi and played by Ossi Oswalda. But this time, she is the daughter of Quacker the Oyster King, and throws a tantrum until her father buys her a prince to wed. The impoverished Prince Nucki sends his servant, Josef, to meet Ossi. Because Josef has borrowed a suit and calling cards from Nucki, Ossi thinks he is the prince and rushes to marry him. Wacky plot twists bring Ossi and the real prince together. Although their mutual desire seems thwarted by her earlier marriage, their real identities eventually emerge, and because their names are together on a marriage certificate, they speedily crawl into bed, to the immense joy of Ossi's father.

In this film too Ossi is aggressive, spoiled, modern, and the mistress of the men in her life. Despite Ossi's assertive behavior, and the jaunty tie she wears to her wedding ceremony, heterosexuality does not meet the same challenge that it does in *Ich möchte kein Mann sein*. Instead, this film addresses the blurring of class boundaries in the industrial world—the same boundaries allegedly challenged by the ready-to-wear industry—and it uses the heterosexual love-match to defuse the tension. Lubitsch sets this narrative of mistaken identity in the world of industrial capital by staging most of the action in the home of Quacker, the

Oyster King (Hake 1992, 85–94). This space is characterized by geometric patterns and masses of people moving as choreographed groups. These people's bodies build what Siegfried Kracauer calls a "mass ornament," a geometric and rhythmic mass constellation (Kracauer 1963, 51) that is an "aesthetic reflex" to the capitalist production process (Kracauer 1963, 54). Much of the style and action of the film, particularly its "almost obsessive display of material objects," constitutes a "celebration of consumption and consumerism" in the Quacker household (Hake 1992, 84–85). Even Ossi is an industrial product; this is shown most clearly in the scene where servants form an assembly line to clean, massage, and dress her (Hake 1992, 87; McCabe 2003, 31–32).

In this industrial context, there are several threats to class integrity. The dominant problem is that the superficial signs of fashion lead an heiress to marry a servant. Because this misrecognition leads immediately to marriage, it threatens a mismatch; a servant marries the oyster princess. This is the implied consequence of a blurring of class distinctions through industry and fashion. As in *Ich möchte kein Mann sein*, this case of mistaken identity is also surrounded by a dramatic irony that diffuses the anxiety about this mismatch. Because the audience remains aware of the mistake throughout the film, the fundamental situation is treated as humorous rather than anxiety-producing. We see the situation differently from Ossi, and laugh at it rather than feel its threat. Furthermore, Ossi's is not the only perspective that the audience is asked to view critically: when Josef, the false Prince Nucki, first enters his new father-in-law's chamber, Quacker sees him as a servant and demands that he blow his nose for him. Upon discovery that this "is" Prince Nucki, Quacker gets angry and scolds Josef for behaving in a position unbecoming to his station. Although initially Quacker recognizes the same thing that the audience does—a servant—he ends up seeing his son-in-law instead. This discrepancy between Quacker's and the external audience's perception of the situation contributes to the humor of the scene.

It is not only through irony that *Die Austernprinzessin* reduces spectators' anxiety around the scene of misrecognition. Because of Josef's constant grotesque behavior—goofy grins and awkward, out-of-place gestures—he never matches romantic ideals of a prince charming. He looks, as Ossi terms it, *blöd* (stupid). Josef's failure to meet princely ideals is particularly clear at the wedding. As others celebrate and dance, Josef makes himself a glutton, eating and drinking absurd amounts from the banquet table with a complete disregard for (or ignorance of) fine table manners. A few cross-cuts to a member of the kitchen staff sneaking food the same way in the kitchen casts this greedy behavior as low-class. When Josef is asked to say a word to his guests, he announces that this is the best food he has eaten in a long time. This emphasizes his inappropriate focus on food as well as his lack of knowledge of polite behavior befitting a prince's wedding day. Ultimately, Josef's grotesque behavior resolves anxieties spectators might have about not recognizing class impostors. Because Josef so clearly stands out, and because spectators have been discouraged from identifying with the dupes in the film, they can feel confident that they know how to identify class outsiders.

Yet the class-mismatch between Josef and Ossi is not the only threat to social distinctions in this film. The purchase of a prince by an industrialist's daughter may also have been seen at the time as a challenge to older social hierarchies by a capitalist order in which commoners can buy nobility. Hake refers to this kind of match as a cliché about nouveau riche Americans (Hake 1992, 85). While the credits' designation of Quacker as the Oyster King of America clearly bears this out, some Germans in the 1910s may also have read this constellation as "Jewish."[6] In Wilhelmine Germany, despite the prevalence of matchmaking and dowries among Jews and Germans of most social classes (Kaplan 1991, 85–99, 103–106), Jewish matchmaking practices were the target of both Jewish and non-Jewish criticism (Kaplan 1991, 99–104). Wealthy Jewish women who "achieved social 'respectability' by marrying into the nobility" were targets of particular scorn (Kaplan 1991, 103). While *Die Austernprinzessin* never claims that the Quackers are Jewish, the matchmaker used by Quacker, whose name is Seligson, and who uses the Yiddish *meschugge* to describe Nucki's and Josef's antics, evokes this ethnic stereotype. Despite these references, however, it is not possible (or essential) to positively determine whether the Quackers are Jewish or not.

While the match between Ossi and Nucki *may* represent religious or cultural intermarriage, it is in any case a threat to traditional distinctions between bourgeois and nobility, which are broken down by Seligson because of Quacker's money. Ossi and her father are also portrayed as crass, thus accentuating their misplaced class ambitions, despite their excessive wealth. Their luxurious trappings, like Josef's frock coat, cannot disguise for the spectator that lack-of-class is on the rise. But also like Josef's, the Quackers' buffoonery makes them seem harmless and absurd. The film thus plays out and belittles the threat to class that Boehn and others fear from the garment industry.

The happy ending of *Die Austernprinzessin* uses the promise of heterosexual love and desire to counter the threats of Josef's posturing and Seligson's matchmaking. The year of *Die Austernprinzessin*'s release, 1919, was on the cusp of a large shift in Germany from arranged marriages to love matches, due primarily to the social and economic impact of World War I (Kaplan 1991, 115). It is in keeping with this shift that *Die Austernprinzessin*'s happy ending of coincidentally discovered love between Ossi and Nucki (after he is brought in drunk to the meeting of the Multi-Millionaires' Daughters against Alcoholism) casts the love match in a positive light. The couple is happy. Josef is happy for them, and proud that he has helped them by signing the marriage certificate in Nucki's name and not his own. Quacker, for the first time in the film, after many assertions to the negative, is finally "impressed." The love match is a success on its own terms. It also circumvents the matchmaker, who has nothing to do with the meeting of the true bride and groom. If they challenge social convention, it is because of love, not money. Thus their match is apparently clean of the taint of Quacker's capital. The love match also dislodges the threat of Ossi's initial misrecognition of Josef.

Die Austernprinzessin evokes a potential for class confusion and blending in a capitalist setting, yet diffuses potential anxiety around it through the manipulation of irony, humor, and the happy ending. The final ideal of the heterosexual love match also integrates potential threats to a social order organized around rigid and visible class distinctions into a more palatable form. Class mobility because of love is preferable to capitalist matchmaking or class imposture. Similar techniques and structures are at work in *Ich möchte kein Mann sein*, which plays with the possibilities of gender confusion only to ultimately reinforce gender difference and heteronormativity.[7] Both films deploy *Verwechslung* and the surrounding irony and humor. Thus, they enable different responses to the anxieties around modern fashion, to the feared erasure of gender and class distinctions and their implications for heterosexual union. On the one hand, the irony in these films insists that modernity has not dissolved class and gender difference. On the other hand, the films' humor and their comic instances of mistaken identity make changes in class, gender, and sexuality pleasurable. In Lubitsch's early work, then, the *Verwechslungskomödie* allows for safe play with the social challenges perceived to be posed by modernization, and its "happy ending" of unveiled identities, clarified (if modified) social positions, and heterosexual love matches restores stability and difference.

Notes

1. I presented a version of this paper at the MLA Convention in New Orleans on December 29, 2001. Many thanks to Gail Finney for coordinating the sessions on German Visual Culture at that conference and for editing this

volume. An even earlier version of this argument can be found in my dissertation, "Mistaken Identity in Wilhelmine, Weimar, and Nazi Film," passages of which have made their way into this article verbatim. I owe many thanks to David Bathrick, Leslie Adelson, and Biddy Martin for their help and feedback, as well as to Christopher M. Clark, Horst Lange, and Naomi and Alex Weinstein, who continue to be thoughtful and careful readers of my work. Thanks are also due Biddy Martin's dissertation group in Fall 1998, my German 207 students at Williams College in Spring 2001, and my German 441 students at University of Nevada, Reno in Spring 2002, who have all generously shared their insights into *Die Austernprinzessin*.

2. For more information on this topic, see Guenther 2004 and Westphal 1992.

3. In the nineteenth and early twentieth centuries, this uniformity was both associated with the industrial revolution and considered "masculine" (Kessemeier 2000, 199, 217, 299).

4. Discourses about the acceleration of time and speed were prominent around the time of modernization and applied to other new technologies, such as those of communication and transportation. See Schivelbusch 1986.

5. See also Kalbus 1935, 121.

6. Thank you to Christian Gundermann for reminding me of this.

7. A similar strategy is present in *Die Puppe* (Lubitsch, 1919), where the *Verwechslung* (between a woman and a mechanical doll, again, both named and played by "Ossi") "cures" the protagonist Lanzelot of his fear of heterosexuality.

Works Cited

Boehn, Max von. *Bekleidungskunst und Mode*. Munich: Delphin, 1918.

———. *Die Mode: Eine Kulturgeschichte vom Barock bis zum Jugendstil*. 1925. Reprint. Munich: Bruckmann, 1976.

Dopp, Werner. *125 Jahre Berliner Konfektion*. Berlin: Ernst Staneck, 1962.

Frank. Review of *Ich möchte kein Mann sein*. *Film-Kurier* (Berlin), May 8, 1920, 1.

Grafe, Frieda. "Was Lubitsch berührt." In *Lubitsch*, ed. Hans Helmut Prinzler and Enno Patalas, 81–87. Munich: Bucher, 1984.

Guenther, Irene. *Nazi Chic? Fashioning Women in the Third Reich*. Oxford: Berg, 2004.

Hacker, Hanna. *Frauen und Freundinnen: Studien zur "weiblichen Homosexualität" am Beispiel Österreich 1870–1938*. Weinheim and Basel: Beltz, 1987.

Hake, Sabine. *Passions and Deceptions: The Early Films of Ernst Lubitsch*. Princeton, N.J.: Princeton University Press, 1992.

Isolani, Eugen. *Die Frau in der Hose: Ein Beitrag zur Kultur der Frauenkleidung*. Berlin: Neues Leben, 1911.

Kalbus, Oskar. *Vom Werden Deutscher Filmkunst: Der Stumme Film*. Altona-Bahrenfeld: Cigaretten Bilderdienst, 1935.

Kaplan, Marion A. *The Making of the Jewish Middle Class: Women, Family, and Identity in Imperial Germany.* New York: Oxford University Press, 1991.

Kessemeier, Gesa. *Sportlich, sachlich, männlich: Das Bild der "Neuen Frau" in den Zwanziger Jahren. Zur Konstruktion geschlechtsspezifischer Körperbilder in der Mode der Jahre 1920 bis 1929.* Dortmund: Edition Ebersbach, 2000.

Kokula, Ilse. "Die urnischen Damen treffen sich vielfach in Konditoreien." *Courage: aktuelle Frauenzeitung* 5, no. 7 (1980): 38–39.

Kracauer, Siegfried. "Das Ornament der Masse." In *Das Ornament der Masse: Essays,* 50–63. Frankfurt/Main: Suhrkamp, 1963.

Krafft-Ebing, Richard von. *Psychopathia Sexualis with Especial Reference to the Antipathic Sexual Instinct: A Medico-Forensic Study.* 12th German ed. Trans. F. J. Rebman. New York: Medical Art Agency, 1906.

Kuzniar, Alice. *The Queer German Cinema.* Stanford: Stanford University Press, 2000.

McCabe, Janet. "Regulating Hidden Pleasures and 'Modern' Identities: Imagined Female Spectators, Early German Popular Cinema, and *The Oyster Princess* (1919)." In *Light Motives: German Popular Film in Perspective,* ed. Randall Halle and Margaret McCarthy, 24–40. Detroit: Wayne State University Press, 2003.

Prinzler, Hans Helmut, and Enno Patalas, eds. *Lubitsch.* Munich: Bucher, 1984.

Prinzler, Hans Helmut. "Berlin, 29.1.1892—Hollywood, 30.11.1947: Bausteine zu einer *Lubitsch*-Biographie." In *Lubitsch,* ed. Hans Helmut Prinzler and Enno Patalas, 8–59. Munich: Bucher, 1984.

Schivelbusch,Wolfgang. *The Railway Journey: The Industrialization of Time and Space in the 19th Century.* 1977. Reprint. Trans. Anselm Hollo. Berkeley: University of California Press, 1986.

Schlüpmann, Heide. "'Ich möchte kein Mann sein': Ernst Lubitsch, Sigmund Freud und die frühe deutsche Komödie." *KINtop 1: Jahrbuch zur Erforschung des frühen Films,* 75–92. Basel and Frankfurt/Main: Stroemfeld/ Roter Stern, 1993.

Spaich, Herbert. *Ernst Lubitsch und seine Filme.* Munich: Heyne, 1992.

Truffaut, François. "Lubitsch war ein Fürst." Trans. Frieda Grafe and Enno Patalas. In *Lubitsch,* ed. Hans Helmut Prinzler and Enno Patalas, 120–122. Munich: Bucher, 1984.

Waidenschlager, Christine. "Berliner Mode der zwanziger Jahre zwischen Couture und Konfektion." In *Mode der 20er Jahre,* ed. Christine Waidenschlager and Christa Gustavus, 20–31. Berlin and Tübingen: Ernst Wasmuth Verlag, 1993.

Weinstein, Valerie Aviva. "Mistaken Identity in Wilhelmine, Weimar, and Nazi Film." Ph.D. diss., Cornell University, 2000.

Westphal, Uwe. *Berliner Konfektion und Mode: Die Zerstörung einer Tradition 1836–1939.* 2d ed. Berlin: Hentrich Berlin, 1992.

Wilder, Billy. " . . . und auf einmal war es Lubitsch." In *Lubitsch,* ed. Hans Helmut Prinzler and Enno Patalas, 122–123. Munich: Bucher, 1984.

9

Cigarettes, Advertising, and the Weimar Republic's Modern Woman

Barbara Kosta

In 1924, when a woman lit a cigarette at the annual Press Ball in Berlin, it sent shock waves through the room. The event was so sensational that it drew the attention of the press. Yet, as Alex De Jonge reports in *The Weimar Chronicle,* "The press commented unfavorably upon her action the next day, but, presumably to spare her feelings, turned her into a man as they reported her action" (De Jonge 1978, 132). What appeared at first to be a provocation soon became a customary sight, as routine as the appearance of the so-called New Woman of the Weimar Republic. In fact, women's increased consumption of cigarettes during the 1920s suggests an intricate relationship between the emergence of the modern woman and women smoking. It is no accident that the newly experienced freedom to smoke publicly and to enhance one's appearance with a cigarette accompanied women's right to vote, women's entry into the public work force, and their increased participation in leisure activities. Despite the controversy that surrounds smoking today, it still holds true, as Richard Klein notes, that "the degree to which women have the right to smoke in society is an unmistakable indicator of the general equality they have achieved, a test of their full membership in civil society" (142). For a woman to smoke during the 1920s meant to break with conventions, to "blow smoke" in the face of traditional authorities and to delight in a pleasure that remained socially taboo for women until its acceptance in the 1960s. What draws my attention to that brief moment at the Press Ball in Berlin is not only the fact that a woman smoked but also that in accounts of the experience the transgressor was transformed into a man. Indeed, what appears on the surface as the simple work of camouflage has profound social connotations.

Among the many accessories worn by the modern woman of the 1920s, a cigarette casually, yet strategically and indispensably, accented her look. A woman's cigarette was as characteristic as her *Bubikopf* ("bob") hairstyle and a knee-high skirt. It suggested a certain "sex appeal," implied a love for the movies, and displayed an insatiable appetite for fashion magazines and a desire to be modern. An air of liberation, eroticism, self-assertion, progress, and independence accompanied the image of a woman with a cigarette (often accentuated by showing her in a smoking jacket). This image threatened to make gender boundaries opaque during an era that was poised between a desperate compulsion to regulate gendered behavior and the need for a renegotiation of social practices. Along with other newly savored opportunities, a woman with her cigarette in hand entered a domain traditionally enjoyed by men. The cigarette symbolized access to and full membership in the public sphere and modernity. It also signaled a way of life that was fast-paced and public. Despite the warnings women received concerning the health hazards of smoking, particularly when the habit exceeded thirty cigarettes a day, cigarettes stood for freedom from the constraints of the traditional gender divide ("Das Rauchen der Frauen," 41).[1] August Sander's photograph *Radiosekretärin* (1931), which shows a fashionably dressed garçonne holding a cigarette, represents a figure who allegedly turned her back on domesticity and the traditional economy of womanhood. Moreover, for the female consumers addressed in the Virginia Slims cigarette slogan of the 1970s, "You've come a long way, baby," the path that promised a new life course started in the 1920s with the advent of modernity, a consumer culture, and a sophisticated visual culture.

While cigarettes may have been an expression of modern woman's newly found pleasure and a sign of a more liberated femininity, they also were regarded as a symptom of cultural degeneracy against which nationalists and antimodernists rallied. Thus in the realm between too much smoking and not smoking at all lies the discussion of gender and modernity in the uncertain years of the Weimar Republic. Attitudes toward smoking tobacco fell on opposite sides of the cultural divide: there were those who repudiated the abandonment of traditional values and those who welcomed their demise. Robert Hofstätter, a gynecologist and vigilant opponent of women's smoking habit, and author of *Die rauchende Frau: Eine klinische, psychologische und soziale Studie* (The woman who smokes: a clinical, psychological and social study, 1924), may serve as an example of modernity's discontents. Couched in his findings on how women's health was affected by the hazards of smoking is a suspect etiology of cultural decline. Hofstätter claims that upon closer observation ("nähere Analyse"), pathology underlies women's habitual smoking. With the exception of those who occasionally smoke as a consequence of unconscious, innocent mimicry, he claims that female smoking illuminates the "dark continent" to reveal a great measure of uncertainty and personal despondency:

> The happy and contented woman never smokes, or at least never heavily. Women who are heavy smokers developed the habit at a time when they were especially unhappy. . . . In many cases, heavy smoking is a sign that a woman is unhappy with her gender role, and she sometimes has within herself the avowed tendency [to believe] that women have the same rights as men. Thus smoking, in the spirit of Alfred Adler's theory, would be considered a "masculine protest." (Hofstätter 1924, 190)[2]

The reference to Alfred Adler, the Viennese psychologist and contemporary of Freud, undoubtedly pertains to his theory of the inferiority complex and the notion that feelings of inferiority are overcompensated in an egocentric striving for power and overbearing behavior at someone else's expense. Thus women who smoke actually suffer from low self-esteem: they delude themselves into thinking that they share the same privileges as men, when in reality they smoke in order to compensate for unfulfilled needs. Hofstätter cites cases in which smoking is associated with sexual perversion and concludes that women who are heavy smokers fear their calling as women:

> The architecture of the female body and mind steers women with absolute certainty to the path to happiness: Child, Wife, and Mother. The rejection of woman's fate derails women to such an extent that they seek salvation in mimicking men's lifestyles. And as absurd as it sounds, the wish for equality with men finds symbolic expression in smoking! (Hofstätter 1924, 238)

In Hofstätter's estimation, nicotine wreaks havoc when it comes to performing traditional gender roles, in that it eventually dulls women's senses and threatens their ability to love (Hofstätter 1924, 238–239). His fierce criticism of women smokers sheds light on an understanding of pleasure that is linked inextricably to structures of power and privilege and to nationalist discourses and the female body. Smoking as a form of self-gratification, self-indulgence, and self-assertion, which is independent of the family and men, unsettles a long-standing economy of sexual difference that narrowly defines the pursuit of pleasure along gendered lines. Those who protested women's smoking snubbed their noses not so much at the stench of tobacco as at modernity and its alleged threat to the family and traditional womanhood. Hofstätter's observations reveal an image of femininity that he considered at risk both physically and spiritually.

In contrast to Hofstätter's polemic against women smokers, the plethora of visual, cinematographic, and literary representations of women smoking in the 1920s functionalizes the cigarette to signal a profound pact with modernity. Whether in Irmgard Keun's 1931 novel *Gilgi—eine von uns* (Gilgi—one of us) or Marieluise Fleisser's 1931 novel *Eine Zierde für den Verein* (A credit to the club) or Joe May's 1929 film *Asphalt*, the cigarette marked the modern woman. Yet, even in these various fictional settings, the meaning of the cigarette depends significantly on the hand that holds it. The vamp, arguably, wielded her cigarette differently than the harried office worker or the trendy girl. Thus the cigarette requires interpretation. In an essay entitled "Die Zigarette," which appeared in *Die perfekte Dame* (The perfect lady, 1928), the unidentified author provides an astute semiotic reading of smoking that intimates the social value of the cigarette and establishes a kind of smoker's grammar. What follows is a description of the dramaturgy of smoking:

> The cigarette actually fulfills the mission of a multifaceted playmate. It distracts, diverts, soothes; it is used to flirt, is lovingly turned between fingers or is crossly tossed aside. . . . Its blue smoke dissolves the awkwardness of a question. It serves as an excellent weapon—naturally more for attacking than defending. In addition, if need be, it creates a protective wall. It supports insecurity, emphasizes stylishness and a masculine attitude. It only looks ridiculous if overstated. . . . It shouldn't be emphasized, it has to fit in. (73)

As much as the cigarette became a defining ingredient of women's modernity, so too did advertising. Women constituted a new market for profits during the interwar years, and the modern woman fit well into the emerging consumer culture that contributed to shaping her identity. Exploiting the new markets produced by social change and technology, tobacco advertisers targeted the female epicure and capitalized on the image of the New Woman as smoker. Much like the cinema that joined in reinforcing a new female image, advertisers too constructed, staged, and circulated images of the modern woman for a female audience while cultivating new needs. In other words, advertisers commodified the female body and skillfully exploited a discourse of femininity based on progress and consumption. With a function similar to that of the display case or display window, which became popular in the late 1800s, advertisements exhibited products and lured the consumer into a phantasmagoric world of commodities that promised transformation of the self. The advertisement mobilized the gaze and aroused desire; it mirrored identities, compensated for lack, and, in a modified form, turned the "Lacanian mirror-stage [into a] 'window-shopping stage'" (Davis 2000, 106).

With women's increased participation in consumer culture and the new stresses on gendered identities, the intersection of women, advertising, and smoking proves interesting for examining the ways in which cigarette advertisements participated in the various narratives of the modern woman. Admittedly, there is one common thread in all of these representations: the modern woman smoked, and marketing strategists joined forces to make sure that she did. They clearly recognized the significance of female shoppers and the need to channel their desires for commercial purposes. Advertisers produced images for the female gaze while attempting to dictate women's tastes. Yet, because of women's position as consumers, the female gaze arguably became more differentiated. The diverse images allowed for experimentation and opened channels for self-fashioning, while contributing to a new understanding of womanhood. Since smoking, along with sports, driving, and wearing pants, had been considered taboo for women only a decade earlier, the infraction of social norms and the representation of women smoking went hand in hand with expanding the catalog of images and thereby challenging conventional identity constructions that advertisers inevitably exploited and enabled. The undeniable correspondence between women smoking and the emergent sense of agency women experienced in the 1920s calls for rereading and complicating the potential impact of advertisements. This does not mean that all cigarette advertisements featuring women smokers promoted women's agency or autonomy but rather that the extraordinary range of images allowed for new experiences of identity.

What began as a relatively small market at the turn of the century blossomed by the 1920s into a full-fledged campaign to entice women to smoke. Advertisers were well aware of the discourses that evolved around women smoking and the suspicion of female pleasure in the culture at large. To detract from critics of smoking, dissenting opinions may have been incorporated into advertisements themselves and submitted to the injunctions of experts who advocated for female smokers. For instance, in an appeal to historical knowledge to justify smoking, the ad for the Haus Neuerburg brand Ravenklau portrays a learned man, encircled by books and composing a letter by candlelight. Promoting the interests of the tobacco industry, the "letter" directly addresses female smokers and encourages them to ignore any rebuke of their habit and to remember that life's pleasures are short-lived:

> Madame, even if the foolish world condemns you for smoking, I would like to advise you not to stop this harmless diversion. This is what a perceptive author wrote in 1700 to a woman who smoked. He believed that smoking is healing, it leads to states of reflective consciousness and reminds one that "all riches, fame and beauty in the world dissipate, like smoke dispersed in the wind." (*Die Dame* 1925, 43)

The ad plays on the emancipatory impulse that resides in the gesture of smoking; emphasizes the feminine qualities of its implied audience; and alludes to the medicinal qualities of the product, in order to allay women's anxieties about their susceptibility to the sensual pleasures of smoking. Thus the ad placates potential critics of women smoking.

Other marketing strategies used to increase a company's consumer base included competitions. The A. Batschari cigarette company in Baden-Baden launched a campaign for its Tufuma brand. Female smokers were invited to send a photograph with their first name and a few catchy lines about smoking; the most original phrase would win. "Dear Ladies," begins the ad in *Die Dame,* a fashion magazine whose audience may be described as middle- and upper-middle-class women, "We would like to get to know our Tufuma smokers." Indeed, the epistolary address of the advertisement and the focus on personal experience drew the cigarette into the realm of the private, and the private into the realm of the public. Another publicity campaign to increase sales included collector's cards (*Sammelbilder*). Cards with images of film stars were most popular. Indeed, the use of film celebrities speaks to the significant role cinema plays in the promotion of cigarettes. Film served as a valuable forum for product placement in addition to cultivating tastes and promoting images of smoking. In many instances films featured cigarettes, not as props, but as significant players in their narratives. The Hanover-based Constantin cigarette company featured smoking and moviegoing as an existential component of modern life: "What fulfills the need for pleasure in human beings is the harmonious balance that we seek in a total detachment from daily life. These days the cinema and cigarettes offer it—they are two complementary elements that play an important role in our lives" (Weisser 2002, 93). Cigarettes and movies both were associated with leisure, providing a respite from life's hectic pace—not to mention an occasion to fantasize and reinvent oneself. The cigarette was viewed as an antidote for all occasions. Like movies, cigarettes served as a calmative for the overloaded nervous system of modernity's participants.

Compared to the United States, Germany was late in developing a mass-produced, commodity-based marketplace, but Germans were quick to learn from Americans who studied commercial psychology and perfected the art of advertising. In *Der Weg zum Käufer* (The way to the buyer), Kurt Friedländer acknowledges the value of psychological training for advertisers. "Psychology," he writes, "studies the thoughts and sensibilities of the individual and the masses, which the businessman then tries to influence" (Friedländer 1923, 4). In order to produce a successful ad, Friedländer lists a number of factors that warrant consideration: the use of color and light, isolation (whole-page ads), size, repetition, contrast, location, staging motion, and evenly balancing text and illustration. Of equal importance is the appeal to an inherent sensibility (*Wohlwollen*), as well as the appeal to what Friedländer calls "a suggestive moment" (Friedländer 1923, 53). Each word and each brushstroke come together to produce an ensemble of messages. With each image, advertisers taught consumers how and where to spend as well as why. The ads promise a lifestyle, spark dreams, and make up for a sense of lack.

Thus German advertisers actively studied consumer psychology and, like their American counterparts, made the female consumer their favored subject of inquiry. Advertisers claimed that women, along with children, were far more susceptible to ads than men, therefore turning images of women as well as those of the female consumers into advertising's obsession (Davis 2000, 80). Technology allowed for tobacco companies to mass-produce their wares and to provide quality differences and a wide range of prices in order to attract all classes of female smokers. Women preferred their new stimulant light and aromatic, which explains their partiality to light tobacco. New, milder brands that appealed to a female customer received names such as *"Gerty, Miriam, Sybilla, Daphne, Vera, etc."* and "the stylish, self-confident woman [accordingly became] the bearer in word and image of a brand-name consciousness" (Weisser 2002, 49). These brand names affirmed a contemporary image.

A number of trade manuals of the 1920s reveal that advertisers perceived their task as designing an essentialized female character and thereby streamlining the image of woman, as though there were a stable and coherent female subject. Despite advertisers' desire to standardize the image of the female consumer, the female consumer was neither as transparent nor as one-dimensional as some advertisers would believe. It could be said that the various representations that advertisers produced to attract female smokers even expanded the repertoire of images of women and thus opened new avenues for the performance of gender. By this I mean that advertisers produced images that showcased a product but also offered an array of opportunities for identification. Instead of coalescing or standardizing the image of woman, ads function as a mirror of identity, fragmenting images into diverse fantasies of the self. The multiple "idealizations" of the modern woman thus caused a dispersal of what was typically considered "traditional" femininity. Using the cigarette as their prop, women could play with femininity in various guises.

In "Maskerade im Alltag: Ein beliebter Damensport" (Masquerade in daily life: A favorite woman's sport), an essay that appeared in a 1929 issue of *Das Magazin,* a popular mainstream magazine, the author wonders how women spent their day in a time before sports, flirting, smoking, and going to the theater without a chaperone. Leading the list of recently acquired liberties, the essay draws attention to the latest favorite pastime, "a new social game" for the modern woman called "masquerade." The author lightheartedly blames film for introducing women to the art of masquerade. "It [film] aroused the desire in all women's hearts to appear different, to imagine wanting to be different than one is. The way to do it is through masquerade" (4119). The author suggests that film had complicated the desires of the new woman and aroused the frivolous tendency in women (and children) to take on various guises and personas. The images that accompany the article show women dressed as "salon Tiroleans, Ski-Girls, Pirates, Farmers and a sheik's daughter" (4119–4123). In other words, it was not only clothes that made the woman but also, more significantly, performance as well. Of equal significance is the fact that the author distinguishes between an inner self and an appearance. This assumption, read against the "intended" grain, gains in theoretical capital when considering the many representations of the new woman in advertisements of the 1920s. The discreet difference between "being" and "appearing" suggests the dissolution of a coherent identity, and even calls into question the possibility of a stabilized "self" that exists underneath the appearance. The chance to masquerade and to take on a number of identities speaks to a new understanding of the boundaries of identity that the modern woman tested and enjoyed.[3]

In "Womanliness as Masquerade," published in 1929, Joan Riviere attempts to solve the puzzle of the new woman who unsettles traditional gender expectations. This new woman is neither homosexual nor heterosexual; Riviere calls the women she analyzes "intermediate types." She writes:

These women are excellent wives and mothers, capable housewives; they maintain a social life and assist culture; they have no lack of feminine interests, e.g. in their personal appearance, and when called upon they can still find time to play the part of devoted and disinterested mother-substitutes among a wide circle of relatives and friends. At the same time they fulfill the duties of their profession at least as well as the average man. It is really a puzzle to know how to classify this type psychologically. (Riviere 1986, 36)

In her lengthy discussion of one such case, Riviere describes a woman who suffers from anxiety after her public lectures. In order to overcome her anxieties, she seeks affirmation from male colleagues, turning them into father figures and reinstating their masculinity through flirtation and by masquerading femininity. Underlying the art of female masquerading, Riviere alludes to a fear of being charged with having masculine traits and of retaliation. She tackles this case as a psychoanalyst of her time and hypothesizes about the various phases of sexual development that may have gone awry.[4] Discussions of gender and masquerade have evolved since Riviere's insightful attempt to address gender and "unconventional" expressions of femininity that puzzled, shocked, affronted, and excited a 1920s audience. Most notably, she argues that masquerading does not imply the existence of an essential female self beneath the disguise:

The reader may not ask how I define womanliness or where I draw the line between genuine womanliness and the "masquerade." My suggestion is not, however, that there is any such difference; whether radical or superficial, they are the same thing. (Riviere 1986, 38)

Riviere's keen analysis of gender lays the ground for a more contemporary understanding of gender and performance. To borrow Judith Butler's understanding of its construction, gender is based on the repetitive performance of socially scripted gender assumptions. The recurrent performance of these assumptions naturalizes their "truth" value.

Women's propensity to perform, alluded to in *Das Magazin* and theorized by Riviere about the same time, may be understood as an opportunity for women to take on many roles and to play with gender identity, an opportunity that ultimately defies the traditional, cultural interpretations of gender into which women were corseted. The proliferation of identities through performance and play, the dream worlds that advertisements offered, and the different versions of the new woman that they projected actually may have complicated the performance of identity within the arena of daily life and contributed to an expansion of the repertoire of identities within a given field of social practices. The proliferation of visual representations of women in various guises helped to redefine notions of gender and subjectivity in the same way that the display window transformed the experience of the street and its female public.[5] In other words, advertising in women's magazines plays an influential role in formulating, maintaining, and altering how readers understand the construction of socially acceptable gender norms while engaging subjectivities in different ways. This unfolding of possibilities certainly coexisted with capitalism's push toward standardization, which writer Vicki Baum lampooned in her description of the fashion slave and copyist Yipsi, who in her quest to be original conforms zealously to the mandates of the industry.[6] Mass culture secured an audience while trying, however successfully, to invent it. The question is, then, what types of images did it convey?

An ad designed for the cigarette brand Waldorf Astoria in 1925 expresses elegance and urbanity in the style of New Objectivity, which is known aesthetically for its "precision without atmosphere, for cool, subdued colors, a harsh metallic sheen and elegant contours" (Sembach 1986, 10). The swirl of smoke and the silhouette of the pageboy hairstyle balance the geometrically designed graphic image. The cigarette becomes an integral feature of the model's hand. At the same time, the rising smoke signifies an extension of the sleek, sensual curve of the arm. A sense of unobtrusive luxury reigns, evoked by the English name of the cigarette. In contrast, the Batschari tobacco company borrows iconography for its ABC brand from Spain. Drawing upon tradition and appealing to the exotic while acquiescing to modernity, the female figure, draped in a mantilla, holds a fan with the company's insignia—the ABC brand known throughout Europe. Her elongated body in a virginal white dress and the excessive flowing lace around her red cap resemble a cigarette. The female figure not only represents and adds to the commodity's appeal, the ad also conflates the cigarette with the female body and feminizes the product. The female body lights up the cigarette as much as the cigarette enhances the woman's appearance. The slippage between the modern female body and the product suggests an ontological relationship between the modern woman and smoking. A number of advertisers create a similar association. An advertisement for Manoli's Heliotrop brand describes the cigarette as "slim, elegant, mild, light and aromatic" and thereby feminizes its commodity. By the same token, the brand name Mercedes and the woman or "product vehicle" bear the same signifier.

If cigarettes communicate subtexts, they not only accent gestures, but

Figure 9.1. Ad for Waldorf Astoria cigarettes, 1925.
Courtesy *Die Dame,* 1925.

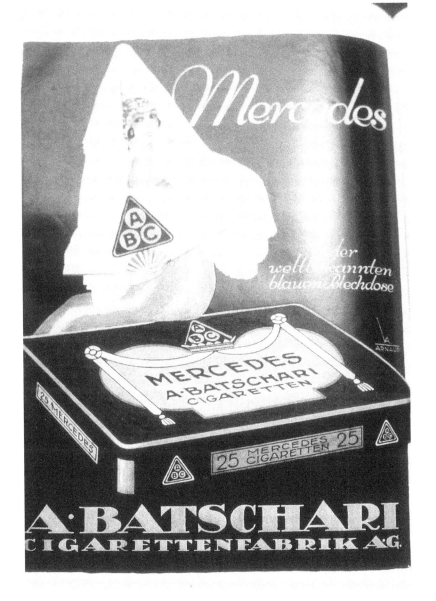

Figure 9.2. Ad for Mercedes Batschari cigarettes, 1926.
Courtesy *Die Dame*, 1926.

underscore certain narratives. The narratives in the following examples reveal female protagonists absorbed in various activities, while enjoying a cigarette. The ads project an aura of self-sufficiency and self-gratification. Because ads play a role in the public sphere, they expand a woman's space beyond a room of her own. In these ads, female pleasure goes public.

The correlation of smoking with luxury and leisure is built into a number of advertisements. In a study of American advertising in the 1920s, Simone Weil Davis shows that modern identity is rooted in leisure and consumer practices: "Advertising increasingly positioned selfhood as resident among an individual's leisure pursuits" (Davis 2000, 5). In other words, a new social identity emerges from the surface of the images. Perhaps *Die Dame*, the Berlin-based Ullstein fashion magazine from which most of the advertisements discussed here are taken, caters especially to more exclusive forms of leisure. These cigarette ads, sketched or painted, capture a moment much like a candid snapshot, its protagonists seemingly unaware of the gaze they serve. An ad for Halpaus Privat, for instance, an exclusive upscale brand, links cigarette smoking with solitary leisure and self-indulgence. The advertisement looks into the private sphere to display an elegantly dressed woman with bobbed hair stretched out on a divan, shielded from the outside world by a partition. The attribute "a noble cigarette" and the exclusive upper-class setting work together to lend sophistication to smoking. The partition and the inclusion of the designation "private" in the product's brand name highlight an intimacy between the product and the activity and set the product's user apart from the masses. While reading a book, the female smoker draws on her chic cigarette holder. The combination of smoking and reading—two activities that traditionally were deemed bad for women's health—work together to enliven the imagination and heighten the sense of private pleasures.

The advertisement for Abdulla cigarettes, known for its light Turkish blend of tobacco, employs other visual strategies to attract the female gaze. Striking an elegant pose in a bathing suit, an ideal image of a youthful, modern female is featured as athletic, small-breasted, and narrow-hipped. She sits relaxed; her elbow is perched on her hip, and her arm is casually extended with a cigarette balanced between her fingers. As Richard Klein notes: "As a general rule, the farther one holds the cigarette from one's body, the more confident and peaceful the pose" (Klein 1993, 176). The body language and visual composition exude a palatable nonchalance that counterbalances the hectic pace long associated with the modern woman's metropolitan existence. Self-contained, introspective, the figure takes pleasure in her solitude and in the mo-

**Figure 9.3. Ad for Halpaus Privat cigarettes, 1927.
Courtesy *Die Dame*, 1927.**

ment that the cigarette provides for musing. The image does not convey the sense of boredom that Kracauer alleges modernity has stolen, but an artificial drawing-out of time. The cigarette allows one to linger and punctuate the moment. It suspends the passage of ordinary time. The sparse text reads, "Abdulla super cigarettes," with the letters "a" in Abdulla harmonizing and alluding to an Arabic script. The prominent red color unifies the brand name, the image, and the tip of the burning cigarette, and the ensemble of image and text turns smoking into a harmonious and aesthetic experience.

With tobacco being imported, for the most part, from Turkey, it was common for advertisers to employ "oriental" stereotypes to lend an air of exoticism to their product. The mosque-like architecture housing the tobacco company Salem-Aleikum in Dresden, the hub of the tobacco industry in Germany in the 1920s, epitomizes the transplantation of a stereotypical Orient onto German soil and reinforces the exotic aura surrounding smoking.[7] Another Abdulla ad capitalizes on an "oriental setting" to feature the modern woman who smokes. Sitting cross-legged on a large red pillow with her hands relaxed in her lap and a cigarette leisurely propped between two fingers, the female figure dreamily blows smoke rings into the air. Her posture and introspective gaze evoke an association of the cigarette with an opiate, a narcotic

Figure 9.4. Ad for Abdulla cigarettes (1), 1925.
Courtesy *Die Dame*, 1925.

that produces a state of ecstasy, and plays off of the similarity between the words "smoke" and "ecstasy" (*Rauch, Rausch* in German). The ad draws on orientalist fantasies of sensuous solitude, narcissistic pleasure, and a state of reflective consciousness and interiority. The atmosphere intimates personal fulfillment and also self-discovery away from the stress of urban life. As fashion does, the ad "promotes the illusion of selfhood through consumption" (Hake 1997, 194). Similarly, the woman occupies a space alone, which stands in sharp contrast to the traditional image of a female identity configured in relation to a male or within the context of the family.

It is interesting to note that these advertisements do not conform to the numerous cinematic images of women smoking. In films, it was typically the vamp who mastered the art of smoking and surrendered to its excesses. Her mastery of the object intimated a mastery of the man. The cigarette is transformed into an erotic prop, a symbolic instrument, and a scintillating wand. There was hardly a film that did not show the vamp or the ultramodern woman drawing on a cigarette as she attracts the male gaze and simultaneously contemplates her prey. Time freezes when the vamp lights a cigarette. While she takes pleasure in being looked at, turning herself into the spectacle, she invites the male gaze to indulge itself and its fantasies. Lighting the cigarette always takes place self-consciously. It signals taking control while feigning activity and lack of interest. The provocative gesture suggests peril for the vamp's male audience, as in "this girl is going to vamp that man," a neologism that according to a 1925 essay in *Das Magazin* on the "Vamp" derives from American linguistic sloppiness (Weinand 1925, 86). This article opens with an image of a woman's arms gloved to the elbow, decorated with ornate bracelets and holding a cigarette.

The cigarette's smoke veils the vamp and lends her a quality of exoticism, mystery, and emancipation that is dangerously sexual. The woman stands for addictive desire (*Sucht/Sehnsucht*). With a cigarette, she toys with transgression and the shifting border of gender determination and prohibition. As Richard Klein observes: "Cigarette smoking is both a source of visible sensual pleasure and an emblem of women's erotic life. At least this is how it appears to men, for whom the sight of women smoking is both threatening and intensely, voyeuristically exciting" (Klein 1993, 160).

What is striking about many of the cigarette ads that targeted the female consumer is that the female body, though commodified, is not sexualized the way it often is in films. On the surface, it is withdrawn from the circulation of the male gaze and an economy of difference, while playing on the social significance of smoking and its symbolic

Figure 9.5. Ad for Abdulla cigarettes (2), 1925.
Courtesy *Die Dame*, 1925.

power. These ads emphasize personal pleasure, fantasy, and reflection in the service of commodity culture. Yet at the junction of competing political, social, and market interests and the ambivalences that characterized Weimar culture stands the consumer, whose choices are directed, but open, and who is called upon to decipher images that unleash a battery of associations. These images may reinforce the conventions or work to expand them. In both cases, the images have, as Roland Barthes perceptively notes in "Rhetoric of the Image," a projective power so that "the one lexia mobilizes different lexicons" dependent on the reader. Or in this case, remembering the image of the woman reposed on the divan, shall we say they are dependent on the smoker?

Notes

1. The author of "Das Rauchen der Frauen" points to the health hazards as well as to the moral and financial repercussions for women who smoke. In fact, smoking, in this author's view, is equated with treason, since the Dawes Plan recommended that alcohol and nicotine consumption be used to measure Germany's standard of living. Because of the population's indulgence in these products, the author claims that the country will have to pay higher reparations. The nationalist rhetoric against smoking found its most formidable advocate in Hitler, who pronounced: "Deutsche Weiber rauchen nicht" (German women don't smoke).

2. Except where otherwise indicated, translations are my own.

3. Petro argues that photojournalism and popular fashion magazines must be read alongside cinematic representations of gender relations. For my own argument, I would like to refer to Petro's discussion of the representation of the masculinized Weimar woman as she is introduced in the fashion magazine *Die Dame* by the writer Anita, a fashion editor. Anita emphasizes that the masculine attire of the modern woman is a self-conscious masculine masquerade. She writes: "Today, however, the man is neither strong nor weak but too realistic, too neuter; he has 'no time' for his soul and for his wife. For this reason, the suffering woman responds ironically to this neutered being by parodying his masculinity; she makes fun of these men whenever she is among those who are like her" (quoted in Petro 1989, 113–114).

4. See Vicki Baum's 1928 novel *Stud. Chem. Helene Willfuer* for what may be considered a literary illustration of the "intermediate" female type. Baum resolves the narrative by having the protagonist Helene, a professional single parent, marry her professor, who is much her senior and most definitely a father figure. Thus she successfully merges the various identities that are conceived of as being contradictory and therefore in conflict.

5. See Janet Ward Lungstrum, "The Display Window: Designs of Desires of

Weimar Consumerism," *New German Critique* 76 (Winter 1999): 115–160. See also "Die Frau vor dem Schaufenster." The editor's advice to prenuptial men is if they want a glimpse into the soul of their fiancée, they should take them for a stroll through the streets and secretly observe their reactions to the many display windows that adorn the metropolis, in this case Frankfurt. These display windows are regarded as windows to the souls of women. In other words, the "dark continent" of the female psyche is illuminated in the presence of the display of commodities, and the picture is not pretty. The features of a once-innocent *Backfisch* become "ugly, greedy and envious" (*hässlichen, habsüchtigen, neidischen Züge*), and a "childishly demanding spite" (*kindisch verlangender Trotz*) manifests itself. In other words, an innocent female Jekyll turns into a greedy Hyde. The author portrays various types of women in relation to the display window and does a symptomatic reading of their character and marriageability. He particularly warns against those types of women who are drawn to chocolate displays and those who visit bookstores. Those who frequent flower shops are the most eligible spouses and best future mothers.

6. Vicki Baum, "People Today," in *The Weimar Republic Sourcebook* 665 (originally published in 1927 in *Die Dame*). See also Sombart 1986.

7. The first German cigarette factory was established in Dresden in the mid-nineteenth century.

Works Cited

Barthes, Roland. "Rhetoric of the Image." In *Image-Music-Text*, trans. Stephen Heath, 32–51. New York: Hill and Wang, 1977.

Baum, Vicki. *Stud. Chem. Helene Willfuer*. Berlin: Ullstein, 1928.

"Das Rauchen der Frauen." *Frauen-Weckruf*, no. 4 (April 15, 1925): 41.

Davis, Simone Weil. *Living Up to the Ads: Gender Fictions of the 1920s*. Durham, N.C. and London: Duke University Press, 2000.

De Jonge, Alex. *The Weimar Chronicle: Prelude to Hitler*. New York and London: Paddington Press, 1978.

Die Dame. Berlin: Ullstein, 1925.

"Die Frau vor dem Schaufenster." *Frankfurter Hausfrau*, February 20, 1924.

"Die Zigarette." In *Die perfekte Dame*, ed. Paula von Reznicek, 73. 1928. Reprint. Bindlach: Gondrom, 1997.

Dimenburg, Edward, Anton Kaes, and Martin Jay. *The Weimar Republic Sourcebook*. Berkeley: University of California Press, 1994.

Friedländer, Kurt. *Der Weg zum Käufer: Eine Theorie der praktischen Reklame*. Berlin: Julius Springer, 1923.

Hake, Sabine. "In the Mirror of Fashion." In *Women in the Metropolis: Gender and Modernity in Weimar Culture*, ed. Katharina von Ankum, 185–201. Berkeley: University of California Press, 1997.

Hofstätter, Robert. *Die rauchende Frau: Eine klinische, psychologische und soziale Studie.* Vienna and Leipzig: Hölder-Pichler-Tempsky, 1924.

Klein, Richard. *Cigarettes Are Sublime.* Durham, N.C.: Duke University Press, 1993.

Lungstrum, Janet Ward. "The Display Window: Designs of Desires of Weimar Consumerism." *New German Critique* 76 (Winter 1999): 115–160.

"Maskerade im Alltag: Ein beliebter Damensport." *Das Magazin* (November 1929): 4119–4123.

Petro, Patrice. *Joyless Streets: Women and Representation in Weimar Cinema.* Princeton, N.J.: Princeton University Press, 1989.

Riviere, Joan. "Womanliness as Masquerade." In *Formations of Fantasy*, ed. Victor Burgin et al., 35–44. London/New York: Methuen, 1986.

Schmitz, Dawn. "Only Flossy, High-Society Dudes Would Smoke 'Em: Gender and Cigarette Advertising in the Nineteenth Century." In *Turning the Century: Essays in Media and Cultural Studies*, ed. Carol A. Stabile, 100–121. Boulder, Col.: Westview Press, 2000.

Sembach, Klaus-Jürgen. *Style 1930: Elegance and Sophistication in Architecture, Design, Fashion, Graphics, and Photography.* Trans. Judith Filson. New York: Universe Books, 1986.

Sombart, Werner. "Wirtschaft und Mode: Ein Beitrag zur Theorie der modernen Bedarfsgestaltung." In *Die Listen der Mode*, ed. Silvia Bovenschen, 90–105. Frankfurt/Main: Suhrkamp, 1986.

Sturken, Marita, and Lisa Cartwright. *Practices of Looking: An Introduction to Visual Culture.* New York and Oxford: Oxford University Press, 2001.

Weinand, Hans. "Vamp." *Das Magazin*, September 13, 1925, 86.

Weisser, Michael. *Cigaretten Reclame: Über die Kunst, blauen Dunst zu verkaufen.* Bassum: Döll Verlag, 2002.

10

Montage and Identity in Brecht and Fassbinder

Patrick Greaney

In an essay on Douglas Sirk, Fassbinder describes Sirk's 1957 film *Tarnished Angels* in terms that could also be read as an apt presentation of Fassbinder's own films: "Nothing but defeats. This film is nothing but a collection of defeats" (Fassbinder 1992, 85). Almost all of Fassbinder's films and plays present the gradual destruction of their central characters, and it is hard to disagree with Kaja Silverman when she insists on Fassbinder's "absolute refusal . . . to provide affirmation" (217). This absence of "affirmation" and the predominance of defeat and destruction coincide in Fassbinder's films with the repeated demand, in his writings on the cinema, that filmmakers present utopia, hope, and "strange, wondrous secrets of the universe" (Fassbinder 1992, 101). Fassbinder concludes his essay on the planned film version of Gustav Freytag's *Soll und Haben* (*Debit and credit,* 1855) with this long sentence on what film could be:

> This is exciting entertainment, that is, entertainment that entertains and is exciting and does not bore the audience, or stultify it, or confirm its assumptions, which calls into question and provokes questions, which is capable of revealing the illusory quality of things that seem safe and sure, which is also fun and enjoyable, and at the same time makes the person who is enjoying it actually want to discover the gaps and flimsy patches in his own reality, to recognize some of the contradictions that make up our reality. (Fassbinder 1992, 117–118)

Das ist spannende Unterhaltung, das heißt Unterhaltung, die
unterhält und spannend ist und nicht langweilt und nicht ver-
dummt und nicht bestätigt, die in Frage stellt, Fragen provoziert,
die im scheinbar Abgesicherten das "scheinbar" transparent zu
machen fähig ist, die dennoch Spaß macht, Freude, und nicht
zuletzt dem, der den Spaß hat, Brüche und falsche Klebestellen
in der eigenen Wirklichkeit zu entdecken, Lust macht, ein paar
Widersprüche zu erkennen, aus denen unsere Wirklichkeit be-
steht. (Fassbinder 1984, 39)

For Fassbinder, film should entertain without confirming reality as it
is, and it should reveal reality's apparent seamlessness to be an illusion. Elsewhere, Fassbinder writes, "Alles in Einzelteile zerlegen und
neu zusammensetzen, das müßte schön sein. Man kann immer nur aus-
gehen von dem, was ist. Keine Utopie ist eine" (To cut up everything
into pieces and reassemble it, that would be great. One can only begin
with what is. No utopia is one) (Fassbinder 1984, 25).[1] That which is—
"das, was ist"—would be completely taken apart, and this process would
allow for a utopia that is not an ideal, other world, but the possibility of
reassembling the world as it is, a possibility that remains to be realized,
as Fassbinder's use of the subjunctive indicates. In both of the essays
from which these passages are quoted, Fassbinder presents the utopian
aspect of film in the vocabulary of montage. As the coincidence of cutting and utopia, montage appears in these texts as the key to understanding the simultaneity of destruction and liberation in Fassbinder.

There has not yet been a reading of montage in this sense in Fassbinder, but such a reading has been central to the reception of one of
Fassbinder's predecessors in German theater and film: Bertolt Brecht.
The pages that follow will focus on an early Brecht play, *Man Equals
Man* (*Mann ist Mann*, 1924–1926) in order to show how that play and
Walter Benjamin's reading of it offer a model for understanding Fassbinder. The discussion of Brecht will be followed by an analysis of a
scene from Fassbinder's film *In a Year of Thirteen Moons* (*In einem Jahr
mit 13. Monden*, 1978) and by a consideration of the potential uses of the
notions of montage and montageability in discussions of queer identity.

Brecht's Reassembly Line

Brecht's early play *Man Equals Man* presents the disassembly and reassembly of Galy Gay, its central character. Walter Benjamin summarizes Brecht's play as follows:

No sooner has [Galy Gay] walked out his own door to buy fish for his wife than he meets some soldiers belonging to the Anglo-Indian army who have lost the fourth man in their unit while plundering a pagoda. They all have an interest in finding a substitute as quickly as possible. Galy Gay is a man who is unable to say no. He follows the three of them without knowing what they want with him. Bit by bit, he assumes possessions, thoughts, attitudes, and habits of the kind needed by a soldier in a war. He is completely reassembled [*ummontiert*]. (Benjamin 1999, 369)[2]

As Galy Gay "appropriates" the "attitude" of the soldiers, he is completely transformed. "The nature of his transformation," Benjamin writes by way of an introduction to his citation of an "interlude" from *Mann ist Mann*, "is explained in the following statement":

Herr Bertolt Brecht behauptet: Mann ist Mann.
Und das ist etwas, was jeder behaupten kann.
Aber Herr Bertolt Brecht beweist auch dann,
Daß man mit einem Menschen beliebig viel machen kann.
Hier wird heute abend ein Mensch wie ein Auto ummontiert,
Ohne daß er irgend etwas dabei verliert.
Dem Mann wird menschlich nähergetreten,
Er wird mit Nachdruck, ohne Verdruß gebeten,
Sich dem Laufe der Welt schon anzupassen
Und seinen Privatfisch schwimmen zu lassen. (Brecht 1988, 2:123)[3]

Herr Bertolt Brecht maintains man is man, a view that anyone can claim to have. But then Herr Brecht also can prove that one can do as much as one likes with a human being. Tonight you are going to see a man reassembled like a car without his losing anything in the process. One comes humanly close to man; he is emphatically, not annoyingly, asked to adapt to the way of the world and to let his private fish take a swim.[4]

The claim "man is man" restates the principle of identity, "A = A" or "A is A," which at least since German Idealism has been interpreted not as a declaration of abstract identity, but as the articulation of a synthetic identity, an identity that includes difference.[5] The first "A" is different from the second "A," and the equal sign becomes the marker of mediation or synthesis. The song emphasizes the place of difference in identity by interpreting the sentence "Mann ist Mann" as a statement about the possibility of transformation. A claim of identity is followed by an insistence on a "proven" transformation. The two aspects of the statement are not contradictory, since transformation appears as a complement to identity: "But then Herr Brecht *also* can prove that one can do as much as one likes with a human being." Galy Gay's identity includes the openness to transformation and to being "reassembled," and the title's apparent insistence on identity, read through the lens of the interlude, also indicates this openness. The interlude emphasizes that Galy Gay's transformation is not to be understood as a loss: he is "reassembled like a car without his losing anything in the process." In the comparison to an automobile, Galy Gay has already surrendered some of his humanity, but his renunciation appears in the interlude not as a loss, but as a "letting be": "he is asked . . . to let his private fish take a swim."

Once Galy Gay has been released from his private life, he embarks on the adventure of being "reassembled" or "remontaged" (*ummontiert*), with the following effect: "Herr Bertolt Brecht hofft, Sie werden den Boden, auf dem Sie stehen / Wie einen Schnee unter sich vergehen sehen / Und werden schon merken bei dem Packer Galy Gay, / Daß das Leben auf Erden gefährlich sei" (Herr Bertolt Brecht hopes that you will see the floor on which you are standing vanish under your feet like a snowfall—and notice with the porter Galy Gay that life on earth is dangerous) (Brecht 1988, 2:123). The force at work in the reassembly of Galy Gay corresponds to this more general desubstantialization, in which foundations melt "like a snowfall," a single layer of snow. This loss of foundation is "dangerous," free of any guarantee, and has its ultimate realization in the song's own statement regarding the transformation of Galy Gay.

As indicated by both the interlude and the play's subtitle—*Mann ist Mann: Die Verwandlung eines lebendigen Menschen in den Militärbaracken zu Kilkoa im Jahre Neunzehnhundertfünfundzwanzig* (Man equals man: the transformation of a living man in the military cantonment of Kilkoa in the year nineteen hundred and twenty-five)—Galy Gay undergoes a transformation. Galy Gay is particularly well suited to transformation; he has a "weiches Gemüt" (weak or malleable disposition), as we learn from his wife in the play's first scene, and the soldiers of the Anglo-Indian army sense this (Brecht 1988, 2:95). One of them says, "So einer verwandelt sich ganz von selber. Wenn ihr den in einen Tümpel schmeißt, dann wachsen ihm in zwei Tagen zwischen den Fingern Schwimmhäute" (Brecht 1988, 2:224) (His kind change of their own accord, you know. Throw him into a pond, and two days later he'll have webs growing between his fingers. That's because he's got nothing to

lose [Brecht 1979, 31]). In Jesse's joke, Galy Gay appears as a potential
amphibian, whose ability to transform would allow him to give up, if
necessary, his humanity.[6]

In *Man Equals Man*, the transformability of Galy Gay exceeds each
of the forms that he assumes. He is always "gebraucht und . . . also
brauchbar" (used and accordingly usable) (Brecht 1988, 2:224). In these
lines from the 1938 version of the play, we see that Galy Gay's specific
way of being used—his conscription—does not exhaust his usability,
which appears here as distinct from the ways in which he is used. *Man
Equals Man* does not celebrate Galy Gay's assimilation into the military, but rather the ability to be assimilated that exceeds every assimilation and that shows how Galy Gay could have become something completely different. It would be a grave misreading if only the first aspect
of *Man Equals Man*—his assimilation—were to be emphasized without
a simultaneous insistence on the second, the ability to be assimilated.
Brecht's 1953 text "Bei Durchsicht meiner ersten Stücke" ("In looking
through my first plays") is helpful here: "Das Problem des Stückes ist
das falsche, schlechte Kollektiv (die 'Bande') und seine Verführungs-
kraft, jenes Kollektiv, das in diesen Jahren Hitler und seine Geldgeber
rekrutieren, das unbestimmte Verlangen der Kleinbürger nach dem
geschichtlich reifen, echten sozialen Kollektiv der Arbeiter ausbeuten"
(The problem of the play is the false, bad collective [the "gang"] and its
seductive force, that collective which in these years Hitler and his financial backers recruited, thus exploiting the petite bourgeoisie's undefined
desire for a historically mature and true social collective of workers)
(Brecht 1988, 23:245).

This late statement by Brecht accentuates the doubleness of Galy
Gay's transformation, whose presentation Brecht changes as the meaning of mass movements changed in the 1920s and 1930s.[7] The play aims
to show both the "bad collective" and how it exploits the "Verlangen,"
the "desire" or "demand," for another collective. This other, "undetermined" demand appears in *Man Equals Man* as Galy Gay's constant
transformation, his transformability that exceeds every individual role
and group. Instead of affirming any individual "man" in its title or any
group or collective, *Man Equals Man* affirms the transformation that
allows one "man" to become another; it affirms the *ist* in the title *Mann
ist Mann* that is not a copula or an insistence on constancy but, instead,
a marker for the possibility of change. *Man Equals Man* insists on this
other sense of being, of *sein*, that allows for every state and every "man"
to become different. The verb form *ist*, far from serving as a marker for
sameness, "stands in for operations performed on persons . . . that involve above all the transformation of posture and gesture," as Brigid

Doherty writes in her interpretation of the equal sign in one of the play's earlier titles, *Mann=Mann* (451). *Man Equals Man* presents an "undetermined demand" for a collective that does not yet exist; the play presents Galy Gay's entry into a "false, bad collective" at the same time that it insists on Galy's excessive transformability, which indicates the demand for another, "true" collective.

Butchered Identity

Fassbinder's 1978 film *In a Year of Thirteen Moons* presents the last five days in the life of the transsexual Elvira/Erwin. After her sex reassignment surgery, Elvira occasionally cross-dresses as a man to find a job as a butcher (without success) and when she cruises for sex (and is beaten up, in the film's opening sequence, when a group of hustlers discover that she is not a man). Elvira/Erwin's acts of estranging herself from her sex and gender develop an ability that Erwin cultivated when he worked as a butcher's apprentice; he had, we read in Fassbinder's project for the film, "eine große Fähigkeit . . . sich von dem, der da mit Fleisch arbeitet, zu entfernen und irgendwo, und wo genau das war, wußte er selbst nicht, mit anderen Dingen beschäftigt, glücklich zu sein" (Fassbinder 1984, 54) (a great ability to separate himself from that person working with the meat and to be happy somewhere else, he wasn't exactly sure where, occupied with other things entirely [Fassbinder 1992, 185]). Erwin is able to find happiness not in his work, but in an estrangement that places him "somewhere" unknown. The self from which Erwin the butcher distances himself appears here as "he who works with meat/flesh," and the film constantly foregrounds the word *Fleisch* and its double meaning of animal meat and human flesh.

One of the film's most well-known scenes presents Elvira as she leads her prostitute friend Zora through a slaughterhouse, a scene that is meant to reinforce the analogy made earlier in the film between the flesh of slaughtered cows and Elvira's monstrous, transformed body. But it is also a scene marked by disturbances in the construction of this analogy. The simultaneous creation and undoing of an analogy offer an ideal point of departure for an analysis of what Fassbinder calls the "gaps and flimsy patches" of reality. The scene opens with a very approximate match on action: one shot shows Elvira and Zora leaving a bar, walking from frame left to frame right, and the next shot shows them turning the corner, walking into the slaughterhouse from frame left, but then continuing the movement from left to right that began in the previous shot. The match on action, even in its brokenness, aims to create the illusion of a seamless transition from the bar to the slaughterhouse—and at the same time to emphasize the impossibility or falseness of that continuity. These editing choices exemplify what Fassbinder calls "revealing the illusory quality of things that seem safe and sure" and showing the "gaps and flimsy patches in reality" (Fassbinder 1992, 117). The scene thus opens with an insistence on the place of discontinuity in what seems to be most continuous. The foregrounding of a technical cut coincides with the thematization of cutting as we are shown the flaying and dismemberment of the cows, a process that is demonstrated at length during the remainder of the scene while Elvira, in a voiceover, relates her biography. The scene's powerful analogy between Elvira and the cows' flesh arises simultaneously with a series of ruptures that emphasize the jumps and gaps in every analogy and the difference implicit in every identity, just as in Brecht's *Man Equals Man* the copula that joins the title's first "man" to the second appears primarily as a gap. Montage thus creates and forbids two relations: the classical Hollywood construction of film continuity and the analogy of animal flesh and Elvira's body. Montage binds together and keeps apart, and Fassbinder emphasizes the artifice of the bonds that montage creates.

A reading of Elvira's transgendered body as montaged reveals how she exceeds every identification and every montaged arrangement—and thus allows for her surgery to appear along with the montaged film as more than a mere thematic medical operation. Elvira's body, like the film *In a Year of Thirteen Moons,* is the result of a process of cutting and splicing that Fassbinder does not attempt to hide. Elvira has been montaged together; she is, like Brecht's figures, used and thus usable, montaged and thus montageable. In Brecht's version of Marlowe's *The Life of Edward II,* Edward's guards say of the deposed king, "His body can take more than ours," and the reading of montage in Fassbinder reveals how his queer and/or female bodies can do and be more than what they have been forced to do and be (Brecht 1988, 2:84). A similar emphasis can be found in Benjamin's interpretation of the title *Man Equals Man:* "Mann ist Mann, das ist nicht Treue zum eignen Wesen, sondern die Bereitschaft, ein neues in sich selbst zu empfangen" (Man equals man: that is not faithfulness to one's own essence, but the readiness to receive something new in oneself) (Benjamin 1972, 2:527).

This preparedness to receive "something new in oneself" is double, because the "in" of "in sich selbst" (in oneself) could be read either as "in" or "into" and the "sich selbst" as both accusative (suggesting movement) and dative (implying stasis); the "readiness to receive something new in/to oneself" can be read both as "readiness to receive something from outside into oneself" and "readiness to receive something already there in oneself." Galy Gay both receives something from the outside—his uniform, his new habits, his new name—and brings to light something inside him—his attitude or stance that allows him to take on the roles given to him. By the end of the play, nothing is left of Galy Gay but this ability or *Haltung*. Rainer Nägele's reading of Brecht's *Keuner* stories shows how *Haltung* is "that which subsists and remains under all transformations, and yet . . . is itself a principle of transformation" (119), and the same can be said of Galy Gay's attitude, which subsists beneath his transformation into a soldier—his being used—as his transformability, his usability. This reading of *Man Equals Man* takes account of the ability that allows Galy Gay to be assimilated into the Anglo-Indian army but that could also have allowed for a different kind of transformation; his openness undoes the illusion of the completion of identity by figuring within himself the ability to become something else. Erwin/Elvira's spontaneous decision to change his gender and sex as well as her cross-dressing reveal a similar openness, which is exploited and ultimately leads to her destruction; but, as with Galy Gay, her excessive exposure is a *Haltung* or "attitude" that could have allowed for a different transformation. Her exposure is a capacity for change.

Such a reading of the fissures and breaks within figuration and identity responds to the task set for queer theory by Lee Edelman in his 1998 essay "The Future is Kid Stuff: Queer Theory, Disidentification, and the Death Drive." Edelman writes of queer theory as "the perpetual disappropriation of propriety" and of the necessity of exploring "the possibilities of acceding to our construction as figures bodying forth, within the logic of narrative, the dissolution of that very logic" (26–27). He insists on "our queer capacity to figure the undoing of the symbolic and the subject of the symbolic" (28). Edelman formulates the task that is essential to a reading of Fassbinder—a queer theory that can take account of the breaks within the false appearance of identity and continuity. A reading of montage and the ability to be montaged in Fassbinder reveals how his central characters can be said both to have an identity and to call into question identity itself; Elvira's exposure allows her both to be who she is and to remain open to becoming something else. Similar processes can be seen at work in more recent queer cinema, especially in the films of Ulrike Ottinger and Hans Scheirl, whose thematization and use of montage reveal a "wish to escape from crystallized identity" (as one character says in Ottinger's *Madame X*, 1977/1978) and the necessity of "remember[ing] the extra selves— waste products of identity" (in Scheirl's *Dandy Dust*, 1998). Their films and Fassbinder's utopian, destructive cinema aim to expose the false seamlessness of our identities by insisting on the presence and power of those gaps that bind identities together, making them possible and, at the same time, leaving them exposed to their destruction and transformation. Reading queer montage in their texts and films means identifying the discontinuity necessary for the montaged construction of continuity, the exposure that makes every identity always something other than itself.

Notes

1. This translation, and all the following uncredited translations, are mine.
2. The German text can be found in Benjamin 1972, 2:666.
3. In Brecht's play, the "Zwischenspruch" follows and comments upon the intertitle "Die Verwandlung eines lebendigen Menschen in den Militärbaracken zu Kilkoa im Jahre Neunzehnhundertfünfundzwanzig," which is also the subtitle to the play; see Brecht 1988, 2:123.
4. This is my prose translation, which draws on the verse translation of the interlude that can be found in Brecht 1979, 38.
5. See Hegel 1970, 8:237–238; Hegel 1970, 6:41–44.
6. Brigid Doherty points to this line as a sign of Galy Gay's malleability (Doherty 2000, 462).
7. See Brecht 1988, 2:406–410 for a reconstruction of the many versions of *Mann ist Mann.*

Works Cited

Benjamin, Walter. *Gesammelte Schriften.* Ed. Hermann Schweppenhäuser and Rolf Tiedemann. 7 vols. Frankfurt am Main: Suhrkamp, 1972.
———. *Selected Writings.* Ed. Michael W. Jennings et al. Vol. 2. Cambridge, Mass.: Harvard University Press, 1999.
Brecht, Bertolt. *Plays, Poetry, and Prose.* Ed. John Willet and Ralph Manheim. Vol. 2, *Man Equals Man and The Elephant Calf,* trans. Gerhard Nellhaus. London: Eyre Methuen, 1979.
———. *Werke: Große kommentierte Berliner und Frankfurter Ausgabe.* Ed. Werner Hecht et al. Berlin and Weimar: Aufbau and Frankfurt/Main: Suhrkamp, 1988.
Doherty, Brigid. "Test and Gestus in Brecht and Benjamin." *MLN* 115 (2000): 442–481.
Edelman, Lee. "The Future Is Kid Stuff: Queer Theory, Disidentification, and the Death Drive." *Narrative* 6, no. 1 (January 1998): 18–30.
Fassbinder, Rainer Werner. *The Anarchy of the Imagination: Interviews, Essays,*

Notes. Ed. Michael Töteberg and Leo A. Lensing and trans. Krishna Wilson. Baltimore: Johns Hopkins University Press, 1992.

———. *Filme befreien den Kopf: Essays und Arbeitsnotizen*. Ed. Michael Töteberg. Frankfurt am Main: Fischer, 1984.

Hegel, Georg Wilhelm Friedrich. *Werkausgabe*. Frankfurt am Main: Suhrkamp, 1970.

Nägele, Rainer. *Reading after Freud: Essays on Goethe, Hölderlin, Habermas, Nietzsche, Brecht, Celan, and Freud*. New York: Columbia University Press, 1987.

Silverman, Kaja. *Male Subjectivity at the Margins*. New York: Routledge, 1992.

11

Activism, Alterity, *Alex & Ali*
Writing Germany's First Gay Sitcom

Thomas J. D. Armbrecht

The following essay is somewhat untraditional for a scholarly article because it is based in part on an experience that I had in the late 1990s as a screenwriter for German television. Although I am a professor of French language and literature in the United States, I have had the opportunity to write concepts and scripts for two sitcoms and a police drama for German television. In writing this essay, my objectives are twofold. First, I want to explain how I used creative writing—as opposed to critical analysis—to examine the representation of cross-cultural, gay, and lesbian identities in Germany. Second, I want to analyze my experience with the German television industry in order to underline the importance of the media as a cultural force in contemporary Germany.

Rather than analyzing my own work, I will explain what I attempted to do in the programs that I conceived as a way showing how screenplays can become a sort of *mise en action* of otherwise abstract theories. I will then discuss the reactions to my work from the German television industry in an attempt to interpret the cultural significance of its reactions. In order to facilitate my analysis, I will draw comparisons with other programs on German TV and refer to interviews conducted with people who work in the entertainment industry.

Putting the *Heim* in *Unheimlich* or the *Family* in *Unfamiliar*

In the summer of 1996, I was in the proverbial right place at the right time, which in this particular instance was Munich, Germany. I was staying with a friend who had recently begun an internship at Hofmann & Voges Entertainment, when I was told that the firm wanted to develop a "gay sitcom." Since I was a queer scholar and activist who coincidentally had several weeks of free time at his disposal, the opportunity to write something was irresistible. To understand why this experience is worth recounting, it is necessary to state my intellectual motivation for participating in it and, more importantly, to understand the state of German popular entertainment at the time.

I have written about the textual representation of sexuality in the writings of early-twentieth-century authors Marguerite Yourcenar and Julien Green. In *At the Periphery of the Center: Sexuality and Literary Genre in the Works of Yourcenar and Green*, I examine the structure of their texts—specifically, the interplay of dialogue, narration, paratexte,[1] and, in the case of theater, of stage and acting directions—in order to determine how these authors created gay and lesbian characters when there existed little textual precedent for doing so. My screenwriting can hardly be compared to the literary works of either Yourcenar or Green, but my research has shown that the constraints of a genre change the way a story is told and the way that characters are drawn. Although this might seem evident, I found through my work on Yourcenar and Green that the authors wrote about gay characters differently in drama than they did in prose. In their novels, for example, both writers used a quasi-epistolary format as a way of removing their authorial presence from the narrative, thereby allowing the characters to narrate their own tales.

Because it seemed appropriate to test some of the theoretical work that I had done by writing in a highly structured genre myself, I decided to use the opportunity of scripting a sitcom to investigate the advantages and disadvantages of writing about gender and sexuality. In both the United States and Germany, contemporary sitcoms are, at their most basic, twenty-two-minute (without commercials), episodic programs that take place in the same locale and feature the same characters in every show (Holzer 1999, 11). In good Aristotelian tradition, the primary storyline of each episode has three "acts," which correspond to Aristotle's beginning, middle, and end, and which together form a "complete action." The first two acts present the problem and then escalate it with a series of what Aristotle refers to as "recognitions and reversals." (Essentially, these are plot complications.) The final act resolves the problem and ends the storyline. In each show there is usually a principal plot and a subplot, both following the same sort of development and generally relating to each other. The show itself is usually framed with a "teaser" at the beginning and a "tag" at the end. Respectively, these devices whet the audience's appetite by alluding to the episode's principal conflict and provide a final moment of poetic justice with one last "twist" of the plot at the very end. (Both devices are on the periphery of Aristotle's "complete action.")

A cardinal rule of sitcoms is that order must be restored by the episode's end. This effectively maintains the show's "situation," allowing everything to start out the same way at the beginning of each program. This return to order, along with the rigidity of a sitcom's structure, implies a kind of stability. Given the fact that homosexual people are often regarded as "unstable," either because they live unorthodox lifestyles or because by their very existence they destabilize categories of gender and sexuality, I saw a sitcom about a gay family as a chance to create dramatic tension between format and subject. I also saw it as an opportunity for a subtle form of activism, in that the gay family featured in my show would, as the genre mandates, always return to "normal," thereby establishing a gay family as the norm. This seemed worth doing not only to combat stereotypes but also to normalize the idea of a gay family for the general public.

Of course, even though there had not yet been a gay sitcom in Germany, networks were experimenting with such shows in the United States. Examining these programs provides the context in which my show was written, for the German television industry watches its American counterpart closely and usually imitates successes (Holzer 1999, 40). In terms of American television's representation of gays and lesbians, 1997 was "post-*Ellen*," but "pre-*Will & Grace*."[2] Although this distinction might seem trivial, there are aspects of each show that make it significant, not only in the context of network television but also in the context of American public consciousness. *Ellen* was the first sitcom to have a gay protagonist. Although the character played by Ellen DeGeneres did not start the show openly gay, she came out after several seasons. Unfortunately, her "sexualization" of the show, which viewers claimed transformed it into a program that was more about identity politics than comedy, was deemed to have caused the failure of the series (Smith 1999, 35). As was evident from reactions of the media at the time, while American audiences might not have been against the idea of an out lesbian on television, they certainly didn't want to know about the character's personal life. (Ironically, however, they were all too happy to know about actress Ellen DeGeneres's personal life; the well-publicized failure of her relationship with actress Anne Heche was tabloid fodder for many months.)

Will & Grace represented the next step in gay and lesbian visibility on television. As with its predecessor *Ellen*, the show contained a good deal of queer content. *Will & Grace* also revealed itself as the manifestation of certain lessons learned after *Ellen*'s demise. Although out from the beginning, the show's eponymous male protagonist was not just single, but practically asexual. He did not have a boyfriend, and it was his status as a gay man (who lived with a woman) that provided much of the show's comedy. Moreover, while unabashedly gay, Will was not particularly physically identifiable as such; he fit the "straight-looking, straight-acting" stereotype that can imply internalized homophobia. (It probably was no coincidence that Eric McCormack, the actor playing the character, was self-declaredly heterosexual, which removed any "real life" gravitas from his character.) Rather than imbuing Will with any threateningly queer characteristics, he was given a "super-queer" alter ego in the form of Jack, who was his flamboyant and effeminate best friend. Although neither *Will & Grace* nor *Ellen* are subjects of this article, it was within the interstice that came between a failed sitcom with a sexual/political protagonist and a successful show with an asexual/apolitical one that *Alex & Ali*, the show that I wrote for German television, was created.

Undoubtedly, the press and success generated by *Ellen* (thirty-seven episodes of which were shown in Germany) was responsible for Hofmann & Voges's interest in a gay-themed sitcom (*Ellen*, Internet Movie Database). As conventional thinking goes, Germans are less prudish than their American counterparts, so that sexual content does not bother them as much. Although there was no precedent for a gay sitcom on German television, there had been several films with gay and lesbian characters, which indicated that German audiences were indeed ready for such programs. *Der bewegte Mann* (*Maybe, Maybe Not,* 1994) and *Kondom des Grauens* (*Killer Condom,* 1996), two movies based on Ralf König's popular comics, did reasonably well at the German box office and received some distribution outside Germany. A number of English-language films with gay themes, like 1994's *The Adventures of Priscilla, Queen of the Desert,* were hits all over the world, Germany being no exception. Hofmann & Voges Entertainment, among other production companies, wanted to capitalize on this trend in producing a gay sitcom. Moreover, they wanted the sitcom to be specifically German and to have some aspect that would distinguish it from its American equivalents.

Although I had never done any screenwriting before and had not even watched that many sitcoms, the challenge of writing a television program in an American genre but with a German premise appealed to me. I considered writing a sitcom as the proof of the theoretical pudding that was my scholarly work. I was specifically interested in how an author could avail himself of a particular literary genre—and of the

various textual constraints specific to it—in order to make a taboo subject like homosexuality entertaining enough to interest a general audience. While neither Yourcenar nor Green was interested in a popular
audience per se, they had grappled with essentially the same problem
when learning to work within an established literary tradition in order
to write about a subject that did not have much of a history or even a
lexicon on which they could rely. As Yourcenar herself notes in the introduction to her novel *Alexis ou le traité du vain combat* (*Alexis, or the
Treatise of Vain Combat*), the only language that existed for writing about
same-sex sexuality was either medical or obscene: "The writer who is
looking to [write about homosexuality] honestly . . . barely has a choice
between two or three means of expression, which are more or less defec-
tive and sometimes unacceptable" (Yourcenar 1982, 4).[3] Her task was,
therefore, to discover a new "means of expression" within an established tradition that would be more appropriate to her subject matter.
My efforts to write a gay sitcom seemed to be analogous.

Unlike my attempt to queer a mainstream literary genre, homosexuality itself was untried literary ground for authors like Yourcenar and
Green. Appropriately, in his novel *Le malfaiteur* (*The Transgressor*),
Green remarks that the most typical way of writing about homosexuality was in fact *not* to write about it, but to rely instead either on allusion or on the implicit: "Know then that when a male writer (*écrivain*)
tells his reader of a person with whom he is taken, of a creature incomparably beautiful and good, of a unique and delicious being, know . . .
that he is writing about a man" (Green 1982, 292).[4] Neither Green's nor
Yourcenar's analysis would work for the medium of television, of course,
nor would the literary tropes (like the aforementioned epistolary framework) that they used to accomplish their tasks. Writing in the late twentieth century, however, I had the benefit of familiarity and precedent,
both personally and with regard to my audience; while gay sexuality was
still somewhat taboo, audiences were neither offended by the mention of
it, nor were they completely ignorant of the subject. This did not mean,
however, that German audiences in particular were comfortable enough
with homosexuality to welcome it as the subject of a television sitcom,
nor that they were sufficiently interested in the topic for such a show to
withstand the financial pressures of the television industry.

I decided, therefore, that my task was to make the premise of the
show both universal enough (that is, familiar and therefore nonthreaten-
ing) to appeal to a large variety of viewers, and specifically German
enough to make it different from American and other imported programs
on German television. It was ironic that my status as an outsider—both
to German culture and to German television culture—allowed me the

perspective to perceive common aspects of Germany that I found odd (and sometimes humorous), which I believed would also amuse German audiences when presented in a comic light. To this end, I decided to make the status of outsiders in Germany the focus of the show, rather than to concentrate exclusively on gay and lesbian culture. As recent theoretical writing on Germany has made clear, the concepts of German identity and *Heimat* ("homeland") remain important in post-*Wende* literary and political culture (Kelly-Holmes 2000, 99). Despite having some of the most liberal social policies in Europe, Germans still struggle with narrowly defined ideas about who is a German and what constitutes Germanness. I felt that a character who was not only prototypically German (according to culturally agreed-upon signifiers) but also gay would seemingly personify this kind of paradox and would make a compelling protagonist for a program. Accordingly, Alex embodied many German physical stereotypes (he was tall and fair) and came from a privileged cultural milieu (he was rich, but not snobby). Conversely, I decided to make Alex's amorous interest an inverse image of sorts; Ali was the son of a Turkish *Gastarbeiter* ("guest worker") and grew up in the underprivileged Turkish neighborhoods of Munich.

Of course, these characters raised the highly subjective and controversial issue of who and what is German. In creating them, I attempted to use my training in cultural studies as well as personal observation to identify visual representations of Germanness that would translate effectively to the small screen. I found it particularly frustrating, however, to discover that in attempting to isolate visual signifiers that represent what is "German" or what is "Turkish," it is difficult to avoid reductionism and reliance on stereotypes. As Barthes says in his book about Japan, *Empire of Signs*, rather than writing about any real place, he is simply "isolat[ing] somewhere in the world (*faraway*) a certain number of features," out of which he forms a "system" that he calls "Japan" (Barthes 1982, 3). Perhaps because of my discomfort with the fact that sitcoms often rely on the interplay of prototypical characters within well-established situations, I began to empathize more with the challenges faced by Yourcenar and Green, who felt as though language and precedent constrained them when writing about gay and lesbian characters. Much screenwriting employs characters that are easily recognizable as prototypes of whatever group to which they supposedly belong. In representing a minority group, particularly one that previously has been represented either unfavorably or not at all, then the principal task—before issues of plot and comedy—is either to avoid or to subvert what an audience thinks it already knows (I discovered that the latter option was more interesting).

My solution was to use stereotypes in a way that would at first seem familiar to the audience, but which would subtly challenge (and possibly change) their preconceptions about the groups these stereotypes were claiming to represent. I therefore created a situation comedy whose situation might be described by the word *unheimlich* ("uncanny"),[5] not because it was frightening, but because it was the opposite of *heimlich* ("secret, concealed") (Freud 1953). *Alex & Ali* would be about an unconventional family that could be considered *unheimlich* because its secret (homosexuality) was out in the open. This family would be a strange reflection (or double) of a "typical" German family—familiar and yet unfamiliar—and would thereby fascinate the audience with an uncanny version of itself.[6]

The show also plays on the familiar/unfamiliar binary typical of the uncanny in that it follows in the footsteps of many popular sitcoms, like *All in the Family*, *The Donna Reed Show*, *The Simpsons*, or any other number of shows that have dominated comic programming during the history of television both in the United States and abroad. The difference is, however, that *Alex & Ali* is about a nonnuclear family, with nontraditional people filling the traditional roles. Alex, the aforementioned stereotypical German, is in a relationship with Ali, the German-born son of immigrant Turks. Together they take care of Alex's children from a previous marriage to Ute, who is still very involved in the couple's life. These characters are joined by Ingrid, Alex's mother, and Deniz, Ali's brother, both of whom meddle in the couple's affairs. Ali's best friend Rudi rounds out the cast as a flamboyant loudmouth who encourages Ali to continue living almost as though he were single, despite the fact that he and Alex have been together for almost five years. Plots revolve around typical family issues: fidelity, problems at work and at school, personal insecurities, annoying relatives, and other issues common to such programs.

The most "unfamiliar" aspect of *Alex & Ali* is, of course, that problems typical to the genre are played out between two men. While Ali does not resemble Donna Reed, he does occasionally act like her. In fact, except for the fact that Alex and Ali are men, they live a fairly traditional life—perhaps even an enviably traditional one. Alex is an architect, and Ali more of a stay-at-home mom. Ali is shown, for example, fixing dinner in the kitchen several times during the first episode, whose plot revolves around his finding an incriminating telephone number in Alex's pocket while doing the laundry. In some ways Ali is even more (stereotypically) German than Alex: he is excessively interested in order and cleanliness in his house. (In one episode, for example, a conflict arises when Alex uses the wrong towel to dry his hands, ignoring the fact that there is one for dishes, another for glasses, and a third for hands, as in many well-ordered German households.) Family celebrations and other *rites de passage* specific to German culture are also featured in various episodes, like the "Feuerzangenbowle" (a spiced-wine drink served with ceremony and ritual) and the "Sissi movies" (about the Empress Elisabeth, starring Romy Schneider), which figure prominently in a holiday show.[7] By using some stereotypes to subvert others (depicting a very German-seeming Turk, for example), and by incorporating rituals and objects specific to the traditional German milieu in this untraditional family, *Alex & Ali* attempts to appropriate certain social signifiers in order to transcend issues of ethnicity and sexuality.

Noticeably absent from the program's plots are issues of discrimination or homophobia. I was pressured by the production company to avoid such supposedly "overly serious" issues since the show was, after all, a comedy. Such conflicts were also seen as potentially alienating (or perhaps, more accurately, guilt-inducing) to audiences. Avoiding what I considered to be the most realistic and significant topics contradicted my training and instincts as an academic and activist. The more I worked to refine the script, however, the more I realized that, given the demands of the industry (about which I will write more momentarily), the only way to include a message in the show was through positive example. I began to accept that there could be some benefits to portraying gay men on television as a monogamous, well-adjusted couple whose main task in life is to deal with the same day-to-day problems (albeit on an exaggerated scale appropriate to sitcoms) that most of the audience members supposedly dealt with. Doing this depended on believing that making a gay family seem normal on TV would in turn make real-life gay families seem more normal, which in a way was the lesson learned from the show *Ellen*. This program had been significant in part because it succeeded in showing many viewers comparatively ordinary gays and lesbians for what was probably the first time. The darker side of the message was that once the show dealt with more serious subjects, such as discrimination and loneliness, viewers lost interest.

Unfortunately, the television industry is not particularly interested in socially responsible programming, let alone gay activism. The principal motivation of both the production company and the network for which I worked was financial. If I could write an enlightened show that caught viewers' attention, then fine; if not, well, then there would have to be changes. It would be unfair to vilify either Hofmann & Voges or Radio Television Luxembourg (RTL), the network that bought the series and paid for the pilot episode; their willingness even to entertain such a project was still rather rare in Germany at the time. Moreover, their bottom lines were not higher for this project than for any other; their discrimination was financial, rather than social. Unfortunately, however, their choices were informed by the public's taste, as they perceived and (more likely) created it.

"Totally Normal Guys"

Creating a new television series is a notoriously slow process. Since networks and the production companies have to invest so much money even before filming the pilot episode, they employ a "test-market" to validate every aspect of the series at every step of its development. Even so, the amount of time that it took RTL to commit to the series and to begin filming it was unusually long. The script was rewritten several times, partly to increase the number of jokes and, more problematically, to reorient the pilot episode so that it was centered more around Alex than Ali. Although this did not present a problem in theory, since the characters are in a relationship with each other and "equally gay" (as if such a thing were quantifiable!), the production company's motivation for reorienting the show was that they felt that audiences would identify more closely with Alex, since he was "straighter-looking, straighter-acting," and, most importantly, not Turkish. Somewhat unconsciously, I had written the series so that Ali was the protagonist. To me he was the most interesting character, since he embodied the greatest combination of cultures; here was a man who personified the nexus of the heterosexual/homosexual, German/Turkish, rich/poor, masculine/feminine communities represented by the other characters on the show. If anyone was the face of the "new Germany"—indeed, of the new reality of most Western European countries—it was Ali, a twenty-first-century *Weltbürger* ("world citizen") par excellence.

Although I thought that Ali would appeal to almost any viewer, industry professionals based their appraisal of the show and its characters on more tried and true criteria, like sex appeal. They seized on Alex's archetypical masculinity (and perhaps upon his former heterosexuality) and rewrote the show to please those whom they assumed would be its principal consumers: women aged eighteen to forty-five. At one point during the casting, they even considered casting a German to play the role of Ali (who, it will be remembered, is Turkish), because they could not find any "suitably attractive" Turks (Romey 2002). The disturbing irony of casting a German to play a Turk in a show that was about—or was at least motivated by—breaking down cultural barriers was of no concern to either the production company or the television network. As long as Ali *looked* Turkish enough for the audience to understand his position in the show, they were satisfied. Fortunately, however, Volkan Bydar, the actor whom they found to play Ali, not only looked but also was Turkish. In fact the entire show was well cast with actors who not only looked their parts but also were open to and excited about acting in a show about a gay male couple, regardless of their own ethnic backgrounds or sexual orientations.

Not all cast members tested particularly well, however. Viewers who saw a rough cut of the show hated Alex's ex-wife, Ute, who was played by the actress Joey Cordovan. Although this was blamed on a variety of factors, from Cordovan's acting to the costumer's choices, it is my opinion that the audience's dislike was due to misogyny, but not necessarily their own. During the pilot episode's numerous rewrites, the character of Ute had taken on increasingly stereotypical qualities of the ex-wife: whiny, lovelorn, capricious, demanding, and so on. She was also pitted against Alex's mother, Ingrid, who was similarly portrayed as meddlesome and domineering. Although audiences tended to like Ingrid, who was played by a well-known actress of "Boulevard Theatre," Kathrine Ackermann, her character also depended on various preconceptions of females that stood in direct opposition to the show's modern ideas about gender roles and sexual identities. Admittedly, looking back over drafts of the script, I see that the seeds of these misogynistic characters were sown in my original ideas for them. I find it quite disturbing, however, that the entertainment professionals with whom I worked saw fit to capitalize on this kind of stereotype in order to position the female characters in backward opposition to their "enlightened" gay male counterparts. Was this polarization of the characters employed because humor depends upon, as Freud claimed, "the ability to find similarity between dissimilar things" (Freud 1960, 9)? If so, did it mean that the characters needed to be reduced to stereotypes to make them funny?

Unfortunately, much of what is on television in both the United States and Germany seems to argue that stereotypes are indeed more humorous. Even successful shows like *Ally McBeal*, whose value was debated by many feminists, rely on audiences' preconceptions of gender as much as they challenge them. The ultimate fate of *Alex & Ali* also reinforces this idea: as of 2005, the show has yet to be aired on German television, but instead continues to be reinvented (and remarketed) in increasingly watered-down versions. First it was retitled *Ganz Normale Männer* (*Totally Normal Guys*), and then the characters were changed. Although it still featured a gay couple, both men were German. Its current incarnation, which is under development, is about a heterosexual couple (both German), and is told from the point of view of a *woman*. How this show can even be considered to be based on *Alex & Ali* is unclear, unless one views it as the equal and opposite version of the original concept.

It is difficult for me as the author of the concept and original scripts for the show to know how to interpret or to react to *Alex & Ali*'s itinerary. Obviously, I am disappointed, although not because the show as I conceived it has not yet been shown on television, but rather because my work not only became a project that I do not believe in but also actually perpetuates aspects of television that I disliked in the first place. Despite this experience, I have, however, continued to write concepts and screenplays. My most recent show, *Der Schwule Bulle* (*The Queer Cop*), is about a gay detective who uses his powers of empathy to solve homicides. This show was written with a certain kind of homophobia in the mix from the very beginning, however. The protagonist[8] is again conventionally heterosexual in appearance and behavior and is intended to appeal to female viewers aged eighteen through forty-five. His partner plays only a peripheral role in the show; their relationship, which is somewhat visible, is the "hook," although the premise is hardly different from *Schimanski, Magnum, P.I.*, or any of the other *Krimis* ("crime shows") that are perpetual favorites of German television audiences: the crimes that they solve are "bourgeois murders" that happen in an affluent milieu. The only thing "gay" about the show is the protagonist's sexuality.

Rather than see this as a meaningless project that capitalizes solely on the exoticism of a gay character, however, this type of programming may speak to an essential difference between German and American television, as well as a misconception of German sexuality on my part. In the United States, politics has become part of the way that Americans define themselves; a person's point of view is determined by the culture—or subculture—with which s/he is identified, be it Hispanic, Italian American, gay, disabled, or whatnot. I wrote *Alex & Ali* with this in mind: it was the characters' "different" perspectives in "normal" situations that made them compelling. I assumed that audiences would find the concept of a gay family curious, because they would assume that a gay family, while still a family, *was* different from their own. I now wonder, after writing *Der Schwule Bulle* (which, while far more traditional and in my opinion less interesting, is scheduled to have thirteen episodes filmed),[9] whether German audiences do believe that gay families are different enough from their own to merit a show about them. Having a homosexual protagonist is acceptable, but that does not mean that they want to know what the couple does behind the proverbial closed doors. Americans seem more comfortable than Germans with the idea of sexuality as a defining feature of a character, perhaps because they are less comfortable with the idea of homosexuality in general. Germans, on the other hand, are more comfortable with homosexuality, but less accepting of it as the subject of a television show, unless of course the show is specifically about sexuality, like the television station Pro Sieben's popular program, *Liebe Sünde*. A sitcom about a multicultural gay family like *Alex & Ali* fails to titillate because it is not erotic. It also fails to captivate, since homosexuality is perhaps not inherently funny to the German public.[10]

What is disturbing about both the German and American television industries, however, is the subliminal effects that they have on their viewers. While it would be naive to think that the media in either country is concerned primarily with the education of its public, it is rather shocking to consider the insouciance with which the industries send troubling social messages in order to enlarge the audience. If the only homosexual characters (not to mention bisexuals or transgendered characters) on television are mere reflections of the public's preconceived ideas about them, then they are reinforcing these very stereotypes, not to mention gender roles in general.[11] The fact that test audiences considered Alex and Ali's romantic kiss to be more offensive than the violent crimes featured in *Der Schwule Bulle* is problematic. In this case, it is unfortunate that the German television industry relies so heavily on the American model, whose discomfort with sex is seemingly expressed through a love of violence.

In many ways, the recent appearance of homosexual characters on German television is indicative of this culture's evolving attitudes towards sexuality. In the years after the *Wende*, television networks have found themselves faced with the challenge of creating programming for a very heterogeneous public. Germans raised on Western entertainment, with its capitalist-driven programming, have a different "entertainment education" than those from the former GDR, whose media were censored by the government (Naftzinger 1998, 225).[12] (This distinction, of course, does not take into account the growing immigrant populations' television-viewing habits and preferences.) National networks' current difficulties with representing sexuality on television must be due at least in part to the fact that their audiences come from varied backgrounds and have correspondingly differing views of many subjects, including sexuality. Today's programming represents a two-steps-forward, one-step-back approach; networks are finally showing gays and lesbians on TV, but they are still struggling to create characters with integrity that will at the same time be of interest to the general public. Of course, not even the worldwide media leader, the United States, has succeeded in doing this, which may mean that it will be the

Germans (with some help from American writers) who will show the way after all.

Notes

1. Cf. Gérard Genette's *Seuils* (1987).

2. I am referring, of course, to two popular sitcoms that were shown on American network television. *Ellen* ran from 1994 until 1998, but by 1997 (after Ellen's coming out in April of that year), it was clear that the end was near. The series *Will & Grace* began in 1998.

3. All translations are my own, unless otherwise indicated in Works Cited.

4. The French words *personne* and *creature* are both feminine words, which Green argues an author could use to make it seem that he was talking about a woman (since adjectives describing them would also be feminine), when in fact, the gender remained unspecified.

5. I am not using this word in the strictly Freudian sense, which implies an eerily simultaneous feeling of discomfort and familiarity and is usually used to describe tales of the occult or supernatural. The effect of watching a gay family on television may, however, have provoked such feelings in less tolerant viewers.

6. According to Freud, doubles often produce uncanny sensations, particularly when they skirt the line between fantasy and reality, as the realism inherent in the medium of television arguably does (Freud 1953, 219).

7. See the essay by Dagmar C. G. Lorenz in this volume, "Gender, Imperialism, and the Encounter with Islam: Ruth Beckermann's Film *A Fleeting Passage to the Orient.*"

8. Unfortunately, since the show has not yet been aired, I am forbidden by contract to discuss the particulars of the program, including details like the characters' names.

9. Since I wrote this, *Der Schwule Bulle* has had its name changed, and its pilot episode was shown on "SAT1" on October 28, 2002. The episode was called "Mit Herz und Handschellen" ("With heart and handcuffs" [!]). After the pilot was shown along with the pilots of several other prospective programs, an online poll called "Happyoderend" was conducted to select which show should be made into a series. "Mit Herz und Handschellen" was one of three selected.

10. Whereas it might be considered as such to an American public, whose appetite for comedy programs about gays and lesbians indicates that the only way they feel comfortable dealing with this subject is through humor.

11. Gays and lesbians are often represented as inversions of the masculine/

feminine binary that seems to define heterosexuality; that is, the men are effeminate, and the women are "butch."

12. For more on this topic, see, for example, Stevenson and Theobald 2000 or Nowell-Smith and Wollen 1991.

Works Cited

Adventures of Priscilla, Queen of the Desert. Written and directed by Stephen Elliott. Distributed by Gramercy Pictures, 1994.

Ally McBeal. Fox Television, 1997–2002.

Aristotle. *Poetics.* Trans. S. H. Butcher. New York: Hill and Wang, 1961.

Armbrecht, Thomas J. D. *At the Periphery of the Center: Sexuality and Literary Genre in the Works of Yourcenar and Green.* Forthcoming. Amsterdam: Rodopi Press, 2006.

Barthes, Roland. *Empire of the Signs.* Trans. Richard Howard. New York: Noonday Press, 1982.

DeGeneres, Ellen. "The Puppy Episode." *Ellen.* ABC, April 30, 1997.

Ellen. Internet Movie Database. Online: http://us.imdb.com/Details?0108761 (accessed June 21, 2002).

Evans, Jeff. *The Guinness Television Encyclopedia.* Enfield: Guinness, 1995.

Freud, Sigmund. *Jokes and Their Relation to the Unconscious.* 1905. Reprint. Trans. and ed. James Strachey. New York: Norton, 1960.

———. "The Uncanny." Vol. 17 of *The Standard Edition of the Complete Psychological Works of Sigmund Freud,* trans. and ed. James Strachey, 219–252. 1919. Reprint. London: Hogarth Press and the Institute of Psycho-Analysis, 1953.

Genette, Gérard. *Seuils.* Paris: Editions du Seuil, 1987.

Green, Julien. *Le Malfaiteur.* Vol. 3 of *Œuvres complètes.* Paris: Bibliothèque de la Pléiade, 1982.

Holzer, Daniela. *Die deutsche Sitcom: Format, Konzeption, Drehbuch, Umsetzung.* Bergisch Gladbach, Germany: Lübbe, 1999.

Kelly-Holmes, Helen. "Advertising Discourse and Constructions of Identity." In *Relocating Germanness: Discursive Disunity in Unified Germany,* ed. Patrick Stevenson and John Theobald. New York: St. Martin's Press, 2000.

König, Ralf. *Der bewegte Mann.* Dir. Sönke Wortmann. Orion Classics, 1994.

———. *Kondom des Grauens.* Dir. Martin Walz. Troma Films, 1996.

Naftzinger, Joseph. "Radio and Television in the East: A Continuing Odyssey of Change." In *After the Wall: East Germany since 1989,* ed. Patricia Smith. Boulder, Colo.: Westview Press, 1998.

Nowell-Smith, Geoffrey, and Tana Wollen, eds. *After the Wall: Broadcasting in Germany.* London: British Film Institute, 1991.

Romey, Taçlan. Producer of *Alex & Ali,* Hofmann & Voges Entertainment. Telephone interview, June 15, 2002.

Smith, Evan S. *Writing Television Sitcoms.* New York: Perigee, 1999.

Stevenson, Patrick, and John Theobald, eds. *Relocating Germanness: Discursive Disunity in Unified Germany.* New York: St. Martin's Press, 2000.

Will & Grace. NBC, 1998–present.

Yourcenar, Marguerite. *Alexis ou le traité du vain combat. Œuvres romanesques.* Paris: Bibliothèque de la Pléiade, 1982.

12

Gender, Imperialism, and the Encounter with Islam

Ruth Beckermann's Film
A Fleeting Passage to the Orient

Dagmar C. G. Lorenz

Unlike most conventional documentary films, Ruth Beckermann's *Ein flüchtiger Zug nach dem Orient* (*A Fleeting Passage to the Orient*, 1999), rather than presenting mere facts and footage about a historical figure or event, foregrounds in its gender-conscious internal journey through space and history encounters among different mentalities and subjectivities. The key figure, Elisabeth, empress of Austria and queen of Hungary (1837–1898), provides access into discussions of history and cultural memory, serving to problematize contemporary versions of the past designed for popular consumption. Beckermann, present only as a voiceover, engages in a dialogue with the late nineteenth century as a historical vantage point from which a better understanding of her own time can be achieved. In her narrative she dismantles the popular image of Elisabeth, also known as Sissi or Sisi, and provides a narrative of modern Austria that challenges the "Habsburg myth" (Magris 1966).[1] Beckermann's Sisi is a fugitive from marriage, Austrian society, and the Habsburg court, a woman trying to escape the constraints of her rank and marital status. She is cast as a traveler, a somewhat ambivalent patron of travelers and the misunderstood and marginalized: women, Hungarians, and Jews. The historical Elisabeth, the narrator points out, collected women's pictures, her closest associates were Hungarian, and she had a monument erected to Heinrich Heine on one of her estates. Writing and collecting images connect the empress with the filmmaker, as does the focus on women. A series of Egyptian women's faces is presented in the film, reflecting different ideals of beauty and degrees of modernity. Yet another link is suggested by Elisabeth's admiration for

Heine's satires. In *Die Mazzesinsel* (The matzoh island, 1984) and her essays, including "Beyond the Bridges," Beckermann pays special tribute to the pre-Shoah traditions of Jewish satire and cabaret and places herself within this tradition.

The film was occasioned by the 1998 "Sissi" revival that marked the centennial of Elisabeth's assassination, and both were major media events.[2] Elisabeth, styled as nineteenth-century Austria's fairy-tale princess, *mater dolorosa*, and tragic victim, had always been of interest to the media and in 1998 she was celebrated in exhibits, publications, and films.[3] Among other things the Sisi mania was a diversion from contemporary developments leading up to the formation of an Austrian government that included the xenophobic Freedom Party (FPÖ). In the already-troubled 1990s, images of Habsburg splendor came in handy to deflect from political turmoil. The tourist-friendly version of the past foregrounded a nostalgic Austria, a fatherly Franz Joseph I, and a glamorous Empress. By showing a difficult and fragmented Elisabeth and deconstructing the deceptive image of the golden past, Beckermann undermines the dominant narrative of Austro-Hungary. The passages quoted from Elisabeth's writings describe an empire in decline and a society guided by outdated religious, social, and family values. In addition the film reveals the inability of imperialist Europe to live up to its intentions and make a lasting impact on its colonies; for Austria, the imperialist phase ended after World War I, and it ended for the other colonial powers after World War II.

Edward Said asserts that, in contrast to France and Great Britain, German-speaking countries had a primarily imaginary relationship with the Muslim world.[4] Considering the Austrian involvement in the Baghdad railroad project and the support of the Young Turks against the Armenians, Said's statement is not entirely correct. However, it is true that for writers and artists such as Adalbert Stifter, Karl May, Hugo von Hofmannsthal, Gustav Klimt, and Else Lasker-Schüler, Oriental cultures represented sensuality, adventure, and freedom from occidental norms. A modern version of the idealized orient, coupled with postcolonial sensitivities, informs late-twentieth-century writing and films. This view combines the argument that European civilization oppresses women and non-European cultures with the notion that the colonized groups, if left to their own devices, would have fostered less tyrannical lifestyles. Such views have led to the assumption that somewhere else— either in the past, as in Bachofen's *Mutterrecht* (Gynecocracy), or in a different culture, as in Lea Fleischmann's *Dies ist nicht mein Land* (This is not my country, 1980)—an alternative to the restrictions of European culture can be found. Hence the popularity of the escape to "the Orient" in film and literature.[5]

Already in Bachmann's *Der Fall Franza* (The case of Franza, 1979), however, the search for freedom in the Orient ends tragically for the woman. Bachmann's protagonist escapes to Egypt from her despotic Austrian husband, a former Nazi doctor, and from post-Shoah Austria still overshadowed by its fascist past. But rather than finding a reprieve from misogyny and racism, Franza confronts ethnocentrism and genocide in ancient Egyptian artwork and modern Egyptian society. In Cairo she meets a former Nazi physician apparently sheltered by the authorities, is raped by a European, and dies from injury sustained during the ordeal. The oppression of women seems universal. The story of Hatshepsut, the only woman pharaoh, whose successor removed her face from every monument, and the blatant mistreatment of women in public suggest that gender oppression is common in the Middle East.

Considering the patriarchal structures shared by Jewish, Christian, and Muslim societies and the worldwide oppression of women, it must be expected that the experiences of European women in the Middle East differ from the adventures of men, tourists, journalists, and would-be conquerors.[6] Even though European women participate in the colonizing culture, they lack the authority and freedom of movement European males enjoy. As travelers in a patriarchal, non-Western society, women are perceived as doubly other: as Europeans because of their language, dress, and features, and as women they are accorded little or no authority. They are the objects of potential domination and conquest. In conjunction with her perceptive discussion of the diary of Rifa'an al-Tahtawi, an Egyptian who traveled to Europe in 1826, Nina Berman discusses the importance of a writer's own experience and self-assessment for his or her representation of the "other" (Berman 1997, 346–347). Disapprovingly, al-Tahtawi in his diary characterized the position of French women as dominant, implicitly endorsing his own more radically gendered society, and he described French males as subordinate and unmanly (Berman 1997, 348).

At the very least, Empress Elisabeth roaming the streets of nineteenth-century Cairo must have been perceived as an oddity, no less so than Beckermann recording the street life of late-twentieth-century Egypt with her camera. A statement by Elisabeth, quoted in the film, reveals the monarch's even more profound alienation from Catholic Habsburg Austria and her family. She states that she felt more at ease in Egypt than in Vienna, and it is implied that Beckermann agrees with her to a certain degree, aware of the extent to which the celebrated empress was the victim of her circumstances. On September 10, 1898, the sixty-year-old Elisabeth was murdered while in Switzerland by an obscure Italian anarchist who had planned to assassinate the Prince of Orleans but ended up stabbing Elisabeth when the prince did not show up as planned.[7]

Even though Elisabeth does not figure prominently in traditional historiography, much has been written about her, and her fate continues to attract attention.[8] People close to her wrote about her, her favorite daughter Marie Valerie, and her reader and companion on her journeys to the Mediterranean and to Egypt, Constantin Chrestomanos (1867–1911) (see Sardent 1914; Rödhammer 1983). Following her engagement to Franz Joseph, supposedly a love match, and her spectacular wedding in 1854, Elisabeth was the object of adulation and gossip. Her eccentric way of life, which included the avoidance of her family and in-laws and her approval of her husband's mistress, gave rise to widespread rumors. After less than six years of marriage and the birth of three children, Elisabeth left Vienna. Her love for Hungary and her support for the cause of Hungarian equality were as controversial as her prowess as an equestrian and sportswoman, her literary pursuits, and her constant travels. Her solitude and the importance she placed on physical beauty and elegant clothes raised eyebrows as well. Her thoughts, collected in *Frei sollen die Frauen sein: Gedanken der Kaiserin Elisabeth von Österreich* (Women should be free: Thoughts of Empress Elisabeth of Austria), show her commitment to personal autonomy and her disdain for traditional gender roles (Daimler 1998).

With particular attention to gender and minority status Beckermann examines the correlation between privilege and victimization, problematizing common assumptions about prominence by showing the dangers inherent in popularity and the scapegoating of those perceived as powerful. In comparison with twentieth-century stars, Elisabeth calls to mind the tragic fates of personalities such as Marilyn Monroe and John Lennon. By including the sequence of women adorning themselves for their weddings and also providing references to the advantages Western achievements have brought to non-European populations, Beckermann uncovers the complicity between colonizers and colonized and reveals that power is not unilateral. Noting, moreover, that the Orient itself contributes greatly to the phenomenon of orientalism, she presents concurrent images of a fundamentalist rally, the expression of unabashed male dominance. By the same token, her portrayal of the victimization of Greeks and Jews at the hands of Egyptian nationalists in the 1950s suggests that the perception of victimhood depends on the position of the observer. The differentiated perspective of Beckermann's film precludes simple judgments about colonialism and political autonomy, personal freedom and oppression.[9] Rather, the film reveals that there is a great deal of injustice and oppression involved in the supposed freedom fights—national and religious freedom is not to be confounded with personal freedom.

Beckermann uses the aesthetic possibilities of her medium to the fullest for the purpose of recasting history, employing narrative, still photography, historical footage, and her own film work. Period photographs and documents are juxtaposed with dynamic street scenes in contemporary Egypt. A mural shows Franz Joseph I at the opening of the Suez Canal with the French empress Eugénie by his side; Elisabeth did not attend the affair. As emperor of Austria and king of Hungary, Franz Joseph ranked highest among the aristocratic guests and served as the figurehead of the colonial nations.[10] Sand dunes provide a contrast to the pomp and circumstance. Elisabeth's visit to the port city of Ismaliya two decades after the opening ceremonies is contrasted with the exploits of her husband. The narrator explains that after a few days of pageantry the town reverted to the dusty provincial place it had always been and still is. This is how Elisabeth and Beckermann saw it.

The film repeatedly evokes the destruction of Egypt's colonial grandeur. At one point the narrator describes the amenities of the Shepherd's Hotel in fin-de-siècle Cairo, but all viewers see is a filling station that occupies the location of what had been a gathering place for the elegant world. Both the hotel and the gas station, however, are symbols of the West, one of an elite cosmopolitan culture, the other of the car and oil industry. Among images of former splendor are the classical gardens in Alexandria, reminiscent of Vienna's formal parks. Contrasting their delicate beauty is a rally of clamoring men in traditional Islamic clothes carrying the insignias of their various religious brotherhoods on the birthday of the Prophet. The disparity suggests the loss of a budding modern civilization and calls for a reevaluation of the postcolonial condition.

Gender is a major aspect of Beckermann's views on history, power, nationality, and identity. Like most women's biographers, Beckermann tries to recover a life overshadowed by the male experience, a life led in relative obscurity, protected from intruders by the empress herself. Elisabeth preferred to travel incognito using names such as Countess Hohenems and Mrs. Elizabeth Nicholson. There are few solid facts about her life in obscurity.[11] Thus the popular media had the opportunity to cast her as a traditional wife and mother. Beckermann's goal is to unravel rather than reconfigure the Elisabeth myth along with other nineteenth-century myths. The picture of the empress shown most frequently in the film is that of a modern woman in a plain striped top without imperial accoutrements. The quotations from Elisabeth's writings and the notes by Chrestomanos provide insight into Sisi's way of thinking. An uncompromising critic of convention who had no illusions about the dismal state of the empire, Beckermann's Sisi comes across as a complex and progressive woman.

Compared to the straightforward, often aggressive approach in documentary films by male directors, Beckermann's use of the camera seems defensive and probing rather than domineering. Often the camera serves as a tool to fend off intrusive stares and approaches. The viewer is reminded of Beckermann's film *Die papierene Brücke* (*The paper bridge*, 1987), where the audience witnesses the filmmaker's camera being smashed during the filming of a demonstration against the presidential candidate Kurt Waldheim in 1986. Most remarkable, though, is Beckermann's way of representing women. She focuses on the face rather than the body and is sensitive to different kinds of beauty rather than privileging one particular beauty ideal. The empathetic portraits of women stand in striking contrast to the way women are depicted on the posters in Cairo's Freedom Square, which are scanned by the camera.

The unfamiliar setting of Arab culture and the filmmaker's own precarious position prove advantageous for examining the role of the European woman in a traditionally exoticized culture, whether she is an Austrian empress of the nineteenth century or an Austrian Jewish filmmaker of the twentieth. The film establishes visually and through Beckermann's disembodied and deterritorialized voice that the woman's position is not conducive to colonizing and exploiting others. In her radical exclusion, the narrator is unable to interpret and comment on the street scenes and the conversations and interactions. It is impossible to forge a cohesive story because the narrator has no access to the material stories are made of. The very structure of Beckermann's film conveys that both Elisabeth of Austria and Ruth Beckermann, even though they assumed the male-defined roles of travelers and explorers, did not and could not reproduce the orientalist pose of male adventurers and filmmakers.[12] One need only compare Elisabeth's travel party of fourteen with Franz Joseph's magnificent entourage at the opening of the Suez Canal, or Beckermann's small film crew with the armies of actors, technicians, specialists, and extras working for a male filmmaker like Werner Herzog, to appreciate the difference.[13] In contrast to the European men who have the wherewithal to dominate the unfamiliar world, European women lack the institutional, social, and political support to overcome their colonized status, not only in their societies of origin but also in other patriarchal settings. Thus *Ein flüchtiger Zug nach dem Orient* offers little sympathy for Third World men supposedly suffering under the domination of imperialist powers.

Rather than examining the spaces of Egyptian men, the sphere of Arab and European women is shown to be under siege. Elisabeth's incognito shielded her only for a short while—her attempt to retreat into anonymity failed. The situation is similar for Beckermann, who finds herself spied upon by the hotel personnel and accosted at every turn, even though her camera records the male approaches, the "hellos," "welcomes," and "where-are-you-froms." The mere desire on the part of a woman to be given space to go about her business provokes suspicion. Not unlike the late "Lady Di"—Diana, Princess of Wales—Elisabeth too was hounded by reporters and political spies sent after her from Vienna, and her admirers considered it a distinction to be privy to her secrets (Daimler 1998; Déon-Bessière 1998). A trophy and a target, Elisabeth resented the way her personal freedom was compromised. As a European woman in the Middle East, Beckermann is similarly vulnerable. No European male, certainly no professional or dignitary, would be subjected to tirades, invitations, and questions such as the ones men of just about any status direct at Beckermann.

Beckermann's experience as a Jew growing up in post-Shoah Vienna adds another important dimension to the search for an alternative history in *Ein flüchtiger Zug nach dem Orient*. Informed by this experience, Beckermann approaches the Habsburg era with a critical attitude. She realizes that Sisi, the cultural icon, has been created to replace the problematic empress in accordance with an agreeable version of the past. Beckermann discovers a Sisi with whom she can agree on her views about the empire, Central European society, and the oppression of women. The empress's preference for the Hungarian people, who were oppressed under Habsburg rule, and her choice of a young Greek man as her travel companion establish a sense of appreciation on the part of the filmmaker.

Whether because Sisi's unconventional education had spoiled her for playing the role of the emperor's obedient consort or because she was revolted by the bigotry at court, she did not "fit" into the Austria of the Victorian era, just as Beckermann and her peers, those highly educated and cosmopolitan children of Holocaust survivors, did not fit into the Second Republic of Austria. Beckermann quotes Elisabeth as saying that she wanted to traverse the world and make Ahasver appear like a homebody, to travel the oceans like a "weiblicher Fliegender Holländer" (female Flying Dutchman). These statements are conjoined with images of the ocean overcast with heavy clouds, which is boldly traversed by Beckermann's camera. A synaesthetic correspondence between Beckermann's film and Elisabeth's words is established, which calls to mind the transcontinental perspectives of Austrian Jews who also look for places of refuge on the other side of the ocean, in Israel and the United States. There is, moreover, a parallel between the Jewish experience of extinguishing cultural specificity through assimilation and Elisabeth's flight from herself into obscurity. Finally, the filmmaker is intrigued by Elisabeth's desire to hire death-row candidates as her ship's crew, and by her way of immortalizing herself as if she were already dead.

In her deliberately created marginality, Beckermann's Elisabeth comes across more like a Jewish Sisi than the Madonna-like apparition surrounded by an aura of ageless beauty that the young Chrestomanos perceives when first meeting her. Beckermann's Elisabeth is a flâneur, a women's advocate, and a free spirit who traveled from the "static world of the Habsburgs into the mobility of modern life."[14] The reading of history against the Austrian and Egyptian consensus in *Ein flüchtiger Zug nach dem Orient*, presented alongside countless casually made but profoundly critical comments, as well as sensitivity to the situation of minorities, draw attention to Beckermann's Jewish background. There is an affinity between Beckermann and Elisabeth traveling in Egypt, the farthest destination on the monarch's flight from her dynastic and family obligations (Hamann 1998). For Beckermann, Egypt in terms of its culture and politics represents the most remote terrain she has explored to date. Yet insofar as Egypt is an important site of ancient and modern Jewish history, *Ein flüchtiger Zug nach dem Orient* ties in seamlessly with Beckermann's earlier films, *Wien Retour* (Return trip to Vienna, 1983), *Die papierene Brücke* (The paper bridge, 1987), and *Nach Jerusalem* (Toward Jerusalem, 1990). These works were devoted to Jewish memory in Vienna, Eastern Europe, and Israel. Similarly, *Ein flüchtiger Zug nach dem Orient* also confronts Jewish history and examines the dangers lurking in a hostile present.

Jenseits des Krieges (East of war, 1997), filmed at the controversial exhibit in Vienna, *Vernichtungskrieg: Verbrechen der Wehrmacht 1941–1944* (The war of elimination: crimes of the Wehrmacht 1941–1944) in October and November 1995 foregrounds memory and new dangers. The exhibition venue was the Alpenmilchzentrale (Alpine Milk Center), in the Weyringergasse 3611, Vienna 1040, since none of the Vienna museums was willing to host the controversial event. Beckermann interviewed World War II veterans about their war experiences and asked them about their reactions to the pictures at the exhibition showing German soldiers committing atrocities. Easily identified as a Jewish woman, Beckermann intruded, as it were, into the male realm of war, violence, and cruelty and confronted the members of the dominant culture from her position of vulnerability. She did so in a direct manner, without the aggression and disdain with which Claude Lanzmann in his film *Shoah* (1985) approaches former Nazis. Only the spatial arrangement makes Beckermann's intellectual and emotional distance obvious. She stands apart from the debating men, as an outsider who is privy to cultural insider information and who nonetheless does not share the reactions of the majority. In her acceptance speech for the Mannes Sperber Prize, Beckermann notes that a Jew is like an anthropologist studying the natives: "I see folklore dresses in the opera and at the symphony. I watch newscasts that deem politicians singing folk songs or praying newsworthy. I am baffled at how satisfied people are that the popular provincial film, this genuinely German-Austrian genre of the 1950s, celebrates a never-ending comeback as reality show. . . . I do not understand the majority of my age cohort, realize that I never understood them. Why are their envy, their hatred, and their resentment so great? Why are they so cowardly? Why so sad?"[15]

In *Ein flüchtiger Zug nach dem Orient* Beckermann and her camerawoman Nurith Aviv crossed the Mediterranean as they did in *Nach Jerusalem* to examine people and conversations. There are similarities between the Israel scenario and the exploration of Egypt in *Ein flüchtiger Zug*. In both cases the European woman acts as an intruder. She works in a precarious position, an outsider to the male spheres of work and religion. Filming spontaneously without professional actors, Beckermann has no control over how situations and conversations will evolve. Her commentaries are made by a gentle but determined female voice separate from the images and voices captured on film. There is no public space for anyone speaking in this register and yet saying the things she says. Beckermann's voice makes critical and personal revelations and is at risk of being drowned out by the crowds or of incurring popular wrath if it were heard. Again, an assumed affinity with Elisabeth can be noticed. Beckermann observes that Franz Joseph must have really loved Elisabeth, because prominent women like her, unwilling to conform, would normally have been institutionalized.

The exceptional role of the two women is also apparent from their attitude toward representation and the arts. Instead of being photographed or filmed, they collect and produce images. Beckermann emphasizes her own desire for and enjoyment of images, knowing that her assigned place in a Muslim as well as an Austrian society would be among the edible Barbie dolls displayed in the candy stores or on man-made posters. Yet neither for herself nor, Beckermann implies, for Elisabeth is a position of complete self-assurance possible to achieve within societies that do not validate the work and experience of women. Being denied the respect owed an autonomous person and not even having the options of blending may explain Elisabeth's extreme caution with Egyptian merchants. Beckermann points out that the empress was exceedingly afraid of being taken advantage of despite the fact that she could have afforded almost anything she desired. Her assumption that she was cheated seems to have derived from her awareness that she was denied the kind of validation a man of like rank would have enjoyed.

Sisi functions as Beckermann's imaginary counterpart. Stories about Elisabeth's journey to Egypt in 1885 are juxtaposed with images in the film,[16] and the voiceover tells Beckermann's own story against images of street, market, and coffeehouse scenes. The clash between the narrative and the images, the reminiscences about Elisabeth's era and the present, create a sense of disorientation and alienation.

The opening of *Ein flüchtiger Zug nach dem Orient*, showing the crossing of the Mediterranean Sea, cites Beckermann's earlier film *Nach Jerusalem*. In that film as well the destination, Israel, is represented as a dusty, noisy, hot, and sunny country with men dominating the public sphere. In neither setting does the filmmaker find a place of comfort, even though *Nach Jerusalem* contains motifs reminiscent of her work on Central and Eastern Europe. In *Ein flüchtiger Zug nach dem Orient*, "Jewish Cairo" with the Ben Ezra synagogue at its center is passed by—it is a Jewish site without Jews that Elisabeth probably did not visit. Other than occasional memory flashes, there are no traces of a Jewish past. The absence of Jewish life and the progressive disenfranchisement of European culture in Egypt make Egypt the most alien place in the works of Ruth Beckermann, the place where her status as outsider is complete.

Segregated according to the patriarchal precepts of Islam, the public sphere in Cairo—coffee shops and streets—is populated by men dressed, for the most part, in Western-style clothes. As the narrator states, they enjoy the leisure women are denied. Women are partly or completely covered up and do their errands discreetly and hurriedly, relaxing only among themselves, mostly inside buildings or at a business venue, and occasionally in the company of a male "protector." Beckermann and Nurith Aviv clearly transgress against the gender code. They are tolerated to a certain extent, but just barely. The narrator explains that the authorities forbid them to take pictures of the poor and of men in traditional garments. Such images are considered detrimental to the reputation of Egypt abroad. Then there are the stares and calls designed to chase the women intruders away. The exaggerated servility of the shopkeepers—one of them, a spice dealer who speaks German—and the provocative statements of the boys on the bridge across the Nile River reveal latent hostility toward the women. Empress Elisabeth, impeccably dressed, tall and slender, who used to walk for hours through the city streets, must have been, Beckermann speculates, just as exposed in a society that reduced her, regardless of rank, to the status of European female.

The conspicuousness of the European woman traveler in the Middle East—Israel and Egypt—is captured brilliantly in Beckermann's films. This motif supports the isolation of the Jewish filmmaker in an environment similarly inhospitable, such as at the Vienna war crime exhibit. Revealing the vulnerability as well as the strength of nonconformist women and of Jews in the Islamic as well as the Christian public, Beckermann relates to the empress by way of the traveler's otherness, an otherness that ultimately must be accepted and embraced as Elisabeth must have done. Perhaps precisely because of her refusal to conform and her long absences, Elisabeth became a constant presence in Austrian culture. There is a similarity with the memory of Jewish Vienna: it has remained constant despite its destruction during the Shoah, and over time, despite continued antisemitism, it has been embellished, packaged, and turned into a tourist attraction (Beckermann 1994, 304–305).

At first glance the empress seems an unlikely choice for a Jewish filmmaker as a partner in a dialogue about history, Austria, imperialism, power, and gender roles. Yet, the vanishing of the real Elisabeth, concomitant with the rise of the mythical Elisabeth, calls to mind a similar paradox that concerns Beckermann and her family: the absence of Austrian Jews from the post-Shoah Second Republic and the ever-present, ever-increasing memory of the murdered Jews. Hence Beckermann's interest in the making of the "star" Elisabeth, whom she compares to Greta Garbo and other stars who came to shun the public. Just as Elisabeth's youthful images were inserted into family and ceremonial photos next to those of the aging emperor in order to show the public an intact imperial family, the reproduction of pre-Shoah Jewish images and speech suggests a continuity that is in effect illusionary. The success of Beckermann's own documentary volume of Vienna Jewish life during the interwar period, *Die Mazzesinsel* (The matzoh island, 1984) is a case in point. By 1992 this photo documentary of the second district had gone through four editions.

Ein flüchtiger Zug nach dem Orient uncovers an infrequently discussed break in history, characterized by violence similar to that of 1930s Austria, the expulsion of Jews and Europeans from Egypt and other Muslim countries. Describing the famous Shepherd's Hotel, Beckermann informs the viewers that in 1952, on "Black Saturday," as she—

but hardly Egyptian historians—would call it, the hotel was burnt down along with other properties that belonged to non-Egyptians.[17] These brief comments alluding to a postcolonial ethnic cleansing are part of an oppositional narrative that undermines the nationalist version of history—Egypt's triumphant liberation. Placing her narrative alongside Austria's deceptive postwar history, Beckermann suggest that other developments might have been possible and desirable. She uncovers the injustices and the suffering caused in nationalist revolutions. As was already the case in her anti-Zionist narrative in *Die papierene Brücke*, *Ein flüchtiger Zug nach dem Orient* also juxtaposes a utopian cosmopolitan model with the actually achieved national state. Beckermann reveals the violent ruptures and the destruction that even in the name of progress and patriotism are hard to justify. Her films convey the notion that nationalism has left the societies under scrutiny—Austria, Israel, and Egypt—intellectually and spiritually impoverished without improving the status of the oppressed—women, the poor, and minorities.

Growing up in post-Shoah Vienna, Beckermann, like any young person at the time, enjoyed Ernst Marischka's romantic *Sissi* films, which starred Romy Schneider as Elisabeth and Karl-Heinz Böhm as Franz Joseph I: *Sissi* (1955), *Sissi, die junge Kaiserin* (Sissi, the young empress, 1956), and *Sissi—Schicksalsjahre einer Kaiserin* (Sissi—fateful years of an empress, 1957).[18] In *Ein flüchtiger Zug nach dem Orient* Beckermann acknowledges her initial fascination with the cult figure Sissi that inspired her own critical reception. Rather than establishing a diametrically opposed counterimage to the Sissi character of films and popular children's books (see Schuster 1998), Beckermann discovers cultural possibilities and ways of life that fell by the wayside when nationalism became the dominant paradigm worldwide.

In *Ein flüchtiger Zug nach dem Orient* Beckermann accesses a phase in Austrian history commonly associated with Jewish assimilation and the emancipation of Jews and women, which is also a presumably optimistic era to which Jews contributed in great measure. She juxtaposes the experience of Austria's most prominent woman with her own perspective as the child of Holocaust survivors—the perspective of one who is *unzugehörig*, who does not belong. Focusing on the similarities rather than the differences, she discovers an Elisabeth who, like the Austrian Jews, was co-opted against her will and instrumentalized for political purposes even in her absence. In the 1950s the glorified image of Sissi, who in reality was depressed and lonely, was used in the famous *Heimatfilme*, popular patriotic films intended to erase the memory of National Socialism and the Holocaust. Again, the parallel with the opportunistic use of Jewish history is striking. Oblivious to the plight of survivors and exiles, and notwithstanding continued antisemitism, the Austrian cultural industry availed itself of Sigmund Freud, Arthur Schnitzler, Karl Kraus, and Hermann Broch and claimed as its own even Jews who were not born in Austria and never came back to live there, such as Elias Canetti and Paul Celan. The very lack of a continuous story in *Ein flüchtiger Zug nach dem Orient* undercuts the notion of a continuous Austrian history from the Austro-Hungarian monarchy by way of Austro-Fascism and National Socialism to the postwar Habsburg myth evoked in the *Sissi* films. On a visual level these films suggested such a continuity, which was supported by the cast. Magda Schneider, who appeared alongside her Sissi-daughter Romy, had already been famous in the Nazi years, and Karl-Heinz Böhm, who played the emperor, was a known entity as well. Thus the *Sissi* films forged a comfortable image of Austria at home and abroad.[19] By sidestepping and deconstructing the epics of the user-friendly *Sissi* films designed to reintroduce Austria into the community of civilized nations, Beckermann calls into question the cultural narratives that minimize the Shoah.[20] At the same time, the representation of a repressive Egypt void of any traces, any memory of the modern cosmopolitan culture Elisabeth promoted calls to mind Europe's religious fanaticism and its fascist history. Beckermann's film and its title suggest how rare and ephemeral this culture was, both in Europe and elsewhere, before it was forcibly transplanted by nationalism, chauvinism, and old and new religious zeal.

Notes

1. Sisi is the name the Empress used; Sissi was the name that was assigned to her in Marischka's films and gained popularity over Sisi.

2. Empress Elisabeth was born Eugenie Amalie Elisabeth of Wittelsbach in 1837, the third daughter of the eight children of Duke Maximilian and Duchess Ludovika in Bavaria. Scandal and tragedy were common in her extended family.

3. See, for example, the diary of Elisabeth's secretary Chrestomanos and Elisabeth's diaries. For references to recent publications about Elisabeth, see the Works Cited section below.

4. "At no time in German scholarship during the first two-thirds of the nineteenth century could a close partnership have developed between Orientalists and a protracted, sustained national interest in the Orient" (Said 1979, 19).

5. Said cautions: "Appeals to the past are among the commonest strategies in interpretations of the present. What animates such appeals is not only dis-

agreement about what happened in the past and what the past was, but uncertainty about whether the past really is past, over and concluded, or whether it continues, albeit in different forms, perhaps" (Said 1994, 4).

6. Berman compares the experiences of Karl May, Hugo von Hofmannsthal, and Else Lasker-Schüler, describing the fluctuation between male and female narrative perspectives in Lasker-Schüler as a strategy to which the colonized person, in this case the woman, resorts to escape the image imposed on her by the colonizer (Berman 1997, 317).

7. Seyrl examines the circumstances of and the reaction to Elisabeth's assassination in detail. See also the notebook of Elisabeth's murderer, Luigi Luccheni (1873-1910) (Luccheni 1998).

8. In Tapié's rather traditional Austrian history Elisabeth does not even figure marginally.

9. Cf. Said: "Neither imperialism nor colonialism is a simple act of accumulation and acquisition" (Said 1994, 11).

10. Said discusses the cultural events on the occasion of the opening (Said 1994, 114-117).

11. See Jäger's acclaimed *Weltgeschichte*. Franz Joseph is represented in two portraits and referred to throughout. There is no index entry for Elisabeth.

12. Slibar presents a case study of Alma Karlin, an early-twentieth-century woman traveler, a "Columbus-like spirit" (Slibar 1998, 119). Like Elisabeth, Karlin "was completely on her own in every sense, and it was a matter of her ingenuity to reach the remote and inaccessible parts of her routes" (Slibar 1998, 125).

13. Herzog's *Aguirre: The Wrath of God* (1972) was shot in Peru despite tremendous difficulties, sparing no human efforts; *Fitzcarraldo* (1982) was produced in the Amazon jungle.

14. "Aus der statischen Welt der Habsburger ins moderne bewegte Leben" (Beckermann, *Ein flüchtiger Zug nach dem Orient*). Except where otherwise indicated, translations are my own.

15. "Ich sehe Dirndlkleider in Oper und Musikverein, ich sehe Nachrichtensendungen, die Volkslieder-absingende oder betende Politiker für newswürdig erachten. Ich komme aus dem Staunen gar nicht raus, wie zufrieden die Menschen damit sind, dass der Heimatfilm, dieses genuin deutsch-österreichische Genre der 50er Jahre, nun als Reality-Show in Endlosschleife sein Comeback feiert. . . . Ich verstehe die meisten meiner Altersgenossen nicht, merke jetzt deutlich, dass ich sie nie verstanden habe. Warum ist ihr Neid, ihr Hass, ihr Ressentiment so groß? Warum sind sie so feige? Warum so traurig?" (Beckermann 2001, 5-6).

16. Carl Schorske comments on the fin-de-siècle fascination with Egypt: "That mysterious land promised access to the womb of culture and the tomb of time, to the original and the hidden, the voiceless (infans) childhood of humanity. In the fin de siècle it was the finds of archeologists that

aroused anew the desire to decipher the culture of the Nile, as the philolo-gists had done a century before. The archeologist's work swept the edu-cated public in its wake" (Schorske 1998, 205).

17. Chahine's *Alexandria—Why?* thematizes a young man's flight from the violence at the end of World War II and the collapse of Alexandria's multicultural society.

18. Marischka also wrote a novel based on his films.

19. In the interwar era the interest in Elisabeth continued (see Tschuppik 1929), as it did also in the Nazi years (see, e.g., Aretz 1938), despite occa-sional attempts to reduce her popularity (see Corti 1934).

20. Clément examines the nonconformist and rebellious character of the "Sis-sified" empress.

Works Cited

Al-Tahtawi, Rifa'. *Ein Muslim entdeckt Europa: Die Reise eines Ägypters im 19. Jahrhundert nach Paris.* Ed. Karl Stowasser. Leipzig: Kiepenheuer, 1988.

Amtmann, Karin. *Elisabeth von Österreich: Die politischen Geschäfte der Kaiserin.* Regensburg: F. Pustet, 1998.

Aretz, Gertrude. *Kaiserin Elisabeth von Österreich in zweihundert Bildern.* Vi-enna: Bernina-Verlag, 1938.

Bachmann, Ingeborg. *Der Fall Franza.* München: dtv, 1981.

Bachofen, Johann Jakob. *Das Mutterrecht.* Mit Untersuchung von Harald Fuchs, Gustav Meyer, and Karl Schefold. Ed. Karl Meuli. Basel: Schwab, 1948.

Beckermann, Ruth. "Auf der Brücke: Rede zur Verleihung des Mannes Sperber-Preises, Wien, 16/10/2000." *German Quarterly* 74, no. 1 (2001): 1–7.

———. "Beyond the Bridges." In *Insiders and Outsiders: Jewish and Gentile Culture in Germany and Austria,* ed. Dagmar C. G. Lorenz and Gabriele W. Weinberger, 301–307. Detroit, Mich.: Wayne State University Press, 1994.

———. *Die Mazzesinsel. Juden in der Wiener Leopoldstadt.* Vienna: Löcker, 1984.

———. *Jenseits des Krieges.* Vienna: Döcker, 1998.

———. *Unzugehörig.* Vienna: Löcker, 1989.

Berman, Nina. *Orientalismus, Kolonialismus und Moderne: Zum Bild des Orients in der deutschsprachigen Kultur um 1900.* Stuttgart: Verlag für Wissenschaft und Forschung, 1997.

Chrestomanos, Constantin. *Die letzte Griechin: Die Reise der Kaiserin Elisabeth nach Korfu im Frühjahr 1892 erzählt aus den Tagebuchblättern von Constan-tin Christomanos.* Ed. Robert Holzschuh. Aschaffenburg: Eduard Krem-Bardischewski Verlag, 1996.

Clément, Catherine. *Sissi, l'impératrice anarchiste.* Paris: Gallimard, 1992.

Corti, Egon Caesar Conte, ed. *Elisabeth, die seltsame Frau: Nach dem schrift-*

lichen Nachlass der Kaiserin, den Tagebüchern ihrer Tochter und sonstigen unveröffentlichten Tagebüchern und Dokumenten. Graz: Styria, 1934.

——. *Elisabeth von Österreich: Tragik einer Unpolitischen.* Munich: W. Heyne, 1997.

Daimler, Renate. *Diana und Sissi: Zwei Frauen—ein Schicksal.* Vienna: Deuticke, 1998.

Déon-Bessière, Danièle. *Sissi & Diana: Du rêve à la tragédie.* Paris: Buchet-Chastel, 1998.

Elisabeth, Kaiserin von Österreich. *Drei Gedichte von Elisabeth, Kaiserin von Österreich.* Ed. Felix Weingartner. Vienna: Universal-Edition, 1938.

——. *Frei sollen die Frauen sein—: Gedanken der Kaiserin Elisabeth von Österreich.* Ed. Renate Daimler. Vienna: C. Brandstätter, 1998.

——. *Tagebuchblätter.* Ed. Verena von der Heyden-Rynsch and Ludwig Klages. Frankfurt am Main: Insel, 1993.

Fleischmann, Lea. *Dies ist nicht mein Land: Eine Jüdin verläßt die Bundesrepublik.* Hamburg: Hoffmann und Campe, 1980.

Hamann, Brigitte. *Elisabeth: Kaiserin wider Willen.* Munich and Zürich: Piper, 1998.

Jäger, Oskar. *Weltgeschichte in 4 Bänden.* Vol. 4, *Geschichte der neuesten Zeit 1789-1900.* Leipzig: Velhagen und Klasing, 1912.

Lanzmann, Claude, dir. *Shoah.* Paris: Films Aleph, Historia Films, 1985.

Luccheni, Luigi. *"Ich bereue nichts!"* In *Die Aufzeichnungen des Sisi-Mörders,* ed. Santo Cappon. Vienna: Zsolnay, 1998.

Magris, Claudio. *Der habsburgische Mythos in der österreichischen Literatur.* Salzburg: Müller, 1966.

Marie Valerie, Archduchess of Austria. *Marie Valerie von Österreich: Das Tagebuch der Lieblingstochter von Kaiserin Elisabeth, 1880-1899.* Ed. Martha and Horst Heinrich Schad. Munich: Langen Müller, 1998.

Marischka, Ernst. *Sissi: Ein Roman nach den Filmen Sissi; Sissi, die junge Kaiserin; und, Schicksalsjahre einer Kaiserin.* Hamburg: Im Bertelsmann Lesering, 1959.

Rödhammer, Hans. *Elisabeth, Kaiserin von Österreich und Königin von Ungarn.* Linz: Kulturverein Schloss Ebelsberg, 1983.

Said, Edward. *Culture and Imperialism.* New York: Knopf, 1994.

——. *Orientalism.* New York: Vintage Books, 1979.

Sardent, Marie de. *Elisabeth von Bayern: Kaiserin von Österreich und Königin von Ungarn.* Halle: E. Thamm, 1914.

Schorske, Carl E. *Thinking with History: Explorations in the Passage to Modernism.* Princeton, N.J.: Princeton University Press: 1998.

Schuster, Gaby. *Sissi. Eine Prinzessin für den Kaiser.* Bindlach: Kinder-& Jugendbücher Loewe Vlg., 1998.

Seyrl, Harald. *Der Tod der Kaiserin: Die Ermordung der Kaiserin und Königin Elisabeth von Österreich-Ungarn am 10. September 1898 im Spiegel der zeitgenössischen Darstellung.* Vienna: Edition Seyrl, 1998.

Slibar, Nava. "Traveling, Living, Writing from and at the Margins: Alma

Maximiliana Karlin and Her Geobiographical Books." In *Transforming the Center, Eroding the Margins,* ed. Dagmar C. G. Lorenz and Renate S. Posthofen, 115–131. Columbia, S.C.: Camden House, 1998.

Tapié, Victor Lucien. *Die Völker unter dem Doppeladler.* Graz: Styria, 1975.

Tschuppik, Karl. *Elisabeth Kaiserin von Österreich.* Vienna: H. Epstein, 1929.

Filmography

Beckermann, Ruth, dir. *Die papierene Brücke.* Vienna: filmladen, 1987.

——. *Ein flüchtiger Zug nach dem Orient.* Vienna: filmladen, 1999.

——. *Jenseits des Krieges.* Vienna: filmladen 1997.

——. *Nach Jerusalem.* Vienna: filmladen, 1990.

Beckermann, Ruth, and Josef Aichholzer, dir. *Wien Retour.* Vienna: filmladen, 1983.

Chahine, Youssef, dir. *Alexandria—Why?* Script by Mohsen Zeyed. New York: Fox Lorber Films, 1979.

Die Mazzesinsel. Juden in der Wiener Leopoldstadt. Wien: Löcker, 1984.

Herzog, Werner, dir. *Aguirre: The Wrath of God.* Berlin: Filmverlag der Autoren, 1972.

——, dir. and prod. *Fitzcarraldo.* Berlin: Filmverlag der Autoren, 1982.

Lanzmann, Claude, dir. *Shoah.* Paris: Films Aleph, Historia Films, 1985.

Marischka, Ernst, dir. *Sissi.* Wien: Herzog Film, 1955.

——. *Sissi, die junge Kaiserin.* Berlin: UFA Film, 1956.

——. *Sissi—Schicksalsjahre einer Kaiserin.* Berlin: UFA Film, 1957.

PART III
Political Dimensions

13

Cartographic Claims

Colonial Mappings of Poland in German Territorial Revisionism

Kristin Kopp

As a condition of the peace settlements marking the end of World War I, Germany was forced to relinquish vast stretches of land at the periphery of the nation.[1] With their country stripped entirely of its colonial holdings overseas and forced to cede great territorial expanses on the European continent, Germans were devastated by their dramatically relocated—and reduced—national "place" in the world. The peace of Versailles thus quickly gave way to a revisionist war, as Germans fought for the return of their lost territories. This was a battle fought on two fronts, both militarily at the nation's borders and cartographically on the world's map. For while rogue militias engaged in bloody border skirmishes (particularly in the east), German geopoliticians fought to convince an international public of the illegitimacy of the newly located borders. This latter battle was largely conducted on a field made available by the representational power of cartography.

As a reduced and abstracted representation of a geographic landscape, the map offers the only means of constructing and communicating a territorial imagination of the nation (see Pickles 1992; Robinson and Petchenik 1976). While other visual and scriptural media may convey qualities of the landscape, only on a map do we see the contours of borders, the extension of territory, in other words, the experience of *structured and located spatiality*. This visual function rendered maps crucial for German revisionists and their opponents, and accounts for the prominent role played by maps and atlases in the postwar arena of popular culture. The visual aspect of maps also accounts for a new genre—the persuasive map—developed in this period. Distinguished from its forerunners by the introduction of various graphic symbols indicating change over time (most notably the arrow), and also by the use of noncartographic images to impart connotative meaning, the persuasive map overcame the limitations of static representation to gain the power of narration. In the struggle to legitimate competing versions of the "rightful" location of German national space, such narrative maps were increasingly mobilized as tools of persuasive communication.

Within the field of critical geography, recent work has addressed the important question of the map as a socially constructed, argumentative text. The late J. B. Harley was a central figure in this disciplinary development, a cartographic theorist who convincingly showed that even those maps commonly held to be the most objectively "scientific" nonetheless remain the cultural products of subjective agency and textual authorship (see Harley 1988; Harley 1992). Cartographers make decisions about the geographic area they will represent and how they will frame it. They determine what features of this landscape will be addressed, whose statistics will be appealed to in determining the distributions of such features, and what visual signs will be used to represent them.

For the cultural scholar, this understanding of the map as the product of such strategic choices means that all maps can be "read" and that the meanings they impart to space can be interpreted. While scientific cartographers may focus on questions of mimetic accuracy, we sidestep this ontological morass by instead examining the *map as text*.

Such an understanding means recognizing that the map, like all other cultural products, does not contain a singular and static, internally identifiable meaning but instead that various manipulations of formal features link the map and its meanings to the various social discourses in which it circulates. We can thus examine the ways in which the map intervenes—as it makes arguments and chooses sides—in these discourses. Such a reading must proceed from a critical interpretation of the map's formal features—its *textual strategies*. What follows is a consideration of the most fundamental elements of the persuasive cartography apparatus, followed by a close reading of revisionist maps in which they are deployed.

In order to render the three-dimensional curve of the earth's surface in two dimensions, the mapmaker must make use of a mathematical cartographic projection. This process always leads to relative distortions of territorial size and shape; different projections will render different distortions, and thus can be chosen to support various spatial arguments (the Mercator projection, for example, is well known for having exaggerated the size of the Soviet Union in Cold War mappings of "the Russian menace" [Ager 1977, 4]). Choices made in framing the depicted region can also present strong visual arguments. While the central position on a map generally privileges a certain point of view (a criticism leveled at Eurocentric maps—those depicting Europe as the center of the world—in school textbooks), there were also reasons to favor other locations. A position left of center, for example, was frequently chosen in order to conceptually emphasize Germany's location in *Western* Europe.

Obviously unable to represent all of the multitudinous objects and features present in any given landscape, the cartographer then makes crucial, strategic decisions about what to include on—and *what to exclude from*—the map. These inclusions and exclusions inscribe "realities" upon the space represented and construct understandings and expectations of the social practices that take place there.[2] Revisionist maps, for example, frequently used bold colors to depict the distribution of ethnic Germans in the contested territories, while failing to indicate the presence of Poles in these regions.

Another effective means of cartographically "erasing" the Polish population involved strategies of shading and coloration. The practice whereby regions are demarcated and distinguished from each other via contrastive coloring is standard in cartography, frequently employed to visually organize political maps (where each country or state is shaded a different color). Topographical maps, meanwhile, deploy a more nuanced version of this code. Typically, a finite set of colors is used to represent altitudinal strata, where brown, for example, might indicate elevations from 500 to 1,000 feet. Within the region shaded brown, all difference is eliminated: whether an area is 500 feet, 700 feet, or 900 feet, it appears brown on the map. This homogenizing tactic was often used to depict population distributions. If a particular map uses red to indicate that a region is inhabited 30 to 60 percent by Germans, a homogenous pool of this color could easily cover up the fact that large stretches of the territory in question contained populations that were 70 percent Polish.

Within the space created by the borders of the map, the meaning of any sign must be negotiated by the reader with respect to its location. Suddenly, words themselves become spatialized signs serving multiple functions: the proper noun "The Alps" may thus indicate the name of a mountain range, while its letters are contorted to also indicate the territorial coverage of this geographical feature. The spatialized word hereby assumes an analogic character similar to that found in concrete poetry. Pictorial images located in the space of the map must also be read with an awareness of the meanings they attribute through such analogic argumentation. In the maps examined below, the deployment of visual graphics was particularly pronounced as the revisionists fought to communicate a German identity to the contested territories through visual means of suggestion.[3]

Having suffered defeat in many of its colonies soon after the outbreak of the war, the Germans were anticipating some degree of colonial loss. They were not prepared, however, for the complete dispossession outlined in the Versailles Treaty, when the Allies stripped Germany of all of its colonies in Africa, Asia, and the Pacific. In justifying this decision, the Allies gave account of reported atrocities perpetrated by the Germans in their colonies, emphasizing the tragic fate of the Herero tribe (which had been decimated by the Germans in a genocidal war earlier in the century), as well as various forms of forced labor and seizures of tribal property. Such severe mistreatment of the natives, the Allies argued, proved that Germans were unfit to participate in the esteemed European mission of bringing civilization and progress to the rest of the world.

This series of accusations dealt the nation a strong psychological blow, but the loss of large territorial regions in Europe was arguably more traumatic for the German nation, its financial and social ramifications far exceeding those arising from the overseas dispossessions. With the surrender of Alsace-Lorraine to France, stretches of Schleswig to Denmark, and—most important for my discussion here—the ceding of Posen and large portions of West Prussia to the newly reinstated Polish state, Germany lost some 13 percent of its previous European territorial expanse. This loss of land also resulted in an enormous loss of inhabitants—approximately 6.5 million, including 3.5 million identified as ethnic Germans (Tiessen 1924).[4] More than 700,000 of these Germans, suddenly finding themselves reduced to a minority group in Poland, would flee to assumed safety within the reduced borders of their own country (Bessel 1993, 224).[5]

The lost eastern territories had been the landscape of German *Ostkolonisation* ("eastward colonization") in the late medieval period, had been annexed by Prussia in the Polish Partitions of the late eighteenth century, and had most recently been the target of Bismarck's *Innerkolonisation* ("internal colonization") campaign to strengthen German presence and control in the predominantly Polish region. Now, the loss of this territory came to be depicted as a wound in the body of the nation, a wound that metonymically represented the traumatic loss of German space both in Europe and overseas—and a wound whose refusal to heal would later feed the National Socialist desire to "regain" Poland.

Although proponents of colonial expansion overseas and *Innerkoloni-sation* in the Prussian East had only seldom found common ground for cooperation in the prewar period, they now found it advantageous to conceptually link their two projects in pressing for revisions of the Versailles Treaty. According to their new logic, Germany's long history of successful colonization in Eastern Europe provided the moral justification not only for the return of the lost Polish territories to Germany but also for the return of its overseas colonies. Germans should be readmitted as equal partners in the European colonial mission, because their nation could demonstrate a history of colonization as long, rich, and successful as that of its European counterparts—a history Germans depicted as one in which a primitive, barbaric Polish East had been transformed into organized, fertile, and civilized European space as the result of successful German colonial *Kulturarbeit* ("cultural labor").

For the continental revisionists, this strategy had the benefit of privileging the category of *space* over that of *race* in the East, thereby marginalizing considerations of the ethnic makeup of the populations inhabiting this space. This allowed them to conveniently ignore the problematic issue of regional population statistics, as these clearly demonstrated overwhelming Slavic majorities in the contested areas (Herb 1997, 13–45).

In 1925, the geopolitician Albrecht Penck provided a pseudoscientific conceptual model of German space that gained broad currency in the popular discourse of the interwar period. Penck argued the existence of both *Deutscher Volks-und Kulturboden* ("land of the German Volk" and "land of German culture"). While *Volksboden* denoted areas then dominated by German-speaking Germans, *Kulturboden* referred to territory no longer under German control, and not even necessarily inhabited by Germans, but exhibiting traces of past German cultural labor. Penck claimed that such German intervention was recognizable in the orderly organization of crop fields into straight rows, as well as in the presence of farmhouses that were sturdily built and *behaglich* ("comfortable, cozy") (Penck 1925, 64). Germans, according to Penck, could lay claim to regions exhibiting such agricultural and architectural characteristics, for this land had only been uplifted from the depths of Slavic barbarism due to the strong force of German civilizational engagement. The ideological connections to European colonial discourse are not accidental.

With the intent of intensifying and naturalizing the validity of this auspicious spatial construction among their fellow populace, German revisionists unleashed a concerted propaganda campaign. They wanted Germans to imagine the space of their nation in a very specific way, as a landscape created and defined by German cultural practice, as a territory which, so understood, naturally and inherently exceeded the artificial and arbitrary borders of the *Stumpfnation* ("the amputated nation"). In this campaign, the collective spatial imagination of Germany was at stake, and the new genre of "persuasive maps" was developed as a primary instrument of public influence.

School textbooks were the first targets. Here, the goal was to naturalize the validity of the prewar German borders, in order to maintain an identification with this particular silhouette among the nation's youth (Herb 1997, 101). The Twentieth Convention of German Geographers agreed in 1921 that the outline of the former border must be indicated on every map, advocating "that only those works for which this is the case be used for instruction in all school grades" (Herb 1997, 79).[6]

Meanwhile, schoolchildren were being educated to respect the strong science reflected in these textbooks. An educational film from 1928 entitled *Karten und Kartographie* (Maps and cartography) follows all the stages of cartographic production from statistical land surveying to the final color printing of the maps. Not only is strict precision and scientific objectivity stressed, but perhaps above all, the progressive, almost autonomous nature of the technology involved is emphasized. We see enormous, complex machines deployed in the etching of cartographic plates, serious men in white lab coats, and animated film segments reviewing critical geometric principles. The maps in the school atlas, the final product presented to the viewer at the end of the film—and replicated on the student's own desk—are thus rendered highly scientific. These are not texts whose legitimacy is to be questioned; they are instead rationalized products of the most modern technologies.

The student was thereby educated to accept maps as "mirrors of nature," and this apparatus of authority was mobilized in the validation of the prewar German border. The repetitive encounter with this border outline constructs what Benedict Anderson terms the "map-as-logo" (Anderson 1983, 175). Identified so strongly with a particular shape, the "logo-map" takes on the autonomous character of a piece in a jigsaw puzzle, wholly detachable from its geographic context, and *fundamentally immutable in its shape*.

In the popular *Diercke Schulatlas für höhere Lehranstalten* (Diercke School Atlas) of 1928 (ten years after the end of the war!) we find that the prewar German border has been inscribed in blood red onto an otherwise pastel-colored map (*Diercke Schulatlas für höhere Lehranstalten*, 68–69). Where other borders are indicated in the standard black of cartographic convention, this anomalous choice of color carries specific connotative meaning. Etched in red, this border becomes the bloody site of national struggle, the open wound that refuses to heal.

The agenda, then, of the geopolitician was to take this immutable shape, this analogic representation of the spatially conceived nation, and to fill it with emotional identity and persuasive meaning. Their task was to deliver an immediately comprehensible, provocative message—one that insisted upon the dual nature of this space as German *Volks-und Kulturboden*—and they could deploy a variety of media in doing so. In interrogating the rhetorical strategies of persuasive, geopolitical maps, I build on Jürgen E. Müller's understanding of the *Medientext*, as a site in which meaning is created in the fusion and interaction of multiple media, and in the multiplicity of reading practices that they simultaneously evoke. "Reading" such texts necessitates a contextualization sensitive to both historical discourses as well as the social function of genre. The geopolitical map would have been read at the conjuncture of scientific authority and politics. Some of these maps restricted themselves to the traditional conventions for cartographic symbols, scale and projection, and thus would have mobilized a greater degree of scientific authority. However, the geopolitical map frequently also made use of photographs, paintings, sketches, diagrams, et cetera—elements not admissible within the field of scientific cartography. These geopolitical maps thus functioned in a completely different way: by importing visual images into an otherwise sparsely delineated cartographic frame, the message of the medial import, both denotative and connotative, was mapped onto the region in question. This geographic space was thus inscribed with new meaning.

I take here several examples from Paul Kuntze's *Volksbuch unserer Kolonien* (The German Volk's Colonial Reader), an extremely popular history of German colonialism first published in 1938, with a second, reedited version appearing four years later. Emphasizing the cooperation between overseas and continental revisionists, this book on German overseas colonization opens with a rather lengthy section depicting a successful history of German colonization in Eastern Europe.

The map of "Die Ostkolonisation der Deutschen Ritterorden" (The eastern colonization of the German Teutonic knights) (Kuntze 1938, plate 2) is a highly complex, intermedial text (see fig. 13.1). It first orients the viewer with a recognizable outline of northern Europe, Scandinavia, and the Baltic region, and then separates this space into two distinct categories. Land is unambiguously marked as either black or white by means of a digital code frequently deployed in cartography, allowing the map to reduce and homogenize this geographic region under the meaning of one sign. Thus, within regions where black indicates Teutonic colonization, differences are erased: there is no perceivable variation in the level of Germanic presence, the density of its population, or the duration of its control. Instead, Teutonic control appears

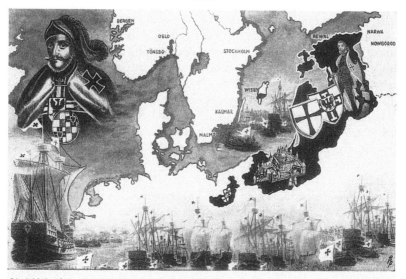

Die Ostkolonisation der Deutschen Ritterorden. Links Ulrich von Jungingen, rechts ein Schwertritter. Neben den Wappenschildern die Marienburg. Die Seebilder stellen die Seeschlacht des Deutschen Ritterordens vor Wisby dar

Figure 13.1. Die Ostkolonisation der Deutschen Ritterorden [The eastern colonization of the Teutonic knights].
Reprinted from Paul H. Kuntze, *Das Volksbuch unserer Kolonien*. Leipzig: Georg Dollheimer, 1938. Plate 2.

statically timeless, well defined in its area of coverage, unchallenged, and absolute. Three symbols are mapped onto this homogenized space reinforcing the singular meaning of Teutonic domination: the Marienburg demonstratively bridges both halves of Prussia (which was divided by the Polish Corridor in the postwar period!), while the shields and the image of the knight serve to maintain the visual density of the Teutonic sign throughout the region. Meanwhile, history and meaning are washed from the remainder of the European continent, which now serves as the blank projection screen for a soft-gray memory-scape of Germanic naval grandeur.

In addition to pictorial images and symbols, the geopolitical map often deployed the spatialized printed word, mobilizing the visual function enabled by the space created by the map. While such analogic denotation was common cartographic practice, it is strategically manipulated in the map entitled "Die Lebensräume des Deutschen Volkes" (The living spaces of the German Volk) (Kuntze 1938, 9). Here, the words "Deutsches Reich" are meant to analogically indicate the east-

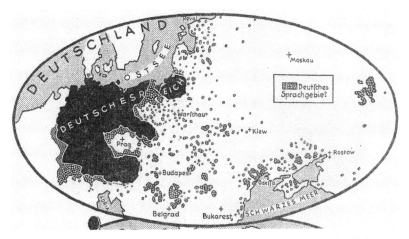

Figure 13.2. Die Lebensräume des deutschen Volkes [The living
spaces of the German Volk].
Reprinted from Paul H. Kuntze, *Das Volksbuch unserer Kolonien.*
Leipzig: Georg Dollheimer, 1938, 9.

west expanse of the German nation (see fig. 13.2). Here, however, rules
of morphology are broken, strongly suggesting an analogous geographical violation. The spatial wedge so awkwardly dividing the word "Reich"
thus seems to indicate the unnatural separation of the territory this
word labels.

Most maps we encounter—including those here under consideration—
do not exist for and of themselves, but are incorporated into larger textual frames, usually books, textbooks, and atlases, but also propaganda
posters, documentary films, and advertising pamphlets. This additional
layer of inter-mediality is best shown in one final map from the colonial
Volksbuch, which also highlights the map's ability to present and manipulate a narrative of change through time.

The map of *Die deutsche Ostkolonisation* (The German colonization
of the east) (see fig. 13.3) is comprised of five main elements (Kuntze
1938, 10). Moving from the west to the east, there are three labeled
territorial categories: a solid black *Volksgebiet* ("region of the Volk"),
a shaded *Kulturboden* ("land of German culture"), encircled areas of
"scattered German settlement," and a line indicating the extent of
German Law in the medieval period. The map thus offers a tiered system represented by progressive shades of black mapped onto a white
emptiness. The fifth element, the arrows, serves to connect and frame
these spaces.

A key feature indicating narrativity, as defined by the literary theorist

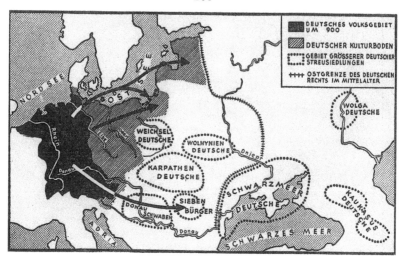

Figure 13.3. Die deutsche Ostkolonisation [The German colonization of the east].
Reprinted from Paul H. Kuntze, *Das Volksbuch unserer Kolonien*.
Leipzig: Georg Dollheimer, 1938, 10.

Gérard Genette, is the transformation of a given situation from its original state.[7] Within the space of the map, the capability for such narrativity is introduced by the symbol of the arrow. Through an indication of movement, the arrow claims a "before" and an "after"—a transformation.

The arrow is thought to have made its first appearances in strategic military cartography as well as in depictions of the tribal migrations, but later it became a standard feature of postwar geopolitical maps, particularly in response to Karl Haushofer's 1922 programmatic article "Die suggestive Karte" (The suggestive map) in which he called for the development of dynamic visual symbols that could be deployed in maps in order to enable them to deliver strong political messages.

The arrow is a powerful tool, for it, like the spatialized word, can be analogically modified to add various connotations to its meaning. Do straight, wide, bold swashes suggest quick, massive action? Or do thin lines, doubling back upon themselves, indicate frustration, hesitation, and defeat?

This map of German colonization of the East reveals only the steady, forward movement of what we will presume to be Germans migrating—or colonizing—eastward. This is not a narrative of trial and error, of advancement and retreat, nor of a singular massive bombardment, but of unhesitating, incessant eastward flow. The arrows reach around the claimed eastern territory, forming a visually organizing, encompassing frame—a frame left provocatively open on its eastern end.

The author of this map creatively modified these arrows, adapting their color to embed their origins deep within the center of the *Volksgebiet*. It is therefore not marginal, displaced Germans who are being represented, but *Kerndeutsche* ("true Germans") from the Heartland, where the Rhine and Danube serve as the inexhaustible spring from which this eastward flow originates.

Identified and dated in the legend as "Volksgebiet um 900," this solid black, homogenized region extends provocatively far to the west of the Rhine, where the map insists upon a strict—and *unchanging*—black and white territorial distinction. There is no ambiguity, no transitional or overlapping space at the French border in the west.

Meanwhile, the blackness seeps eastward, resulting in a large gray region identified as "Deutscher Kulturboden." This is undated in the legend, and upon logical consideration, extremely perplexing. Recalling that Penck's term was understood to refer to land currently displaying signs of *past* German cultural influence, but *no longer* controlled by a German majority presence, how are we meant to understand this region on the map? As land already left behind by the Germans in 900? As land which would become marked by German culture after 900? Perhaps—as *Kulturboden* in 1938?

The third territorial category maintains this temporal ambiguity. Large encircled areas are meant to indicate an unspecified density of "scattered German settlement." But are we to understand that the Volga Germans were already in Russia in 900? Shortly thereafter? Even a biased interwar history of *Ostkolonisation* hesitates to speak of any German settlement in this area prior to the mid-sixteenth century (Kötzschke and Ebert 1937, 149–155), and current accounts maintain that German communities did not appear in this region prior to the 1760s (Dralle 1991, 134–147).

In this map, German cultural presence is visually stamped onto territory otherwise depicted as empty. While German agency is represented by unhesitating arrows and progressive densities of black, the indigenous Slavs are rendered invisible. They are present only as landscape—and thus rendered synonymous with the natural raw material upon which German will has been exercised. The geopolitical map emerges as a distinctly colonial text.

And it is a colonial text conspicuously manipulative of cartographic conventions of the temporal code. For this map conflates several centuries into one image, suspending them in a simultaneity that historically never existed. The narration records a series of territorial additions (while omitting losses, setbacks, and defeats), thereby constructing an expansive—and *expanding*—mental map of the German nation.

Placed back within the textual context from which this map is taken, text and visual image interact to produce a more highly disciplined meaning. For the surrounding text sets the semantic frame within which the visual image is to be approached, while the map spatially locates and referentializes the import of the text:

> Arguably, the most important colonization, even if it didn't go overseas, is represented by the German colonization to the northeast and the southeast in the early medieval period. Here, the Germans seized control of the eastern lands they had abandoned during the great migrations, while also regaining the ancient German seacoast. In this eastern territory the future great states of Austria and Prussia, the creators of German history in the modern period, came into being [*entstanden*]. Without this colonization, without the fresh energies that accumulated here [*die sich hier bildenden Kräfte*], the growth [*heranwachsen*] of Germany to its current greatness, unity, and culture would never have been possible. Let us also think to the future! (Kuntze 1938, 9–10)[8]

In this text, land colonized in the east becomes the new originating source of an organically conceived German nation. The semantic resonances of *entstehen, heranwachsen,* and *sich bildende Kräfte* additively inscribe a natural inherency upon the narrative depicted on the map. Reading this text, the arrows come to resemble the naturally spreading roots of a healthy national organism.

A close observation of each of the final sentences in this textual frame reveals a temporal conflation paralleling that depicted on the map. In a repetition of text-internal, temporal deictic shifts originating in the past and extending into the present, actions which began in various moments of the past are discursively drawn into the text's present. The result is not merely a sense of continuity, but of a temporally flattened *simultaneity.*

In this intermedial *Medientext,* the visual image and linguistic text interact, mutually enhancing their rhetorical power. Delivering similar messages in different codes, these media reinforce the validity of the imagination of German space they attempt to convey. Glancing back to the map, we are left with the final moral imperative of this intermedial text—the necessity of national rejuvenation in eastward expansion.

In the year following the first publication of Paul Kuntze's *Volksbuch unserer Kolonien,* the contested Polish territories would become the stage for that act of military aggression marking the beginning of World War II. Revisionist cartographers could claim a certain degree of success, for the German ethnic-national identity that they had worked so diligently to inscribe upon the space of the East was now leading to its logical conclusion—forceful political incorporation into the German state. Both German enthusiasm for this annexation as well as the world's apathetic response to it were conditioned by the cartographic construction of legitimate German "place."

Notes

1. This article is a reworking of a paper originally presented at the German Studies Association convention in October 2000. I would like to thank the members of the Berkeley-Tübingen-Vienna research collaboration for German and Austrian cultural studies, and particularly Klaus Müller-Richter, who strongly supported my work on this project.

2. Consider, for example, the current Falk-Plan of Berlin, one of the most widely sold street maps of the city. Here, one finds that iconic symbols are used to prominently mark the location of churches, but not of synagogues (which are located only by name on the map, where the fine black lettering used blends in with that of the surrounding street names). Meanwhile, every McDonald's fast-food outlet is indicated, but not those stands selling German bratwurst or Turkish dönerkebabs. This map is hereby making significant arguments, inscribing certain social meanings upon our understandings of the city: in Berlin—as mediated to us by the Falk-Plan—churches are institutionalized parts of the landscape; they have been rendered equivalent in status to schools, hospitals, and post offices by the use of visually comparable symbols. Synagogues, meanwhile, are ascribed to some different degree or category of importance through the lack of such a visual marker. And even if the map's reader doggedly avoids all American fast food while in Berlin, the map still silently communicates to him or her a greater sense of reliability and permanence of the McDonald's chain than of those local equivalents which were somehow not worth representing.

3. The deployment of pictorial images in postwar persuasive cartography represented a return to the aesthetic of the Baroque period, when portraits, cartouches, and vignettes were widely used on maps to assert territorial dominion (see Brancaforte 2001).

4. Germans identified through language statistics.

5. See also Roos 1966, 54. According to Roos, the 1910 census figures list 1,080,000 Germans in the ceded Polish territories, with only 335,000 remaining after these regions were incorporated into the Polish state.

6. This is Herb's translation of the *Verhandlungen des 20. Deutschen Geographentages zu Leipzig, vom 17. bis 19. Mai 1921*. Berlin: Dietrich Reimer, 1922.

7. Gérard Genette, *Narrative Discourse Revisited*, trans. Jane E. Lewin (Ithaca, N.Y.: Cornell University Press, 1988), 19.

8. Wohl die bedeutendste Kolonisation überhaupt, wenn sie auch nicht über See ging, stellt die deutsche Nordost-und Südostkolonisation des frühen Mittelalters dar. In ihr ergriffen die Deutschen wieder von den in der Völkerwanderung verlassenen Osträumen Besitz und erwarben die uralte germanische Seeküste wieder zurück. In diesem Ostraume entstanden die späteren großen Staaten Österreich und Preußen, die Gestalter der deutschen Geschichte neuerer Zeit. Ohne diese Kolonisation, ohne die frischen Kräfte, die sich hier bildeten, wäre das Heranwachsen Deutschlands zu seiner heutigen Größe, Einheit und Kultur gar nicht möglich gewesen. Denken auch wir an die Zukunft!

Works Cited

Ager, John. "Maps & Propaganda." *Bulletin of the Society of University Cartographers* 11, no. 1 (1977): 1-15.

Anderson, Benedict. *Imagined Communities: Reflections on the Origin and Spread of Nationalism*. London: Verso, 1983.

Bessel, Richard. *Germany after the First World War*. New York: Oxford University Press, 1993.

Brancaforte, Elio Christoph. "Reading Word and Image: Representations of Safavid Persia in the Maps and Frontispieces of Adam Olearius (ca. 1650)." Ph.D. diss., Harvard University, 2001.

Diercke Schulatlas für höhere Lehranstalten. Braunschweig: Westermann, 1928.

Dralle, Lothar. *Die Deutschen in Ostmittel-und Osteuropa*, 134-147. Darmstadt: Wissenschaftliche Buchgesellschaft, 1991.

Harley, J. B. "Deconstructing the Map." In *Writing Worlds: Discourse, Texts, and Metaphors in the Representation of Landscape*, ed. Trevor J. Barnes and James S. Duncan, 231-247. London: Routledge, 1992.

———. "Maps, Knowledge, and Power." In *The Iconography of Landscape: Essays on the Symbolic Representation, Design and Use of Past Environments*, 277-312, ed. Denis Cosgrove and Stephen Daniels. New York and Cambridge: Cambridge University Press, 1988.

Haushofer, Karl. "Die suggestive Karte." *Grenzboten* 81 (1922): 17-19.

Herb, Guntram Henrik. *Under the Map of Germany: Nationalism and Propaganda 1918–1945*. London: Routledge, 1997.

Kötzschke, Rudolf, and Wolfgang Ebert. *Geschichte der ostdeutschen Kolonisation*, 149-155. Leipzig: Bibliographisches Institut, 1937.

Kuntze, Paul H. *Das Volksbuch unserer Kolonien*. Leipzig: Dollheimer, 1938.

Müller, Jürgen E. *Intermedialitat: Formen moderner kultureller Kommunikation.* Munster: Nodus Publikationen, 1996.

Penck, Albrecht. "Deutscher Volks-und Kulturboden." In *Volk unter Völkern, Bücher des Deutschtums 1,* ed. Karl C. von Loesch and A. H. Ziegfeld, 62–73. Breslau: Hirt, 1925.

Pickles, John. "Texts, Hermeneutics and Propaganda Maps." In *Writing Worlds: Discourses, Texts, and Metaphors in the Representation of Landscape,* ed. Trevor J. Barnes and James S. Duncan, 193–230. London: Routledge, 1992.

Robinson, Arthur H., and Barbara Bartz Petchenik. *The Nature of Maps: Essays toward Understanding Maps and Mapping.* Chicago: University of Chicago Press, 1976.

Roos, Hans. *A History of Modern Poland: From the Foundation of the State in the First World War to the Present Day.* 1961. Reprint. Trans. J. R. Foster. New York: Knopf, 1966.

Tiessen, Ernst. "Der Friedensvertrag von Versailles und die politische Geographie." *Zeitschrift für Geopolitik* 4 (April 1924): 203–220.

14

Face/Off

Hitler and Weimar Political Photography

Lutz Koepnick

In, or shortly before, August 1927 Heinrich Hoffmann took six famous photographs of Adolf Hitler showing the future dictator in rhetorical poses. The initial purposes of these six shots, it has been suggested, was didactic. They were intended to serve Hitler as a mirror image, allowing the aspiring demagogue to improve his physical self-presentation. Not before long, however, these six images were also supplemented with electrifying captions and disseminated as postcards in order to reach the widest audience possible. In addition, they appeared in various illustrated photojournalistic tabloids, new journalistic venues that enjoyed unprecedented popularity in Weimar Germany particularly during the second half of the 1920s (Gidal 1972; Weise 1997).

Five of Hoffmann's six images show Hitler in medium shots in front of a black studio background, his body and face slightly turning away from the camera. In all of these shots, Hitler's hands probe different gestural possibilities while his arms define a volatile force field of dramatic action. In one picture, Hitler's right arm stretches all the way out to the corner of the frame. Twice we witness Hitler turning the palms of his hands upside down so as to ask rhetorical questions and reject commonplace answers. In yet another picture, Hitler's left hand forms a fist as if to pound his message home, and in picture five his right hand points toward the camera in an effort to enforce the channels of communication.

In all five of these photographs Hitler's body wants to be its own message. What we see is Hitler trying to boost the cause of the nation by presenting his body as a rhetorical instrument of signification. What

we see is a body that wants to speak, to articulate matters more effectively, persuasively, and loudly than verbal expressions could ever do. All
five images present Hitler as a man of steadfast resolve and uncompromising determination; a man shaping chaos into order and instilling the
ordinary with charismatic power; a man who is pure energy and whose
will therefore should and always will triumph over what meets his eyes.

Picture six adds another tone to Hitler's exercises in political body
language. Hitler here not only bends forward and turns closer toward
the camera but also the index finger of his right hand seems to directly
address the camera, reaching out to us through the frame or luring us
into the image in order to join his cause. Hitler's countenance and eyes,
on the other hand, take on the outlook of a shifty seducer. Unlike images one through five, picture six can barely be seen as an image asking
the viewer to place his or her life in Hitler's hands. Who, after all, would
ever trust a man who uses his body as a blatant instrument of seduction
and aggression? Who could ever be inspired by a man who desires to
play on our emotions the way others play the keys of a piano?

At first there are good reasons to assume that image six tells the
truth about what we can see and, more importantly, what might be hidden in the other images of the 1927 series. This at least must have been
Charlie Chaplin's impression when he encountered Hoffmann's series
for the first time in the early 1930s and simply understood these pictures as evidence of Nazi madness. In his autobiography Chaplin recalled: "I could not take Hitler seriously. Each postcard showed a different posture of him: one with his hands clawlike, haranguing the
crowds, another with one arm up and the other down, like a cricketer
about to bowl, and another with hands clenched in front of him as
though lifting an imaginary dumbbell. The salute with the hand thrown
back over the shoulder, the palm upward, made me want to put a tray of
dirty dishes on it. 'This is a nut!' I thought" (Chaplin 1964, 319–320).
In Chaplin's view, Hoffmann's six images portrayed Hitler as a ridiculous creature void of taste, tact, and self-control. Hitler here came out
as a man of excessive affects and unrestrained expressiveness, a man
lacking self-reflection and therefore lacking what makes humans human, namely language and articulation. All rhetoric, Hitler's body in
these six pictures—we could extend Chaplin's impression—preceded,
transcended, or eliminated rhetoric altogether.

The task of this essay is to argue against this kind of intuitive reading, not to downplay the ruthlessness of Nazi politics, but on the contrary to achieve a more complex understanding of how Hitler's movement employed photography in the 1920s to proliferate its political
agenda. To ridicule these images as a self-revelatory freak-show misses

the point. Their whole ambition was to obliterate the very possibility of the ridiculous. Hoffmann's camera in these six images, I suggest, aspired to define the political as a self-referential space of ongoing motion in which mesmerizing surface designs, strategic self-performances, and desensitized forms of seeing undid the legacies of bourgeois culture and public debate. This camera sought nothing less than to eliminate the structuring binarisms of bourgeois life, such as interiority versus exteriority, authenticity versus dissimulation, truth versus lie. While much of this essay will be devoted to discussing the formal strategies involved in achieving this objective, the following pages will not seek to unmoor Hoffmann's six images from their historical foundation and hence obscure the rich historical milieu—the interplay of photographic discourses and practices—from which Hoffmann's work with Hitler emerged. On the contrary, what I call Hoffmann's metaphoric system of the camera is best understood as one of many responses to the challenges of Weimar politics and visual culture, and it is only by reconstructing this system's historical context that we can fully understand its political dimensions.

In late 1919, the *Berliner Illustrierte Zeitung* (BIZ) propagated photography as an emphatically modern interface between the public and the private, the dangerous and the trite: "The photographer travels the world for you, bringing it closer to you. He stands at the crater's edge as the volcano erupts, negotiates the rapids of the Niagara, climbs to the very tip of skyscrapers, flies in an airplane over the Himalayas, comes under fire in the trenches, and braves shoot-outs between the Spartakists and the government troops. . . . So make way for the photographer! Open all roads and doors to him!" (quoted in Weise 1997, 60). Less than a decade later, many of these programmatic visions had become the order of the day. Weimar culture indeed made way for photographers, their public success resting in no small way on remarkable breakthroughs in camera technology and reproduction techniques in the mid-1920s. The introduction of the first lightweight 35-mm camera in 1925 revolutionized the way the photographic medium could capture moving objects in imperfectly lit surroundings. Leica "Model I" and Ernemann "Ermanox" cameras emancipated the photographer from changing negative plates after every shot and handling unwieldy tripods. The act of taking a picture thus gained significantly in flexibility, as much as it could turn much more effectively the transient, ephemeral, or dangerous into lasting impressions. Empowered by the advent of new equipment, photographers were thus able to approach the volcanoes of public and private life in novel ways and to feed the rapidly expanding hunger of Weimar's tabloid press.

Due to the extensive use of photographic images during World War I, photography in the immediate postwar era was often closely associated with the war experience (Hüppauf 1993). The spread of lightweight cameras clearly reinforced this kind of thinking; their arrival invigorated in particular right-wing theorists such as Ernst Jünger in their effort to link photography to the understanding of modern society as a warlike horizon of total mobilization. Unlike previous photographic equipment, 35-mm Leicas and Ernemanns offered Weimar photographers an unprecedented means of coupling images of speed and collective mobility with post-liberal strategies of visualizing power and displaying social stratification. Lightweight cameras captured stunning pictures of urban masses and flying airplanes, of car races and dangerous encounters. As importantly, however, their very technological design as well as the sheer flood of pictures they produced for Weimar tabloids were welcomed as powerful testimony to the ways in which World War I had changed social relationships and reconfigured dominant modes of visual perception.

In what follows, I read Hofmann's 1927 images of Adolf Hitler as a symptomatic event actively embedded in Weimar discourses on total mobilization and photographic reproduction, discourses in which the image of modern warfare served as a blueprint for new perceptual realities and modes of cultural address. This reading will have considerable consequences for our understanding not only of Hitler's oratorical qualities but also of the role of the body, of somatic expressiveness, and of the nexus between motion and emotion in Nazi mass politics. Far from invoking antimodern valorizations of emotional over rationalistic modes of social integration, Hoffmann's camera engages that which Ernst Jünger in 1930 called the "modern type," metallized body machine whose "gaze is calm and fixed, trained to observe objects which are grasped in conditions of high speed" (Jünger 1981, 126).[1] Hitler's body in Hoffmann's images is a self-alienated body for which experiences of photographic self-objectification and the presence of prosthetic eyes, of lightweight cameras capturing fast-paced movements, are about to become the norm. Hoffmann's images thus mark what I consider a crucial turning point in Nazi politics during which the agitator Hitler embraced what Helmut Lethen has called Weimar's peculiar codes of cold conduct and detached self-stylization. In contrast to Hitler's earlier use of the photographic medium, Hoffmann's images enlist strategies of artificial self-realization, of protective performance and distanciating masquerade, for the sake of mobilizing the nation. Vis-à-vis the artificial eye of Hoffmann's camera, Hitler in these six images of 1927 emerges as a shrewd political actor who aspires to conquer the

Weimar public sphere as a sphere of impersonal and socially distant interaction.

Voice/Image

Briefly after his first meeting with Adolf Hitler in 1922, Heinrich Hoffmann photographed a Nazi rally at the Circus Krone in Munich. This 1923 image shows the building's interior, bathed in dramatic chiaroscuro effects and packed with hundreds of mostly male listeners, directly facing the camera. Spotlights illuminate the crowd from above as it appropriates this space of entertainment for the purpose of political bonding. What we see, however, is not an ecstatic crowd, or a crowd of intoxicated onlookers beside themselves in the face of the prophetic appearance of a political leader. Instead, what we see is a community of solemn listeners, standing shoulder to shoulder, completely focused on that which is withheld from our own gaze. What we see is an assembly of people too immersed in what they hear in order to engage in any kind of lateral interaction. The crowd in Hoffmann's images is an immensely silent crowd, silenced by what is ghostly present only in a handwritten caption in the picture's upper left corner: "Hitler is Speaking!"

Later circulated as a propaganda postcard, Hoffmann's 1923 image invited the Munich crowd to see itself through the eyes of both their ambitious political leader and the photographer's camera. It is thus difficult to think of any other photograph, political in nature or not, which would define the off-frame as a more salient and projective space than this particular picture does.[2] Animated by what remains invisible, Hoffmann's "Hitler is Speaking!" urged the viewer to imagine and inhabit the emptiness on the other side of the camera. As importantly, however, Hoffmann's image, by trying to visualize Hitler's charisma as a sonic event, emulated modernist aesthetic strategies that sought to re-inscribe synaesthetic forms of perception. Hoffmann's image captured sound as image. It displayed the visible as an allegory of invisible sound waves in the hope of transporting the auratic voice of Hitler to distant onlookers.

We should not mistake Hoffmann's visual strategies in "Hitler is Speaking!" though, for some kind of modernist aesthetic experiment. After all, it simply followed Hitler's own early conception of charismatic leadership, his specific ways of employing his body to appeal to his followers. As is well known, Hitler started out his political career between 1919 and 1923 as a sly agitator whose trademark was his voice, not his appearance. Eager to revive a nation that had lost face due to the Versailles Treaty, Hitler fashioned himself as the inner voice of the

German conscience (Schmöller 2000, 50–54). Acoustical properties—the rhythm of speech, the guttural registers of his vocal organ—were meant to produce a redemptive experience of community and self-presence. Hitler at the same time largely rejected any attempt to circulate photographic portraits of him among the public (Hoffmann 1955, 42). This camera shyness no doubt reflected juridical exigencies resulting from the fact that Hitler at various moments during the early 1920s was subject to police investigations and searches. But there are also good reasons to assume that Hitler resisted cameras because of his strategic fear that photographic images, due to their origin in mechanical reproduction, could dispel the magnetism he was eager to develop in his performances as a speaker. Although photographic images in later years would play an essential role in engineering the "Hitler myth" (Herz 1994; Kershaw 1987), in the eyes of Hitler the agitator of the early 1920s mass-circulating images potentially thwarted his self-invention as a charismatic leader whose sonic presence could shape new communities. Hitler's voice coupled emotion to motion; the spaces it filled were experienced or presented as spaces of becoming and self-transformation. When fixed in the form of a photographic representation, Hitler's sight by contrast potentially thwarted the transformative powers of his vocal appearances. Photographic images replaced becoming with being, presence with absence, immediacy with mediation. As a consequence, Hitler's image—and so the apparent rationale of Hitler's early campaign style—had to be protected from cameras and mass reproduction so as to warrant the Führer's most valuable property, the aura of his voice.

As I shall argue in the following pages, worlds lie between Hoffmann's image of 1923 and his six photographs of 1927 in terms of their negotiation of the relationship between frame and off-frame, between voice and body, between visual pleasure and political mobilization. Whereas Hoffmann's camera in 1923 hid Hitler's body from sight, in 1927 it tried to put it up as a preview of coming attractions. Whereas the image of 1923 staged a stunning dialectic of presence and absence so as to convey the unmediated intensity of Hitler's voice, the 1927 series sought to locate Hitler's charisma in the visual language of his body. In the 1923 image, the crowd in front of the camera figured as an anagram of Hitler's voice and invisible body; the 1927 series, by contrast, viewed speech and orality as occasions to stage Hitler's corporeal appearance as spectacle. I will have more to say shortly about how Hoffmann's photograph of 1923 and his series of 1927, respectively, evidence fundamentally different concepts of photographic temporality and address, of representing time, motion, and memory within the frame of a photographic reproduction. First, however, I want to discuss some of the crucial differences between these sets of images in terms of what Weimar sociologist and philosopher Helmuth Plessner—one of the key witnesses in Lethen's study of cold conduct during the Weimar era—in 1924 theorized as the dialectic of becoming and being, of our inclination for reality versus our desire for illusion. It is against the background of Plessner's contemporaneous political anthropology, that is, Plessner's reflections on artificiality, self-restraint, ritualized behavior, and the limits of community, that the chasm between Hitler and Hoffmann's politics of charisma in 1923 and 1927 becomes the clearest.

Face/Mask

Outlined in the 1924 treatise *The Limits of Community,* Plessner's anthropology considered human psychology as inextricably caught between conflicting drives, one toward being, reality, and identity, toward being fixed and determined, and one toward becoming and ongoing self-redress, away from fixation and the imperatives of public self-disclosure: "We want ourselves to be seen and to have been seen as we are; and we want just as much to veil ourselves and remain unknown, for behind every determination of our being lies dormant the unspoken possibility of being different. Out of this ontological ambiguity arises with iron necessity two fundamental forces of psychological life: the impetus to disclosure—the need for validity; and the impetus to restraint—the need for modesty" (Plessner 1999, 109). Torn between our desire for visible form and our wish to escape visibility, the human soul according to Plessner is constantly threatened by the risk of ridicule as much as it suffers from the strictures imposed by communal modalities of life. On the one hand, it is the fate of our soul that it wants to become something, but in being something it has to realize that it betrayed or left behind what it hoped to become in the first place. When coupled with communal expectations of self-presentation and authenticity, this split between the real and the imagined exposes us to the danger of being ridiculous, understood as the presentation of something contradictory as if it were free of contradiction. On the other hand, if unable to manage this conflict between being and becoming, the human soul cannot but remain enslaved to what Plessner senses as the life-denying grounds of community: its hostility against clear distinctions, its bent for stifling immediacy and amorphous sameness, its inability to foster self-restraint and thus unleash the powers of movement and transformation. Governed by love and familiarity, the communal sphere knows of no alterity. It does not allow the soul to become other, and it thus arrests us forever in our ambivalence between self-revelation and self-concealment.

The solution Plessner suggests in order to overcome the predicaments of the soul's drives is for the person to step out of the communal sphere and take on the protection of an artificial mask. Unlike nineteenth-century visionaries of communal authenticity, Plessner recommends that we endorse distant social interaction and rule-governed behavior, ceremonial self-enactment and prestige, to avoid the disappointments of intimacy and self-disclosure. Learn how to play, so goes Plessner's advice, learn how to interact with strangers under the sign of game-like rules, and you will overcome the paradoxes of human existence. Turn cold and shut out too much intimacy, draw definite lines between self and other, forget nature and revel in the artificial, and you will be able to appear in front of others without being immobilized by the laws of appearance. Ironic though it may seem, in Plessner's anthropology the privileged site at which we can objectify ourselves and thus achieve reciprocal protection from each other is the public sphere. It is the stage of publicity and its various mechanisms of coordinating social behavior that helps us avoid ridicule and defeat the oppressive ambivalence of our soul. In particular in its modern, technologically mediated form, publicity enables the subject to unrealize the contours of subjectivity, beat identity at its own game, and hence enjoy the pleasure and power of being invisible while being looked at from all sides.

Helmut Lethen has persuasively argued that behavioral codes of cold conduct such as Plessner's must be seen as typical products of social instability and cultural disorientation (Lethen 1994, 7). The Weimar emergence of codes of emotional restraint and performative self-enactment, I suggest, is also what separates Hoffmann's 1923 image of the Circus Krone rally and Hoffmann's 1927 series of Hitler as thespian rhetorician. My point here is certainly not to put forward that Hitler or Hoffmann were ardent readers of Plessner's philosophical anthropology; nor that Plessner, in spite of his friendship with Carl Schmitt, should be seen as a spokesman of the Nazi movement. What I do want to argue, however, is that Hoffmann's photographs of 1923 and 1927, respectively, are marked by fundamentally different conceptions of public visibility and social integration—conceptions and differences that can be illuminated with the help of Plessner's 1924 work.

Concepts of society, in Plessner's view, are inextricably linked to the development of a public sphere that relies on modern technologies of mediation and reproducibility, and in which anonymous people pursue their interests according to game-like rules and shared codes of communication. Hoffmann's "Hitler is Speaking!" of 1923, by contrast, aims to reinscribe that which preceded the publicness, anonymity, and self-interest of modern society: the spirit of communal integration, emotional intimacy, and unmediated reciprocity. At first, "Hitler is Speaking!" recalls medieval and baroque analogies between the human body and the body politic. The image—like those of many ideologues within the Nazi movement—reveals a corporeal and corporist thinking about the political according to which individuals are primarily conceived of as constituent parts of a greater, sentient, and organic whole (van der Will 1990). Upon further reflection, however, we come to realize that Hoffmann's use of the body metaphor is far more complex and ironic than its function in the work of ultranationalist thinkers such as Burke, Spencer, Wagner, Chamberlain, and Rosenberg. For Hoffmann's 1923 image is not only meant to show the triumph of communal over social integration, the intimate over the anonymous, the organic crowd over the abstract mass. Instead, it intends to reinvent organic communality with nothing other than the tools of modern publicness and the camera's prosthetic gaze. By locating Hitler's visual appearance off-frame, Hoffmann's photograph presented Hitler's charisma as a site of becoming and change, not of being and self-identity. The Hitler of this picture escaped Plessner's desire for visibility and in so doing steered clear of how acts of self-disclosure can congeal energies of transformation and subject us to the dangers of being ridiculed.

Hofmann's Hitler of 1923 emerged as a man of immediacy who could appear in front of the crowd without wearing a mask or performing according to a code. The photograph showed him as a leader of unrestrained affects unscathed by what Plessner considered the pitfalls of standing naked in front of fellow humans. The costs of this process of allegorization, however, of emancipating Hitler from direct visibility, are considerable. For how can we not think that Hitler's invisibility, his unwillingness to appear in front of the camera and play out his act, stands in direct relationship to the static, the frozen, the lifeless character of this crowd? In its paradoxical attempt to engineer the organic and protect Hitler from visual fixation, Hoffmann's camera in 1923 establishes a repressive structure of exclusion and separation whose symptoms resurface quite visibly in the lonely faces of the crowd, their solemnity, their absence of excitement. In Hoffmann's crowd, the separate are being unified as separate. What produces Hitler's charisma in this picture in the same breath also consumes it. So intimate is the crowd's relation to the unseen that it has nothing left to relate to itself. As a result, Hoffmann's community reveals all the negative traits that caused Plessner to hail society: absence of clear distinctions; stifling sameness; inability to envision, let alone realize, any form of alterity. At once enabling and overcome by Hitler's aura, Hoffmann's crowd is therefore clearly not a force of becoming and political activism. It is impossible to imagine this crowd conquering the streets so as to over-throw the order of the day. No modern community, the picture seems to communicate to us, can do without its leader, yet no picture can ever show us both in one and the same frame without betraying the spirit of emotional intimacy, without draining the transformative powers of charisma, and hence without essentially flunking the task of political mobilization.

"When the German engages in politics," Plessner wrote in 1924, "nothing appears to him with a light heart because he does not dare to play. In this way, he acquires that grim extremist attitude that over-compensates for his inner frailty, overemphasizes the importance of methodological discipline in the sciences, education, and military training, and overevaluates the rationalist thesis that one must anticipate the principles determining one's success in order to achieve happiness in the world" (Plessner 1999, 57). No matter how grim and forced the results, in Hoffmann's picture series of 1927 we witness Hitler daring the art of political playacting, not simply in order to resolve Plessner's dialectic of being and becoming, but to find new ways of feeding his charisma through the channels of modern publicness. Unlike the 1923 postcard, the 1927 images are no longer driven by the imperatives of emotional proximity, authentic self-disclosure, and hence communal integration. On the contrary, these images enact what Plessner called our fundamental right to distance, our need for cool and calculating un-realization. In the view of professional actors such as Chaplin, the Hitler of these six photographs might have looked crazed and void of self-restraint. But in identifying bad acting with bad politics, Chaplin of course invoked a hierarchy of values whose very legitimacy was to be undone by Hitler's foray into the art of wearing a political mask. For Hitler's objective in exploring the artifice of publicness was not simply to replace the procedural rules of political action with cinematic codes of self-stylization, that is, simply to subjugate political, ethical, or social discourses to aesthetic conventions and discourses. Instead, Hoffmann's pictures of 1927 urge us to think of Nazi media politics during the late Weimar Republic as an attempt to subjugate *all* existing value systems to the dictates of one new and central metaphor, a new kind of imperative that defers all value in favor of metaphoricity itself. To wear a social mask, in Plessner's view, meant to defeat the dilemmas of desire and community and hence overcome our unsettled position between the mandates of being and becoming, between our impulses to be seen and to hide from visibility. To embrace the artifice of publicness and of socially distant interaction enabled the drawing of firm lines between self and other, the familiar and the foreign. The 1927 picture series promotes this bliss of public masquerade, of cold self-performance, to the central metaphor organizing all aspects of political, social, economic, and aesthetic life. If Futurism sought to aestheticize politics by centering all discourses around the metaphor of the machine (Hewitt 1993, 133–160), then Hoffmann's images of 1927 tried to subjugate competing value systems to the central metaphor of the public mask and its constitutive relationship to the camera's prosthetic eye.

In his biography of Hitler, Ian Kershaw describes how Hitler, in the course of the second half of the 1920s, became a consummate actor in order both to uphold the aura increasingly attached to him by his followers and to keep in check the internal conflicts of the Nazi movement (Kershaw 2000, 280). But Hitler's predilection for acting, Kershaw is quick to add, was not solely confined to his public appearances. Quoting some of Hitler's closest associates, Kershaw suggest that playacting and self-performance were Hitler's order of the day even in the niches of his private life. As the former Gauleiter of Hamburg, Albert Krebs, recalled critically when trying to understand how Hitler succeeded in swaying his followers in private as much as in public: "The art of the mask and dissimulation should not be forgotten. It made it so difficult to grasp the core of Hitler's being" (quoted in Kershaw 2000, 281).

Krebs's suggestion that Hitler's masklike behavior be read as a symptom of histrionic and hypocritical inclinations at once illuminates and misses the central point of Hoffmann's pictures of 1927. Unlike the 1923 image, which kept Hitler out of sight in order to solve the rhetorical problem of disseminating aura to the masses, the 1927 series disavows any meaningful distinctions between interiority and exteriority, the public and the private. Instead, Hoffmann's images promote a discursive order that centers all discourses around the eye and the metaphor of the camera and that wants us to believe that whatever cameras may present to you is what you get. Cold conduct, ceremonial self-performance, and prosthetic vision here render concepts such as histrionics and hypocrisy irrelevant. For once masklike behavior and self-reification become the norm to fortify us against the messy aporias of desire, and once vision becomes relocated to a technological plane severed from any human observer to undo the predicaments of organic communality, then nothing will remain of the bourgeois dialectic between emotion and symbolization, truthfulness and dissimulation. Hoffmann's images of 1927 legitimate a process that erases former binarisms in favor of a performative system of metaphoricity in which the very notion of fixed values becomes impossible. The images establish the camera and its production of masklike conduct to the central metaphor of political action, a process that instead of simply replacing one value system ("politics") with the help of another ("aesthetics") results in a constant deferral of any central value in the first place. Like Jünger's concept of total mobilization (Jünger 1991), Hoffmann's system calls for ongoing intensities subordinating everyone and everything to the restless dictates of a postliberal order. In fact, I suggest, Hoffmann's system of the camera and Jünger's notion of total mobilization are inextricably intertwined, one at once relying on and sustaining the other. I now turn my attention in the remainder of this essay to how Hoffmann's camera established this system in more formal terms, how Hoffmann's practices of reframing the political differed from other contemporary photographic strategies, and how his photographic practice articulated the links among masklike conduct, movement, and mobilization.

Time/Frame

In August 1919, a cover photograph of the *Berliner Illustrirte Zeitung,* showing President Friedrich Ebert and Minister of Defense Gustav Noske in swimming trunks as they enjoyed their vacation at the Baltic Coast, produced a heated debate about the limits of photographic journalism and its public responsibilities. Less than a decade later, such arguments would strike the German public as deeply anachronistic. In the wake of the proliferation of photographic images in the second half of the 1920s, the availability of cheaper and more flexible cameras after 1925 to mass audiences, and the commercial successes of photo essays and photographic coffee-table books toward the end of the decade, opinions about the limits and functions of the photographic image had undergone dramatic changes. What in the immediate postwar years had appeared to many improper and potentially subversive, in the second half of the 1920s became the norm of Weimar commercial display culture and visual pleasure. To succeed as a political figure now increasingly meant to be ready to be photographed at all times, whether in public or in private settings, whether aware of the presence of a camera or not.

The work of two outstanding Weimar photographers, Erich Salomon and August Sander, is useful to recall here, not only in order to illustrate how photographic practice in the course of the 1920s renegotiated the boundary between the private and public but also to better understand the specificity of Hoffmann's work with Hitler. Salomon and Sander pursued fundamentally different strategies of putting a frame around the world and hence arresting fleeting realities. Their work was driven by contrasting conceptions of how to triangulate the relationships among photographer, the object of photography, and the viewer, formal conceptions that indexed competing "world-views" and political affiliations. Unlike Hoffmann's 1927 images of Hitler, however, neither Salomon nor Sander were ready to give up certain distinctions of liberal society, and it is in their thinking about the meaning of the photographic frame and the mechanical image's temporality that we can find helpful categories to explicate the formal design and political implications of Hoffmann's system of the camera in further detail.

In 1931 Salomon wrote, "The photojournalist's activity, if he wants to be more than a mere manual laborer, is a constant struggle, a struggle for the image, and as with hunting, he only gets the booty if he is possessed with the passion of the hunt for the image" (Salomon 42). And a passionate hunter Salomon was indeed. Salomon gained notoriety in the course of the late 1920s as a result of his many tricks to take candid pictures of famous politicians in unexpected settings. Salomon's photographs of European leaders as they let loose in late-night gatherings or showed unforeseen emotions—or the lack therefore—during League of Nations meetings quickly captured the tabloid press and prompted enormously positive responses. So notorious and popular, in fact, was Salomon's hunt for candid shots that his prey started to engage in guessing games about his presence and his latest strategies of infringing upon the remaining taboo areas of representation.

Though equipped with advanced photographic technology, Salomon in most situations still had to deal with exposure times of a quarter-second or longer, which made the use of a tripod necessary. To ensure that his subjects did not know when he was shooting, Salomon developed all kinds of strategies to blend into the background (Hunter 1978, 10). The visual shapes and compositional principles of Salomon's pictures closely reflected the challenges of their production. To borrow Leo Braudy's terminology, Salomon's camera pursued an open form of representation that saw photography as a momentary frame around an ongoing reality, which invited the viewer to enter the frame and enjoy its multiplicity of meanings and motions. In order to achieve this open form, Salomon had to rely first and foremost on his mastery of timing. Despite prolonged exposure times and moving subjects, few of Salomon's shots reveal blurry figure motion. Rather than simply break up movement into discrete elements and thus anticipate decisive moments, the hunter Salomon understood how to align his perception with the prey's movement and trigger his shutter whenever his subjects would almost imperceptibly pause their motion—during instants of attentive listening, for instance, or when briefly halting their gait to peruse their surroundings. Chasing intimate and unposed aspects of public life,

Salomon thus succeeded with his photographic practice, not because he viewed time and movement as a series of discrete and quantifiable moments, but on the contrary because for him the experience of movement and time was one of flux and synthesis, one to which photographers had to attune themselves in order to show the world as one of variable intensities. Only he who could yield to the alterity of his prey and become other, only he who could develop mimetic relationships to a world of qualities rather than quantities, could get and would deserve the booty.

Nothing could have been more foreign to August Sander's work of the 1920s than the idea of photography as a hunt for candid booty. Culminating in the encyclopedic project *Antlitz der Zeit: Sechzig Aufnahmen deutscher Menschen des 20. Jahrhunderts* (Faces of the times: sixty photographs of twentieth-century Germans), Sander's Weimar work relied on the explicit cooperation of his photographic subjects, on their willingness and desire to display important aspects of their private life as public identity in front of the camera. To capture social poses and self-performances—the deliberate presentation of cultural and professional markers—was at the heart of Sander's mission. What we see in Sander's shots is how people of different status, class, and regional background want to be seen in public and how this self-seeing informs their individual subject positions. The typical Sander subject appears in front of Sander's camera as if trying to demonstrate something essential about his or her existence between the private and the public. Like actors in Brecht's Epic Theatre, Sander's workers, farmers, teachers, academics, artists, musicians, judges, and politicians do not evoke sympathetic identification or emotional solidarity on the part of the viewer. Instead, their *gestus* catalyzes detached reflection about the extent to which public imperatives of visualization permeate the private sphere and cause Sander's subjects to understand even their everyday life as a site of ongoing role-play and self-performance. What interests us about these characters is not their psychological makeup and emotional interiority, but how they seek to assume their respective positions in society by negotiating self-images, prescribed cues, personal expressions, and dominant templates of identity. In Sander's best work, this negotiation of conflicting impulses and imperatives in fact is often shown as dissonant. By highlighting symbolic background elements or cropping images in counterintuitive ways, Sander's most memorable shots reframe their subject's self-framings, reveal their secret contradictions or point toward excessive pompousness, and thus communicate a certain air of irony.

This is not the place to discuss the anachronistic underpinnings of Sander's attempt to map the increasingly unrepresentable and abstract relationships of modern industrial culture. What should be of greater interest in this context, however, is how Sander used the photographic frame in order to capture time and space and thus establish peculiar relationships between photographer, the photographed, and the viewer. Returning to Braudy's terminology, we might think of Sander's work as committed to a closed form. Though dedicated to recording their subject's self-perception, Sander's images foreground the extent to which the world we encounter in photographic reproductions is one produced for and by omniscient cameras. In contrast to Salomon's understanding of the frame as a temporary window on transient realities, Sander's frames produce the world of the photographed in the first place. Rather than allow the viewer to freely wander into and through the images' pictorial space, Sander wants to grip us and focus our attention onto the seemingly self-sufficient meanings staged within the frame. Unlike Salomon, Sander does not allow us to enter the image as a voyeuristic onlooker navigating unstable image spaces in search for something or someone that might order it for us from within. As he frames and reframes his subject's exhibitionism, Sander instead asks us to become complicit with his own attempt to construct visual structures in a world which in the absence of photographic cameras would overwhelm us as chaotic.

Sander's compositional principles correspond to the use of photographic equipment quite unlike that deployed by candid photographer Salomon. As importantly, Sander's principles resulted in an articulation of time and movement fundamentally different to Salomon's aesthetic of the snapshot. Even though Sander's gear was clearly superior to what had been used during the advent of photography in the mid-nineteenth-century, his images recall the products of early photographers who—due to lengthy exposure times—positioned their subjects in relatively isolated settings and relied on their contemplative stillness. As Walter Benjamin argued in 1931, early photographs had a phantasmatic and hallucinatory quality. Everything in them was meant and designed to last. Rather than extending a mortifying shock to the real, the camera here recorded how the photographed, by holding still and thus simulating death in face of the camera, prepared for his own afterlife. A similar exorcism of time and death can be witnessed in Sander's work of the 1920s. In stark contrast to Salomon, whose struggle for the image was a struggle with temporal flux and transient motion, Sander hoped to lay bare that which survives the moment, a survival not only of the life of the photographed, but also of its death.[3] Sander's camera was not concerned with nourishing the mass media's cult of personality and catering to the short attention span of Weimar tabloid readers. It is part of the beauty and melancholy of Sander's portraits of the 1920s that, unlike Salomon's celebration of presence and attentive looking, these pictures sought to transcend time altogether and recall the present from the vantage point of the eternal.

Salomon's and Sander's work of the late 1920s represent two important coordinates within the force field of Weimar photography. Their respective photographs and recording strategies point toward fundamental different conceptions of how to use the photographic frame in order to organize the viewer's attention, how to define the boundaries between the public and the private, and last but not least how to negotiate the relationships among time, transience, motion, and photographic memory. Hoffmann's 1927 series of Hitler, I suggest, does not simply inhabit a position somewhere between Salomon's quest for open form and Sander's preference for closed form, nor does it lie between Salomon's mimetic hunt for right moments and Sander's attempt to outdo death with the eye of his camera. Instead, Hoffmann's series articulates a thinking about the meaning and effects of the photographic image that strives to invalidate the very system according to which Salomon and Sander defined their individual projects in the first place. Hoffmann's 1927 images of Hitler neither allow the viewer to step into the scene of the picture, roaming freely in search of various nodes of meaning, nor do they encourage the viewer to become a detached observer and identify the irony of certain acts of self-performance. Hoffmann's photographic frame neither opens a self-effacing window onto Hitler nor emphasizes its power to produce the photographed to begin with. And finally, Hoffmann's camera neither maps temporal flux by becoming other, nor does it seek to exorcise the ephemeral by preparing the photographed's afterlife. What Hoffmann offers us instead is a photographic practice that allows the photographed itself to step out of the frame towards the viewer and enact what we can call with Roman Jakobson conative forms of visual communication. These are imperative modes of cultural address that can neither be challenged by the question "Is it true or morally right or not?" nor allow for challenge, dissent, or contingent reception.[4] Aggressively gesticulating in face of and toward the camera, Hoffmann's Hitler in this series of six shots contests the limits of the photographic frame in order to become his own frame. He caters to and in fact incorporates the gaze of Hoffmann's camera with the aim to display his body as a sight that would exceed the defining power of any frame of representation. His intention is to become a self-sufficient window that would bring into view nothing but himself and thereby allow him to touch and activate the viewer directly. Hoffmann's Hitler does not grow into the picture and thus transcend time, nor does Hoffmann's series provide memento moris of what is transient and ephemeral. Rather, in these six pictures Hoffmann's camera allows Hitler to establish visual relationships that redefine public space and time as a site of all-inclusive intensity and activism, a site that knows no pause, fatigue, and hesitation, a site of fierce decisions and commitments from which none shall escape.

Unlike Salomon or Sander, Hoffmann in the series of 1927 no longer understood photography as a medium indexing the real or mapping social hierarchy. It became a strategic weapon—a projectile undoing bourgeois empathy, engendering discipline, and demarcating firm lines of belonging. In his late Weimar reflections on pain and danger, Ernst Jünger provided the vocabulary to explicate this peculiar employment of photography. For Jünger, photography was not only directly linked to the experience of modern technological warfare, it also represented the rise of a second consciousness, that is, a new regime of technologically mediated self-alienation, which enabled modern subjects to armor themselves and develop anaestheticized relations to danger and violence (Huyssen 1995; Werneburg 1994). Modern seeing for Jünger was both inherently aggressive and structured by the cold gaze of objectification: Hoffmann's images of 1927, I suggest, were designed to carry both photography and politics beyond what Jünger called the bourgeois "zone of sensibility" (Jünger 1989, 208) and thus establish Jünger's second consciousness as a decisive relay station for right-wing mobilization. In these photographs Hitler steps through the frame of representation, neither to evoke fear and trembling, nor simply to stir people's emotions, but to test and train the imperviousness of his followers' eyes. As if trying to become one of Jünger's bullets, Hitler stages himself as a source of danger and violence with the aim to allow his viewers to experience themselves as objects and overcome bourgeois receptivity, ambivalence, and emotional intricacy. The purpose of these images, in other words, was not to aestheticize politics, but to anaestheticize it, aesthetics here being understood in its original sense as primarily concerned with the sensory aspects of perception.[5] Exercises in cold conduct, Hoffmann's images of 1927 presented Hitler as a calculating agitator for the sake of engineering a viewing subject whose eyes become invulnerable and prosthetic, whose senses feel no pain, and whose body can thus be subsumed to the task of total mobilization.

Death/History (Photography/Film)

Since the inception of photography in the mid-nineteenth century, critical writing on the photographic image has continually emphasized its curious complicity with stasis and death. We do not photograph something we would like to forget, as the protagonist of Mark Romanek's 2002 thriller *One Hour Photo* summarizes this discourse, but whatever we capture with our camera turns aleatory presents into corpses documenting the pastness of the past. So intimate is photography's relationship with death that media theorists such as Vilém Flusser, for instance, consider photographical images as antithetical to both human freedom and historical consciousness. Forcing us to tailor our own behavior and appearances to the eye of the camera, photography tends to shove us into the realm of posthistory. Unless they try to play against the logic of the camera, photographic images, according to Flusser, "absorb the whole of history and form a collective memory going endlessly round in circles" (Flusser 2000, 20).

We may not want to follow Flusser's philosophy of the photographic image in its entirety, but Hoffmann's series of 1927 is best understood as an attempt to outwit the camera's rigidity so as to evacuate death from the photographic image, lodge time in the technical image itself, and thus, instead of proclaiming the end of history, position photographic practice as an integral moment of political mobilization. Neither mirror nor window, Hoffmann's images sought to move vision beyond itself in order to move the viewer against the order of the day. They intended to remake the laws of seeing in the name of remaking history and breaking what was perceived as the circular time of the Weimar Republic.

When writer and critic Berthold Viertel received Hoffmann's postcards in his Hollywood exile in 1937, his first impulse was to scoff at Hitler's theatrical poses. In an article for *Die Neue Weltbühne*, Viertel described the choreography of Hitler's body as one lacking spontaneity and authenticity. Everything about Hoffmann's 1927 Hitler, according to Viertel, is unnatural and contorted, is marked by striking and hence laughable disjunctures between ambition and realization. Though meant to stir the masses' emotions, these images remind Viertel of promotional film stills clumsily reconstructing a crime after the fact. In retrospect, however, Viertel's ridicule might appear out of focus given the fact that the whole purpose of Hoffmann's images—as I have argued in the preceding pages—was to obliterate the very possibility of the ridiculous. Seeking to deconstruct both Hitler's masquerade and the work of Hoffmann's camera, Viertel overlooked the fact that Hoffmann's images of 1927 themselves were practiced deconstruction. To laugh at something that denied the grounds for laughter, to deride as inauthentic that which performed and capitalized on the performativity of all identity, is itself in danger of approaching the ridiculous.

Yet Viertel was certainly right in understanding these six images, not in individual isolation, but as part of a film-like series—as motion pictures. "The mail," Viertel wrote, "has delivered an Adolf-Hitler-film into my house, or at least something that could offer a surrogate for such a thing. To be sure, it is only a series of six picture postcards as they are offered for sale in Germany in order to educate and elevate the people. However, this series of images, each print showing a different pose, can be experienced as a continual sequence of pantomimic action. . . . I am placing these six images side by side and showing to myself an Adolf-Hitler-film" (quoted in Herz 1994, 109). The telos of Hoffmann's metaphoric system of the camera of 1927 was not only to reconfigure the relationships between the photographed and the photographic off-frame, and to reorganize the political as an all-inclusive image space structured by desensitized forms of looking. As importantly, it was to liberate the photographic image from its association with death, memory, and melancholia, and thereby erase given binarisms of value (public/private; aesthetics/politics; face/mask; emotion/expression; community/society; photography/film). As they redefined photographic images as motion pictures and movement-visions, Hoffmann's images of 1927 endorsed a system of image production that constantly deferred central values with the intention to fight stasis and energize the masses. They emulated the protocols of a film camera to reinvent the political as a self-referential space of ongoing movement and invigorating presence.

No wonder, then, that Photo-Hoffmann in August 1930 sought to swamp the German market with Hitler flipbooks, presenting the mere act of looking at passing images as a mobilizing experience of the first order. As an ad promoting these "Daumenkinos" (thumb cinema)— the German for flipbook—insinuated: "The living picture of Adolf Hitler—80 shots of a speech by Adolf Hitler create, when flipped through quickly and in sequence, a moving image which offers a lifelike reproduction of the vivacious speech of our Führer" (quoted in Herz 1994, 113).

Notes

1. Except where otherwise indicated, translations are my own.

2. For more on the photographic off-frame, see Metz 1990.

3. For more on the relationships among photography, death, and the afterlife, see in particular Cadava 1997.

4. On the "conative" functions of language, see Jakobson 1987, 67–68.

5. For more on anaesthetics and its relationship to fascism, see Buck-Morss 1992.

Works Cited

Benjamin, Walter. "Little History of Photography." Vol. 2 of Benjamin, *Selected Writings: 1927–1934*, trans. Rodney Livingstone et al. and ed. Michael W. Jennings, Howard Eiland, and Gary Smith, 507–530. Cambridge: Belknap Press, 1999.

Braudy, Leo. *The World in a Frame*. Garden City, N.J.: Anchor Books, 1977.

Buck-Morss, Susan. "Aesthetics and Anaesthetics: Walter Benjamin's Artwork Essay Reconsidered." *October* 62 (Fall 1992): 3–41.

Cadava, Eduardo. *Words of Light: Theses on the Photography of History*. Princeton, N.J.: Princeton University Press, 1997.

Chaplin, Charles. *My Autobiography*. New York: Simon and Schuster, 1964.

Flusser, Vilém. *Towards a Philosophy of Photography*. Trans. Anthony Mathews. London: Reaktion Books, 2000.

Gidal, Tim. *Deutschland—Beginn des modernen Photojournalismus*. Lucerne: Bucher, 1972.

Herz, Rudolf. *Hoffmann & Hitler: Fotografie als Medium des Führer-Mythos*. Munich: Klinkhardt & Biermann, 1994.

Hewitt, Andrew. *Fascist Modernism: Aesthetics, Politics, and the Avant-Garde*. Stanford: Stanford University Press, 1993.

Hoffmann, Heinrich. *Hitler Was My Friend*. Trans. R. H. Stevens. London: Burke, 1955.

Hunter, Peter. *Erich Salomon: The Aperture History of Photography Series*. New York: Aperture, 1978.

Hüppauf, Bernd. "Experiences of Modern Warfare and the Crisis of Representation." *New German Critique* 59 (Spring/Summer 1993): 41–76.

Huyssen, Andreas. "Fortifying the Heart—Totally: Ernst Jünger's Armored Texts." In *Twilight Memories: Marking Time in a Culture of Amnesia*, 127–144. New York: Routledge, 1995.

Jakobson, Roman. *Language in Literature*. Ed. Krystyna Pomorska and Stephen Rudy. Cambridge, Mass.: Harvard University Press, 1987.

Jünger, Ernst. *Der Arbeiter: Herrschaft und Gestalt*. 1932. Reprint. *Sämtliche Werke: Zweite Abteilung*. Stuttgart: Klett-Cotta, 1981.

———. "Photography and the 'Second Consciousness': An Excerpt from 'On Pain.'" Trans. Joel Agee. In *Photography in the Modern Era: European Documents and Critical Writings, 1913–1940*, ed. Christopher Phillips, 207–210. New York: Metropolitan Museum of Art/Aperture, 1989.

———. "Total Mobilization." Trans. Richard Wolin. In *The Heidegger Controversy: A Critical Reader*, ed. Richard Wolin, 119–139. New York: Columbia University Press, 1991.

Kershaw, Ian. *The "Hitler Myth": Image and Reality in the Third Reich.* Oxford: Oxford University Press, 1987.

———. *Hitler: 1889–1936. Hubris.* New York: W. W. Norton, 2000.

Lethen, Helmut. *Verhaltenslehre der Kälte: Lebensversuche zwischen den Kriegen.* Frankfurt/Main: Suhrkamp, 1994.

Metz, Christian. "Photography and Fetish." In *The Critical Image: Essays on Contemporary Photography,* ed. Carol Squiers, 155–164. Seattle: Bay Press, 1990.

Plessner, Helmuth. *The Limits of Community: A Critique of Social Radicalism.* 1924. Reprint. Trans. Andrew Wallace. Amherst, N.Y.: Humanity Books, 1999.

Salomon, Erich. *Berühmte Zeitgenossen in unbewachten Augenblicken.* Stuttgart: J. Engelhorns Nachfolge, 1931.

Sander, August. *Antlitz der Zeit: Sechzig Aufnahmen deutscher Menschen des 20. Jahrhunderts.* Munich: Kurt Wolff Verlag, 1929.

Schmöller, Claudia. *Hitlers Gesicht: Eine physiognomische Biographie.* Munich: Beck, 2000.

van der Will, Winfried. "The Body and the Body Politic as Symptom in the Transition of German Culture to National Socialism." In *The Nazification of Art: Art, Design, Music, Architecture and Film in the Third Reich,* ed. Brandon Taylor and Winfried van der Will, 14–52. Winchester: Winchester Press, 1990.

Viertel, Berthold. "Ein Hitler-Film." *Die Neue Weltbühne* 33, no. 2 (1937): 1331–1333.

Weise, Bernd. "Photojournalism from the First World War to the Weimar Republic." In *German Photography 1870–1970: Power of a Medium,* ed. Klaus Honnef, Rolf Sachsse, and Karin Thomas, 52–67. Cologne: Dumont, 1997.

Werneburg, Brigitte. "Die veränderte Welt. Der gefährliche anstelle des entscheidenden Augenblicks: Ernst Jüngers Überlegungen zur Fotografie." *Fotogeschichte* 51 (1994): 51–67.

15

"Send in the Clowns"

Carnivalizing the Heil-Hitler Salute in German Visual Culture

Peter Arnds

Clowns are grotesque blasphemers against all our pieties.
That's why we need them. They are our alter egos.
— Dario Fo, quoted in James Fisher,
The Theater of Yesterday and Tomorrow:
Commedia dell'Arte on the Modern Stage

After 1945 there was a resurgence of carnivalesque forms in neo-picaresque culture dealing with the Nazi period, with novels like Günter Grass's *Die Blechtrommel* (*The Tin Drum*), Thomas Mann's *Felix Krull*, and Heinrich Böll's *Ansichten eines Clowns* (*The Clown*); films like Volker Schlöndorff's *Der Unhold* (*The Ogre*) and Agniezska Holland's *Europa, Europa;* and the photography and paintings of Anselm Kiefer. Postwar carnivalesque culture has the three functions of (a) liberating culture from fascist aesthetics, (b) representing fascist aesthetics through its very own opposite, and (c) breaking postfascist taboos. Harlequins, clowns, fools, and the picaro—these grotesque and, in the eyes of Nazi ideologues, degenerate figures—disappeared almost entirely during the Third Reich, a period that forms the climax of modernity, if by modernity we understand the bourgeois era that emerged from the Renaissance. The rise of the bourgeoisie is accompanied by a repression of popular culture, a development that in Germany manifests itself in such details as Gottsched's banning of the clown from the stage. Carnivalesque figures both in real life and in the arts become increasingly marginalized, and only in Romanticism do we observe a movement that runs counter to this increasing bourgeoisification of culture. Harlequins, clowns, fools, and the picaro are social outsiders and reconfigurations of the trickster archetype. They surface throughout the twentieth century in art that tries to challenge bourgeois life and its official discourses. The Bakhtinian distinction between the classical and the grotesque may help in explaining the functions of this twentieth-century art that attempts to disturb the established norms of the official culture.

An art that revives the figure of the clown (Böll's Hans Schnier), the
picaro (Thomas Mann's Felix Krull), or the tramp (Charlie Chaplin's
vagabond) is art that subscribes to the discursive norms of the grotesque
body, to a tolerance of madness rather than its exclusion following the
dictates of bourgeois notions of sanity, to a nomadic rather than a sed-
entary lifestyle, to a body in the act of becoming rather than a body that
is closed, frozen in time.

This study examines parodies of the *Sieg-Heil* salute in visual culture. The works at the center of this analysis are Volker Schlöndorff's
adaptation of Günter Grass's *The Tin Drum*, particularly the famous
scene in which Oskar Matzerath sits under a rostrum and disrupts a
Nazi party rally, and Anselm Kiefer's paintings and photo series that
parody this gesture. I will demonstrate that in parodying the Hitler salute, twentieth-century visual art subverts a gesture that expresses the
imperialist visions of a ruling elite through popular traditions that are
as timeworn as the salute itself. Although Schlöndorff and Kiefer are
pivotal to this study, they should be viewed within a broader cultural
framework. Particular attention should be paid to the time when these
parodies were produced as well as to the origin of the artist. It is one
thing for non-German artists like Mel Brooks, Charlie Chaplin, or
Roberto Benigni to carnivalize the National Socialist iconography, but
it is an altogether different challenge for a German artist like Kiefer to
break the postwar taboo on the reenactment of fascist practices by posing in drag and attempting to walk on water while doing the *Sieg-Heil*
salute in the late 1960s. One must also distinguish between parodies of
the Third Reich during the war, such as Chaplin's *The Great Dictator*
(1940) and Ernst Lubitsch's *To Be or Not to Be* (1942), which in their
relative ignorance of the full range of Nazi crimes are somewhat naive,
and post-Nazi representations, which conflate the horrific with the
farcical while being fully conscious of the horrors committed by the
Nazis. To perform the Hitler salute in a work of art after 1945, especially in Germany, meant to tamper with a taboo gesture, an act that
triggered reactions of the sort experienced by Anselm Kiefer when he
presented Germany with his series of Hitler salutes. In many cases even
the place where the salute is performed holds a deeper significance. In
his artwork *Occupations*, when Kiefer stretches out his arm in front of
the Colosseum, he alludes to a tradition of imperialism that links the
Roman Empire with the Third Reich.

In non-German carnivalizations of the Hitler salute the gesture is
parodied; its seriousness is broken down into farce. Holland's *Europa,
Europa* (1991) features a scene in which the rigidity of the Hitler salute
collapses into a sort of Chaplinesque tap dance. In one of the beginning

scenes in Benigni's Holocaust farce *Life Is Beautiful* (1998), the protagonist Guido, driving a convertible without brakes, is headed straight for a crowd with banners saying "Hail to the King." When he sways his arms urging everyone to clear the way, the crowd, mistaking him for the King, hails him with outstretched arms, a scene that exemplifies the blindness of the masses and is possibly copied from Chaplin's *The Great Dictator*. Here too the clown figure, the little Jewish barber, is mistaken for the ruler. Chaplin's film repeatedly parodies the Hitler salute. It shows the Venus de Milo and Rodin's Thinker in a *Sieg-Heil* position, thus commenting on the subjugation of art and culture to Nazi ideology. Another memorable scene from this film is the little dance that Hitler (Adenoid Hynkel) and Mussolini (Napaloni) perform as they want to shake hands but fail to do so because they are trying to out-salute each other. Mel Brooks's *The Producers* (1968) contains the famous musical number entitled "Springtime for Hitler," where the Hitler salute is performed as a cancan dance. In Lubitsch's *To Be or Not to Be* the Hitler look-alike responds to a chorus of *Heil Hitler* with "Heil myself!" and the phrase becomes comically defused as it is uttered between kisses (cf. Insdorf 1982, 72).

The carnivalization of this gesture is not limited to film. Albert Bloch's painting *March of the Clowns* (1941) reflects a vision of the end of fascism. The center of this circus scene shows a Hitler puppet hanging from a swastika at the end of a stick carried by a clown, one among a host of characters from American popular culture. It is especially ironic that Hitler, who was so fascinated with circuses, is hanged in one of them. The swastika that carries him is dominated by a Star of David and the stick serving as Hitler's gallows is held at such an angle that it immediately conjures up the *Sieg-Heil* salute. There are other figures in the circus cortege who perform the Hitler salute: a skeleton and a man with a walking cane. They are pointing toward the end of fascism, death, and destruction in the same way that the *Sieg-Heil* salute was intended to point toward the victorious outcome of the war, the end of world domination by the Jews, and the vision of the Thousand-Year Reich.

Conflating the Hitler salute with grotesque images involving the figure of the clown evokes the specifically European tradition of the carnival and its uncrownings of the ruling authorities, first and foremost the State and the Church, by the powerless. To temporarily uncrown those in power was the task of the carnival as it was of the fool at court (cf. the excellent study of this figure in Welsford 1935), of the harlequin of the *commedia dell'arte*, and symbolically still is today of the circus clown, who is a contemporary relic of the two earlier figures. In this conflation of the serious with the humorous the former is as steeped in tradition as the latter. Although a CIA file from 1942 claims that the German Nazis copied the salute from American college-football cheerleaders, Julian Borger has pointed out that the historical consensus is that Hitler took the *Sieg-Heil* salute from Mussolini. Mussolini in turn had copied it from the old Roman "Ave"-salute, a fact that Anselm Kiefer alludes to in his photograph series *Occupations* (1969).

Yet the Hitler salute also has its roots in the occult tradition. It was a symbol used by the Thule Society founded in 1918 by Adam Rudolf Glauer, or Baron Rudolf von Sebottendorf, as he called himself. The society named itself after an ancient Nordic island also known as "Hyperborea," which was thought to have been inhabited by superhumans, the original Aryan race. Thule discipline required their disciples' blind obedience to their enlightened master, a fact that Sebottendorf called the *Führerprinzip* ("Führer principle") (Sklar 1977, 46), which was derived from ancient Oriental Freemasons and prefigured what the Nazis later came to call *Kadavergehorsam* ("blind obedience") ("Be between the hands of your sheikh like a cadaver in the hands of him who washes him") (Sklar 1977, 34). This god-like master was to be greeted with the words *Sieg Heil*. In the early 1920s Hitler was introduced to Munich occult circles as the "long-promised savior" above whom "there hovers a star" (Sklar 1977, 52 ff.). Undoubtedly, in his painting *March of the Clowns*, Albert Bloch seems to allude to this vision of Hitler as the messiah leading Germany to victory, primarily to a victory over the Jews, when he creates his parodistic counter-vision of the Jewish victory over Hitler. He places orthodox Jews in the audience surrounding Hitler hanging from his own swastika, above which hovers the Jewish Star of David.

What is specifically under attack in visual art that parodies the Hitler salute? It is primarily its rigidity that becomes the target of a clown-like figure in all these visual representations. For the fascists the gesture implied the unity of purpose and warranty of their own power. Although by itself it may be expressive of an iron will, if used by the masses the monotony and synchronicity of this gesture become the ultimate expression of a loss of individuality and therefore of the people's powerlessness vis-à-vis those who govern them. Breaking down the Hitler salute therefore entails a reempowering of the individual, a process that is possibly best exemplified in Agnieszka Holland's *Europa, Europa*. When Solly, alias Josef Peters, joins a napola and takes the oath of allegiance, he is welcomed by a triple *Sieg Heil* with outstretched arms, which he has to imitate. But when he steps into the shower room and finds himself alone in front of the mirror, after performing a couple of heel-clicking rigid salutes he reasserts his individualism by breaking into a tap dance, during which his arm relaxes into a mere waist-high wave.

The movie *The Tin Drum* (1979), unlike Grass's novel (1959), places a good deal of emphasis on the choreography of the Hitler salute. What starts as the classical image of a mass of arms all pointing rigidly in the same direction is dissolved by Oskar's subversive rhythms. The rigidity of the salute is broken down through the following choreographic sequence: (a) although still pointing in one direction the arms of the masses start waving; (b) then people start facing each other in order to dance a waltz triggered by the subversive rhythms of Oskar's drum; their arms are no longer parallel but are raised against each other before they go down and are placed around their partners' waists and shoulders; and (c) Gauleiter Löbsack is the only one who tries to uphold the rigidity of the Hitler salute. At this point something funny happens in the movie scene: it starts raining and for a moment Löbsack interrupts the rigidity of his salute by turning his palm up toward the falling rain. This image of catching rain in his palm is in its affirmation of a life-giving natural power the very opposite of the Nazi salute, which conjures up associations with execution and dealing out death.

For the Nazis, the rigidity of the salute reflected the Faustian quest of the German soul. Highlighting the discursive norms of the classical body, the salute reinforces a virility that, due to the Nazis' despair in view of the degeneracy of the modern age, may have become questionable. In contrast to the grotesque body found in an abundance of popular culture, including the literature of carnival, the classical body is limited, self-sufficient, closed, not open at its orifices, and, above all, inflexible and frozen in time. Arno Breker's statues in particular reflect this ideal human body in art. Breker did for sculpture what Leni Riefenstahl achieved for film. With the Olympic Games of 1936, antiquity's ideal of beauty became adopted in theory and practice (Wolbert 1982, 88). Through her images of the marathon runners and the decathlete Erwin Huber, Riefenstahl establishes a link between antiquity and the Germany of her time. The Nazis' adoption of the Greek ideal of the perfect body paved the way for their rejection of the degenerate body. Unlike the grotesque body, whose principle features are the gaping mouth, protrusions such as the huge nose, and a transformability that forever promises the renewal of life, "all the events taking place within [the classical body] acquire one single meaning: death" (Bakhtin 1984, 321). By opening his palm and wildly throwing his arms around picking up dirt at the end of Schlöndorff's scene, Löbsack exemplifies this transition from the classical body expressive of death to the life-affirming principle of the grotesque body.

As an extension of the erect body of classical antiquity, the Hitler salute functions as a *pars pro toto* that distinguishes itself from the bent-over body that the Nazis associated with the Jewish body (Wildmann 1998, 79). Walter Benjamin spoke of the "bucklicht Männlein," man bent over by the burden of patriarchally determined history. The bent-over back expresses man's alienation from nature, and according to Siegfried Kaltenecker, while Benjamin attempted to straighten man through critical thinking, the Nazis tried to straighten man through violence (Kaltenecker 1995, 91). The Nazis' ambition to straighten out man to his original natural shape from the time preceding the malaise of civilization was therefore one reaction of modernity to the ubiquitous symptoms of its own degeneracy. As Bernd Jürgen Warneken has shown, the disciplining of the body into an erect one was a sign of bourgeois emancipation, a sign of the citizen's autonomy of will over his own body in the age of Enlightenment (Warneken 1990, 45).

What held true for the beginnings of the bourgeois age had even more validity for National Socialism, this period of the bourgeoisie *in extremis*, where an erect body was considered to reflect a strong charac-ter and a strong will. Among the sports that had a primary function in straightening the body was gymnastics, which gained increasing signifi-cance during the nineteenth century, a time when the disciplining of the body pervaded not only the military but all other institutions of discipline: school, where the erect posture was introduced for the pu-pil's desk, and even the workplace (Warneken 1990, 48). What started as a trend to liberate the individual was perverted by the Nazis into a general subjection of the body. The Swing Movement in postfascist Germany then became a reaction to the Nazis' perversion of the erect body posture, a disruption of the erect body back into relaxation. In the rostrum chapter of Grass's novel, this juxtaposition of erect bodies next to their relaxation is a central motif. Oskar Matzerath sits inside the rostrum and drums the rhythm of a Charleston, "Jimmy the Tiger," which Schlöndorff turns into a waltz.

Schlöndorff's scene shows to what extent Grass's book plays with mythical material and to what extent it is indebted to several European cultural traditions that involve a buffoon-like figure. Oskar corresponds to the typical trickster archetype, who is common to all cultures and can be reincarnated as a clown, fool, or harlequin. Like Thomas Mann's Felix Krull, Oskar compares himself on several occasions with the Greek Hermes, with whom he shares the powers of enchantment and disenchantment. Considering his position on the margins of society, his insanity and lack of physical growth, he has to enchant the Nazis in order to survive the constant threat of euthanasia, but at the same time he repeatedly disenchants them through his subversiveness. His carnivalesque disturbances are directed against the two principal authorities, the State (during the rostrum scene) and the Church (through blasphemy and other forms of desecration, such as fondling Baby Jesus's penis). Hermes and Oskar both play an instrument and are artists in the sense of *ars* as "skill," "artifice," "craft." Lewis Hyde has defined tricksters as "joint-disturbers," since the word "art" is also related to the Latin *articulus* and the Greek *arthron*, joint. But he points out, "not that they are much involved with making the firm and well-set joints that lead to classical harmony. What tricksters like is the *flexible* or *movable* joint" (Hyde 1998, 256).

Oskar's drumming can be read as a relic of the charivari tradition, in which as much clamor as possible was performed on pots and pans to announce the devil to the community and drive it away (Sanders 1995, 154). Oskar's secret performance defines itself in opposition to the official Nazi culture. He temporarily displaces a music that in Wolbert's words is classical and Prussian, *parademäßig* ("parade-like") (Wolbert 1982, 148) by a music that belongs to the discursive norms of the grotesque body, the body that gives up its classical rigidity. In Schlöndorff's scene, we can see this not only in the dissolution of the Hitler salute into waving and waltzing but also in the Nazi marching step which cannot help but follow the wild rhythm Oskar has introduced with his drum. Oskar's deflation of the ruling group's power and consequent empowerment of the people corresponds to the traditional function of the historical fool, who was to remind the ruler of his limitations as a human and of the presence of his inferior subjects to whom he was responsible. This was also the intention of the Feast of Fools (*festa stultorum*), which with its "parody and travesty of the official cult, with masquerades and improper dances" (Bakhtin 1984, 74) meant to empower temporarily those officials in the Church who normally had little to say.

By disrupting the sinister party rally through his comic diablerie, Oskar is also playing the role of the typical harlequin, whose origins go back to the spectre-devils and clown-devils of the early Middle Ages before this figure became a predominantly clownish character in the *commedia dell'arte* of the Italian Renaissance. The *commedia dell'arte* arose in the late Renaissance, was performed until the eighteenth century, and still leaves its mark on the twentieth century, in literature, the performing arts, and visual culture. At the turn of the twentieth century the avant-garde in Germany and Russia adapted *commedia* motifs for their anti-bourgeois theater, and the work of such American comedians as Buster Keaton, W. C. Fields, Oliver Hardy, and above all Charlie Chaplin with his swinging cane, funny hat, and floppy shoes follows the tradition of the *commedia* (cf. Madden 1975, 27; Green and Swan 1986, 10, 132).

Like the *commedia, The Tin Drum* makes use of certain stock characters, for example the doctor (Hollatz) and the courtesan (Raguna). Just as *The Tin Drum* destabilizes the official rational discourse of its time, the *commedia dell' arte* had its own counterpart, the *commedia sostenuta,* or learned drama performed from a written text. Like Grass's masterpiece, the *commedia* was rich in heteroglossia, from the Venetian merchant's dialect to the elegant Tuscan to low vernacular. It was a satire of the upper and lower strata of society, one of whose favorite themes was adultery (cf. Oskar's mother Agnes), an endless source of ridicule and shame (steeped in carnival and its uncrownings), and it featured lecherous old men (cf. Matzerath and Maria). The most common plot, however, was based upon a threat posed to two young sweethearts by an overly protective parent. Only a servant could bring about their union, which entailed a carnivalesque reversal of high and low, of servant over master.

In *The Tin Drum* the lowly is centralized in the figure of Oskar himself, his perspective from the bottom. In Schlöndorff's rostrum scene Oskar's association with the lower social sphere is tied to the Bakhtinian concept of the grotesque body with its images of the lower bodily stratum. Like Rabelais's *Gargantua and Pantagruel* and Grimmelshausen's *Simplicissimus,* Grass's book teems with scatological images that form part of the low-class ambience. Schlöndorff pays tribute to this fecal atmosphere by having Oskar step into a turd before he climbs into the rostrum. Grass's novel is not exclusively a love story but rather depicts the repeated decrowning of the powerful by the low in the form of Oskar. The figures of the *commedia* were all tricksters, *arte* standing for the talents and skills of the actors but also for commercially profitable "trade." *Commedia* intends to alienate its audiences through its exotic elements, its shapeshifting characters with their fluid nature, like Mercury, that are completely opposed to official culture. In the French *commedia,* the lunatic Harlequin and his fellow clown Pulcinella became the subversive counterparts to absolutism as epitomized in Louis XIV, the *Roi-Soleil,* who finally banned the *commedia* in France.

As fellow clowns, Bebra and Oskarnello are Grass's version of Harlequin and Pulcinella. In the role of Harlequin the circus clown Bebra, who is "descended from Prince Eugene, whose father was Louis XIV"

(Grass 1990, 114), is the wise fool joined to the ruler Hitler and corresponds to the traditional courtly pattern in which the lunar Harlequin is the counterpart to the Sun King. Like Oskar after the war, Pulcinella, the Neapolitan version of the Harlequin, was hunchbacked and was usually portrayed with sticks in his hands (Oskar's drumsticks), either a dagger or macaroni, and was "a great beater of others and much beaten himself" (Oreglia 1968, 93). A peasant from the region around Naples, we see him come back to life in Oskar, who forges his papers to "Oskarnello Raguna, born on October 21, 1912 in Naples" (Grass 1990, 326), when he joins the war front theater. By screaming "glassware from the reign of Louis XIV" (Grass 1990, 329) to pieces, another memorable scene in Schlöndorff's movie, Oskar not only offers his services to Nazi rule, participating in the German destruction of France, but unconsciously also engages in a subversive culture opposed to the official culture of absolutism and the reign of the Sun King. Oskar's girlfriend Roswitha Raguna, herself from Naples, is the great somnambulist, which also evokes the French tradition of the *commedia*, the *Théâtre des Funambules* (Theater of the High Wire) and its very own Harlequin, Pierrot, a central image of the artist and as such much abused by society.

The rostrum scene evokes the grotesque marketplace spectacles of the Middle Ages and the Renaissance with their theater scaffoldings, an atmosphere that Grass copied from Rabelais's "*Chronicles of Gargantua*," "in which . . . the sacred and the profane are levelled and are all drawn into the same dance" (Bakhtin 1984, 160). Bakhtin's categories of the marketplace, billingsgate, that is, the language of oaths and curses, and images of the lower bodily stratum, all conjoin in this scene. The medieval mystery plays are an important source of the grotesque concept. In these plays the stage represented the cosmos as then envisioned, with its notions of paradise and hell. As Bakhtin informs us, beneath "the platform representing the earth there was a large opening, indicating hell, covered by a broad curtain decorated with a huge mask of the devil (Harlequin)" (Bakhtin 1984, 348). It was from this opening that Satan's devils would spring into the world. In the rostrum scene Oskar sits precisely in the spot the devil had occupied in the medieval mystery plays, under the stage, one of the many allusions to Oskar's satanic nature. This is where his similarity with Hermes is truly evident; he is both messenger of the gods, in that he tries to disrupt the satanic event, and also to be found in the underworld. Sitting inside the rostrum Oskar is located at the very center of the hell created by the Nazi party, which emanates from the center, the rostrum, to the periphery, thus trying to draw in the whole population. The gullible Germans on the periphery, who fall for the satanic charm of the Nazis, do not have the same insight as Oskar at the center.

In connection with the iconography of hell inscribed into the rostrum scene it becomes worthwhile looking at the word "carnival." If the term signifies a holy site (*karne*) to which the dead (*val, wal*) are led (Bakhtin 1984, 392) rather than a farewell to flesh (from *carnis*, flesh and *vale*, farewell), there is a close proximity between carnival and the idea of hell. The image of being swallowed that is so abundant in carnival would then imply being swallowed by hell, and indeed "Carnival hell was seen in various forms . . . a giant devouring children," as we can see in many folktales, or "an oven for the baking of fools" (Bakhtin 1984, 393–394). The rostrum scene combines the carnival with hell in two ways. On the one hand, there is the suspension of serious officialdom through Oskar in his satanic position, a suspension that is typically carnivalesque because it reinforces the official power structures by temporarily subverting them. On the other hand, the spectator cannot help but think of Nazism itself as a sort of hellish carnival, in which the face of history has become grotesquely distorted and the delineation between rationality and irrationality has become blurred.

After 1945 no representation of the Third Reich, no matter how humorous, manages to escape the shadow of Auschwitz. Among the most macabre images conflating the comical with the sublime in postwar German visual culture are the paintings and photographs of Anselm Kiefer. Kiefer shares with Grass an interest in the archetypal, in German myth, and in mixing Nazi iconography with Christian motifs. More than anywhere else in his œuvre, Kiefer in harlequinesque fashion conflates the sublime with the profane in his photos and paintings in which he performs the Nazi salute, primarily in *To Genet* (1969), *Heroic Symbols* (1969), and *Occupations* (1969). He tells the entire story of Hitler and National Socialism through the economy of this one gesture. Like the satanic, dionysiac side of Oskar Matzerath, who has been compared with Hitler himself, there is a saturnine and dionysiac element in Kiefer's seemingly irrational return to a taboo gesture and an ideologically polluted cultural heritage. Although his salutes have been interpreted not as irony but, for example, as reflecting the artist's fascination with the mystique of "a glamor related to the underlying violence of the saluting figure" (Brooks 1990, 114), I would argue that Kiefer's hypnotic gesture is highly carnivalesque in its subversive power. Like old Cronus, Saturn is the god who has always ruled time. As he raises his arm, in one moment Kiefer releases himself and his audience from the flux of time that favors forgetfulness, bringing them face to face with a repressed past.

While his Holocaust paintings may command one to silence, Kiefer's *Occupations* caused a major uproar among Germans. This is a set of photographs and paintings in which, by making the *Sieg-Heil* salute, Kiefer "occupies" various symbolic locations in Europe, all territories occupied by the Nazis during World War II. The interesting thing about Kiefer's salutes is that unlike many of his predecessors and unlike Schlöndorff ten years after him, he does not break down the rigidity of the salute but seems to reenact it in all its seriousness. It is, however, through the context in which he performs the salute that it becomes the target of parody. In a caption over one of his *Occupations* he informs the spectator that "between summer and autumn of 1969 I have occupied Switzerland, France, and Italy."

The monstrousness of world imperialism is revealed through the contrast of one—usually dwarfed—person, Kiefer himself, performing the Hitler salute in such timeworn places as the Colosseum, the Foro Romano, or facing the ocean as did Caspar David Friedrich in his painting *The Wanderer over the Mist of Sea* (1817), thus linking the imperialism of the Roman empire to that of Germany, linking Romanticism to Nazism, and generally questioning the concept of ownership with regard to these places. This is similar to what Charlie Chaplin does in *The Great Dictator,* in the famous scene where Hynkel, dreaming of his imperialist goals, plays with the globe, an air-filled balloon, which then bursts, a scene that has been seen in the tradition of the *commedia* (Green and Swan 1986, 133); or the scene in which Hynkel (Hitler) and Napaloni (Mussolini) choke on English mustard, an allusion to the fact that they are trying to devour more than they can chew.

Although the Hitler salute is not broken down physically in Kiefer's work, he tries to break it down mentally both in his own mind as well as in the minds of his German audience. By reenacting the Hitler salute, Kiefer is pointing out to his fellow Germans that the Nazi past, its crimes, and its iconography have hardly been worked through. The rigidity of the salute still haunts everyone's mind, and as profane as this gesture may seem, this profanity is necessary in order to awaken public consciousness to a repressed past. One cannot but agree with Andreas Huyssen, who argues that with his Hitler salutes Kiefer points out that in a Germany which after the war has not been able to create new national images it was a necessity for art to reflect and work through "the burden of fascism on images" (Huyssen 1989, 34).

In his series *To Genet* (1969), Kiefer poses in drag—the dappled garment of the harlequin?—in front of his bathtub while performing the Hitler salute, an image that implies the idea of Hitler as the messiah walking on water. The drag defuses the masculinity of the salute, whose angle and rigidity in their bluntest symbolism resemble the erection of a penis and imply the idea of imperialism as a result of male ambitions for power linked to an aggressive male sexuality. This context is further defused by Kiefer through a slight tilt of his hand, also visible in his watercolors *Heroic Symbols* (1969). His hand is either tilted downward with the palm facing down, thus creating a rupture in the erectness of his arm and hand, or the palm is facing sideways. In either case the effect is similar to Schlöndorff's scene in which Gauleiter Löbsack turns up his palm in order to feel the falling rain.

I would argue that in these photographs and watercolors Kiefer too locates himself in the tradition of the *commedia*. While Oskar corresponds more closely to Harlequin or Pulcinella performing *lazzi*, Kiefer resembles Pierrot, whose "pantomimic energies are devoted to the expression of his inner life" (Green and Swan 1986, 136). The sad reflectiveness of the figure manifests itself in the immobility of Kiefer's salutes, frozen in photographs or paintings and thus inviting the spectator to reflect upon the past, while this reflectiveness is stifled through the turbulent choreography in Schlöndorff's rostrum scene.

Initially, West German art critics assumed that Anselm Kiefer was a nationalist painter. Kiefer, however, defended himself against accusations that his art was neofascist by saying, "I identify myself neither with Nero nor with Hitler. However, I must sympathize with them just a little bit so as to understand their madness" (Winter 1988, 70). His art, which expresses a sense of shame that he feels deeply for his own culture, provides him with the possibility of acting out and working through the fascist past rather than partaking of the collective amnesia of the parent generation. In an interview he once pointed out that one "cannot show things as they are; you have to ironize them or they are not supportable. The only way to sustain life is to laugh about it" (quoted in Rosenthal 1998, 10).

The provocative work of Kiefer and the jocularity in Schlöndorff's rostrum scene raise questions of permissibility and functionality of black humor, satire, parody, even laughter in representations dealing with the Nazi past, as well as the question whether such art should be the prerogative only of the victims and their children trying to come to terms with their trauma. As images of the Holocaust became known after the war, they initially commanded general silence. To break the spell of this seriousness with laughter would by most people's common sense be a major affront toward the victims, and yet for those struggling for survival in the camps and those who did survive, humor often remained their only weapon. As Terrence Des Pres argued in defending artistic responses to the Holocaust that employ a sense of humor, "it's not fear and sorrow we need more of, but undaunted vision. The paradox of the comic approach is that by setting things at a distance it permits us a tougher, more *active* response. We are not wholly, as in the high seriousness of tragedy, forced to a standstill by the matter we behold" (Des Pres 1991, 282). And as Nietzsche once put it, "even if nothing else today has any future, our *laughter* may yet have a future" (Nietzsche 1966, 150).

In their position vis-à-vis the powerful, the clown, the harlequin of the *commedia*, and the fool at court conjoin: the clown pokes fun at the mighty, the harlequin uncrowns them through his *lazzi*, and the witty fool reminds the ruling elite of their limits and potential abuse of power. If one of the main features of the trickster and his various reincarnations is that they are joint-disturbers, who create a subversive culture in opposition to official culture, thereby challenging the latter, David Bennent (acting in the role of Oskar) and Kiefer adopt the roles of such figures. Both Kiefer's provocative salutes in the late sixties and Schlöndorff's daring scene contribute to a process that has been given the rather unfortunate name *Vergangenheitsbewältigung*, or "coming to terms with the past." By breaking a postwar taboo, that of performing the salute with apparently serious intent, Kiefer attempts to call upon his audience to engage in *Vergangenheitsreflexion*, "reflecting upon the past," long before the German public seemed to be ready for it. For Schlöndorff, reaching a German audience was a lot easier. His movie appeared at a time when, thanks to the dissemination of Marvin Chomsky's *Holocaust* miniseries on German television in January 1979, the German public could finally talk more openly about the Holocaust. And yet, Schlöndorff's turbulent rostrum scene does not incite his spectators to the same kind of serious reflection on the German past achieved by the motionlessness of Kiefer's Hitler salutes.

Works Cited

Bakhtin, Mikhail. *Rabelais and His World*. Bloomington: Indiana University Press, 1984.

Borger, Julian. "How Cheerleaders Gave Birth to Sieg-Heil." *Guardian Unlimited*, July 28, 2001. http://www.guardian.co.uk/international/story/0,3604,528696,00.html (accessed September 16, 2005).

Brooks, Linda M. "Portrait of the Artist as Hero: Anselm Kiefer and the Modernist Semiotics of Fascism." Vol. 2 of *Mimesis in Contemporary Theory: An Interdisciplinary Approach*, ed. Ronald Bogue, 99–125. Philadelphia/Amsterdam: John Benjamins, 1990.

Des Pres, Terrence. *Writing into the World: Essays, 1973–1987.* New York: Viking Penguin, 1991.

Fisher, James. *The Theater of Yesterday and Tomorrow: Commedia dell'Arte on the Modern Stage.* Lewiston, N.Y.: Mellen, 1992.

Grass, Günter. *The Tin Drum.* Trans. Ralph Manheim. New York: Vintage, 1990.

Green, Martin, and John Swan. *The Triumph of Pierrot.* University Park: Pennsylvania State University Press, 1986.

Huyssen, Andreas. "Anselm Kiefer: The Terror of History, the Temptation of Myth." *October* 48 (1989): 25–45.

Hyde, Lewis. *Trickster Makes This World: Mischief, Myth, and Art.* New York: North Point Press, 1998.

Insdorf, Annette. *Indelible Shadows: Film and the Holocaust.* Cambridge: Cambridge University Press, 1982.

Kaltenecker, Siegfried. "Weil aber die vergessenste Fremde unser Körper ist: Über Männer-Körper Repräsentationen und Faschismus." In *The Body of Gender, Körper, Geschlechter, Identitäten,* ed. Marie-Luise Angerer, 91–109. Vienna: Passagen Verlag, 1995.

Madden, David. *Harlequin's Stick, Charlie's Cane: A Comparative Study of Commedia dell' Arte and Silent Slapstick Comedy.* Bowling Green, Ohio: Bowling Green University Press, 1975.

Nietzsche, Friedrich. *Beyond Good and Evil: Prelude to a Philosophy of the Future.* Trans. Walter Kaufman. New York: Random House, 1966.

Oreglia, Giacomo. *The Commedia dell'Arte.* New York: Hill and Wang, 1968.

Rosenthal, Nan. *Anselm Kiefer: Works on Paper in the Metropolitan Museum of Art.* New York: Metropolitan Museum of Art, 1998.

Sanders, Barry. *Sudden Glory: Laughter as Subversive History.* Boston: Beacon, 1995.

Sklar, Dusty. *Gods and Beasts: The Nazis and the Occult.* New York: Crowell, 1977.

Warneken, Bernd Jürgen. "Bürgerliche Emanzipation und aufrechter Gang: Zur Geschichte eines Handlungsideals." *Das Argument, Zeitschrift für Philosophie und Sozialwissenschaften* 179 (1990): 39–52.

Welsford, Enid. *The Fool: His Social and Literary History.* New York: Farrar and Rinehart, 1935.

Wildmann, Daniel. *Begehrte Körper: Konstruktion und Inszenierung des "arischen" Männerkörpers im "Dritten Reich."* Würzburg: Königshausen and Neumann, 1998.

Winter, Peter. "Whipping Boy with Clipped Wings." *Evaluating Anselm Kiefer.* Special issue of *Art International* 2 (1988): 66–70.

Wolbert, Klaus. *Die Nackten und die Toten des Dritten Reiches.* Gießen: Anabas Verlag, 1982.

16

Visual Signaling Systems in East German Political Cabaret

The Case of Berlin's Distel

Michele Ricci

In October 1953, East Berlin's *Distel* (Thistle) cabaret opened its doors for its first show, *Hurrah! Humor ist eingeplant!* (Hurrah! Humor is planned for!). That political cabaret had found fertile soil in East Germany was confirmed only a year later, when Dresden's *Herkuleskeule* and the *Leipziger Pfeffermühle* joined the *Distel* as East Germany's leading professional cabarets. Although reviewers gently ridiculed the theaters for failing to make good on a promise of political sharpness—Budzinski referred to the "stumpfer Dorn" (dull thorn) and the "süßer Pfeffer" (sweet pepper)—these cabarets found both state approval and a popular following that assured their survival and success for the duration of East Germany's history (Budzinski 1982, 279). In 1990, former cabaret director and theorist Mathias Wedel looked back upon this phenomenon, observing that "the state needed a cabaret in order to show that even taboos could be handled publicly. We cabaret members needed the aura of the shrewd antagonist. The public needed us, because our played opposition obliged it to nothing—certainly not to opposition. And we all needed the censors: they were the reliable mediator between our inclination to joke and the state's demands of discipline, partiality, and allegiance" (quoted in Fensch 1995, 219).[1] As Wedel's statement suggests, cabaret in socialist East Germany was charged with mediating the needs and interests of several parties at once—including those of the state, the audience, and the artist. Though Wedel's summary of these needs may not be exhaustive, his statement importantly reveals that the interests served by East German cabaret were as varied as the parties that it served.

By taking account of cabaret's function as mediator among different factions and their differing interests, we begin to approach an understanding of the vital role played by the *Distel* and its counterparts in East Germany. But this revelation, in turn, raises new questions: How did this mediation take place? What were the contents of these messages, and what was the form of these several vectors of communication along which directives could be conveyed and received? Rudolf Hösch, echoing his contemporary Manfred Berger, referred to socialist cabaret as a "'special aesthetic system of signals, that through pleasurable means makes [our] public aware of the contradictions in the development of our socialist society'" (Hösch 1972, 208). While Hösch's statement primarily addresses the programmatic goals of socialist cabaret, it offers a concept—the signal—that captures the cabaret's unit of communicative currency. Notably, this signal belonged to a system of many, and moreover, it was designed to convey a particular meaning. Some two decades later, Michael Fleischer revived this notion of the cabaret as signaling system, unfolding its significance in particular for the Eastern European stage: "Cabaret is a *zeichenhaftes* ['sign-filled'] phenomenon." Fleischer's signs, like Hösch's signals, were understood to bear meaning, though Fleischer additionally emphasized the variety of givers and receivers in this matrix. Moreover, Fleischer's theory underscores the variation in the form of the cabaret's sign: "The formulation that [cabaret] is a multimedia message in fact carries currency" (Fleischer 1989, 74).

Whether upholding the ideals of socialism against the unsatisfactory forms of its realization or assuming a profoundly subversive stance, political cabaret of East Germany indeed employed a system of signals or signs to convey meaning from text writer, director, and actor to the viewer, which at the same time was capable of circumventing the censors' watchful eyes. Scholarship to date dealing with the nature of political cabaret in East Germany, including works by Klaus Budzinski (1982), Michael Fleischer (1989), Hanne Castein (1990), and, most recently, Dietmar Jacobs (1996), has focused on verbal signals, considering methods used to couch political themes in witty, pointed, yet accessible lines. Without disputing the centrality of the spoken word as "signal" in GDR political cabaret, we must acknowledge that other forms of signals, namely on the visual level, deserve our attention, including stage sets, props, and the gestural aspects of acting. By reviewing statements on the theory and purpose of the visual elements of cabaret written mainly by *Distel* affiliates, I reveal the fundamental programmatic role the visual component was to play in conveying meaning.

Through examining examples of specific modes of visual signaling and instances of the practical implementations of these signals, I explore the forms and goals of their use, with particular attention to the advantages and limits of employing—and studying—this sensory level as a communicative tool for the East German cabaret.

Though aspects of this inquiry may apply to East German cabaret as a whole, certain conditions determined by particular geography, economics, audience, and directorial philosophy underlie the decision to consider one GDR cabaret in isolation. East Berlin's *Distel,* founded by Erich Brehm as the first significant East German cabaret, forms the focal point for this inquiry. This particular cabaret lends itself to study not only for what it affords but also for its limitations. The copious treatises, manuals, and articles on cabaret theory and practice produced by several members of the *Distel*'s directorial staff—including Brehm, Otto Stark, and Gisela Oechelhaeuser, along with Hösch—provide an important link between the abstract ideas of satire in the socialist state and their actual manifestation on stage. At the same time, due to its location in the heart of the East German capital, the *Distel,* known as East Germany's *Hofkabarett* ("court cabaret"), was at once the showcase of the GDR, while also being subjected to constraints that its counterparts in Leipzig and Dresden were spared. This extreme combination of heightened prestige and control—as the pride of the East and yet dangerously near to the West—provides a provocative backdrop for the potential uses and abuses of visual signaling systems in GDR cabaret.

The *Distel* was born into an era of Eastern European socialism when interests were anything but unambiguous. Three months after Stalin's death in March of 1953, East Germany's general secretary of the SED (*Sozialistische Einheitspartei Deutschlands,* Socialist Unity Party), Walter Ulbricht, was summoned to Moscow and instructed to begin a "New Course" involving a more moderate policy, with the central aim of reuniting the two Germanys. Meanwhile, tensions among workers displeased with SED policies were mounting, and by mid-June had culminated in strikes and demonstrations. Yet, far from a harmonious force giving voice to a common demand, these protesters advocated a spectrum of often conflicting agendas, and strains of democratic, nationalistic, and reformed socialist thinking issued from these masses.[2] By autumn, Soviet-led initiatives to move toward creating a single German government were thwarted by Konrad Adenauer's solid victory in the September 6 general elections in the Federal Republic of Germany. Rejected by their Western brothers, dissatisfied with their own lots, bitterly divided on the course to take, and ultimately powerless in the face of unyielding state authoritarianism, the East Germans found themselves in a precarious situation. "East Germany in 1953 was thus a deeply divided and fractured society" (Pritchard 2000, 220).

The *Distel*'s founding in 1953 marked the ultimate triumph of those believing that "entertainment of the populous must be taken seriously, and that a small vent must be created for the everyday dissatisfactions" of life (Jäger 1973, 214). More specifically, this vent was "to give a degree of expression to the public opinion, while at the same time channeling this opinion" (Jäger 1975, 119). That is, the cabaret presented the mired state a twofold political opportunity: a forum for both venting and learning. Tailored to affect the contemporary audience on these two levels—the cathartic and the didactic—this particular brand of socialist satire required a new name. Brehm, in his humorous text on the theory and how- to of GDR cabaret entitled the *Die erfrischende Trompete* (The refreshing trumpet), posited a notion of *helping* satire, which aimed at once to show mistakes and setbacks, while also working toward the goal of improvement within the system (Brehm 1964, 22–23). This Eastern version, in distinction to Western satire, was also characterized as "positive," namely, as defined in terms of *what it stood for* as well as what it stood against (Castein 1990, 92). In its very definition of socialist cabaret, the state's programmatic goals allowed for a vent for public grievances, while smartly couching those grievances as born of a desire to fulfill socialist ideals.

That cabaret members—at least on paper—affirmed the connection between programmatic goals and cabaret performances was reflected by former *Distel* director Otto Stark's claim: "The starting point [of cabaret] is the goals of our Party" (quoted in Castein 1990, 93). Beyond celebrating cabaret's role in encapsulating programmatic messages, cabaret advocates also seemed convinced that its signals actually would reach their target. Former *Distel* actress and director Gisela Oechelhaeuser felt that "with the help of political satire we can convey value conceptions, come to terms with false value conceptions, and accomplish our part in the carrying through of societal ideals of socialism. We cabaret actors must effect a consciousness-raising, since the consciousness of our public is constrained to some degree within our [sphere] of influence" (Oechelhaeuser 1985, 8–10). Whether presenting either a retrospective justification for previously established methods or an actual gesture to interpret cabaret's role in socialist society, cabaret theory nonetheless upheld the socialist ideals. Yet, perhaps even more striking than the way that this conviction permeated the theory is the corresponding assertion that these ideals could be translated into theatrical terms. That is, every scene, every line, and every move on the cabaret stage were seen to lend themselves to achieving the directive of didactics and catharsis—from the socialist cabaret's inception to the collapse of the GDR.

At the same time, as Wedel suggested, the objectives of the cabaret troupe did not merely mirror those of the state. Indeed, the cabaret's subversive potential could not have been lost on the players—and its use is perhaps best affirmed by the state's systematic attempts to guard against such tactics. The state's concern that undesired messages might issue from the *Distel* numbers via both spoken and visual signals is demonstrated above all by its particular mode of censorship. For not only were certain censors assigned to read all cabaret texts in advance, they were also present for dress rehearsals, observing how each number was actually *played*. "So that in performance the approved texts would not acquire hidden or contrary meaning through director's interference, mimicry or gestures, a party bureaucrat appeared at rehearsal" (Budzinski 1982, 278).

By distinguishing the interests of the state and of the cabaret troupe, we create a basis for reading the cabaret's visual symbols and inferring their intended role and use on stage. A final and perhaps most important component in this signaling system, capable of revealing the intended role of the signals and their possible reception, is the audience itself. Admittedly, it is with extreme difficulty that we characterize the *Distel* audience, given changes in material and societal conditions over the history of the GDR, as well as the nature of documentation of public opinions of this group. Historian Mike Dennis, for example, cites a sociological study of 1990, in which some 1,500 citizens of the former East Germany expressed opinions about socialism. According to the findings, a majority were satisfied or very satisfied with their social security system, jobs, child care, and housing (Dennis 2000, 157). At the same time, this group acknowledged dissatisfaction with their material standing, as well as with their standard of living relative to the West. While such studies may reflect their own biases, they do caution us not to assume that the public's perspective was necessarily diametrically opposed to that of the state.[3]

The climate of 1953 reveals that—as the state well knew—the audiences filling the *Haus der Presse* at East Berlin's Friedrichstrasse Station represented highly varied perspectives. In addition to serving as a so-called *Ventil* ("vent or safety valve") for expectant socialists, who were frustrated that society was not in fact advancing toward prescribed ideals, this cabaret must have been received as—if not conceived as—a forum for all kinds of cathartic expressions, comprising the eclectic interests of those groups who were on strike that very summer. While it is difficult to gauge how explicitly the state or cabaret troupe catered to these various clusters of public opinion, we can at least imagine that it was possible to do so, and that perhaps in the very ways that it deviated from programmatic goals, the cabaret might have spoken to these other interests, creating a *Ventil* for them as well.

Whether intentional or not, the cabaret was offering satisfaction to this diverse audience, as documented by regular sellouts, advance ticket sales of up to a year, and the opening of the *Distel*'s second house in Hohenschönhausen in 1976 to meet incredible audience demand. And, while we must suppose that audience sentiments had evolved from the days of the *Distel*'s opening through to the building of the Berlin Wall in 1961 and Erich Honecker's appointment as first secretary in 1971, it is plausible to assume that they still echoed the varied opinions of viewers in the mid-50s, however tempered. Additionally, the state's initiative, providing blocks of tickets to factories and other organizations to attend culture events, may well have helped assure a variety of perspectives among viewers. Hence, the cabaret's signals—purposefully or incidentally—were aimed at an audience both thankful to be present and in search of not one kind of *Ventil* but several. Only in light of this complex constellation of interests and perspectives associated with the GDR cabaret's inception can we infer the potential uses and (perhaps unwitting) functions of any cabaret signs—including the visual. Here, I focus on the visual elements for one, because they have undeservedly gained only minimal attention, and secondly, because they offer additional signaling possibilities that speech alone cannot convey.

As programmatic texts reveal, the gestural aspects of acting were long recognized for their great potential to transmit messages. In an article of 1969 entitled "Über die Bedeutung der Kabarett-Regie" (On the meaning of cabaret-directing), Karl-Heinz Tuschel upheld the importance of nonverbal elements of GDR-style acting: "If the cabaret aims to penetrate deeper into mankind, it must turn to modes of behavior as its main object. . . . Real modes of behavior, especially [those that] interest the cabaret, *zeichnen sich* ['distinguish themselves'] in the everyday often through the fact that their actual content is expressed *less through words, and more through actions, bodily-motor reactions, [and] facial gestures*" (Tuschel 1969, 10, emphasis added). Frank Kleinke similarly insisted on the centrality of the visual: the "goal of the game of gestures is the production of optically-perceivable processes and images for the viewers, from which they can arrive at the way of thinking and behavior of the figures on stage" (Kleinke 1990, 21–22). And, more directly, Kleinke asserted the value not only of dialogue but also of "staging the texts as *sehenswert* ['worth seeing']" (Kleinke 1990, 21–22).

In the *Distel* case, the visual focus of GDR cabaret was unfolded—at least theoretically—in two important ways. Heinz Lyschik, long-time *Distel* dramaturge, actor, and text writer, distinguished the *Distel* from other GDR cabarets as a group that "put a great value on [the idea that] something would be *gespielt* ['played'] instead of *berichtet* ['reported'], on demonstrating instead of telling." According to Lyschik, this particular method was understood as a means to allow the audience to be present and participating in the action, rather than merely to be listening (Lyschik 2001). This deliberate shift toward a less centrally verbal style of cabaret might be read as evidence of the *Distel*'s distinctive conception of the cabaret in a socialist state. The point acquires added dimension when we consider that the *Distel,* as it exists now in a post-Wall Germany, has adopted the journalistic style previously popular among its counterparts.

The second facet of a visually focused approach to directing at the *Distel* concerns the building of individual characters. In a telling statement, Oechelhaeuser distinguished the cabaret acting method from that of the theater as analogous to the difference between a *caricature* and a *portrait* (Oechelhaeuser 1985, 305). Whereas the portrait shows the figure in a normal and well-developed sense, the caricature represents the special and particular, by deliberately deviating from the norm it posits. By establishing this tension between the norm and the anomaly, the caricature provokes the audience to critically evaluate seemingly unambiguous conditions (Oechelhaeuser 1985, 29–30). Helmut Hellmann, a former *Distel* cast member, added to this notion of caricature that "the figure must be *drawn* with a few strokes, sometimes exaggerated, and without shadowing" (author's interview with Hellmann). The primary practical reason dictating this method was the time constraint—two- to three-minute sketches hardly allowed for building a complex character. Yet, there is also the sense that, as Oechelhaeuser put it, the "imperative of pregnancy"—which she extended not only to character creation but also to stage sets, props, gestures, and mimicry—was itself an essential characteristic of socialistic cabaret (Oechelhaeuser 1985, 26). That is, some value or message rested precisely in this method of rapid communication itself, as well as in the simple, direct delivery it afforded.

The *Distel*'s commitment to playing over reporting, in addition to creating a caricature over a developed role, is exemplified by the "Tante Emma" character, played by Ilse Maybrid, who became a regular in shows of the 1980s. Emma was found in the marketplace, attempting to hawk her wares with exaggerated gestures and screaming. She was indeed a caricature, whose purpose was reinforced not by the depth of her role, but by the regularity with which she appeared to audiences, establishing a kind of predictability. In fact, the frequent use of stock characters, including the sailor Kuddeldaddeldu, the Russian soldier Alojscha, and other types, such as the American, underscores the way that visual recognition of certain characters helped to quickly evoke again the experiences with which they were associated. Hellmann revealed the importance of this visual association, even above recollection of particular lines or songs, by observing that the audience "clung to certain roles" (author's interview with Hellmann).

But in acting out over reporting, Emma did even more than recreate the marketplace experience. Depicted in the process of trying to sell what were invariably useless, silly, or ridiculous objects, Emma was a means of pointing to the materiality of the objects themselves. In the show *Ein Glück, daß wir es haben* (How lucky that we have it!), which opened in 1981, Emma stood before the audience sporting a metal gismo, with braces over her shoulders and flaps over her head. The object was dubbed a *Gleichgewichtsstabilisator* ("balance stabilizer"), intended to help an intemperate comrade make his way home from a bar without injury. Emma was charged with showing how things worked and why one might (or might not) wish to own them. Combining a kind of slapstick humor with a direct, didactic objective, the Emma character, through the use of her props, could instruct the audience in a skeptical role vis-à-vis goods, sales, and capitalism as a whole. Moreover, by demonstrating the ridiculousness of the available goods, she might have brought to a frustrated audience's mind something that they would much rather have had available to them. In the case of the *Gleichgewichtsstabilisator,* the objective of both thematizing and alleviating popular frustration was facilitated by the ambiguous form of the prop itself, which at first glance actually looks like a flying machine.

The "Transit" skits offer a second example of this complex effect of staging over reporting. In this number, featured in 1978's *Hurrah ist eingeplant!* (Hurray is planned in!), Irma and Horsti, a West Berlin couple (played by actors Hanna Donner und Helmut Hellmann), traveled to the GDR to visit relatives. Like Emma, these characters were revived in other *Distel* shows, drawing laughs for their characterization of Western snobbishness and disdain, while giving voice to valid criticisms of the East (Jelavich 2000, 169). This impression is enhanced through the visual performance of the scene, particularly illustrated by the uncomfortable look on the wife's face as she held in her lap the Mercedes hood ornament belonging to their otherwise structureless car. Likewise, her husband, with a steering wheel propped upon his knee, leaned forward with a casual air of contempt. The transparency of the car read as a metaphor for the transparency of the figures. In addition,

Figure 16.1. "Tante Emma," 1981 *Distel* performance of *Ein Glück, daß wir es haben* (How lucky that we have it!). Photo by Adelheid Beyer, Berlin. Printed with permission of the *Distel* Cabaret.

the very crudely sketched drawing of an East German city behind—and notably slightly below—the actors functioned as if to offer a glimpse into the minds of this West German couple, belying their conception of a cheerless, primitive East Germany.

Furthermore, the very staging of this scene, as opposed to its recounting, created for the audience the experience of East meeting West. By this process, the audience was provided with a reminder of this very fact of separation, perhaps of relatives or loved ones lost to the other side, as well as of the bitter echoes of the West's choice in 1953, in which capitalism—and democracy—won out over socialism. Like a kind of no man's land, the stage in "Transit" offered itself as a space to think about the material, physical and ideological separation between "them" and "us." Indeed, one might imagine that the numerous restagings of "Transit," and the audience's resultant growing familiarity with the characters, further complicated the notion of separation, to the point where the "other" paradoxically became intensely familiar.

As illustrated above, the use of props, sets, and costumes was inextricably linked with the way in which the staging of scenes occurred. Therefore, it should come as no surprise that cabaret theory explicitly accounted for their appropriate role in enriching the cabaret's system of signals. A general rule of thumb, echoed by Oechelhaeuser as well as Kleinke, was to use visual elements economically. "Director and actor . . . must carefully control the use [of props and costumes] so that the enjoyment of a played text could be incomparably greater than that of a written text" (Oechelhaeuser 1985, 26). And similarly, Kleinke recommended that stage sets, costume, props and technical elements be used to effect a "shortening, condensing, rendering crudely, or typification." When applied specifically to a given scene, this meant that one should use "the most symbolic thing." For example, when showing a cleaning lady "as she dusts off her boss's Lenin-volumes, it is logical what she should have in hand" (Kleinke 1990, 8–9). Implicit in this frugal and often selective use of props and costumes is the assumption that, as with acting, the signals should be few, well chosen, and clear. Their impact and effect rested precisely in their crude simplicity. Additionally, these deliberately "simple" props, by their very nature, might have suggested something about the message that they were to carry. Was the message as direct and simple as the props were, or was the message so complicated that the props should not detract from its apprehension?

That the props served as more than a humble handmaiden to the scene's verbal political message is affirmed by their noted importance in achieving theatrical effect. Such signals were not imparted by the merely basic, most characteristic prop, but by distorting the given prop by degrees. Kleinke spoke of the use of *analogous props*—such as a spoon for a reporter microphone—in this context (Kleinke 1990, 8–9). By means of this substitution, the analogous prop unleashed a host of potential signals, such as surprise or laughter, while at the same time conveying a kind of austerity and spontaneity typical of the cabaret format. Moreover, this very substitution attracted attention to the prop, not merely for its use, but also for the distinction between its identity and its function. When Wolfgang Haarhaus recommended that stage sets, props, and costumes "should not be real, they should only look as though they were the required object," his unspoken rationale suggested a value in addition to that of pregnancy (Haarhaus n.d., 73). Namely, he pointed to the analogous prop's ability to stand as something else, while always therefore underscoring the very fact that it is only a substitute for something absent. The *Distel*'s Kuddeldadeldu character, played by Heinz Draehn, sported a shaving brush in his hat brim in the place of a flower, offering an illustration of the humorous and potentially thought-provoking effect of employing analogous props.

Besides the use of analogous props, additional distortions by degrees were achieved by the use of exaggeration in props. The *Distel*'s *Bis hierher und so weiter* (Until this point and so forth) of 1964 featured a number entitled "Rock für den Frieden" (Rock for peace) in which this type of exaggeration was employed. Played during a guest performance in Hamburg in what the *Deutsche Volkszeitung* of Düsseldorf called a Beatles parody, this number included three long-haired guitar players, clad in white shirts with black ties, each holding guitars of progressively greater size. From the smallest—the size of a ukulele—to the largest— around which the musician could hardly get his arms—the guitars formed the focal point of the number. Haarhaus, using the comparable example of an oversized sofa into which one sinks, maintained that the use of exaggerated props evokes surprise and humor. One could equally imagine these oversized props achieving Oechelhaeuser's more programmatic goal of conveying the tensions between normality and anomaly. Specifically, size distortion could signal corruption, distorted viewpoints, ridiculousness, or decadence—in other words, the false value concepts of which Oechelhaeuser spoke, and which at once could be turned subversively onto the critical state itself.

Costumes, too, were subject to the doctrine of austerity. Both Haarhaus and Kleinke emphasized the imperative of simple dress, including the use of few and suggestive pieces, such as a white coat for a scientist. As *Distel* photos reveal, attractive but no-frills outfits were the standard, communicating simplicity and frugality, while also creating continuity between sketches, thus marking the actors as actors rather than im-

Figure 16.2. "Two Angels Deliberate," 1976 *Distel* performance of
So wahr mir. Spott helfe (So help me, mockery!).
Photo by Helmut Raddatz, Berlin. Printed with permission
of the *Distel* Cabaret.

mersing them in their roles. Yet the *Distel* also exercised more variation
and calculation in costuming than cabaret theory would recommend. A
number in 1976, "So wahr mir. Spott helfe" (So help me, mockery!),
featured a discussion between two angels who, far from being simply
clad, donned black robes, fabric wings upon their heads, and ringlets of
hair (quite obviously fashioned from paper). In this type of routine, the
costume did more than suggest. Rather, it reflected an effort to transform the characters into angels, in part distinguishable because they
would not reappear in their angel costumes in the next scene. From the
didactic standpoint, this type of costume filled in much more detail
than cabaret theory would favor, illustrating itself elaborately for the
audience. More than that, the wigs in particular no doubt aimed to elicit
laughter—above all for their blatant falseness—in a manner similar to
the analogous props.

A second deviation from the doctrine of austerity practiced at the
Distel arose from actors' personal desires to impart their own signals—
namely to look their best. According to Lyschik, the *Distel* employed a
master tailor responsible for making all costumes, and each woman

Figure 16.3. Stage set, 1974 *Distel* performance of *Vorwärts und nichts vergessen* (Forward and forget nothing). Photo by Tassilo Leher, Berlin. Printed with permission of the *Distel* Cabaret.

typically had two outfits at her disposal. In the 1971 number "Der Freizeit eine Gasse" (A free road for free time), for example, Hanna Donner appeared in a stylishly patterned shirt, a short, pleated skirt, and lace-up boots—an outfit clearly designed to maximize attention to the actress's looks. This desire on the part of particular actresses to look attractive could reach an extreme, noted Lyschik, when the tailor was called to produce especially beautiful gowns for them.

As with costumes, the *Distel* set designers practiced the doctrine of austerity, while at the same time attempting to exceed it. From very modest sets like 1974's *Vorwärts und nichts vergessen* (Forward and forget nothing), which was barely adorned but for a few signs primitively attached to the curtain, to 1978's *Einsteigen, bitte!* (All aboard!) set before a crudely painted rendering of a subway station entrance, the 1970s *Distel* experienced a shift toward a more austere style (Otto and Rösler 1981, 356). Evident even in the comparison between these two 1970s shows is the fact that the more simple the background, the more the eye is drawn to the actors on stage. It would seem, then, that the favoring in theoretical texts of these types of sets was based on the conviction

Figure 16.4. Stage set and cast, 1978 *Distel* performance of
Einsteigen, bitte (All aboard!).
Photo by Helmut Raddatz, Berlin. Printed with permission
of the *Distel* Cabaret.

that the set aids the signaling precisely by not hindering it. That there
was a perceived tradeoff imagined between set and texts, for example, is
revealed in Budzinski's account of GDR cabaret, in which he understood the intricacy and richness of the stage set as serving a compensatory role in relationship to weak texts (Budzinski 1982, 286). But if this
was a signal projected from ornate sets, then the reverse might also
manifest itself—namely, that an unadorned stage suggests strength of
other components, such as texts and acting.

Yet the notion of the stage set as either compensation for weak texts
or a complement to strong ones did not comprise the entire view of the
stage's potential in GDR cabaret. As with props, sets at times employed
a direct and active role in the signaling process. This is most vividly
exemplified by the *Distel*'s *Panoptical 67*, which marked the culmination
of radical experiments with multimedia displays, using collage, film,
and animation to redefine the cabaret experience. Specific effects included the use of a screen upon which were projected the thoughts of
the actors who played before it, as well as the combining of the image
of actor Gerd Schäfer—filmed previously—engaged in a discussion

with Gerd Schäfer incarnate. Director Georg Honigmann's use of these new media in cabaret, read as consistent with programmatic objectives, seemed designed to uncover the dichotomies between acting and thinking and between artifice and truth, while also problematizing material reality by visual means.

As significant as the direct role assigned to the sets, lighting, and other stage effects in creating this experience was the contemporary critical reception, which revealed that some still weighed the set against the text. "It seems as though the texts were written to *show* as much as possible and to *say* as a little as possible [emphasis added]" ("Schäfers lustige Schau," 1967). Otto and Rösler likewise commented on the trend toward effects at the *Distel* of the late 1960s: "[T]he *Distel* employed film-blending, live-film combinations, animation, film, and sound montage. . . . But the texts themselves remained the Achilles' heel of all programs" (Otto and Rösler 1981, 353). The degree to which the reviewers reflected the opinions of the audience is uncertain. But unreceptive reviews, combined with the enormous costs associated with this type of production, were followed by the *Distel*'s subsequent shift away from these media. The most radical use of the visual may have broached the limits of its efficacy.

While "mask play, puppets, pantomime and expressionistic dance" were all added to Max Hohl's list of means to "force [individuals] to contemplate," dance deserves attention for its special role in the communication of additional, even subversive signals in GDR cabaret (Hohl 1986, 30–31). Subsumed in the list of visual elements meant to foster a kind of critical thinking, dance—abstract dance in particular—was assigned instructive value for illustrating, alienating, or otherwise creating a standpoint conducive to critical reflection. For one, abstract movement offered training in reading metaphor, because it required the viewer to distinguish the action from that which it signified. Yet as Lyschik and Hellmann noted, dancing had also acquired a particularly subversive function at the *Distel*. Rather than communicating one mode of thinking or rejecting another, dancing—or more precisely *vertanzen*—became a way to deal with censors. In Lyschik's words, the show was able to carry certain messages because "what we could not speak, would be sung. And what was still too politically sharp to sing, would be *vertanzt* [danced]." Hellmann similarly referred to the "*vertanzen* ['dancing'] of a dangerous text" (author's interview with Hellmann). That is, as a means to get a risky text past the censors, the actors would play it incongruously lightly or quickly, creating distraction through visual rhythm changes devised to shift attention away from content. Therefore, dance participated in the direct conveyance of didactic signals while also functioning as an accessory to other subversive signaling processes.

These examples clearly present only a cursory overview of numerous uses of visual signaling during the *Distel*'s history. Nonetheless, they offer a basis for establishing the importance of visual signaling in GDR cabaret, its uses, and, most of all, the variety of messages that these signals were able to bear. Although recreating with complete accuracy the intention behind and reception of certain signals in GDR cabaret is impossible, evidence of the visual signs' ability to convey programmatic, subversive, and other messages offers clues to the cabaret's widespread success and acceptance in East Germany. The flexibility of the visual sign ensured the fulfillment of these disparate needs: to teach, to vent, to criticize, and to laugh.

Notes

My heartfelt thanks to Gail Finney for her insightful critique of this essay. I am also grateful to *Distel* associates Hanna Donner, Helmut Hellmann, and Heinz Lyschik for sharing their memories and invaluable comments, and to Matthias Thiel of the Kabarett Archiv in Mainz for his gracious assistance.

1. Except where otherwise indicated, translations are my own.

2. See Pritchard 2000 for a thorough account of this spectrum of political views in 1953 East Germany.

3. For more perspectives on East Germans' political opinions, see Weber 1985 and Engler 1999.

Works Cited

Brehm, Erich. *Die erfrischende Trompete: Taten und Untaten der Satire.* Berlin: Henschelverlag, 1964.

Budzinski, Klaus. *Pfeffer ins Getriebe: Ein Streifzug durch 100 Jahre Kabarett.* Munich: Wilhelm Heyne Verlag, 1982.

Castein, Hanne. "'Agit-Pro & Contra': Zum Kabarett der DDR." In *Kurz bevor der Vorhang fiel: Zum Theater der DDR,* ed. John Flood, 91–104. GDR Monitor Special Series 7. Ian Wallace, gen. ed. Amsterdam: Rodopi, 1990.

Dennis, Mike. *The Rise and Fall of the German Democratic Republic, 1945–1990.* New York: Longman, 2000.

"'Die Distel.'" *Deutsche Volkszeitung: Düsseldorf,* February 19, 1965, n.p.

Engler, Wolfgang. *Die Ostdeutschen: Kunde von einem verlorenen Land.* Berlin: Aufbau, 1999.

Fensch, Helmut. "Im Kabarett des Ostens: Nachgeschobene Betrachtungen." *die horen: Zeitschrift für Literatur, Kunst und Kritik* 40, no. 1 (1995): 217–221.

Fleischer, Michael. *Eine Theorie des Kabaretts: Versuch einer Gattungsbeschreibung (an deutschem und polnischem Material)*. Bochum: Brockmeyer, 1989.

Haarhaus, Wolfgang. *Bühnentechnik. Beleuchtung. Requisiten*. Leipzig: Zentralhaus für Kulturarbeit, n.d.

Hellmann, Helmut. Personal interview. August 12, 2001.

Hohl, Max. *Über die im Kabarett gebräuchlichen künstlerischen Formen*. Leipzig: Zentralhaus-Publikation, 1986.

Hösch, Rudolf. *Kabarett von gestern und heute: Nach zeitgenössischen Berichten, Kritiken, Texten und Erinnerungen*. Vol. 2. Berlin: Henschelverlag, 1972.

Jacobs, Dietmar. *Untersuchungen zum DDR-Berufskabarett der Ära-Honecker*. Frankfurt am Main: Lang, 1996.

Jäger, Manfred. "So lacht man in der DDR." *Pardon* 14, no. 1 (1975): 28–121.

———. *Sozialliteraten: Funktion und Selbstverständnis der Schriftsteller in der DDR*. Düsseldorf: Bertelsmann Universitätsverlag, 1973.

Jelavich, Peter. "Satire under Socialism: Cabaret in the German Democratic Republic." In *Literarisches und politisches Kabarett von 1901 bis 1999*, ed. Sigrid Bauschinger. Tübingen: Francke, 2000.

Kleinke, Frank. *Kabarett-ABC*. Leipzig: Zentralhaus-Publikation, 1990.

Lyschik, Heinz. Personal interview. August 14, 2001.

Oechelhaeuser, Gisela. *Von der Absicht zum Programm: Beobachtungen, Bemerkungen und Empfehlungen zur Arbeit im Amateurkabarett*. Leipzig: Zentralhaus-Publikation, 1985.

Otto, Rainer, and Walter Rösler. *Kabarettgeschichte: Abriß des deutschsprachigen Kabaretts*. Berlin: Henschelverlag, 1981.

Pritchard, Gareth. *The Making of the GDR, 1945–1953: From Antifascism to Stalinism*. Manchester, N.Y.: Manchester University Press, 2000.

"Schäfers lustige Schau: Zum neuen Programm der Berliner 'Distel.'" *Der Morgen*, June 15, 1967, n.p.

Tuschel, Karl-Heinz. "Über die Bedeutung der Kabarett-Regie." *Unterhaltungskunst* 1, no. 4 (1969): 9–10.

Weber, Hermann. *Geschichte der DDR*. Munich: DTV, 1985.

17

Reframing Celan in the Paintings of Anselm Kiefer

Eric Kligerman

In his evocative reading of Celan's poetry, Derrida asserts that in Celan's lyric, "Every blank space, every breath and caesura defies translation yet calls for and provokes it at the same time" (Derrida 1994, 74). Calling to mind Adorno's statement concerning the implications of poetry after Auschwitz, a fifty-year-old dictum that does not so much forbid representation of the Holocaust but rather incites and challenges artists to configure its absolute horror, Derrida seems to suggest that Celan's poetry taunts its receiver to translate its wounds into voices. A double translation unfolds: one translates not just Celan's lyrical wounds but also the traumatic event that permeates the fissures of the poem. Celan's poetry serves as a template for provocative forms of art in the Shoah's aftermath. Never acquiescing to a cessation of the work of mourning, Celan's poem's constantly provokes the German reader to confront her/his traumatic history.

One such translator of Celan's poetics is the painter Anselm Kiefer. I am particularly interested in Kiefer's paintings from 1981 through 1983, in which he translates the poet's "Todesfuge" ("Death Fugue") into the space of his Margarethe-Sulamith series. What makes Kiefer's translation of Celan's poetry so successful is that the painter is not merely translating the text of the poem into visual imagery but continues to translate the provocative style of Celan's lyric and attempts to incite and disorient the individual standing before his works. The purpose of this analysis will be to examine the development of Kiefer's process of memory work in the early 1980s for the victims of the Shoah in relation to Celan's lyric. I argue that Kiefer transforms Celan's poem into an uncanny transitional object, that is, a transitional object used in the process of mourning that is represented in the mode of the uncanny.

In a manner similar to Celan's momentary denial of the poem's voice, which he describes in the "Meridian" speech—"The poem shows a strong tendency towards silence"—Kiefer puts on display before the spectator's gaze scenes of erasure (Celan 1985b, 192).[1] For both Kiefer and Celan this disfiguring of readability or of the specular forces the spectator to turn inward and remember the historical catastrophe inscribed in the anamnestic spaces of the artwork. Yet one does not undergo a catharsis or purgation in these texts; instead, we experience a series of perceptual assaults. Kiefer, like Celan, denies to the spectator a passive encounter with the artwork; neither invites his respective reader/spectator to enter the space of poetry or painting in order to enjoy a therapeutic experience with the Holocaust. Their goal is to interrupt such a process of therapy through an assault on our perception. While Celan's poems become terser, approaching the point of whispers or gasps, the dimensions of Kiefer's paintings grow, requiring more space and taking up entire walls. Yet Kiefer's use of language in the Margarethe-Sulamith series, like Celan's later poetry, becomes more abrupt, reduced to a single word. As the paintings expand in size, the words almost vanish or are overlooked by the spectator. Kiefer's growing surfaces create a gravitational pull on the observer who is drawn into the breadth of the canvas. The artist is not simply trying to capture the monumentality of historical loss; his goal is also to overwhelm, estrange, and isolate the spectator in these desolate places.

The anxiety-provoking nature of Kiefer's paintings can most clearly be seen in the reviews his artwork received during the 1980s in Germany. At the time when his popularity was expanding internationally, the response to Kiefer from German critics was anything but positive, some going so far as to call him a proto-fascist. Although critical assessments of Kiefer's art often transform the painter into a patient, using such psychoanalytic terms as taboo, obsession, repression, trauma, mourning, and melancholia to discuss his works, I would argue that the reverse is the case. Kiefer is in fact the analyst who places his audience, postwar Germany, into the position of the patient.

In an article written in 1984 for the *Frankfurter Allgemeine Zeitung*, Robert Beaucamp described Kiefer as a *Tabubrecher* ("breaker of taboos"), insofar as his paintings employ the same names, images, dates, and myths that the Nazis used for their political grounding. Characterizing his paintings as mythic constructions running wild, Beaucamp reads Kiefer's works as celebrations of the very national myths the Nazis abused. In particular, Beaucamp criticizes Kiefer's use of National

Socialist architecture in his paintings of the 1980s—*To the Unknown Painter* (1980, 1982)—and sees the artist celebrating the architectural works of Troost, Kreis, and Speer. What Beaucamp fails to mention anywhere in his article is that while Kiefer is using National Socialist architecture in his works, he is at the same time returning repeatedly to Celan's "Death Fugue." The attacks against Kiefer occur at the same time as Celan's poem and themes of the Holocaust spread across his canvases. What then is the "taboo" that Beaucamp sees Kiefer breaking? Beaucamp discusses neither Celan nor the Shoah, and the real taboo that Kiefer has broken is his confrontation with the genocide of the European Jewish community.

Kiefer's artistic development from 1969 to 1980 can be read as a struggle both with his parent's generation, the perpetrators, and with the cultural inheritance left to a German artist living in the aftermath of Auschwitz. Turning to Eric Santner's discussion of transitional objects in his study of postwar German cinema, I assert that we witness in Kiefer's artworks his own search for transitional objects: objects that can be employed to negotiate the compromised position of other cultural symbols poisoned by their association with the National Socialists. The very possibility of identity construction for both the individual and the nation relies on such objects. As Santner claims,

> The core dilemma is that the cultural reservoir has been poisoned, and few totems seem to exist which would evoke such traumatic ambivalence that only a global foreclosure of all symbolic legacies would prevent further contamination. To carry out their labors of self-constitution the second and third generations face a double bind of needing symbolic resources which, because of the unmanageable degrees of ambivalence such resources arouse, make these labors impossible. (Santner 1990, 45)

Such symbolic legacies as the romantic landscapes of Caspar David Friedrich, the legend of the Nibelungen, and the works of Goethe and Wagner have become defiled through their appropriation by the National Socialists. The names, dates, landscapes, and signs that adorn his paintings throughout the 1970s are the "stranded objects" that Kiefer puts on display before his German audience as he attempts to question, critique, and finally decathect from these national symbols.[2] I contend that Kiefer, a member of the second generation, finds in Celan's poetry the perfect incarnation of a transitional object to take the place of the cultural iconography now rendered toxic by the events of the Shoah.

Kiefer's artworks try to reconstruct the boundaries of national identity after the past boundaries had been shattered. As Santner describes the compromised space of identity construction in postwar Germany:

> The conditions under which stable cultural identities may be con-
> solidated have indeed with and since the Holocaust become radi-
> cally different; the symbolic order to which a German is subjected,
> that is, the social space in which he or she first learns to say *"ich"*
> and *"wir"* now contains traces of a horrific violence. [But] the con-
> ventional sites of identity formation have become destabilized,
> have become more and more *unheimlich*. (Santner 1990, 51)

Trying to engage with what Santner calls "the phantasmatic kernel of the Third Reich," Kiefer demonstrates in his work an ongoing confron-tation with the compromised social space in which identity construction unfolds. By conjuring up the ghostly totems of fascism, Kiefer, I be-lieve, transforms the surface of his canvas into an uncanny site in order to question them and provoke Germany's amnesiac state to remember. What is *unheimlich* about Kiefer's artwork?

According to Freud's model of the uncanny, when something shatters a well-known division (interior/exterior, subject/object), the uncanny rises to the surface. The spatial configuration of the uncanny is orga-nized around blurred boundaries and dissolving frames. The modes of estrangement and terror associated with it are produced through the fading of this line. In particular, it is the figure of a phantom crossing the line between the realm of the living and the dead that is the most uncanny image for Freud.[3] However, the uncanny spaces that com-prise Kiefer's canvases do not simply point to Freud's model of the un-canny with its logic of return of the repressed, anxiety, estrangement, and lost vision. I am arguing here that a second type of uncanny un-folds throughout Kiefer's paintings that confront the Nazi past, culmi-nating in the inscription of Celan's poem: I call this moment the *holo-caustal uncanny*. While for Freud it was the uncanny that approached the reader/spectator, this direction is reversed in the holocaustal uncanny. The artist now lures the individual into the space of the dead. The frame of the artwork splits open and our gaze is consumed by some-thing abysmal. Breaking the division between interior and exterior, Kiefer reframes the conventions of his media by doing violence to the frame.

Although the uncanny is a form of anxiety, and anxiety itself is pro-duced through an act of repression, in my use of the holocaustal un-canny I am not arguing that the mechanism of repression is at work. Rather, I am interested in another trait connected to the return of the repressed and thus to the uncanny: the breakdown of representation. As

Freud asserts in his essay on repression that repression denies mental representations (Freud 1957, 148). According to Freud, the traumatic event repressed by the subject remains untranslated in the space of the unconscious as the unconscious tries to circumvent displeasure. But in the holocaustal uncanny, it is not repressive modes of the unconscious that deny the translation of the anxiety-provoking event. Rather, it is the artist who leaves almost invisible the moment of trauma in order to provoke anxiety in the spectator.

I wish to introduce here that representation in Holocaust aesthetics has less to do with the imitation of a traumatic scene than with the reproduction of affect: the "morbid anxiety" of the uncanny (Freud 1963b, 59). We follow the path that the artist sets before us and expect to read or see something; instead, we are led into scenes of erasure, whether in the ripped lines of Celan's lyric or Kiefer's effaced canvases. The aesthetic strategies of these artists follow an anti-therapeutic model; each constructs traumatic scenes that the spectator can neither overcome nor master. Destroying our position as conventional spectators, the artist disrupts the voyeuristic gaze in order to provoke a vicarious experience of trauma.[4]

Before examining Kiefer's translation of Celan's poetics, I will trace some of the steps leading to his encounter with Celan and the Shoah. We can see from the shifting terrain of Kiefer's artworks the transformation of conventional modes of the uncanny to the holocaustal uncanny, culminating in one of Kiefer's most evocative paintings, *Sulamith* (1983). The place where Kiefer juxtaposes painted image with poetic inscription is the moment when he leads the spectator into an uncanny dimension. We remember from Freud that the uncanny is nothing new or foreign but "something familiar and old-established in the mind that has been estranged only by the process of repression" (Freud 1963b, 60). Repression is the protective coat that prevents something from coming to light, so as to spare the subject any discomfort of memory. Through his technique of layering the canvas with various materials and media—wood, sand, lead, ash, photos, quotations, and paint—Kiefer takes the familiar sites of his studio in Buchen, the forests and landscapes of Germany, through an abstraction. It is the poetic fragment from Celan's poem that provides orientation to what unfolds upon the canvas. These spaces become scenes of temporal dislocation as the inscriptions on the canvas, and the images that accompany them, pull us into sites of trauma.

In the early 1970s Kiefer represents the space of his wooden studio in the Black Forest. Referred to as the attic paintings, they depict wooden spaces filled with religious, mythic, and historical iconography:

quotations and symbols from the *Nibelungenlied* and Wagner. We can read these interiors as not simply the places where cultural memory is stored away, but more exactly they signify the places of a repressed memory. These spaces with their Wagnerian themes—and hence with a Wagnerian antisemitism looming in the background—resemble theatrical stages. Our perspective is that of the audience looking at a stage devoid of actors. Kiefer will put on display here the stranded objects of German cultural history. Contrary to Mark Rosenthal's claim that Kiefer is trying to stare down the ghosts of Germany's past and reclaim Germany's romantic tradition (Rosenthal 1987, 22), there is no redemptive moment in these works. Phantoms haunt the surface of the canvases.

In *Nothung* (1973), the name of the magical sword in the *Nibelungenlied*, the artist takes Wotan's sword found by his son Siegmund in the trunk of a tree and thrusts it into the wooden floor of his studio. Above the sword is the name "Nothung" and beneath the beam of the ceiling are written Siegmund's words: "Ein Schwert verhiess mir der Vater" (my father promised me a sword). Kiefer now places himself into this chain of inheritors, but he transforms the steel of Nothung into a papier-mâché prop stuck into the stage floor. We are reminded of Freud's insight in his essay "Recollection, Repetition, and Working Through": "The past is the patient's armory out of which he fetches weapons for defending himself against the progress of analysis, weapons that we must wrest from him one by one" (Freud 1963a, 160). Setting these weapons on the stage in order to disarm Germany of its toxic myths, Kiefer's goal is to reveal this repressed kernel of Germany history to the audience standing before his paintings.

The passing on of the father's sword, part of the artist's patrimony, becomes a passing on of his crime: blood stains the blade. This murder weapon leaves its traces upon Kiefer's other canvases: the tainted landscapes, Margarethe's straw hair, and Sulamith's breasts. There is something uncanny about this space, not only because a lost object reappears, but because the object that Kiefer chooses to place into the scene has a Freudian resonance—the phallic image of a bloody sword. Although Freud's *uncanny* has at its core the fear of castration, what is symbolically represented in Kiefer's painting is not castration anxiety but rather the fear of losing the ability to represent oneself, individually or collectively. The symbolic order of his patrimony has been severely damaged. Yet, the cultural legacy has not been rendered totally powerless; Kiefer transforms the sword into a tool to critique this very tradition and to point to the jeopardized position of its cultural signifiers.

During the 1970s Kiefer shifts from the interior spaces of his studio to the landscapes of his homeland, from a personal space to a collective one signifying *Heimat* ("homeland"). Although these German landscapes are infused with flowing golden fields and small towns, they are depleted of their powers to serve as cultural signs of national identity, tainted by the presence of fire and blood. In a painting from 1974 titled *Maikäfer, Flieg* (Maybeetle, fly), Kiefer juxtaposes a burning landscape to a German nursery rhyme, bringing the catastrophic scene illustrated directly into relation to German history. The nursery song begins, "Maybeetle, Fly, Father is off at war, Mother is in Pomerania, Pomerania has burned down." While the nursery rhyme goes back to the Thirty Years War, its pathos intensifies after World War II, when the Eastern Territories, including Pomerania, were lost. Whether Kiefer intended to or not, the painting also intersects with Celan's poem "In der Luft" ("In the Air"), which also employs the rhyme. While poem and painting are encounters with an uncanny moment that confront the historical loss of home, both Celan and Kiefer are also reflecting on their cultural inheritance: How can one write poetry or paint with the cultural material of Germany in the aftermath of the war? Celan's poem begins,

> up there moves the banned one, the
> burned one: a Pomeranian, at home
> in the Maybeetle Song that stayed motherly bright-
> bloomed at the edge
> of all cragged
> cold winterhard
> syllables . . .

> Returned home [heimgekehrt] in the
> uncanny [den unheimlichen] spellbeam,
> where the dispersed ones gather. (Felstiner 1995, 198)

What does it mean to be at home in the "Maybeetle Song"? Celan's poem, like the rhyme, tells of the very destruction of home, of exile and cremation. Home is now located in the sky. While we might hear in the title "In the Air" the line from Celan's "Meridian" speech from 1960, "There is something uncanny in the air we breathe," we should go one step further to "Death Fugue" with its "Grave in the Air." The uncanniness in the air we breathe stems from those who have been turned to ash and smoke. Deprived of graves, the most uncanny are those who have risen upward into the clouds. Despite all that has taken place, Celan intimates that a time of growth out of the burning and of winter is possible as seen in the "summerly" and "bright-blossoming."[5] Celan returns to the most basic language of the nursery rhyme and reflects not on words but rather on their simplest components: syllables. Language, although nursed on pain, begins to re-form. Removing the song from the context of the German landscape, Celan reshapes this childhood rhyme to fit into the context of the Shoah. Pomeranians now become Celan's trope for those Jews banished from their homes and exterminated.

In contradistinction to Celan's poem, which moves up into the heavens, the sky in Kiefer's massive work *Maikäfer, Flieg* makes up only a thin line of the painting. The focus is on the terrestrial. The majority of its surface is comprised of a thick layering of black and white oils that undulate horizontally across the canvas. The spectator is positioned, as it were, at sea with the white oils functioning as the crests of waves. The waves appear to be breaking away from shore and toward the spectator, driving him/her away from the expected safety of the shore. In the precariousness of this scene, we are kept at a perpetual distance from the horizon. But as our gaze approaches the horizon, we realize that the waves are actually the furrows of burnt fields as fire rises from the ground. We move toward a small town resting on the horizon. In reaching the woods, we read the inscription of the rhyme placed on the horizon. The rhyme fixes us spatially and temporally in the painting: Germany, or more specifically, Pomerania, in the war's aftermath. At this thin space and time of dusk, we are immediately brought into the memory of the war, of lost homes, exile and death.

I would argue that at this moment, with this particular gaze, we enter the uncanny dimension of the painting. We cross into the landscape in search of safety. Yet our gaze is confronted with the burned fields of winter. Before we reach the vanishing point of the painting, where the rhyme mediates the space between earth and heaven, our eyes must move across the devastated countryside to get to it. Trees and homes catch fire and parts of the field carry traces of blood. The words themselves seem to be burning, lifting like smoke toward the frame of the painting. By focusing on the destruction of *Heimat* and of the rhyme itself, one wonders if Kiefer is transforming Germany into the victim in the painting. Kiefer, I believe, is not making the loss of Pomerania the painting's subject. The artist does not gaze longingly at his or Germany's past, nor is any self-pity evoked in this painting. In his brutal look at history, Kiefer asks the spectator: What can possibly grow out of this field sown with the ruins of German culture? While a nursery rhyme functions as a link between child and parent, a song before sleep, offering comfort to the child before the parent's departure, there is no comfort in this painting comprised of nightmarish images.[6]

After a series of paintings where art, symbolized by a palette, is equated with a fire that consumes in its path Germany's spiritual heroes, its landscapes, and its legends, Kiefer begins to translate Celan's "Death Fugue" into visual imagery from 1981 through 1983. In a work from 1980 titled *Der gestirnte Himmel* (The starry heavens), Kiefer depicts the tension in this transition from his confrontation with the stranded objects of the artist's cultural heritage and the necessity to represent and remember the victims of the trauma. How can he represent this burning through a contaminated symbolic order? In *Der gestirnte Himmel* Kiefer returns briefly to photography, using a photograph taken from around 1969: the artist poses comically in a white nightshirt, hands on his hips, reminiscent of the photos from *Besetzung*. He appears ghostly as black paint is smeared around his pale outline, crystallizing out of the darkness. Although not performing the Hitler salute, Kiefer evidently is alluding to a time when he investigated the perpetrators of fascism.

Painted across the artist's nightshirt is the image of a palette. Beneath him is scrawled part of Kant's closing lines from the Second Critique: "der gestirnte Himmel über uns, das moralische Gesetz in mir" (the starry skies above us, the moral law within me). Thus, Kiefer's symbol for the artist is no longer equated with burning but with Kant's moral law. Kiefer appears to mock one of the most sublime pronouncements of German idealism in order to turn it on its head. While Kant links his formulation of the moral law to questions of the sublime, which is itself derived from the limits of representation, by placing the palette within himself Kiefer rejects the Kantian dictum against representation, the most sublime of commandments. He makes the breaking of the proscription against representation the new law. Art's imperative is now to represent and memorialize the burning committed during the Shoah.

For Kiefer, the work of memory is analogous to an act of excavation, and as he remarked in an interview, "I think vertically, and one of the plains reached was fascism. Yet I see all of these layers [*Schichten*]. I tell stories [*Geschichten*] in my pictures in order to show what is behind the history. I make a hole and go through it" (West 1988, 75). While Lisa Saltzman may read the layering of material on the canvas—paint, lead, sand, straw, and inscription—as an act of entombment that obscures history and thwarts the work of mourning (Saltzman 1999, 91), I contend that just the opposite is occurring. In his Margarethe-Sulamith series, Kiefer ultimately lures his audience through the layers to what is interred beneath the canvas: the Jewish dead.[7]

In his essay on translation Walter Benjamin remarks that translation transpires during times of crisis. What then in 1980 is the crisis in Germany that brings Kiefer into the role of translator? It is a crisis of memory, in which an excessive focusing on the parent's generation, on the perpetrators, starts to shift toward the memory of the Jewish victims.[8] It is as if the burnings that preceded Kiefer's use of "Death Fugue" opened up a space from which the victims themselves could return. There is nothing surprising in Kiefer's turn to Celan's "Death Fugue." In her discussion of the social function of the poem, Sidra Ezrahi describes "Death Fugue" as a "national obsession" in Germany. The poem reappears throughout anthologies of German postwar literature and its recitation has become a fixture in commemorative events. Ezrahi's critique of Germany's relation to the poem comes closest to naming what Kiefer is trying to break out of: "At some subliminal level the Germans have come to *know* the poem the way a people knows its anthems and its liturgies, learning the words at such an early age and on ceremonial occasions that it has become an incantational procedure rather than an attended text" (Ezrahi 1992, 268). The poem remains something performative, while its content remains repressed.

But Kiefer's use of Celan is anything but performative. Radically transforming Celan's poem, Kiefer's goal is to shock the spectator. He tears and estranges the poem in order to break out of the repetitive mode that had befallen it and that threatened to make the poem into a fetishized object. Reanimating the lines through his act of translation, Kiefer brings out of the depths of memory the victims of the Shoah. While Felstiner discusses how the poem has often been misused in German classrooms as instructors focused on the poem's musicality, attempting to show its expertise in sound but overlooking its traumatic content, Kiefer's paintings are anything but musical (Felstiner 1995, 118). Although the refrains and repetitions of the poem are again placed into the Margarethe-Sulamith paintings, the works are not about rhythm or meter. Kiefer uses the disharmony of material in these works—sand, straw, ash, and oils—to convey the rupture of Jewish life in Germany.

While Kiefer shifts between images of Margarethe and Sulamith in his paintings, I concentrate here exclusively on the figure of Sulamith, Celan's and Kiefer's trope for the incinerated European Jewish community. Although the setting of the Margarethe paintings remains relatively unchanged, burning fields comprised of straw and ash, the Sulamith paintings undergo a conspicuous transformation: they move from ravaged fields, to modern high-rise apartments, to a burial chamber, and finally return in leaden books in *Sulamith* (1990). Kiefer's paintings link the destruction of *Heimat* with the extermination of the

Jews. The burned land carries in its soil the traces of the lost other. While Celan's ghosts are written into his poems as erasures, foreign and fractured words, Kiefer's ghosts materialize in his works through the traces of smoke, ash, hair, and fractured words.

In one of his earliest depictions of Sulamith, *Dein aschenes Haar, Sulamith* (Your ashen hair, Sulamith, 1981), Kiefer duplicates the landscape from an earlier painting, *Dein goldenes Haar, Margarethe* (Your golden hair, Margarethe, 1981), with its fields of burning straw, vanishing sky, small village, and tracks in the field moving toward the horizon. But while in *Margarethe* the inscription sits in the fields, in *Sulamith* the words rise into a thin horizon like the rhyme in *Maikäfer, Flieg*. In their black, childlike scrawl the words appear to lift off the canvas like smoke from the fields. Sulamith becomes the product of the burning as Kiefer captures the moment before she vanishes. In contrast to the verse in "Death Fugue," "there you won't lie too cramped," this narrow slit of sky becomes the receptacle for the incinerated Sulamith. Kiefer accents the land, the place of the crime, not the diffusion of the other in the sky.

In *Dein aschenes Haar, Sulamith,* Kiefer returns to the use of lines; they proceed not straight ahead but diagonally to the left corner of the painting. These visual cues draw our gaze away from the center of the painting and guide us to a liminal space near the horizon. The lines naturalize both our glance and the experience of looking away from the center and toward the side. While we are not taken to this place unwillingly, our expectant gaze is nonetheless subverted. The horizon of the painting is not infinite sky and space: it is a thin, dull-gray line of dusk, similar to many of Kiefer's landscape paintings during this period (*Margarethe* 1981, *Die Meistersinger* 1981, *Nürnberg* 1982). Something phantomlike hovers on the horizon. With the blurring of imagery, the unfocused structures on the horizon, the layering of oils and the use of iconographic material like ash upon the canvas, Kiefer takes his painting through an abstraction. To where do the lines of the painting transport us?

As in *Maikäfer, Flieg,* the quotation provides both locus and time to the decimated landscape. While Celan had used language as his primary mode to estrange the reader, Kiefer turns the opacity of Celan's language upon itself to bring into focus the abstract material and content of his paintings. The line from Celan helps to orient the spectator, both spatially and temporally, within the wide expanse of the canvas. At the painting's vanishing point we are taken to the place of extermination and into the holocaustal uncanny. Theo Buck remarks that although one wishes to see loading ramps in these fields, the spectator is forcing something upon the canvas that is not there (Buck 1993, 30). Yet I believe cultural memory is already influencing the way the spectator reads the burned landscape. These phantom associations of the camps, of deportation lines in the countryside, are engendered not merely by Celan's poem but by the photos that Habermas says have been burned into Germany's memory: the tracks leading to Auschwitz (Habermas 1989, 229).[9] While Celan's poem is set in a concentration camp, in Kiefer's landscape paintings of Margarethe and Sulamith it appears as if we are positioned outside the camp and are about to be delivered by the lines to its gates.

If the Margarethe-Sulamith landscape paintings depict the time and place of the trauma, the next painting in the series, *Dein aschenes Haar, Sulamith* (1981), links Sulamith to contemporary German society as the setting shifts to the city. Sulamith's wounded body returns and sits naked in front of a row of modern high-rise apartment houses. Her cascading, bloody-ashen hair conceals her face and gaze. No eyes peer back at the spectator, who is left to look at the dead. Hair and blood flow downward across her breasts, stomach, and legs towards the edge of the canvas and threaten to pour out of the frame; the traces of the crime are about to cross into the realm of the spectator. Kiefer's layering of hair also extends upward toward the gray sky in the painting, and the artist is again alluding to the photographic images of the piles of hair left behind at the extermination camps. The amassing of hair around Sulamith's crouching body testifies to her inconsolable grief.

Kiefer places at the painting's center Sulamith's breasts, partly covered by her black hair and flow of blood. Our gaze is drawn to the first love object of the child. But the breasts in Kiefer's painting, like those metonymically represented through "black milk" in Celan's poem, are unable to sustain life. The breasts should remind us again of Kiefer's attempts at decathexis and his search for substitute objects. The metaphor of black milk here becomes ashen hair strewn across blood-covered breasts. Kiefer's transitional object for the missing Jews of Germany becomes Celan's poem reconfigured in the space of the painting.

The inscription reverses direction and climbs vertically along her hair, mediating the space between Sulamith's hair and the small backdrop of a darkening sky. Now the name "Sulamith" is missing an "H" as language becomes part of the incineration. The moment when the name becomes erased, concealed, or repressed is also the time when the bloodied body returns like a phantom. The windows facing outward toward the body suggest that the crime and its attempted erasure do not go by unseen. While we may move away from the place and time of death and recall how the Nazis tried to leave nothing behind from their crimes, the traces of the extermination are burned into the present.

These buildings, prefiguring the sepulcher from *Sulamith* (1983), tower above the figure like tombstones as her feet emerge from a swirl of smoky-gray oils. It appears as if the body is rising out of the ground.

At the same time as he was employing imagery from "Death Fugue," Kiefer was also representing the architectural projects under the National Socialists.[10] The two collide in *Sulamith*, where a memorial chamber used to honor the Nazi dead, Kreis's design for German soldiers in the Berlin Hall of Soldiers, becomes a room that commemorates instead their Jewish victims. I would argue that this painting is the culmination of the holocaustal uncanny. The spectator must cross not only the sedimentation of material—oil, ash, straw, and wood—but also the layering of distinct forms of representation: architecture, the photograph of Kreis's design, poetic inscription, and painting itself. Utilizing these multiple boundaries of material and media, Kiefer leads the spectator into the recesses of traumatic memory. He transforms the very instruments that were used to erase traces of Jewish culture and its people into a memorial space of the painting. The fire at the back of the hall resembles a seven-flamed menorah, and there is a name carved in stone in the left-hand corner of the painting: Sulamith. The place signifies both erasure and remembrance. While we may be reminded of the wooden interior and columns from *Nothung*, the space in *Sulamith* is of brick, unable to be destroyed by fire.

The tracks of the field in *Dein aschenes Haar, Sulamith* (1981) turn into the crisscrossing lines on Sulamith's chamber floor. Kiefer returns to the use of classical line formations that take us again toward a center horizon. The artist, however, subverts such a perspective. Instead of the lines on the floor leading to an infinite horizon, we are taken into an enclosed space; our gaze is pulled toward the back recesses of the painting. The vertical lines on the floor resembling railroad tracks guide us into the tunnel of the painting. Blocked by the columns on both sides of the chamber, we cannot move to the left or right and are transported toward the vanishing point. While our vision may at first be overwhelmed by the sheer expanse of the canvas (290 × 370 cm), the back recess of the painting gets narrower. Finally, we reach not an infinite space but flames. Our subject position in the room threatens to be consumed by fire. If Kiefer had left obfuscated the structure at the end of the line in *Dein goldenes Haar, Margarethe* (1981), it is clear in *Sulamith* to where we have been brought. After moving from decimated fields to urban settings to an enclosed room set aflame, at the end of the line we encounter the all-consuming fire of the Holocaust. Kiefer takes us to the innermost narrows of the series, into the claustrophobic space of the chamber: there is no exit. Although the lighting is one of semidarkness, the space is devoid of sky. The place for windows has been blackened, casting the canvas into a perpetual night. With its red brick and flame, the perspective of the room resembles the interior of an oven. Trapped in this space of the burning, we have been drawn into the crypt and toward the flames of cremation.

Even language itself is taken through a vanishing, down to the solitary name on the canvas. Sulamith's name is neither written in the center of the painting nor does it mediate the space between land and sky. Barely perceptible, it is written in the upper left-hand corner, sitting precariously on the edge of the frame between tomb and spectator. The name is scratched into her ashen remains on the blackened ceiling of the chamber. But memory of the dead is not definitive as the faint letters upon the wall run the risk of being overlooked.

While Saltzman employs the works of Abraham and Torok to read the *Sulamith* painting as an act of entombment and repression, the body is not a fetishized object that Kiefer refuses to let go of. Sulamith's body, hair, and blood have all vanished in this painting. The only things present in the chamber are memorial flame and ashen name. It is not the gaze of the other that Kiefer wishes would return in the Sulamith paintings but the other's voice. As Robert Hughes remarks, a voice utters forth from the canvas, "Every square centimeter of those giant canvases is intended to speak" (Hughes 1987, 46). Kiefer, appropriating the spectral language from Celan, provides a voice from beyond the grave.

The return of the voice reminds us of de Man on prosopopeia, which is "the fiction of the voice-from-beyond-the-grave. . . . The fiction of an apostrophe to an absent, deceased, or voiceless entity, which posits the possibility of the latter's reply, and confers upon it the power of speech." De Man continues, "Our topic deals with the giving and taking away of faces, with face and deface, figure, figuration and disfiguration" (De Man 1984, 76). In Kiefer's *Sulamith,* the ghost neither returns a gaze nor shows her face but attempts to speak. Her name echoes in the chamber. For de Man, when the dead speak, "The living are struck dumb, frozen in their own death." It is not a Medusa-like gaze that petrifies the observer, but the voice emanating from the canvas that turns the viewer to stone. By depriving us of the gaze of the other, Kiefer forces us to look at fields of ash, smoke, a wounded body, and a name on the wall in order to provoke us into remembering the significance of these disfigurations in the artworks.

But Kiefer's use of Sulamith does not stop in 1983 in Kreis's vault; she returns in the book project of 1990 entitled *Sulamith.* Kiefer shifts from the canvas to books of lead. His objective is to transform the grave in the air, where the body dissolves and is lost, into a leaden interior, where the body can be given proper burial. Nicholas Abraham asserts that during a "transgenerational haunting," a term that could apply to Germany's relation to the Shoah, "The shameful and therefore concealed secret always does return to haunt. To exorcise it one must *express it in words*" (Abraham 1987, 290). A traumatic event becomes "encrypted" and only through an act of writing, of inscription, can the "phantom effect" of the trauma, the return of the dead, be averted. Yet Kiefer's books are not filled with words or letters; rather, each page of these heavy leaden texts contains strands of black hair and ash: Sulamith's signature. The ghost is returned to the page of the book, not as a word but as a vestige of hair. This lock, indicative both of the remains of the dead and a sign of mourning, is placed into the book that bears the title *Sulamith:* the book becomes a tomb, its title the epitaph. How do we read these books?

With the return of the phantom to its grave, one might try to read closure in Kiefer's traumatic narrative. But it is exactly this sense that the past can be mastered, of a *Vergangenheitsbewältigung,* that Kiefer wishes to undermine. Through the presence of hair and ash, marks of disfigurement, something uncanny dominates these leaden books. Kiefer is engaged not so much in an act of writing as in erasing. We recall Freud's link between the uncanny and dismemberment: "Dismembered limbs, a severed head, a hand cut off at the wrist, feet which dance by themselves—all these have something particularly uncanny about them, especially when they prove able to move of themselves" (Freud 1963b, 49–50). The hair, a trace from the dead, does not leave the page, but the reader, by opening the book, enters into a tomb. While Kiefer first writes the absent other through her name in the tomb, representation switches to metonymic displacement in his book project as hair and ash take the place of the word. The hair, triggering the process of memory work, provokes the spectator to retrace these remnants back from where they came: Kiefer guides us into a traumatic scene.

Rather than try to escape the "phantom effect," Kiefer's goal is to lead the spectator into the scene of a haunting so that the trauma can be both remembered and witnessed. His leaden books, which memorialize the incineration, become signs of a struggle against cultural amnesia. Whether in Kiefer's art or in Celan's poetry, the spectator encounters the interpretive and perceptual limits of the Holocaust. We have reached the limits not of writing or painting but of reading and seeing. At this uncanny moment of a breakdown in perception, when the artist effaces the text, we are confronted with the task of reading traumatic residue. Our subject position of witness shifts to potential victim; one must choose between remaining in the void or stepping back across the frame of the artwork with a testimony taken from the structural chasm of the disaster. In making this turn, the spectator becomes translator and renders what was left disfigured by the artist into a memory of a historical erasure.

Notes

1. Except where otherwise indicated, translations are my own.

2. In one of his earliest projects, entitled *Besetzung* (1969), Kiefer poses in photographs throughout Europe, performing the Hitler salute. While *Besetzung* translates into the English concept of an army's occupation of another land, it is also Freud's term that is translated in English as cathexis.

3. The uncanny arises when this border between fiction and reality is crossed and the specter crosses from one realm into the other: "As soon as the writer pretends to move in the world of common reality he takes advantage, as it were, of our supposedly surmounted superstitiousness; he deceives us into thinking that he is giving us the sober truth, and then after all oversteps the bounds of possibility" (Freud 1963b, 57).

4. I am particularly indebted to Julia Hell's analysis of the anxiety of looking in postwar German literature and art. See for instance her forthcoming article in the *Germanic Review*, "Unification Effects: Imaginary Landscapes of the Berlin Republic," a discussion of Gerhard Richter's *October 18, 1977* paintings and Sebald's *Luftkrieg und Literatur.*

5. As Celan says in his Bremen speech, "It [language] gave me no words for what happened, but went through it. Went through it and could resurface" (Celan 1985a, 128).

6. While Anna Brailovsky is correct to assert that Kiefer's paintings escape an accusation of nostalgia, I would disagree with her position that his works operate within the context of a *Vergangenheitsbewältigung:* a "mastering of the past" that she sees mediated through Brecht's concept of a *Verfremdungseffekt.* Instead of undergoing a distancing before Kiefer's artworks, the spectator's body is constantly being consumed by the sheer magnitude of his canvases and sculptures. Neither Germany's traumatic past displayed in these works nor their monumentality can be mastered or controlled by the spectator's gaze. Kiefer's objective is to thwart or frustrate any notion that the spectator experiences something therapeutic before these artworks.

7. Much of my analysis here implicitly revolves around the question of whether or not there is a *Vergangenheitsbewältigung* unfolding in Kiefer's works. Is Kiefer performing a work of mourning or does his project col-

lapse into melancholia? Saltzman argues that "We do not see the work of mourning beyond the narrow confines of Kiefer's own impoverished sense of self" (Saltzman 1999, 74). Any act of mourning for the Jewish other gets displaced onto the artist, who becomes emblematic of the postwar German subject. I believe Andreas Huyssen comes closest to describing what is unfolding in Kiefer's Margarethe-Sulamith paintings: "In these paintings, where Kiefer turns to the victims of fascism, the melancholy gaze at the past, dominant in the architecture paintings, is transformed into a genuine sense of mourning. And Kiefer's seemingly self-indulgent and narcissistic obsession with the fate of painting reveals itself here in its broader historical and political dimension" (Huyssen 1989, 40). While I agree with Huyssen that there is an active form of memory work developing throughout his paintings, I believe Kiefer wants to undermine the notion that the past can be worked through, that closure is possible.

8. For an overview of this struggle between the two generations see Schneider 1984.

9. See also Kiefer's *Eisen-steig* from 1986, which depicts train tracks resembling the tracks of Auschwitz-Birkenau.

10. See for instance his watercolors *Interior* (1981), *To the Unknown Painter* (1982), and *The Stairs* (1982–1983).

Works Cited

Abraham, Nicholas. "Notes on the Phantom: A Completion to Freud's Metapsychology." Trans. Nicholas Rand. *Critical Inquiry* 13 (Winter 1987): 287–292.

Beaucamp, Eduard. "Die verbrannte Geschichte: Anselm Kiefer und die deutschen Mythen." *Frankfurter Allgemeine Zeitung* 11 (April 1984): 16.

Brailovsky, Anna. "The Epic Tableau: *Verfremdungseffekte* in Anselm Kiefer's *Varus*." *New German Critique* 71 (Spring/Summer 1997): 115–138.

Buck, Theo. *Bildersprache: Celan-Motive bei László Lakner und Anselm Kiefer.* Aachen: Rimbaud, 1993.

Celan, Paul. "Rede in Bremen." Vol. 3 of *Gesammelte Werke*, ed. Beda Allemann and Stefan Reichert, 185–186. Frankfurt: Suhrkamp, 1985a.

———. "Der Meridian." Vol. 4 of *Gesammelte Werke*, ed. Beda Allemann and Stefan Reichert, 187–202. Frankfurt: Suhrkamp, 1985b.

De Man, Paul. "Autobiography as De-Facement." In *The Rhetoric of Romanticism*, 67–81. New York: Columbia University Press, 1984.

Derrida, Jacques. "Shibboleth: For Paul Celan." In *Word Traces: Readings of Paul Celan*, ed. Aris Fioretos, 3–74. Baltimore: John Hopkins University Press, 1994.

Ezrahi, Sidra DeKoven. "'The Grave in the Air': Unbound Metaphors in Post-Holocaust Poetry." In *Probing the Limits of Representation: Nazism and the*

"Final Solution," ed. Saul Friedlander, 259–276. Cambridge, Mass.: Harvard University Press, 1992.

Felstiner, John. *Paul Celan: Poet, Survivor, Jew.* New Haven, Conn.: Yale University Press, 1995.

———. "Translating Paul Celan's 'Todesfuge': Rhythm and Repetition as Metaphor." In *Probing the Limits of Representation: Nazism and the "Final Solution,"* ed. Saul Friedlander, 240–258. Cambridge, Mass.: Harvard University Press, 1992.

Freud, Sigmund. "Further Recommendations in the Technique of Psychoanalysis: Recollection, Repetition, and Working Through." In *Therapy and Technique,* ed. Philip Rieff, 157–166. New York: Macmillan, 1963a.

———. "Repression." Vol. 14 of *Standard Edition of the Complete Psychological Works of Sigmund Freud,* trans. and ed. James Strachey, 141–158. London: Hogarth Press, 1957.

———. "The 'Uncanny.'" In *Studies in Parapsychology,* ed. Philip Rieff, 19–60. New York: Macmillan, 1963b.

Habermas, Jürgen. *The New Conservatism: Cultural Criticism and the Historians' Debate.* Ed. and trans. Shierry Nicholsen. Cambridge, Mass.: MIT Press, 1989.

Hughes, Robert. "Germany's Master in the Making." *Time,* December 21, 1987, 46.

Huyssen, Andreas. "Anselm Kiefer: The Terror of History, The Temptation of Myth." *October* 48 (1989): 25–45.

Rosenthal, Mark. *Anselm Kiefer.* Chicago: Art Institute of Chicago, 1987.

Saltzman, Lisa. *Art after Auschwitz.* Cambridge: Cambridge University Press, 1999.

Santner, Eric. *Stranded Objects: Mourning, Memory and Film in Postwar Germany.* Ithaca, N.Y.: Cornell University Press, 1990.

Schneider, Michael. "Fathers and Sons, Retrospectively: The Damaged Relationship Between Two Generations." *New German Critique* 31 (1984): 3–51.

West, Thomas. "Interview at Diesel Strasse." *Art International* (Spring 1988): 75–83.

Contributors

Nora M. Alter is Professor of German Film and Media Studies at the University of Florida. She is author of *Vietnam Protest Theatre: The Television War on Stage; Projecting History: Non-Fiction German Film;* and *Chris Marker*. She is co-editor, with Lutz Koepnick, of *Sound Matters: Essays on the Acoustics of Modern German Culture*.

Thomas J. D. Armbrecht is Assistant Professor in the Department of French and Italian at the University of Wisconsin, Madison. His translation, with scholarly introduction, of Eric Jourdan's 1955 novel *Wicked Angels* is forthcoming, as is his first book, *At the Periphery of the Center: Sexuality and Literary Genre in the Works of Yourcenar and Green*.

Peter Arnds is Associate Professor of German and Italian at Kansas State University. He is author of *Wilhelm Raabe's "Der Hungerpastor" and Charles Dickens's "David Copperfield": Intertextuality of two "Bildungsromane"; Representation, Subversion, and Eugenics in Günter Grass's "The Tin Drum";* numerous articles on German literature and culture of the nineteenth and twentieth centuries; as well as some poetry and prose.

Gail Finney is Professor of Comparative Literature and German at the University of California, Davis. Her publications include *The Counterfeit Idyll: The Garden Ideal and Social Reality in Nineteenth-Century Fiction; Women in Modern Drama: Freud, Feminism, and European Theater at the Turn of the Century; Look Who's Laughing: Gender and Comedy* (ed.); and *Christa Wolf*.

Patrick Greaney is Assistant Professor of German Studies at the University of Colorado. He has published articles on Hölderlin and Nietzsche and is author of a forthcoming book on poverty and power in modern German and French writing, titled *Impoverished Writing*.

Ingeborg Hoesterey is Professor of German and Comparative Literature Emerita at Indiana University. Among her publications on comparative arts are *Verschlungene Schriftzeichen: Intertextualität von Kunst und Literatur in der Moderne/Postmoderne; Zeitgeist in Babel: The Postmodernist Controversy* (ed.); and most recently *Pastiche: Cultural Memory in Art, Film, Literature*.

Dagmar von Hoff is Professor of German Media Studies and Aesthetics at the University of Mainz, Germany. She is author of *Dramen des Weiblichen: Deutsche Dramatikerinnen um 1800* and *Familiengeheimnisse: Inzest in Literatur und Film der Gegenwart*.

Eric Kligerman is Assistant Professor in the Department of Germanic and Slavic Studies at the University of Florida. He has articles forthcoming on Paul Celan and Daniel Libeskind and on Gerhard Richter's *October 18, 1977* paintings. He is currently finishing a book entitled *Sights of the Uncanny: Paul Celan and the Visual Arts*.

Lutz Koepnick is Associate Professor of German and Film and Media Studies at Washington University. He is author of *The Dark Mirror: German Cinema between Hitler and Hollywood; Walter Benjamin and the Aesthetics of Power,* for which he received the MLA's Scaglione Prize for Studies in Germanic Languages and Literatures in 2000; and *Nothungs Modernität: Wagners Ring und die Poesie der Politik im neunzehnten Jahrhundert*. He is also co-editor, with Nora M. Alter, of *Sound Matters: Essays on the Acoustics of Modern German Culture*.

Kristin Kopp is Assistant Professor of German at the University of Missouri. She is co-editor, with Klaus Müller-Richter, of *Die "Großstadt" und das "Primitive": Text, Politik, Repräsentation*.

Barbara Kosta is Associate Professor in the Department of German Studies at the University of Arizona. She is author of *Recasting Autobiography: Women's Counterfictions in Contemporary German Literature and Film,* and in 2003 she co-edited, with Helga Kraft, *Writing against Boundaries: Ethnicity, Gender, and Nationality*.

Dagmar C. G. Lorenz is Professor of Germanic Studies at the University of Illinois at Chicago. Her recent book publications include *Keepers of the Motherland: German Texts by Jewish Women Writers* and

Verfolgung bis zum Massenmord: Diskurse zum Holocaust in deutscher Sprache. Her edited volumes include *A Companion to the Works of Elias Canetti; A Companion to the Works of Arthur Schnitzler; Contemporary Jewish Writing in Austria; Transforming the Center, Eroding the Margins: Essays on Ethnic and Cultural Boundaries in German-Speaking Countries* (co-edited with Renate S. Posthofen); and *Insiders and Outsiders: Jewish and Gentile Culture in Germany and Austria*.

Jan Mieszkowski, Associate Professor of German and Humanities at Reed College, is author of *The Art of Interest*, a study of literature and political economy in the nineteenth and twentieth centuries.

David James Prickett is presently an associate member of the Center for Transdisciplinary Gender Studies (ZtG) at the Humboldt University, Berlin.

Michele Ricci is Visiting Assistant Professor of German and Andrew Mellon Postdoctoral Fellow at Oberlin College. Her primary research areas include modern German poetry, East German political cabaret, post-unification culture and literature, exile culture, and film studies.

Blake Stimson teaches in the Art History Program at the University of California, Davis. His recent and forthcoming publications include *Visual Worlds* (co-edited with John Hall and Lisa Tamiris Becker), *Collectivism after Modernism* (co-edited with Gregory Sholette), and *The Pivot of the World: Photography and Its Nation*.

Janet Ward is Associate Professor of History and Director of Interdisciplinary Programs at the University of Nevada, Las Vegas. She is author of *Weimar Surfaces: Urban Visual Culture in 1920s Germany*.

Valerie Weinstein is Assistant Professor of German at the University of Nevada, Reno. The essay in this volume is part of a book project on mistaken identity films and the shaping of identities in Germany through 1945. She has also published on German precolonial literature.

Index

Italicized page numbers refer to illustrations.

Ingram Content Group UK Ltd.
Milton Keynes UK
UKHW020614220323
418970UK00008B/597